MONOTHEISM, POWER, JUSTICE

Collected Old Testament Essays

Millard C. Lind

Text Reader Series No. 3

Institute of Mennonite Studies
3003 Benham Avenue
Elkhart, IN 46517

1990

TEXT-READER SERIES

Series Titles:

1. *Essays on Biblical Interpretation: Anabaptist-Mennonite Perspectives.* Edited by Willard M. Swartley, 1984.

2. *One Lord, One Church, One Hope, and One God: Mennonite Confessions of Faith in North America, An Introduction.* Howard John Loewen, 1985.

3. *Monotheism, Power and Justice: Collected Old Testament Essays.* Millard C. Lind, 1990.

This Text-Reader series is published by the Institute of Mennonite Studies with the encouragement of the Council of Mennonite Seminaries. The series seeks to make available significant resource materials for seminary classroom use. By using photographic reproduction and/or desktop publishing technology and marketing primarily through institutional channels, this series seeks to make available helpful materials at relatively low cost.

Priority in accepting manuscripts will be given to material that has promise for ongoing use in the seminary classroom, with orientation toward or interest in the Anabaptist-Mennonite theological tradition.

The Institute of Mennonite Studies is the research agency of the Associated Mennonite Biblical Seminaries, 3003 Benham Avenue, Elkhart, Indiana, 46517-1999.

ISBN 0-936273-16-X
Printed in the United States of America

ACKNOWLEDGEMENTS

"Interpreting the Interpreters," used by permission of *The Other Side*.

"Reflections on Biblical Hermeneutics," used by permission of Herald Press from *Kingdom, Cross, and Community*.

"The Hermeneutics of the Old Testament," used by permission of *The Mennonite Quarterly Review*.

"Refocusing Theological Education to Mission: The Old Testament and Contextualization," used by permission of *Missiology: An International Review*.

"Traditional and Not-So-Traditional Values," used by permission of *Gospel Herald*.

"Theology of Law," used by permission of Herald Press from *Mennonite Encyclopedia*.

"Old Testament Law: A Review Essay," used by permission from *Journal of Law and Religion*.

"The Anomaly of the Prophet," used by permission of Faith and Life Press from *The New Way of Jesus, Essays Presented to Howard Charles*.

"The Concept of Political Power in Ancient Israel," used by permission of the *Annual of the Swedish Theological Institute*.

"Monotheism, Power and Justice: A Study in Isaiah 40-55," used by permission of *The Catholic Biblical Quarterly*.

"Paradigm of Holy War in the Old Testament," used by permission of *Biblical Research*.

"Exasperated Love, an Exposition of Hosea 5:8-6:6," used by permission of *Interpretation, A Journal of Bible and Theology*.

"Prince of Peace: Temple or Palace," used by permission of *Gospel Herald*.

"The Rule of God: Agenda for the City," used by permission of *The Covenant Quarterly*.

"Law in the Old Testament," "Power and Powerlessness in the Old Testament," and "The Economics of God's People," are reprinted from publications of the Institute of Mennonite Studies.

*To my former students
who inspired, encouraged and
criticized me, and from whom
I stole time to write these essays.*

TABLE OF CONTENTS

FOREWORD 1

INTRODUCTION 4

I. METHOD
    1. Interpreting the Interpreters 9
    2. Reflections on Biblical Hermeneutics 13
    3. The Hermeneutics of the Old Testament 24
    4. Refocusing Theological Education to Mission: The Old Testament
       and Contextualization 38
    5. Traditional and Not-So-Traditional Values 55

II. LAW, JUSTICE AND POWER
    6. Law in the Old Testament 61
    7. Transformation of Justice: From Moses to Jesus 82
    8. Theology of Law 98
    9. Old Testament Law: Review Essay............................104
    10. The Anomaly of the Prophet 109
    11. Is there a Biblical Case for Civil Disobedience? 120
    12. The Concept of Political Power in Ancient Israel 135
    13. Monotheism, Power, and Justice: A Study in Isaiah 40-55 153

III. WAR AND ECONOMICS
    14. Perspectives on War and Peace in the Hebrew Scriptures 171
    15. Paradigm of Holy War in the Old Testament 182
    16. Exasperated Love, an Exposition on Hosea 5:8-6:6 197
    17. Power and Powerlessness in the Old Testament: A Book Analysis ..203
    18. Prince of Peace: Temple or Palace? 211
    19. Economics Among the People of God in the Old Testament 215
    20. The Money Tree 227

IV. WORSHIP, MISSION AND COMMUNITY
    21. Worship: Retelling the Story, Covenanting 233
    22. The Rule of God: Agenda for the City 238
    23. Yahweh and Feminine Liberation: A Few Observations from the
       Hebrew Text 254
    24. A Political Alternative: An Examination of Ezekiel's Recognition
       Statements 260

FOREWORD

Since the mid-sixties a steady stream of essays and addresses has come from the pen and heart of Millard Lind. Millard began his teaching career at the Associated Mennonite Biblical Seminaries in 1959. During the early years of his teaching a major portion of Millard's scholarly energies went toward the refinement of his doctoral dissertation, in order to be published. Its final form appeared in 1980, in the Herald Press book, *Yahweh Is a Warrior*. This book represents a landmark in scholarly studies on the topic of Yahweh's warfare as presented in Hebrew Scripture. It has received numerous critical reviews, and has generally stood the test of the scholarly "picking and pruning."

Alongside this major work Millard has turned out numerous essays, some playing a supportive role to his *Yahweh Is a Warrior* thesis, but many pioneering in new directions as well. As the four divisions in the Table of Contents indicate, these essays represent work in at least four areas of probing in the Hebrew Scripture: method; aspects of law, justice, and power; war and economics; and worship, mission, and community. This range of investigation and productivity indicates the holistic perspective of Millard's scholarly concern and theological reflection. In part it also testifies to Millard's role as a churchman, since some of these investigations grew out of specific requests of various church groups or congregations to address a particular issue.

Of the numerous strengths of Millard's writings and contribution as a teacher I mention three:

First, Millard's scholarship goes down deep into the linguistic and comparative religious milieu of the topics of his investigation. Millard has stood against the tendency and temptation of "creaming off the top" the theological goodies. Anyone who has taught in a church institution with its demands of heavy loads in teaching and church constituency portfolios knows what this is about. Millard gave time to his scholarship. One of my fondest memories is seeing Millard in his chair in his home--after recovering from hip surgery--poring over his Hebrew Bible, thus allowing the text to condition his thought more than anything else. Together with careful and creative attention to the Hebrew text, his work also shows engagement with the comparative literature of the Ancient Near East.

This feature of Millard's scholarship had direct bearing upon his teaching style. One of my privileges as Millard's colleague was to co-teach with him the course, *War and Peace in the Bible*. Students soon learned that Millard would not give a quick answer to the probing questions that arise in the study of war in the Old Testament. They learned rather that first we immerse ourselves in the text at depth level. Then we consider analogous literature from Ancient Near Eastern documents. We then see apparent similarity. And finally, when the wits of the weaker begin to droop, comes the famous *Bu-u-t* which is the form critical prologue to the oracle, as it were, "from on high." And then, with all spirits revitalized, we heard the word of God's reshaping of Israel's life and thought--so that the similar is no longer the same, but indeed fundamentally different. For his contribution to the various topics addressed, Millard's work will stand as a pillar in Old Testament scholarship. Against this pillar canon guns will blast and even bull dozers assail, but from generation to generation Millard's contribution will be a light that will not fail and a word that will not be extinguished. This will be so not because Millard has given a new oracle, but because his work allows and enables the oracles of old to be sounded again boldly and provocatively in our time.

The truth of this word shows itself in a second quality of Millard's scholarship. Millard's work, though oriented to literature two-four thousand years old, is not to be catalogued in the section, "antiquity." Rather, it addresses current issues in our culture via the Word of God from of old. The most pressing agenda of our contemporary society and church includes precisely those issues addressed in these essays: hermeneutics, the nature and function of law in society, our view of justice and power, our society's preoccupation with securing us for and against war, our economic self-protectionism, and the bearing of all these matters upon the nature of our worship, mission and community. Part of the reason why Millard's work carries enduring relevance is that his scholarship has been informed by the contributions of sociological studies, especially the political and economic factors that constitute the social structure. Hence, the religious and theological dimensions of Israel's life, evidenced in the Torah and word of the prophets, stands ever in tension with its concrete sociological, political and economic expressions.

The contour of thought and the sequence of these issues, as set forth in this volume, might well form an outline for a biblical theology addressed to the church and world of the twentieth and twenty-first centuries. That such an outline arises from Old Testament scholarship has an important bearing upon the question of the Old Testament's relation to the New. Indeed, Millard's scholarly contribution shows forth the conviction that Israel's faith is closer to Jesus than to the religious thought of its contemporary world. Moses foreshadows Jesus more than he reflects Egypt. Israel's fundamental break with the structures of the empires marks out a people who anticipate Jesus and his followers.

A third outstanding feature of Millard's work as a scholar and teacher is Millard's one-of-a-kind spirit. On the one hand, Millard will stand firm--like Exodus 14:14 tells him to do!--in debate of his views, but at the same time his relational manner shows forth the fruit of the Spirit. Who has come to know Millard and has not felt his love, patience, kindness and gentleness? Millard's writing style evokes the description of "carefulness with patience." His many close relationships to students have exemplified the same qualities, blended together with love and kindness. Out of this primary matrix of qualities has shone through also gentleness and self-control, joy and peace, and as a topping over all, goodness.

In scholarly culture generally it is customary to celebrate birthday and retirement "passages" of older scholars with Festschrifts containing essays from students whose lives and thought have been shaped by the sage's voice upon them. But this is an *alternative* event, true to the theology Millard's work represents. To celebrate Millard's loving labors, we mark the rite of retirement by bringing together the numerous essays that Millard has written, as a gift for the heart and a guide for the mind. So let it be!

Willard M. Swartley
Professor of New Testament
Associated Mennonite Biblical Seminaries
January 1990

INTRODUCTION

There is good biblical precedent for gathering up one's past works and publishing them in a book (cf. Jeremiah 36). Even though I deal with a message which, if heeded, would profoundly change the course of world history, I do not pretend to write with the spiritual intensity nor poetic beauty of the prophets, and I doubt that even in my own circles my writings will take on the character of canon. But is it too much to hope that they might be provocative enough to contribute in some small way to an honest hermeneutic of the Old Testament, an approach informed both by an ecumenical and Anabaptist perspective? With this hope, I accept the invitation of the Institute of Mennonite Studies and the Board of Goshen Biblical Seminary to gather up for publication some of my essays of the past twenty-five years.

All of these essays view the Bible's message as a critique against a power-oriented world community which has a pyramid concept of justice. The Bible is more than a mere critique, however; it is a proclamation of Yahweh's establishment of an alternative community by which the world is made to know the way of Yahweh. The claim is that this is not *a* message, but *the* message of the Bible's multifaceted literature, a literature which is normative for the life of the human community today.

The observant reader will note some development in these essays. In 1982 I was using non-sexist language, though not always successfully, of human beings. Only in 1987 do the essays come through with non-sexist language used of God. Occasionally, perhaps, this results in literary awkwardness.

One of my oldest essays, "The Concept of Political Power in Ancient Israel" (1970), may have emphasized too much the parallelism of Hittite covenants to the Mosaic covenant. However, I used some care even then, and still feel that these analogies form a corrective to certain presuppositions of form critical thought which had earlier challenged the original unity of divergent formal types. More critically, perhaps, the essay was too early to make use of the work of more recent sociologists which helps to make more credible pre-kingship Israelite structures. However, Josephus' concept of theocracy, the exposure of scholarly presuppositions in regard to power, and the significance of covenant as a religious-political institution of a non-violent non-coercive type, still unacknowledged by sociologists, led me to include the essay.

The essays are made up of both a popular and more scholarly type. The popular articles, mostly sermons, were important to me in helping me focus my thought. The more scholarly essays were important as they provided an opportunity for me to engage in ecumenical conversation, an important dimension for one who teaches in a denominational seminary.

I am indebted to my many exceptional students who challenged me to think and rethink the Biblical texts. I owe a great deal to my work setting at the Associated Mennonite Biblical Seminaries, and to the outstanding faculty of which I was a little part. I am especially indebted to the directors of the Institute of Mennonite Studies, Cornelius J. Dyck, Willard Swartley, Richard A. Kauffman and Wayne Pipkin. Willard especially was responsible for proposing this book, and gave generously of his time in the editorial process. Marlin Miller, president of Goshen Biblical Seminary, supported and encouraged my various study projects, and was always ready with his counsel. Gayle Gerber Koontz, as director of our faculty research efforts, was helpful in channeling some research money my way. Ralph Hernley and Goodville Mutual Casualty Company financed a research chair which enabled me to give myself to this work. Paul Conrad made a contribution toward the book's publishing expenses. Sue DeLeon was my efficient typist and computer operator, who often served beyond the call of duty with enthusiasm and cheerfulness. Wilma Cender was responsible for obtaining copyright permissions and the demanding details of preparing the manuscript for press.

I owe a debt to my family, especially to Miriam my wife, who for many years lived on a financial shoestring, who tolerated my inattentiveness when I had my mind on other matters, and who often read and counseled me on a manuscript.

> Millard C. Lind
> Professor of Old Testament
> Associated Mennonite Biblical Seminaries

I. METHOD

CHAPTER 1

INTERPRETING THE INTERPRETERS

For many years, biblical theologians have tried to find the "center" of the Bible. Eichrodt argued that covenant was the principle that held all else together--and he interpreted everything else from that vantage point. Von Rad, on the other hand, regarded salvation history as the interpretative center. Still others hold that the Bible has no single center and must be interpreted from several standpoints.

In the eyes of many Latin American theologians, however, justice is the all-consuming center of the biblical message. Further, they hold that since the biblical message came to a poor, oppressed slave people, only the poor can really understand the message of the Bible. The wealthy and the middle classes cannot hear its good news, because the good news is directed largely to the poor and enslaved. In fact, the biblical message is subversive to the position of the middle and upper classes.

Biblical sociologists have undergirded the claims of the Latin American theologians. Looking at the Bible in light of sociological studies of preindustrial and ancient societies, they see in the Bible the message of social revolution. Even the conquest of Canaan is viewed as a revolt of the lower Canaanite classes against the oppression of Canaanite city-states.

After reading the biblical analysis of such revolutionaries, I find the commentaries of middle-class theologians rather bland and unsatisfying. But have these Latin American theologians really gotten hold of the biblical message? The message of Scripture may indeed be justice. But is it not always a justice rooted in the structures of discipleship?

A few years ago, Emil Brunner wrote that Christianity chooses state law as its law and that justice finds its structures within the state. This is an excellent description of the kind of Christianity that Brunner knew, the establishment type.

Biblical justice, however, is rooted in the structures of a covenant relationship. Biblical justice is rooted in discipleship. And it is only within the covenant structures of the disestablished synagogue and church that justice and love can be seen as complementary rather than competing virtues.

From *The Other Side*, August, 1983, Vol. 19, No. 8.

Unfortunately, many commentators come to the Scriptures with presuppositions closer to the ancient Mesopotamian model than to the Bible. They assume that justice is to be rooted in the state, love rooted in the church. Like the ancient Mesopotamians with whom God's people lived, they assume that the king is the source of all justice.

The Bible, on the other hand, looks to the kingship of Yahweh. Yahweh is the God of justice. Justice is found in covenant and worship, in obedience to God.

So when you read a commentary, when you listen to a preacher or interpreter, consider the presuppositions. What assumptions are being made about the central message of Scripture? What assumptions are being made about justice? Are those assumptions in keeping with the context and setting in which Scripture was written? Are they faithful to the life and times of the people to whom the message was first given?

The biblical message is not easily domesticated. Yet the world is full of people seeking to make Scripture over in their own--or their society's--image.

As you seek to interpret the meaning of Scripture for today, beware of interpreters whose presuppositions will lead you astray.

The question of power and its proper use in the world illustrates another way in which we are often blinded by our own social and cultural context.

In my early seminary days, it was hard for me to understand most of the statements of Jesus in anything other than an individualistic, personal-relational sense. Today, all that is changed.

The change began when I read Martin Hengel in the early sixties and became more acquainted with the Zealots. Then, just last year, I spent some time on the Golan Heights studying the Zealot-Roman wars. And you can't imagine the impact it had when, in the midst of our studies we were unexpectedly enveloped by Israeli war games.

From Gamala, we could look across to Mount Arbel on the western shore of Lake Galilee, another of the ancient Zealot centers. Further west were other Zealot strongholds and the little town of Nazareth. Closer to us, to the north, we could see Capernaum, the center of Jesus' ministry. With modern tanks rolling around us and F-17s roaring overhead, it was clearer than ever that many of Jesus' statements were, in the Jewish-Roman context, vividly political.

I thought, for example, about Jesus' words, "Blessed are the meek, for they shall inherit the earth." However else such a teaching may have been understood, it was surely understood by Jesus' hearers as a radical critique of violent power as demonstrated by the Zealots.

And Jesus surely pointed to a new kind of poltical leadership when he said to his power-seeking disciples, "You know that those who are supposed to rule over the nations lord it over them, and their great leaders exercise authority over them. But it should not be so among you: whoever would be great among you must be your servant, and whoever would be first among you must be slave of all. For the Son of Man came not to be served but to serve and to give his life as a ransom for many" (Mark 10:42-45).

In a dramatic gesture, Jesus offered to Jerusalem this new kind of political leadership when on Palm Sunday he rode into the city on the foal of an ass. But the city rejected the new leadership. Rome crucified him along with the Zealots.

Where are the biblical theologians and sociologists who can interpret for the church the meaning of this radically new political doctrine?

Can we really leave the interpretation of this radical, political document--the Bible--to establishment theologians? Can we leave it to the heirs of Augustine's theory of "just war" and to those who hold that justice must be rooted in the structures of violent power?

Given its original context, does not the interpretation of Scripture need to come out of the traditions of radically disestablished Christianity? Will we not find greater sensitivity to the biblical message in those whose social context and personal commitments are closer to that of Jesus?

I think of the lay order of St. Francis, whose members were strictly forbidden to bear arms. I think of the order of Peter Waldo, which, from the eleventh to fifteenth centuries after Christ, rejected the death penalty, military service, and the whole state apparatus, believing the Sermon on the Mount to be obligatory for all Christians.

I think of the order of the Czech Brethren, who held that "power breeds fear, for power makes it possible to rule, threaten, abuse,...imprison, beat, and kill." I think of the radical wing of the Reformation, which in 1527 produced the first authoritative confessional statement on nonresistance and the rejection of militarism. I think of George Fox and the seventeenth-century reformers in England, of William Penn and the Quakers in North America.

And I think of the radical wing of evangelicalism and of many churches in twentieth-century America, both Catholic and Protestant, which believe that God in Christ has established a new theo-sociological way--and are committed to walking in it.

Will not the radical theo-political vision of the Bible be twisted if we rely entirely for our interpretations on such state-oriented theologians as Wellhausen and von Rad?

Wellhausen sees the state as the structure through which God works much more than through the church. How does this presupposition affect his biblical interpretation?

Von Rad acknowledges to some extent the radical break of Israel with ancient Near Eastern concepts of violent political power. But his presuppositions lead him to deny that this break in the concept of political power had any connections with Israel's history. In his commentaries, he sees the break as a theological reinterpretation of the ancient war traditions long after the historical fact. This theological bias leads him to deny the miracle underlying the story of the exodus. For him, Israel's politics and sociology of power was like that of any other Near Eastern state. It was only her "pietistic" theology that was different.

Can we accept as our biblical interpreters those Old Testament theologians who downplay the debate about kingship in the Bible or who have relegated the anti-kingship arguments to late theological reconstructions? Was not the political reality underlying those ancient arguments decisive for Israel's history? Did not that political reality underlie the political leadership of Jesus and the early church? Do we not need to discover an interpretation of the Bible different from that of the established church?

For twenty-five years people have been asking me, "What commentaries do you recommend?" My answer, for most of these twenty-five years, has been, "Not many."

Don't get me wrong. Almost any commentary can be helpful--if it's read with critical discernment. I encourage my students to read as many viewpoints as possible. But we need always to keep an eye on the text itself. And we need to keep in mind our commentators' presuppositions.

Ultimately, however, what we really need is a new breed of disestablishment interpreters, careful scholars who share the Bible's radical commitment in regard to justice and political power. We need men and women who believe in revelation and who believe that God in Christ has established a new, historical, theo-political order in which all humanity is called to walk.

Only then will we have the commentaries we need.

CHAPTER 2

REFLECTIONS ON BIBLICAL HERMENEUTICS

Guy F. Hershberger demonstrated his interest in hermeneutics as he sought to establish biblical bases for guiding the life and work of the church in the world. He gave careful attention to matters of biblical interpretation, particularly the question of the relation of the Old and New Testaments, in his two major books on Anabaptist-Mennonite ethics.[1] Through his use of sociology, ethics, and history to elaborate the theological message of the Bible, he has contributed significantly to the development of my own thought.

My intention in this essay is to set forth a few reflections on a valid biblical hermeneutic, from a perspective informed by the Anabaptist tradition. These are the reflections of one who seeks to stand within that tradition, and who is in conversation with modern biblical studies within the ecumenical church and synagogue.[2]

By "hermeneutics" I mean the two-fold effort to understand the original language of the Bible within its ancient settings, and then to translate those understandings into modern language in its social context. This view of hermeneutics thus includes both biblical exegesis and biblical homiletics, which have often been considered as separate aspects. Such an approach demands a knowledge of the ancient languages and worlds, a knowledge of contemporary languages and world, and a method for moving from one to the other.

By "Anabaptist" I mean that movement which began in Europe in the sixteenth century as the result of the rise of humanistic biblical studies within a certain social-economic-political milieu. These studies led to the formation of a body of believers who saw themselves set apart from the world in which they lived, by virtue of their faith. They dared to act in freedom from that world, in response to the sovereignty of the resurrected Christ whose living presence they confessed.

A revolution has occurred in biblical studies since the sixteenth century. Textual criticism, literary criticism, form criticism, archaeology, the recovery of whole libraries of ancient literatures--these have all contributed to a knowledge

---

From *Kingdom, Cross and Community: Essays on Mennonite Themes in Honor of Guy F. Hershberger.* J. R. Burkholder and Calvin Redekop, eds., 1976.

of the Bible which is greater now than at any time since the first century. Followers of the Anabaptist tradition, with its genuine interest in biblical authority, should welcome these advances. Within the context of ecumenical debate (a characteristic of sixteenth-century Anabaptism), we need to approach the Bible anew in every generation. Our new knowledge confirms some of the insights of the sixteenth century, though it may set those insights within new perspectives, and may serve to correct others.

Despite, or perhaps because of, the hermeneutical revolution of the past century, there are some Anabaptist understandings that I find helpful in the interpretation of the Bible.[3] They are:

1. The congregation as a hermeneutical community.

2. An understanding of the authority of both Old and New Testaments in a relationship that is not "flat" but historical, that is, a pattern of promise and fulfillment. (I am not sure that the early Anabaptists were as negative to the Old Testament as have been some Mennonites of the past generation.)

3. The emphasis on discipleship, with the consequent demand for discerning between true and false hermeneutics.

4. The challenge to prevailing concepts of political power, grounded in an analogy to the experience of the biblical people of God in their Near Eastern and Mediterranean context.[4]

For me, these points have an abiding relevance for the hermeneutical task of the faithful church.

Hermeneutics as Exegesis and Homiletics

Hermeneutics as we have defined it is divided into two parts, exegesis and homiletics. Exegesis is the attempt to discover what the original language meant. This original meaning is not easy to fix; it may refer to the oral tradition behind the text, or to the meaning of the text as a unit of written tradition, or to the meaning of the unit within a larger edited whole. In any case, we must realize that when we read the Bible we are crossing cultural barriers of both time and space. Bible translations which obliterate these barriers in order to make the Bible read like a modern book may have their uses, but they also have their debit side. They may remove the reader even further from the culture and milieu of which the Bible was a part. The very nature of the biblical faith, centered about certain prophetic-historical events, excludes methods such as allegorizing that deny the Bible's historical character. All readers of the text should make their journey back into the strange world of the Bible, to the extent that their ability and calling permit them.

Biblical hermeneutics also demands a knowledge of today's languages. Along with moving back into history, the reader must move forward into the modern age. One must be able to say, in terms that the modern person can begin to understand, what the mystery of the gospel means today. This problem is compounded when we remember that ours is a missionary task, and that we must communicate the gospel not only to ourselves, but to those who have no commitment to it, those to whom the Bible is utterly foreign. Here we can

learn much from a prophet like Hosea, who seized the central myth of
Baalism, broke it off from its mythological moorings, and used that language to
proclaim the Yahwistic faith; or from Paul, who translated the Hebraically
oriented gospel of Jesus into the milieu of the Greek world.

The Home of Biblical Hermeneutics

Viewing the congregation as a hermeneutical community is an important
contribution of Anabaptism to biblical hermeneutics. This perspective enables
the specialist to see himself as part of a team concerned with the larger
hermenuetical question. It may deliver him from trivial and unprofitable questions in research, although there may be a difference of opinion as to what the
important questions are. It should also help one to realize that we cannot stop
everything to deal with the problem of hermeneutics but that we must deal
with it "on the run." The results must constantly be tested in the midst of the
community in its relation to the world. For the community itself to enter into
the exegetical and homiletical process, the specialist must exercise his skill as a
genuine leader rather than as a dogmatician.

The concept of the hermeneutical community includes also an
epistemological dimension. The hermeneutical question is shifted from "What
does the text mean to me?" to the more basic question, "What does the text
mean to us?" Slight as this shift may seem, it emphasizes that the Bible is a
public book. It is to be used and interpreted within its own public life situation.
Therefore, its historical and sociopolitical dimensions, as well as its psychological implications, are a part of its relevant theological message. Otherwise, if
the Bible is seen only as a book for private devotions, an adequate hermeneutic
becomes impossible.

I do not want to minimize the difficulties of the movement backward to
the Bible and forward to the twentieth century. But by accepting the congregation as the context for the Bible's life situation, the process is quite a different
one from that in which it is assumed that there is no twentieth-century life
situation in which the Bible is truly at home. If the latter is true, the
hermeneutical process is indeed questionable and largely meaningless. It is
only within the life situation of the hermeneutical community that the fundamental analogies are experienced which make the Bible historically credible.

A Biblical Unity

There is a tendency on the part of some modern Mennonites to disregard
the Old Testament. The Old Testament is essential, however, to an
understanding of the New. This is true not only because the Old Testament
community provides the cultural womb for the New Testament, but even more
because of the nature of the biblical faith itself. We cannot understand a
reality outside our own previous experience, except by a process of analogy in
which similarities and differences stand out. The biblical faith, however, witnesses to certain once-for-all prophetic-historic events that never happened

elsewhere and which, therefore, have no analogies outside the biblical stream of history. The history of biblical scholarship is replete with perversions of the biblical faith caused by interpreting the unique, unrepeatable event in the light of the repeatable events (mythologies or philosophies) of surrounding cultures. The "sacral kingship school" of Old Testament science has attempted to reinterpret Israel's origins in terms of the state structures which surrounded Israel (Hooke, 1958). The "mystery religions school" of New Testament science has tried to reinterpret the meaning of Christ's death and resurrection in terms of death and resurrection as celebrated by the mystery religions of the Graeco-Roman empire (Angus, 1925). Anselm in his theory of the atonement used pagan analogies that have distorted the biblical view of atonement in orthodoxy and Fundamentalism to this day. Bultmann, captivated by Heidegger's existentialism, follows a similar method (Neill, 1964:228ff.). But one cannot capture the biblical reality in the mythologies or philosophies of this world without paganizing the biblical faith. If this is true, and if we can understand something new to us only by analogy, where are the analogies by which we may understand the biblical faith?

Our answer is that the biblical stream of history provides its own analogies; this is the importance of the biblical understanding of promise and fulfillment and of typology.[5] When the New Testament church looked for analogies by which to understand the Christ event, they went to the Old Testament: "This is that which was spoken...." No doubt Jesus' own self-understanding was largely shaped by Old Testament analogy. The Old Testament was indispensable for the early Christians not only because it was the matrix for the New Testament community's culture, but because through the Scripture they experienced that newness of the Word of God, which provided analogies for the understanding of the unique event that had happened among them. It is only by use of these analogies within the stream of biblical history that we can escape from a paganization of the Jesus event.

The Old Testament is necessary, however, not only to provide analogies for the faith event, but also because the great themes of the faith, such as the understanding of God, the understanding of the world (creation), sin and salvation, humankind and peoplehood, are presented as continuities in the two Testaments (Brunner, 1963). The New Testament event may alter the character of some of these emphases, but the continuities are dominant, and without the Old Testament we cannot fully understand these themes.

It is also true that the Old Testament is to be understood in the light of the New. But this presupposition is not a dogma to be enforced by an allegorical method. If we merely read the thought of the New Testament back upon the Old, we deny the value of the Old Testament. When, however, we view the Old Testament narrative within the context of the Near East, with its historic struggle between assimilation to and rejection of that culture, it becomes evident that the New Testament as fulfillment is no longer an arbitrary dogma. As a result of biblical research, one can now say that while the Old Testament developed in the ancient Near Eastern environment and the New Testament within the Graeco-Roman environment, neither was really at home in its environment. Both were closer to each other than they were to their environments. Both are to be interpreted in the light of each other, rather than in the light of their environments, though these environments are important to their understanding.

The Bible in the Context of the Ancient Near Eastern and Mediterranean World

Since the time of the church fathers it has become traditional to contrast Jerusalem with Athens. Such a contrast of the Bible with its environment is much more ancient than the Hebrew-Greek clash, however, for in fact it goes back to pre-kingship Israel. This ancient contrast is not so well known, however, because until recently, ancient Near Eastern history was unknown. The Old Testament jutted into the modern world like a rocky promontory from the past; readers of the Bible knew next to nothing of the environment with which it interacted. Thanks to archaeology and the discovery of ancient libraries, this isolation no longer exists. Today the volume of the ancient Accadian literature is at least as great as that of the Greek and Latin literature which has come down to us. This means that we are able not only to compare the Bible with Athens, but to compare the entire story from Abraham through Jesus and Paul with the Near Eastern and Graeco-Roman world. With this larger perspective, we can observe not only the Bible's rejection of outside cultural items, but also its assimilation of many of them.

In contrasting the Bible with its environment, scholars have usually emphasized formal differences. For example, William Klassen has called attention to Auerbach's judgment of the literature of Greek antiquity: "We are forced to conclude that there could be no serious literary treatment of everyday occupations and social classes...of everyday customs and institutions...in short, of the people and its life. Linked with this is the fact that the realists of antiquity do not make clear the social forces underlying the facts and conditions which they present" (Auerbach, 1957:27). Over against this the literature of the Bible "portrays something which neither the poets nor the historians of antiquity ever set out to portray: the birth of a spiritual movement in the depths of the common people, from within the everyday occurrences of contemporary life, which thus assumes an importance it could never have assumed in antique literature" (Auerbach, 1957:37). This difference of form is obviously connected with the content, however, and it is questionable whether emphasis on merely formal categories can adequately portray the real contrasts.

Scholars have also emphasized the formal category of history in attempting to distinguish the Bible from the Near East. Mowinckel makes a typical statement: "While the other peoples experienced the deity in the eternal cyclic process of nature, the Israelites experienced God in history."[6] Certainly there is some truth in this statement, but it is misleading as a generalization. Clearly the gods of the Near Eastern states participated in their people's history also, since they were always considered decisive in the fighting of wars. For example, Assyrian art provides us with an example of the divinity fighting alongside the king. In a relief of Ashurnasirpal there is a complete conformity between the warlike movements of the god and the king. Before the battle, king and god advance with bow drawn toward the enemy. After the battle, both have their bows slung in celebration of victory (Mendenhall, 1973: Figs. 10-13). Thus, we cannot say that Yahweh acts in history and that gods do not act in history. The point is rather to observe *how* Yahweh acts in history as compared to the gods.

The Bible's Self-Consciousness

We are on safer ground for comparative work when we let Israel speak for herself. What was Israel's own self-consciousness of her difference from the nations?

The ancient poetry of the Pentateuch reveals that Israel was strongly aware of such a difference: "Lo, a people dwelling alone, and not reckoning itself among the nations!" (Numbers 23:9, RSV). This self-consciousness is delineated again and again, in the oldest as well as the more recent sources. For example one of the oldest sources of the Pentateuch contrasts Yahweh's call of Abraham with the self-willed character of the primitive democracy of a Babylonian city state (Genesis 11 and 12, tenth century BC). The Book of Hosea, a polemic of Yahwism against Baalism, concludes with an attack on kingship as rebellion against Yahweh, although it is fitting to Baal.

This polemic against kings is found throughout the Bible: Yahweh against Pharaoh in the escape from Egypt (Exodus 1-15); Yahweh against Sennacherib (Isaiah 37:23-29, eighth century BC); Yahweh against the king of Babylon (Isaiah 14:4-21, seventh or sixth century, BC); Yahweh against the prince and king of Tyre (Ezekiel 28:1-19, sixth century BC). Outside of Israel, kingship was considered as "let down from heaven," a blessing of the gods (Pritchard, 1969:265). Within Israel, kingship was regarded as human rebellion, a rejection of the rule of Yahweh (whose will was communicated not through the king, but through his prophets) to become "like all the nations" (1 Samuel 8; 12; cf. Judges 8:22,23; 9:7-15; Deuteronomy 17:14-20).

William McKane has shown how the problem of political power was at the heart of the prophetic conflict with the political wisdom of the ancient Near East. The prophet's

> main concern is not that power should be stripped of the fearful crudity and grossness of which it partakes in the awful insecurity of our works--the world of the twentieth century. He does not principally work for the refinement or ratification of power, for this implies gradualism and is a political rather than a prophetic solution. The prophet urges rather that the concept of a balance of power is unreal, because it leaves God out of the reckoning. The Israelite prophets and the contemporary prophets assert that power is not built in with historical existence in the way that the statesmen suppose. God reserves all power to himself and so the *locus* of power is outside historical exist-

ence. From this flowed the doctrine of instrumentality in the Israelite prophets. God moves the nations like pawns on a chess-board, but he is the only real policy-maker and reserves all power to himself.

In this case the statesman ought not to concern himself with power, for, if this is the situation, all that is left for him as for the rest of us is to know the will of God and do it. Beyond this everything rests with God. The statesman will say that the crudity of the balance of power in our world today is a true reflection of the tensions and perilous insecurity of the international community and that it is the unresolved, intractable problems, daunting in their magnitude and delicacy, which will have to be tackled and solved one by one before there is any betterment. But the prophet believes that faith has a creative potential and can transform a situation. If we had faith in God and loved our neighbor and were prepared to take the absolute risk for the sake of Christ, the world would cease to be an armed camp. (McKane, 1965:129f.)[7]

Yahweh's law and leadership were not experienced through an office of institutionalized violence, but in the reality of covenant relationship and worship, and in the office of the prophet who communicated the divine will to the people. This revolutionary kind of government reached its climax in the suffering servant of II Isaiah who went out to win the nations for Yahweh, armed only with Yahweh's word (Noth, 1956). That his enterprise ended with suffering and death and that it is this psalm of suffering and death which was decisive for the early church's understanding of Jesus shows that both Old and New Testaments are dealing primarily with the problem of political power.[8]

Jesus' own self-consciousness in relation to the nations had to do precisely with the question of leadership and the exercise of power. Jesus declared to his disciples, "Among pagans it is the kings who lord it over them, and those who have authority over them are given the title Benefactor. This must not happen with you. No; the greatest among you must behave as if he were the youngest, the leader as if he were the one who serves. For who is the greater: the one at table or the one who serves? The one at table, surely? Yet here am I among you as one who serves!" (Luke 22:24-27, *The Jerusalem Bible*; cf. Mark 10:41-45; Matthew 20:24-28). The unity of this saying with Jesus' words about the cross should be obvious. The self-consciousness which set off both Old and New Testaments from the nations had to do with the question of political power. The Bible's radical answer to this central question of power gave new structure to the biblical faith and new form to the literature.

This suggests that in our study of the Bible we must interest ourselves in more than the theology of the Bible. Biblical sociology, politics, and psychology are essential to the understanding of the biblical God. Israel had no concept of separation of church and state. Yahweh was Lord of its entire life. Its concept of separation was not between religious life and secular life, but between herself and the nations. This difference of Israel from the nations is the Old Testament paradigm for the "separation" of church and state.

The Kingdom of God and History

Israel testified that this self-conscious difference from the nations was not due to her own acts, but to the action of God in her behalf: "Did any people ever hear the voice of a god speaking out of the midst of the fire, as you have heard, and still live? Or has any god ever attempted to go and take a nation for himself from the midst of another nation, by trials, by signs, by wonders, and by war, by almighty hand and an outstretched arm, and by great terrors, according to all that the Lord your God did for you in Egypt before your eyes?" (Deuteronomy 4:33,34, RSV)

In my opinion the possibility of independent structures for the faithful church stands or falls with the question of the relation of the biblical tradition to the historical event to which it points. If biblical tradition has no fundamental relationship to historical event, then faith today has no real relationship to history either, and we are doomed to a kind of spiritualism which the Bible abhors. Biblical faith claims that God acted in history for the salvation of humankind. If God did not so act in history, then biblical faith is a fraud.

This raises the question of historical method. The significant difference in Old Testament historical method does not lie between Martin Noth and John Bright,[9] but between Noth and Gerhard von Rad. Von Rad argues for the omnicompetence of the analogy of historical event as the fundamental basis of modern biblical criticism.[10] This means that to understand the rise of Israel the historian must get behind the unique claims of the Exodus and Sinai traditions to show that the real history of Israel's beginnings was more or less the same as the origin of nations elsewhere. In von Rad's view, any uniqueness in Israel's religion was not caused by the juncture of word and deed in an actual theo-historical event, but by theological reflection which reconstructed past history.

In contrast to von Rad, Martin Noth writes:

> Yet in spite of all these historical connections and possibilities for comparison, "Israel" still appears a stranger in the world of its own time, a stranger wearing the garments and behaving in the manner of its age, yet separate from the world it lived in, not merely in the sense that every historical reality has its own individual character, and therefore an element of uniqueness, but rather at the center of the history of Israel we encounter phenomena for which there is no parallel at all elsewhere, not because material for comparison has not yet come to light but because so far as we know, *such things have simply never happened elsewhere.* (Noth, 1958:2,3; italics added)

Noth's treatment of the Reed Sea event illustrates his method. His examination of all the relevant sources of the Pentateuch uncovers much contradictory detail, but also one common agreement: the act was Yahweh's alone, and Israel did no fighting at all. This common agreement, Noth feels, is the more remarkable in the light of the contradiction in detail (Noth, 1962:119ff.) This evaluation and examination of the sources is as far as the historian can go, though it is evident that Noth accepts this common testimony. If one were to reject it, he would then need to explain the absurdity and tenacity of the biblical tradition, in face of overwhelming odds from ancient to modern times. A similar question about the assumptions of historical method is also involved in the quest for the historical Jesus.

The Hermeneutical Community and Miracle

The question of miracle is a crucial one, for it involves not merely peripheral events such as healings, but the fundamental events on which biblical faith rests--the Exodus and Sinai, the resurrection and present rule of God in Christ. It is my opinion that miracle is an essential element of biblical faith.

Miracle, however, is not to be understood in terms of the nineteenth-century argument between science and religion, but in terms of the biblical doctrine of creation. From this perspective, miracle is strange and offensive not only to modern man, but to ancient man as well. Had an Egyptian or Mesopotamian thinker encountered the biblical doctrine of creation he most likely would not have understood it; had he come to understand it, he would have been shaken to the foundations, largely because of the biblical assumption of freedom. As Christopher North points out:

> The concept of creation is not obvious, nor does it come naturally to mankind. Everywhere except in the Bible, interpretation of the universe is naturalistic, and worship is, in one form or another, worship of "the great god Pan." This is true of the religion of classical Greece, of "polymorphic" hinduism, of humanism in its various forms, of the current concept of "one single branching metabolizing protoplasm," and of the popular idea of "the life force" as the creative agent in the universe are so many more or less refined forms of what the OT stigmatizes as the worship of Baal, Baal being conceived as the personification of the life process. (1964:14)

This concept of creation originated in Israel not as speculation on what had happened "back there," but through the present experience of the newness of Yahweh's creation of a people. This is evident from the relationship of the creation event to salvation history. In Nehemiah 9:6-37, for example, the thought of Yahweh as Creator is brought to bear upon what appears to be a frustrated salvation history, that is, Israel's slavery to the Persians (Psalm 33; Isaiah 43:19; 65:17).

Remarkably, Israel projected the creative act of Yahweh in her own prophetic-historical experience onto Yahweh's relation to the entire universe, past, present, and future. While by His creative activity Yahweh gives order and regularity to the whole, at the same time he is making all things new in the creation of his people. There is no conflict between Yahweh's regular ordering of the seasons, and the new act of salvation history; both are based on his promise (Genesis 8:21-22 and 12:1-3).

Yahweh's free creative act on behalf of his people was thus a promise of his creative presence both now and in the future. If we can believe in the possibility of miracle in this sense--that God is free to create something new in biblical times, in the present day, and in the future--this is of greatest consequence for a truly biblical hermeneutic, for it enables the break with the immanent cause-effect pattern of the secular historian.

The Hermeneutical Circle

We have now come full circle in our hermeneutic of the Bible. For it is only by the experience of the new creation that we can realistically affirm with the prophets "that power is not built in with historical existence in the way that statesmen suppose" and that "God reserves all power to himself and so the *locus* of power is outside historical existence" (McKane, 1965:129). The experience of creation alone will make us bold to believe--not that our faith has the creative potential to transform a situation, but that God has already acted creatively in the situation, and by our response to that act we can enter into the freedom of his suffering in making all things new.

It was faith of this character that enabled the Anabaptists of the sixteenth century to act in freedom from the power structures and political assumptions of their age. In a similar manner, Guy Hershberger challenges the "colony of heaven" to "the good fight of faith, overcoming evil with good--with love, nonresistance, and the way of the cross, even as Christ overcame the world by going to his cross" (1958d:55).

In the biblical pattern of promise and fulfillment, it is God's new act of covenant in Christ that provides a solid bridgehead which his people may occupy in the midst of the violent history of the twentieth century, in full confidence that his creative word is the determinative power leading to the future.

NOTES

1. *War, Peace, and Nonresistance* included chapters on both Old and New Testaments. Another chapter distinguished between biblical nonresistance and other types of pacifism. *The Way of the Cross in Human Relations* begins with two chapters on biblical foundations, and utilizes Scripture references throughout.

2. In some respects a case can be made that the synagogue has been closer to the teaching of Jesus than has the mainline church. *The Anchor Bible* commentary series, edited by W. F. Albright and D. N. Freedman, is an example of the ecumenical character of contemporary biblical studies.

3. For discussion of Anabaptist hermeneutics, see Bender (1938), Kaufman (1951), Wenger (1938), Klassen (1966a and 1966b), and Yoder (1966).

4. See Riedemann (1970) for an example of the Anabaptist attitude toward government. Two of my former students, David Mann and Frederic A. Miller, have written papers on this subject.

5. See Zimmerli (1965); I have written a response to this book (Lind, 1966).

6. Quoted by Albrektson (1967). Albrektson's book is a criticism of this concept among Old Testament specialists. In my opinion his work does not demolish the point, but qualifies it.

7. I quote McKane at some length because he is not a pacifist nor an Anabaptist, and thus should not be suspect because of his presuppositions. McKane himself rejects the prophetic ethic in favor of the ethic of "responsibility" of ancient Near Eastern wisdom (pp. 129f.). But if McKane is correct in his contrast of these two ethics, it is then evident on which side this puts the ethics of Reinhold Niebuhr, e.g., *Moral Man and Immoral Society*. His ethic is contrary to that of the prophets and Jesus and is more in line with NE statecraft. This is the fundamental issue between the Bible and its environment; this is what Genesis 3 is about. See my paper, "The Anomaly of the Prophet."

8. For the importance of Isaiah 53 to the New Testament interpretation of Jesus, see Dodd (1965). Hooker (1959) may be successful in qualifying Dodd's thesis, but in my judgment does not demolish his argument.

9. For a statement of the differences between Bright and Noth, see Bright (1957).

10. Von Rad makes a sharp distinction between the confessional character of biblical faith and the way the events "really happened." "These two pictures of Israel's history lie before us-- that of modern critical scholarship and that which the faith of Israel constructed--and for the present, we must reconcile ourself to both of them." He holds that modern critical scholarship is "rational" and "objective"; that is, with the aid of historical method and presupposing *the similarity of all historical occurrence*, it constructs a critical picture of the history as it really was in Israel" (italics mine). In a footnote he sympathetically quotes E. Toeltsch: "The means by which criticism is at all possible is the application of analogy....But the omnicompetence of analogy implies that all historical events are identical in principle" (1962:107).

CHAPTER 3

THE HERMENEUTIC OF THE OLD TESTAMENT

At a time when we are examining Anabaptism to rediscover the hermeneutics of the founders of our movement, we ought also to examine the question of the hermeneutics of the Old Testament in the light of where biblical science is today. This paper is an examination of a book edited by Klaus Westermann, *Essays on Old Testament Hermeneutics*,[1] in which thirteen contemporary European scholars contribute essays on this question. Over and beyond this examination, I will attempt to sketch tentatively an answer to the question of the use of the Bible today.

The book sets forth three dogmatic approaches[2] to a Christian understanding of the Old Testament. One of these is that of A. A. van Ruler, whose book *Die christliche Kirche und das Alte Testament* is criticized by two writers, Johann Jakob Stamm and Th. C. Vriezen.[3] Van Ruler views the Old Testament from a Calvinistic point of view carried out with absolute consistency. He sees the Old Testament, with its realism and emphasis on theocracy, as superior to the New with its overemphasis on spirituality and inwardness. As Vriezen points out, van Ruler fails to see that the message of the New Testament is also theocracy, that is, the kingdom of God. He lacks the insight that the central issue is how the theocracy is to be established, not by the sword but by the cross. He overlooks the tensions within the Old Testament itself and interprets the concept of theocracy "along the lines of the false prophets rather than that of the canonical prophets,"[4] as if coercion rather than grace is the main instrument of the Old Testament.

A second dogmatic interpretation of the Old Testament is that of Friedrich Baumgärtel, which in some respects is the opposite of that of van Ruler.[5] He values the New Testament highly because of its spirituality and inwardness and sees the Old Testament as a witness of an entirely different, a non-Christian religion.[6] For him the Old Testament is not an evangelical word, and must be lost by being comprehended in its self-understanding in order that it might be won back. By making a distinction between promise and prediction on the basis of Ephesians 3:6, Baumgärtel rejects the promise-fulfillment tension of the Old Testament as mere human prediction and thus

From *The Mennonite Quarterly Review*, LX, 1966.

deprives both Testaments of their historical character (in the biblical sense of the concept). For him the timeless basic promise, "I am the Lord your God" is alone important, and is the valid foundation for comprehending the two religions, or Testaments "together and as one."

A third dogmatic approach to the Old Testament, yet an approach more inductive and thus more fruitful than the preceding, is that of Rudolph Bultmann.[7] He begins with Johannes Hofmann, *Weissagung und Erfüllung,* who held that not the words of the Old Testament but the history of Israel to which the Old Testament testifies is the prophecy which finds its fulfillment in Christ and his community. Bultmann criticizes Hofmann's view inasmuch as his "prophecy and fulfillment" is really a philosophy of history influenced by Hegel, a process of development in which tendencies already active in whatever takes place attain their realization in the natural course of events. He sees Hofmann as right, however, in his desire to understand history as prophecy; but Bultmann regards Christ as fulfillment, not in that he signifies the goal of historical development, but because he is the eschatological end.[8] Starting at this point, Bultmann examines the concepts which the New Testament picks up from the Old, concepts decisive to the Old Testament and yet which the New Testament interprets in a new sense, i.e., eschatologically.

The first of these concepts is that of covenant which designates the relationship between God and the people. In this designation something real is meant in distinction from such a concept as marriage which describes the relationship of God to his people only figuratively. This covenant, in which God demands the loyalty of the people and the people rely upon the loyalty of God, "originally gained its validity through sacrifice, and is constantly maintained and so renewed by the right sacrificial worship."[9] Thus Bultmann sees the covenant as grounded upon sacrifice, a concept which is challenged today, though no one would deny that sacrifices were made in connection with the covenant. The prophetic criticism of the sacrificial cult is difficult to explain if it was indeed as fundamental to Israel's faith as Bultmann sees it. But more than this, Bultmann feels that there is a contradiction in terms in speaking of a covenant which distinguishes an empirical and historical people and ensures it of God's help, if the validity of the covenant is bound up not with the existence of the empirical and historical people as a people, but with the moral attitude of the individual within the people. The naive consciousness of Israel that the individual gains his security from his membership in the covenant people was thundered against by the prophets, by the Baptist, and by Jesus himself, who held that the covenant depends upon the moral attitude of the individual and that thus, according to Bultmann, the idea of God's covenant with the people is done away with. "God's covenant with a people whose individuals suffice for the moral demands of God as members of the people is an eschatological concept because such a people is not a real empirical and historical, but an eschatological dimension."[10] Bultmann thus holds that the historical covenant of the Old Testament is fulfilled by the eschatological covenant of the New Testament "and to belong to it takes its members out of the world."[11]

The second concept which Bultmann traces across the Testaments is that of the Kingdom of God. In the ancient concept, this consisted basically of two points: (1) Yahweh imposed his will by law and (2) was Israel's protector and helper, directing Israel's war. In the enthronement festival, Yahweh was praised as supreme over all other gods, as lord of the world. In the time of the exile the kingdom of God became an eschatological concept and in the post-exilic period both present and eschatological ideas of the kingdom ran a parallel course. In this period, however, the future age, awaited by the prophets as an historical epoch, now becomes a supernatural era of salvation, preceded by the judgment of the nations.[12] The kingdom which Jesus proclaimed was no longer understood as an Old Testament theocracy, i.e., the dominion of a divine kingdom in liberated land, "but as the wonder of a new era for the word breaking in from heaven."[13] "There only remains the phase 'the dominion of God' and the idea of a community in which God's name is hallowed and his will is operative."[14] "The demands of the Sermon on the Mount, the command to love, do not reveal any sort of interest in people and the organization of the people; the law is overruled by love, and the judge will ask some day in the tribunal only about what 'you have done unto one of the least of my brethren' (Matt. 25:31-46)."[15] But is such a rule of God realizable within this world? "The New Testament has made the idea of the eschatological rule of God its own in such a way that it sees in the existence of the community the realization of the rule of God, the coming into force of the new *aeon*, seeing in the community a dimension which is at one and the same time within and beyond the world."[16] It is present but not in the old sense, not within the history of the people and in the forms of the national community, but beyond it. "It is realized by Jesus' having been made King through his resurrection, and it is a reality where he is recognized as King."[17] He is ruling even now and will rule till the *parousia* when he will give up his dominion to God (1 Cor. 15:23-28). This rule of God and so of Christ is "completely different from what Old Testament prophecy had expected," eschatological and supramundane in its entirety, "and the man who is in it, as it were, already taken out of the world, so that he lives no longer 'according to the flesh,' however much he still lives 'in the flesh' (2 Cor. 10:3)."[18]

The third concept which Bultmann traces is that of the people of God.[19] The kingdom of this world rivals the kingdom of God. The people whose God is king cannot tolerate any earthy king (Judges 8:23). In the judgment of Hosea, Israel's guilt originated in Gilgal where Saul (1 Sam. 11:14 f.) was anointed king (Hos. 9:15). Though the secular kingdom was not greatly opposed by prophecy after it had become accepted through David, yet the inner contradiction of the idea of the people of God and the secular kingdom soon became apparent. Certain necessities go along with a secular kingdom (1 Sam. 8:10 ff.)--civil service, army, taxation, leagues, all of which have nothing to do with the people of God. The prophetic reaction was directed against the forms and consequences of the new state organization.

But it is clear that the kings, if ever they are willing to bear the responsibility for the state, do not have the possibility of carrying on their rule in the cause of the prophetic idea. They have to see to armament and to the fortification of towns; they have to concern themselves with alliances, and so on. By contrast, the prophets cannot be representatives of the idea of the 'people of God' in a form such as would allow it to be implemented in the secular kingdom. They demand the execution of law and justice, but link this demand to the idea of patriarchal, tribal organization which prevailed before the days of the state, and so what they demand inevitably miscarries.[20]

Israel also implemented this idea of the theocracy after the exile, but then this people of God was no longer a state. It was subject to foreign dominion, and could only so live if it wished to be the people of God as an empirical people. This was again demonstrated when the pious turned away from the Hasmonean dynasty when, after freeing the land, this dynasty began to act as a state. It was demonstrated in the same way when the pious voluntarily submitted to Pompey when he entered Jerusalem. "That is to say, the people of God has acknowledged that it can no longer exist as a state, if it wishes to realize itself in that capacity, but only as a religious community, as a kind of church."[21] A Judaism which desires to be both the people of God and a state "is a self-contradictory phenomenon."[22] This contradiction was expressed in the pages from the "Eighteen Blessings" which expect the restoration of the state, not however through warlike activity but by God's miraculous intervention. Also the coming Messiah became sort of a shadowy figure, a symbol, which had to compete with the idea of God's kingship; and the Messiah's era was finally lowered to the status of a prologue to the real salvation era. This attempt to reconcile the idea of the kingdom of God with that of a national state was rejected by the New Testament. The people of God exists no longer as an empirical historical entity, and thus the state, in so far as it is really a state, "is made irrelevant (Rom. 13); it is, so to speak, released from the sphere of interest of the people of God (cf. 1 Cor. 6:1 ff.). From this there then naturally arises the peculiar dual existence of the Christian in church and state with its problems...."[23] After tracing these three themes, Bultmann asks how, for the Old Testament, Jewish history represents prophecy which is fulfilled in the history of the New Testament community.[24] He answers that it is fulfilled in its miscarriage. Israel's interest in being the people of God led toward the idea of a transcendent God and his activity. But instead of conceiving of this in a radical transcendent, eschatological sense, Israel brought this into line with the empirical history of the people, and so there was a miscarriage of history in this contradiction. (1) "The idea of a covenant of God with a people shows itself to be an impossible development within history and becomes an eschatological idea." (2) "The idea of the rule of God is shown to be unrealizable within the world, and the attempt to realize it is reduced to absurdity by the grotesque form of a priestly and legalistic theocracy." (3) "The idea of the people of God shows itself to be unrealizable in an empirical national community, as this requires for its historical existence forms of state organization, law, and authority."[25]

Bultmann thus reinterprets the biblical concept of promise-fulfillment in line with the pauline idea that the Law is a schoolmaster to bring one to Christ. This might be compared to the Lutheran contrast of Law (Old Testament) and grace (New Testament).[26]

We have given considerable space to Bultmann's essay because of its positive contribution, an attempt to trace decisive themes across the two Testaments. We will speak of this positive contribution later, as we try to chart an answer to the hermeneutical problem. Our purpose here is to raise certain questions about Bultmann's method. Bultmann criticized Hofmann for interpreting the Old Testament in line with the Hegelian philosophy of history; has not Bultmann also imported non-biblical philosophic thought in his interpretation of the Old Testament? For example, he says that the conflict of the Old Testament is not merely that of two human ideas, "but as one which belongs to human existence as such--the conflict of being created for God and called to God, and yet of being imprisoned in secular history."[27] This tendency to see the human dilemma as primarily an ontological rather than moral problem is hardly a biblical formulation. This formulation of the human problem affects Bultmann's concept of salvation, as Zimmerli points out. What the Bible means by the Christian being delivered from the world is that he is delivered from the powers of this world, not as Bultmann would have it that he is delivered from history, history which also in the New Testament continues to stand under the tension of promise-fulfillment, i.e., between resurrection and the coming of Christ. By interpreting the Old Testament totally as failure, Bultmann is able "to elevate the Christ-message purely out of history in existential interpretation,"[28] thus remythologizing or philosophizing the biblical message. Bultmann does this because he fails to see the eschatological or "existential" element of the Old Testament and its peculiar relationship to "history," and because he refuses to take seriously the "history" element of the New Testament, an element which is indeed not too apparent if one rejects what the New Testament community accepted, the unity of the New Testament events with the word of promise in the Old Testament.

The articles by Gerhard von Rad, Klaus Westermann, Martin Noth, Walther Zimmerli, Hans Wolff, and Walther Eichrodt are an attempt to approach the hermeneutic of the Old Testament not dogmatically but inductively. These writers find a substantial measure of agreement in the so-called typological method, particularly as this is understood along the lines of promise and fulfillment. I will present here the position of one of its main representatives, Gerhard von Rad, then will give some correctives from other writers, and finally will treat the criticism of Walther Eichrodt.

Von Rad points out that typological or analogical thought is an elementary function of all human thinking, which presupposes an order deep within things. In the ancient Orient, there was thought to be a correspondence between macrocosm and microcosm, "the prototypes of all countries, rivers, cities, and temples exist in heaven in the form of certain astral figures, while those on earth are only copies of them."[29] The Bible, on the other hand, has only vestigial remnants of this view. Its correspondence, instead of the vertical one, is a horizontal, linear one. This analogical understanding of the Bible, due to the influence of rationalism, has been lost to Old Testament scholarship. While for the Reformers there was an emphasis upon the "facts" of the Old Testament, since the day of Michaelis and Semler the emphasis has been on spiritual teachings, truths, concepts of God, of the world, of man, of sin, all of which were extracted from historical statements.

The Old Testament, von Rad holds, is a history book, history brought to pass by God's word. The word of promise and the fulfillment in the event provide the horizontal correspondence. Even the prophetic books are "history" in that the prophets speak the word which will come to pass in the future, in the eschatological age. And even the fulfillments of the prophetic word, history itself, become prototypes to which the new redemptive act will correspond. Thus all is in motion, both prophecy and history, toward the promise of greater things to come.

This relationship of Word of God to history is a pervasive one in the Old Testament. It is characteristic of the Deuteronomic history (Deuteronomy--2 Kings), of the "succession to the throne of David" (2 Sam. 7--2 Kings 2), and, as we have seen, of even the prophetic books. This view is foundational to the thought of the New Testament, and explains the much quoting of the Old Testament by the New Testament writers. According to these writers it was a method used by Jesus himself (Luke 4:16-21). The relation of the two Testaments is therefore not merely that the thought world of the Old Testament is very much like that of the New Testament. "Rather we see everywhere in this history brought to pass by God's Word, in acts of judgment and acts of redemption alike, the prefiguration of the Christ-event of the New Testament."[30] "One must therefore--at last to use the controversial word--really speak of a witness of the Old Testament to Christ, for our knowledge of Christ is incomplete without the witness of the Old Testament.[31]

Claus Westermann, in presenting this biblical relationship of promise and fulfillment,[32] points out that the older orthodoxy with its timeless dogmatics did not recognize history. History of religion, on the other hand, saw only history; it knew no Word of God. The trouble with both was that neither listened to the Bible to discover what it had to say about the relationship of word to history.

Martin Noth[33] deals with the "re-presentation" of the event in the cult, the worshiping individual being caught up again in the event, the means whereby the past became meaningful to the present.

Walther Zimmerli[34] points up the fact that the Patriarchal covenant has become historically credible today through the research of Albrecht Alt, and that the theme of promise-fulfillment may be as old as Moses. The central meaning of this theme is the faithfulness of God: he does that which he has promised.

Hans Wolff[35] compares the Old Testament and its promise-fulfillment emphasis with the ancient Orient, with Judaism, and with the New Testament in an attempt to find the larger context of the Old Testament. It is obvious to all that the home of the Old Testament is not with it mythological environment, the more striking since Israel borrowed her institutions from this environment. Nor does the historical emphasis of promise-fulfillment fit the synagogue with its emphasis upon law. The only larger context of the Old Testament is the church which in the New Testament sees itself as fulfillment, fulfilling the Old Testament goal of the world-wide community of God established by his grace. Moreover, the Old Testament is important to the church in that it prevents the witness to Christ from being corrupted into a philosophy about Christ. It guards the Christian message against transcendentalism and "is an aid to an eschatological existence in the history of this world."[36] Wolff warns against finding too quickly in the Old Testament a God who is foreign to the New.

The only criticism of the typological method comes from Walther Eichrodt,[37] who distinguishes between typology and promise-fulfillment and argues that these methods should not be made the only means of interpretation. He feels that we must emphasize "more strongly the decisive significance of the people of God in both testaments in its vocation to living fellowship with God, and to characterize exegesis as something that proceeds from the analogy of faith or the analogy of communication."[38] This emphasis upon covenant characterizes his great work on Old Testament theology.[39] It is my own conviction that this criticism by Eichrodt needs to be taken seriously, that there is a serious imbalance in the theology of the typologists, and that recent scholarship provides a new possibility for synthesis which by all means should be made. I expand upon this in my concluding remarks.

CONCLUSION

I offer the following suggestions for our own hermeneutical method, as a response to this book.

1. A Biblical Theology

While the distinction between the two Testaments should continue to be recognized, this should not be made as absolute as was done by some a generation ago.[40] Our strong social emphasis must be guarded against a mere humanism by a rediscovery of the Old Testament and the particularism of God's work in history.

2. An Inductive Approach

Every hermeneutic which seeks to make itself the master rather than the servant of the text must be rejected. The Old Testament should not be interpreted in the light of some dogma of the New unless this dogma is itself compatible and pervasive throughout the Old.

3. Typological Interpretation

The typological interpretation (promise-fulfillment) is common to both Old and New Testaments, and is a clue to their relationship.

4. Covenant History

As Eichrodt has suggested, the typological interpretation is inadequate, and must be corrected with an emphasis upon covenant. Today the unity of the typological emphasis of von Rad and the covenant emphasis of Eichrodt has become apparent in the form-critical discovery of George Mendenhall as to the Mosaic covenant.[41] Long ago Albrecht Alt saw the unity of law with covenant.[42] Now we know that salvation history (Heilsgeschichte) is also a part of the covenant form, a point which von Rad now acknowledges.[43] God's acts in history are seen in their true meaning only as foundational to and archetypal of the act of covenant relationship by which he binds himself to his people, and by which his word of promise to Abraham (also a covenant form, but of a different type, characteristic of the early second millennium B.C.)[44] is fulfilled. This unites and gives orientation not only to the concerns of von Rad and Eichrodt, but also answers Friedrich Baumgärtel.[45] For the promise is not merely "I am with you" (covenant), but "I am with you to deliver you" (*Heilsgeschichte* within covenant). Perhaps the term "salvation history" should be replaced by the term "covenant history."

5. The Content of Covenant

But again it is inadequate to see the relationship of the Old to the New Testament in terms of mere covenant form and of the tension of promise-fulfillment between these forms. One must ask concerning the *content* of the Mosaic covenant for it is not the mere form which is fulfilled, but the content. This brings us to the three concerns of Bultmann, which are to be seen, however, not in Bultmann's negative relationship between the Testaments but in a positive relationship: (1) covenant, (2) the kingdom of God, (3) the people of God.[46]

The first of these, the pledge of loyalty of the two parties, has already been discussed. It is only necessary to point out that this covenant is not grounded primarily upon the sacrificial act which would make it dependent upon an act of the people, but upon God's prior act of salvation. The response of the people was indeed necessary but it was to be a response of loyalty to God and to fellow men as suggested by the Ten Commandments and early prophets (see point 6). Since the covenant is based upon the act of God by which he fulfilled his word of promise, this is a positive, an "existential" or "eschatological" act, which nevertheless enters into the history of his people and of humankind, an act which, as can be seen from hindsight, carries the promise of something even greater.

Bultmann's second theme, the kingdom of God, is also a part of the content of the Mosaic covenant, inasmuch as Yahweh is the suzerain, or king of his people. There is quite general agreement that Yahweh was recognized as king

in Israel as early as the period of the Judges.[47] The discovery of the nature of
the Mosaic covenant formula pushes the probability of such kingship back to
the desert period.[48] This kingship is not to be separated from the concept of
covenant relationship (Bultmann's first theme, above), but is part and parcel of
it: "I will be your God, and you shall be my people."

This kingship of God consists basically of three parts: (1) Yahweh's
saving acts of grace for his people; (2) his demand upon his people; (3) and
finally his reward or judgment of his people. Yahweh's acts of grace are acts of
warfare in behalf of his people. Contrary to the Hittite covenant, which
demands that the vassal come to the aid of the suzerain in warfare, the
covenant forms in the Old Testament do not include warfare as a part of God's
demand or law. In the biblical covenant forms warfare is included only with
Yahweh's saving acts even where Israel cooperates, though Israelite
theologians find Israel's warlike action difficult to harmonize with Israel's
archetypal experience of grace (cf. Joshua 24:6-13).[49] Thus humankind's central problem of alienation and warfare is drawn into the very heart of covenant,
and is fundamentally restricted to God's act for his people.

This kingship of God is also God's eschatological or "existential" act, for
again it is not mythologically oriented (kingship over the gods), but is historically oriented. Yahweh is king of Israel in an immediate sense.

Bultmann's third point, the people of God, is suggested by the fact that
Israel had no human king. That this was dogmatically based at an early period
Bultmann has already shown. The fact that Yahweh takes the place of the
human suzerain in the covenant form suggests that this dogma found its roots
in the desert covenant.[50]

While Bultmann is correct in pointing out Israel's rejection of Near Eastern state structures, he is wrong in assuming that Israel could have no structure
of her own. Israel could not be a nation like other nations, because of the
nature of Yahweh and the vocation to which Israel was called. This did not
exclude structure, but substituted covenant structure for the structures of the
Near East. This was a radical displacement, however, inasmuch as it ideally
reserved the exercise of power politics to Yahweh alone and in a utopian fash-
ion replaced the army and police force with voluntary obedience to the
prophetic word, thus giving birth to the peculiarly biblical concept of freedom.[51] Because of the frailty of man, this idealism often resulted in anarchy
and inability to cope with the external enemy. To overcome this, Israel com-
promised the covenant, both in regard to structure and to content (kingship,
etc.). This compromise was opposed by the canonical prophet who, despairing
of the human problem, prophesied of a salvation beyond judgment when the
idealism of covenant would be realized, but only by a new and decisive act of
God, chiefly an anthropomorphic one (Jer. 31:31).

6. The Movement of History

While D. C. Simpson saw the movement of Old Testament history as progressively upward, Bultmann sees it as progressively downward: "The history

of the Old Testament is a history of foundering and failure."[52] While Westermann sees both as dogmatically based outside of the Old Testament, Bultmann nevertheless has a large measure of support within the Old Testament itself, i.e., from the Deuteronomic historian.[53] This biblical historian, however, saw the movement of Israel's history not merely on a declining plane, but as a downward spiral (cf. Judges 2:6 ff.), a spiral which moved toward two crises. The first of these was the Philistine threat when Israel, by an apostasy which threatened the very nature of her covenant faith, demanded a king "like all the nations" (1 Sam. 12). In this first crisis Israel was given a reprieve, and the very apostasy of the people became by a process of divine alchemy a symbol of hope. This hope, however, was crushed by the second crisis, first in the North (722), then in the South (587).[54] This downward movement is directly related by the Deuteronomic historian to the paganizing office of kingship, and thus the movement is closely related to the covenant content outlined above (point 5).

While the general movement of history was downward, and thus negative, Bultmann failed to be inductive in that he did not take into account the upbeat of the downward spiral. While the downbeat was due to the negative response of the people to the Mosaic covenant, the upbeat was due to a new eschatological (or "existential") act of God in fulfillment of the patriarchal covenant, not an act apart from history, but which enters history and thus saves it with an upward swing (Deut. 4:23-31).[55] The prophets saw beyond 722 and 587 this same upbeat of history, arising this time by resurrection, out of death itself (Ezekiel 37), and being nothing less than a new age in which the covenant reality, experienced by Israel so imperfectly, would be fulfilled. Inasmuch, however, as the upbeats of the downward spiral were the saving acts of God and of an eschatological nature, the history of Israel was not merely negative. While the acts of Israel resulted in a movement which was mainly downward, this very movement was saved from time to time by God's eschatological action, an action which thus partook of the same positive quality as the act of fulfillment witnessed to by the New Testament writers (Hebrews 1:1 ff.).

7. The Servant of Yahweh

Finally, this downward movement of history is not seen in the Old Testament as merely of negative value. At this point we must add to Bultmann's themes one which he somehow has overlooked, that of the suffering servant, set forth by Deutero-Isaiah (Isaiah 40-55). This prophet sees Israel not as bearing punishment merely for her own sins, but as vicariously bearing punishment for the sins of others (Isaiah 53). It is this negative yet positive theme which likely Jesus himself, and certainly the New Testament church, used to interpret his life, death, resurrection, and ascension.[56]

8. The New Testament

If we reject the re-mythologization of the New Testament which results from interpreting it in the context of a modern mythology (or philosophy), we must then be prepared to accept the radical result of a Jesus of Nazareth who is pre-eminently a political figure, of a crucifixion, resurrection, and ascension which are political acts, of the establishment of the church which is a political body (Ephesians). This is not a Constantinian solution, however (a compromise comparable to Israelite kingship), but the call to a renunciation of the Machiavellian political ethic, an ethic as old as the human race, and the voluntary acceptance of the political ethic of the Christ, i.e., the cross.

A biblical realism, including a knowledge of the downward spiral of history, should not blind us with a utopian optimism, but the promise of God's eschatological act should release us on the other hand from the paralysis of despair. Keeping in mind our own frailty, our mission should be twofold: (1) to warn that part of the Body which compromises with the Machiavellian ethic that they should not compromise the essence, (2) and to call the world's nations both by example and preaching toward an acceptance of the political ethic of Christ, thus bringing what they regard as politically expedient into tension with the cross. If this seems utopian we can only observe that the Machiavellian ethic, in our present world situation, threatens the opposite, utter chaos. Our situation is in some ways not unlike that of the Deuteronomic historian. We live in hope of a realized eschatology, knowing all the while that we are descending ever closer to the edge of the abyss. If humankind goes over, we can only hope with the prophets that through death via resurrection humankind will yet realize the promise of God.

NOTES

1. K. Westermann, ed. (Richmond, Va., 1965), Eng. trans., ed. by James Luther Mays. These essays were never gathered up in the German, and many of them are no longer readily available in the original language. Except for no. 2, the following notes refer to individual essays included in this book.

2. By "dogmatic approach" I mean a conscious interpretation of the Old Testament on the basis of a dogmatic principle found outside of the Old Testament, i.e., either in the New Testament or in a confessional statement. I do not deny that all interpreters are influenced by thought extraneous to the Old Testament, but make a distinction between those who have that as their conscious goal and those who have as their conscious goal an understanding of the Old Testament on its own terms.

3. Johann Jakob Stamm, "Jesus Christ and the Old Testament," 200-10; Th. C. Vriezen, "Theocracy and Soteriology," 211-23. Cf. van Ruler, *Die christliche Kirche und das Alte Testament* (Munich, 1955).

4. Vriezen, *op.cit.*, 219.

5. Friedrich Baumgärtel, "The Hermeneutical Problem of the Old Testament," 134-59. For a criticism by K. Westermann, cf. "Remarks on the Theses of Bultmann and Baumgärtel, 123-33; J. J. Stamm, "Jesus Christ and the Old Testament," 204. For a fuller view of Baumgärtel's thought, see his book *Verheissung, zur Frage des evangelischen Verständnisses des Alten Testaments* (C. Bertelsmann Verlag, 1952).

6. Westermann, 135.

7. Bultmann, "Prophecy and Fulfillment," 50-75. For criticisms, see Westermann, "Remarks on the Theses of Bultmann and Baumgärtel," 123-33; Pannenberg, "Redemptive Event and History," 314-35.

8. *Op.cit.*, 58.

9. *Ibid.*, 59.

10. *Ibid.*, 60, 61. The quotation from p. 61.

11. *Ibid.*, 63.

12. *Ibid.*,, 65, 66.

13. *Ibid.*, 66.

14. *Ibid*, 67.

15. *Ibid.*, 66.

16. *Ibid.*, 66.

17. *Ibid.*, 67.

18. *Ibid.*, 67.

19. *Ibid.*, 68.

20. *Ibid.*, 69.

21. *Ibid.*, 69, 70.

22. *Ibid.*, 70.

23. *Ibid.*, 72.

24. *Ibid.*, 72.

25. *Ibid.*, 73.

26. *Ibid.*, 74.

27. *Ibid.*, 74.

28. See Zimmerli, *Ibid.*, 119.

29. *Ibid.*, 18. von Rad is quoting B. Meissner here.

30. *Ibid.*, 36.

31. *Ibid.*, 39.

32. "The Interpretation of the Old Testament," *Ibid.*, 40-49.

33. "The 'Re-Presentation' of the Old Testament in Proclamation," *Ibid.*, 76-88.

34. "Promise and Fulfillment," *Ibid*, 89-122.

35. "The Hermeneutics of the Old Testament," *Ibid.*, 160-99.

36. *Ibid*, 198.

37. "Is Typological Exegesis an Appropriate Method?" *Ibid.*, 224-45.

38. *Ibid.*, 245.

39. *Theologie des Alten Testaments* (Berlin, 1948).

40. The following statement is taken from *the Sword and Trumpet* 5:18 (October 1933): "Popular 'Christianity' with its war, divorce, fashions, and numerous other destructive and hurtful errors is built up on the general plan that the Old and New Testament are a unit, and are to be harmonized into the Christian system of religion, while the Mennonite Church and some others hold the opposite view that the Old Testament and New Testament must be contrasted as entirely separate systems, impossible to harmonize into one system, and not intended by the Lord so to be used." The emphasis upon systems itself shows the influence of rationalistic orthodoxy while the emphasis upon difference leaves us with two religions, in this respect comparable to the view of Friedrich Baumgärtel (134-59). For an opposite viewpoint, see Guy F. Hershberger, *War, Peace and Nonresistance* (Scottdale, 1944) 14-39.

41. Cf. George E. Mendenhall, *Law and Covenant in Israel and the Ancient Near East* (Pittsburgh, 1955); also Klaus Baltzer, *Das Bundesformular* (Neukirchener Verlag, 1960).

42. Cf. Albrecht Alt, "Die Ursprünge des Israelitischen Rechts" in *Kleine Schriften zur Geschichte des Volkes Israel*, I (Munich, 1953) 328f.

43. Cf. Gerhard von Rad, *Das Fünfte Buch Mose. Deuteronomium* (ATD, Vol. 18, 1964) 15.

44. Cf. Julius Lewy, "Les textes paleo-assyriens et l'Ancien Testament," *Revue de l'Histoire des Religions*, Vol. 110 (1934) 29-65.

45. See above, 1, 2.

46. See above, 2 ff.

47. Cf. the ancient poetry, Ex. 15:17, 28; Num. 23:23. For the dating of this poetry see Frank M. Cross,Jr. and David Noel Freedman, "The Song of Miriam," *Journal of Near Eastern Studies* 14:237-50 (October 1955); W. J. Albright, "The Oracles of Balaam," *Journal of Biblical Literature*, LXIII: 207-33 (1944). For studies of the Kingship of God, see Werner Schmidt, *Königtum Gottes in Ugarit und Israel* (Berlin: Verlag Alfred Topelmann, 1961); Albrecht Alt, "Gedanken über das Königtum Jahwes," 1945, in*Kleine Schriften zur Geschichte des Volkes Israel* (Munich, 1953) 345-57.

48. Cf. note 26.

49. Patrick D. Miller, "Holy War and Cosmic War in Early Israel" (Thesis, Harvard University, 1963) 76, also recognizes this point. "A precise statement of the obligation of the vassal to fight for the suzerain does not appear in the stipulations of the Old Testament or Israelite covenant. It was, however, a definite and important part of the Near Eastern vassal treaties upon which the Israelite covenant form and content were based." While I agree with him as to this fact, I disagree with him as to the interpretation of this fact. The Israelite covenant form does have

comparisons with the Near Eastern vassal treaty; but surely the *content* of the Israelite covenant is not based upon the Near Eastern treaty form. The fact that the obligation of the vassal to fight for the suzerain was a "definite and important part of the Near Eastern vassal treaties" makes its omission in the biblical covenantal forms the more striking and suggestive. The problem of disapproval toward uncooperating tribes in the Song of Deborah, etc., needs further study. We only note here that neither blessing nor curse is directed toward the tribes, but toward *external* noncooperation and cooperation with Israel (Judges 5:23,24).

50. Cf. George E. Mendenhall, "The Hebrew Conquest of Palestine," in *The Biblical Archaeologist* 15:66-87 (1962), who sees this dogma as a reaction to Near Eastern kingship, a reaction shared by other than Israel as suggested by the Amarna tablets.

51. Cf. *Ibid.*

52. Quoting Westermann, "Remarks on the Theses of Bultmann and Baumgärtel," 124.

53. For a discussion of the Deuteronomic history in English, see D. N. Freedman, "Pentateuch," in *The Interpreter's Dictionary of the Bible*, 3:715-17.

54. Cf. Martin Noth, *Ueberlieferungsgeschichtliche Studien* (Halle, 1943).

55. Cf. D. N. Freedman, *Divine Commitment and Human Obligation* (Reprint from *Interpretation*, October 1964).

56. Cf. Morna D. Hooker, *Jesus and the Servant*, 1-23, for a general survey of New Testament scholars on this subject.

CHAPTER 4

REFOCUSING THEOLOGICAL EDUCATION TO MISSION:
THE OLD TESTAMENT AND CONTEXTUALIZATION

My encounter with the Old Testament in the past 25 years has convinced me that it speaks of the universal mission of the God of Israel not merely in a few texts here and there, but throughout its total message from Genesis to Malachi. If this is true, our task in refocusing the teaching of the OT to the mission of the church is not to recast the OT into a preconceived "missionary mold" (and so to reject the authority of the OT) but rather to be faithful in exegeting it.

However, more than the question of whether the Bible is concerned with a universal message, contextualization raises the questions of what that universal message is and how it relates to the various cultures of the world.

It is difficult to find a widely acceptable definition of contextualization, since the term "is being harnessed to a wide range of mutually exclusive presuppositions." The concern of indigenization was "to make sure that the gospel in every place is clothed with forms appropriate to the local culture"; contextualization goes beyond this by exploring every conceivable way in which the gospel may be related to "the cosmos: the material-spiritual world of human experience" (Glasser 1979:403-404).

Hiebert suggests that contextualization is the adaptation of the gospel to different cultures, knowledge and nature of human beings on the deepest levels, a challenge of the social sciences which is even greater than the challenge of the natural sciences of the last two centuries, and concludes that "we will need to develop not only a Christian soteriology, ecclesiology and eschatology, but also Christian theologies of time, space, ancestors, animals, plants, misfortunes (individual, societal, and cosmic), and guidance for uncertain futures" (1982:12).

These definitions and descriptions of the task of contextualization raise two questions when compared with the results of biblical exegesis:

1) Starting with the biblical point of view, are some concerns more pertinent than others, and thus more directly addressed within the Bible itself? May some problems so clamor for the church's attention because of the nature

From *Missiology: An International Review*, X, 1982.

of Missio Dei that to address more secondary matters at length should be regarded as misspending the church's resources unconscionably, and perhaps even distorting the biblical concern? May constructing theologies of "time, space, ancestors, animals, plants," etc., have to give way to more ethical and existential constructs such as the relationship of the church to society and the state? One might approach such issues from the perspective of Eliade with his mythology of time (loc cit). Or one might procede more existentially, like the young Muganda woman who said, "Many Africans are seeking answers to their questionings, but the church is not playing its full part in helping young people to face the problems of society. To them, God is the God of the church. He is not the God of politics and social life."[1]

2) Then we must ask which direction the adaptation should flow. Is it merely the gospel that adapts to different cultures, knowledge and nature of human beings, or is there also an even deeper level of adaptation and transformation of cultures, knowledge and nature of human beings to the nature of the revelatory event?[2]

In refocusing the teaching of the OT, it seems best to approach the Bible in terms of canon criticism and then survey texts throughout the OT which speak to Yahweh's universal concern as well as to the problem of contextualization. In the relation of the church and its message to the larger society, we should remember that the Western church's present theology began with an African, Augustine, and that other solutions were also offered by earlier African church leaders (Harms 1980:17-51). The choice the Third World churches must make then is not necessarily a choice among the various options presented by the West, but among options debated by the African church leaders of the second to fifth centuries AD, and by the Near Eastern church (OT and NT) even earlier.

The Approach of Canon Criticism

Canon criticism is a recent emphasis in biblical studies to understand the Bible in its final form. It is not anticritical but postcritical; that is, it does not ignore the critical approach but insists that its purpose is to understand the Bible in its present shape (Childs 1979). From the viewpoint of canon criticism, the Bible is 1) universal in the light of a particular experience (Gen. 1-11), 2) particular with a universal goal as a vision (Gen. 12--Jn 21) and 3) universal around a particular experience of a community (Ac--Rv).

The Primeval History

Genesis 1-11 introduces not only our present Bible, but introduced also the first canon, the Pentateuch. Most of it is thought to have stood as the introduction to the oldest literary tradition of the Hebrew Bible. The universal character which these materials give was thus not an afterthought.

What was the process of contextualizing this ancient material? Obviously Genesis 1-11 interprets the revelatory event of Exodus and Sinai in terms of the need of the nations. Israel and its vocation are seen in the context of the world. The overall outline of the material (preflood, flood, postflood) is one used by the ancient Sumerian kingship list (Pritchard 1969:265f). The creation and flood narratives, and the narrative of the confusion of tongues reflect superficially the Babylonian and Sumerian culture. Yet on a deeper level the material is reoriented and dominated by the theological themes of grace and rebellion, judgment and salvation--these derived from Israel's prophetic experience with Yahweh but universalized to show Yahweh's concern for the world behind his choice of Israel. It also reflects Israel's recognition that its roots were in the nations, that Abraham was a foreigner, an Aramean rather than a Hebrew (cf. Deut. 26:5).

This analysis suggests that Israel's theologians proceeded quite differently from those who refuse to relate the gospel to the world, and also from those who regard the task of contextualizing as merely relating the gospel to the world. On the deepest levels, the opposite movement took place: the world was understood and reinterpreted in light of Israel's election.

Genesis 1, 2

That both these chapters are superficially related to a Babylonian background suggests one phase of the movement in contextualization. The opposite phase is involved, however, in the process of what happens to Near Eastern myth as it enters the Bible. Childs defines myth phenomenologically as that (such as the Enuma Elish) which involves a dynamistic concept of the universe (i.e., ultimate reality is identified with the life process), but also involves the cult, with such ideas as mythological time (return to the beginning) and mythological space (the creative center). Most biblical phenomenologists agree that Genesis 1-11 includes mythological remnants broken off from their base and reoriented to biblical event. Biblical language for example uses mythological language to denote divinity ('ĕlohîm) but denies the mythological character of divinity (that ultimate reality is identified with the life process).

Seen from this perspective, all philosophies which identify ultimate reality with the life process show a continuity with ancient Near Eastern mythological thought, a concept which the Bible challenges (North 1964:14). How did ancient NE mythology arise? Jacobsen sees its origins in observations of nature (natural science) and human society (social science) and a projection of these observations as ultimate reality, that which happened in the cosmogonic beginnings (1946:170-173). This would compare to a modern person interpreting ultimate reality on the basis of the natural and social sciences. Genesis 1-2, on the other hand, is an interpretation of man/woman and the cosmos in view of the prophetic-historical event of Exodus-Sinai. Likewise the NT has interpreted the universal in terms of the new event (John 1).

This fundamental break of Genesis 1 and 2 in the interpretation of the universe coincides with another contrast with the Babylonian and Egyptian cosmogonies, cosmologies which are primarily political manifestos to promote and enforce Babylonian and Memphite political power. In the biblical statements, by way of contrast, Yahweh's creative power undergirds the structure of the universal family rather than a coercive nationalism or Israelite empire. The messages of the creation narratives declare that God's rule is free from any tie with colonialism whether political or economic, or of a tie of the younger churches with the coercive politics of the state. The unity of humankind which Yahweh offers is freedom within covenant rule rather than a coercive "unity" provided by oppressive empire and state structures (cf. Col.; Eph.). This contextualization on the deepest level of the universal to the character of the revelatory event is often lacking today.

Genesis 3; 4; 6:1-4

The narratives of the fall depict man/woman's rebellion against the rule of Yahweh to establish their own rule. Chapter 3 is a study in recategorization and new perspective in an analysis of the ancient NE problem (Hiebert 1981:12). This new perspective is symbolized by the tree. In the NE the tree of life is central to the human concern as reflected both in literature and art. The tree represents life and fertility both for now and for eternity. In these chapters this concern is relegated to the edges of the story, at the beginning and the end. Life is still important, but it is dislodged from the central concern by the "tree of knowledge of good and evil."

What is this tree? Since it is nowhere else represented, either in the Bible or in extant NE literature and art, we cannot know. But the emphasis is upon Yahweh's command regarding the tree. Man and woman challenged the command of Yahweh, instigating their own unjust, coercive rule. The text sees this as humanity's central problem--the viewpoint from which the problem of life itself is to be regarded. The central problem is not a scientific one (the control of nature, etc.) but a spiritual-moral problem--humanity's rebellion against the rule of the divine. Humans use their rule over nature as a means to rule over their peers, thus violating the command of Yahweh who is irrevocably linked to the equality of all people under the rule of God.

The message of the primeval history is not primarily creation and fall but God's coming in grace and judgment. The questions "Where are you?" (Gen. 3) and "Where is your sibling?" (Gen. 4) are universals--posed by God as a fitting introduction to the story of the human race. The source of the writer's pattern for this universal vision of Yahweh's concern is apparent in the fact that the questions parallel the vertical and horizontal concerns of the Ten Words (Ex. 20:1-11, 12-17; and Mk. 12:29-31). Is it not evident here that contextualization moves both ways? The roots of the material are for the most part Babylonian, but it is radically reshaped by the central expressions of Israel's prophetic experience with Yahweh--which itself is seen as Yahweh's searching question to humankind.

Crediting the first city and technological development to Cain and his descendants (4:17-22) was due not to the writer's blind prejudice against cultural development but to the ancient experience that the city was built on serfdom and slavery (see Job 24:12) and that the city-state built its empire on the villages of the countryside. Humans used their domination of nature to dominate others. The story of the fall climaxes in the revenge song of Lamech (4:23-24) and in the military guild described in 6:1-4, a society undergirded by its myth of divine-human procreation (Margulis 1970:292-304).

Perhaps Israel's own story in the time of Solomon had taught our editor/writer that technological and cultural development does not issue in human justice but oppression. More likely the Canaanite city-states, or Israel's servitude in Egypt had given the same message. For those with eyes to see, the evidence was all around, as it is today. Nevertheless our author stresses that in the midst of such oppression some begin to call on the name of Yahweh (4:26), and in the midst of a militarized and violent society one finds grace in Yahweh's eyes (6:7). Yahweh does not desert the human race, but by judgment and grace leads it ever toward justice. This material gives us a vision not only of the human fragmentation but of Yahweh's concern for the total society, and of the place of righteous people within it in leading that society toward justice.

Genesis 9-12

Genesis is usually divided into two sections--the primeval and patriarchal histories. According to the type of material, this division is correct, but in view of the ancient literary traditions, it is not. They divide between the pre-flood and post-flood periods, the latter including the patriarchal era, extending to the time of the traditionalists themselves. The flood divided the old from the new age.

The base of the new post-flood age was Yahweh's providential promise (Gen. 8:20-22) and covenant with all humanity (9:8-17). This covenant also included the animal world (9:8-10). What once was the reason for the flood-- that every imagination of the human heart was evil continually (6:5)--would now be the reason Yahweh would never again destroy every living creature (8:21).

The new age whose base was Yahweh's providential promise to all humanity had as apex Yahweh's call and election of Abraham--Yahweh's answer to the problem of humanity's rebellion, more specifically, the new focal point for the unity of the peoples who had been scattered by their arrogance and pride (11:1-9). The particularism of Israel is depicted by the oldest Pentateuchal tradition not as a further fragmentation of humankind, but God's answer to this problem. All the rebellious families of the earth, upheld by providential promise, would bless themselves in the people whom Yahweh has blessed, a people whose destiny is to bless others.

The oldest Pentateuchal tradition contrasts two particularisms, both portrayed as having possible universal significance: the Mesopotamian city-state with its autonomous, self-seeking decision making (11:1-9), and the Abrahamic people, led and blessed by Yahweh (12:1-3). Just as the first passage emphasizes Yahweh's judgment, fragmentation and scattering of the people (11:5-11), so the second passage by grammar and diction climaxes in a universal blessing of the earth's families (12:3).

Many commentators regard this ancient tradition as reduced to writing in the 10th century BC when the Davidic-Solomonic empire was at its zenith. If so, the writer may have used this ancient tradition to warn Jerusalem that the universalism of Yahwism is not to be achieved by the self-serving decision making of a city-state with its social stratification and empire-building propensities but by the covenant leadership of Yahweh whose name is associated with freedom rather than bondage (Ex. 3:13-17), whose goal is that all nations might bless themselves in their relationships with Israel. Our editor/writer saw the election as Yahweh's primary act to contextualize the world in divine grace. It is evident that this is the most fundamental movement in the contextualizing process.

The Ancestral History: Genesis 12-50

Not only is the particularism of the Abraham people presented as an alternative to the city-state pyramidal social order; more than this, the orientation of this people is not "blood and soil" but God and people, with God as leader. Land is obviously important to a people, but land as well as community and social significance depend on Yahweh's promise and fulfillment. This theme runs like a red thread throughout the patriarchal materials (Gen. 12:1-3,7; 13:14-16; 15:5,7,18; 18:10; 26:24; 28:3f, 13-15; 32:12; 35:9-10; 48:16).

This orientation of land to the divine relationship is congruent with the fact that the earliest canon did not include the story of the occupation. While land is important as promise, its fulfillment is not essential to peoplehood. Israel was a people before entering the land and continued to be one long after the land was lost. It was not essential that fulfillment of the promise of land be a part of the earliest canon.

What was true of the earliest canon may also have been true of the literary tradition of the Pentateuch. Some scholars see this earliest tradition as extending through the conquest down to the time of Solomon. A growing number of critical scholars, however, hold that this earliest literary tradition ends with the Tetrateuch. If this is true, then not only the earliest canon but also Israel's earliest literary tradition (10th century BC) closes the story before the conquest, and thus demonstrates a striking decline of interest in the conquest (Wolff 1966:133).

The interest of this literary tradition was not a nationalistic one. Its message was rather that Israel was to be Yahweh's blessing to the nations and the conquest did not fit the message. A large percentage of the people for whom this literary tradition was intended were of Canaanite origin. An anti-Canaanite polemic runs throughout the material, but it is against the fertility cult rather than ethnocentric or nationalistic. This promise-fulfillment motif carries a powerful message for the transformation of nationalism by the Missio Dei.

Just as the Abraham people are the apex of the base of the universal post-flood providential promise, so the patriarchal narratives continue with Yahweh's blessing of the earth's families through the Abrahamic people. "I loved

Jacob, and I hated Esau" must be exegeted in Malachi but should not be super-
imposed on Genesis. In Genesis, blessing moves out from the Abraham
people to the surrounding nations. Lot makes his decisions on the basis of
what he sees rather than by faith (Gen. 13) and his decision making gets him
into trouble. Even then, however, the god of Abraham saves Lot, traditional
progenitor of Ammon and Moab (Gen. 18; 19), and involves Abraham in this
decision.

But Yahweh's decision included more than Lot; it had to do with the
entire Canaanite population of Sodom and Gomorrah. At this point the
ancient literary tradition clarifies the vocation of the Abraham people: Yahweh said,

> Shall I hide from Abraham what I am about to do, seeing that Abraham
> shall be a great and mighty nation, and all nations of the world shall bless
> themselves by him? No, for I have chosen him, that he may charge his
> children and his household after him to keep the way of Yahweh by
> doing righteousness and justice (18:17-18).

Abraham then keeps this way of Yahweh by standing between Yahweh's
wrath and the Canaanite cities: "Will the judge of the whole earth not
administer justice?" (18:25). The vocation of the people of God to the nations
is here stated by the biblical writer with great clarity and force. Here is a clear
challenge to the NE ḥērem, the utter destruction of the Canaanite city, implemented so often in the book of Joshua. Certainly this program of justice, so
central to the early biblical writer, should be central also to the ecclesia's contextualization of the whole earth in the justice of God.

In the Isaac-Ishmael conflict, though Isaac is chosen, Ishmael, son of the
Egyptian woman, is also blessed by Yahweh (21:15-21). In the narrative of
chapter 20, the vocation of Abraham again becomes clear in relation to
Abimelech "king of Gerar": "Now then, restore the man's wife, for he is a
prophet, and he will pray for you, and you shall live" (20:7). In the Jacob-Esau
narratives, the election of Jacob does not preclude a blessing also for Esau,
progenitor of Edom (Gen. 27:27-29). These narratives also propose that as a
result of Jacob's wrestling with God, Israel's relation to Esau is to be that of a
servant-vassal so that peace may be restored (32; 33). The Joseph narratives
maintain that intertribal policies should be dominated by forgiveness since
Yahweh overrules for the divine salvation purpose even the evil that people do
(45:4f; 50:19), salvation which included the Egyptians who said, "You have
saved our lives" (47:25).

The story of Genesis is also an obstacle story: Sarah is lost to Pharaoh's
harem in Egypt (12); she is barren and Ishmael poses a threat (16). The concept of child sacrifice (22), Rebecca's barrenness (24), Jacob's flight to Aram
(27), Rachel's barrenness (29), Jacob's slavery to Laban (29-30), the threat of
Esau (32), the disruption caused by the Joseph episode--all threaten the continuity of the community for which Yahweh intervenes. The climactic threat
and intervention is slavery in Egypt and the Exodus, an experience which

becomes a new beginning of their peoplehood. This vulnerability of the community of faith and dependence upon Yahweh's intervention is an important understanding for the church in its task of contextualizing the world in God's grace.

Exodus, Sinai and the Wilderness: Exodus-Numbers

The two central pillars of the OT are the Exodus and Sinai events which were responsible for the reorientation of the primeval history and for the shaping of the patriarchal history. These two themes deal with the fundamental needs of any state--freedom from foreign powers and internal order--yet the different character of these two primary events from the usual origins and structure of a state set Israel apart from the ancient states of the NE (cf. Num. 23:9). Their relevancy for contextualization is that they clearly establish the independent political character of the people of Yahweh.

The Exodus Theme: Exodus 1-15

The fundamental problem of Moses was the problem of leadership of any state--political legitimacy. When the Hebrew confronted him with this question, Moses fled (Ex. 2:14). His call is concerned with the same question: "Who am I that I should go to Pharaoh, and bring the children of Israel out of Egypt?" (3:11). Moses' political task was legitimated by the fact that Yahweh had sent him and would be with him (3:10-11). The calls of all the prophets should be understood in terms of this question of political legitimation. This legitimation made it possible for Moses to confront Israel's leaders and Pharaoh, and for the prophet to confront people and king. The Scripture is explicit on this modern-day problem of the church.

Nonviolent Resistance

The ancient narrative of the Exodus is the earliest and best narrative of a nonviolent resistance movement in history. Beginning with the account of five women who oppose the genocide of a totalitarian state, the issue is drawn simply: "But the midwives feared God, and did not do as the king of Egypt commanded" (1:17). Chapter 5 sets forth the pattern of resistance with such detail that one wonders whether it formed a pattern for subsequent events. First Moses and Aaron--Yahweh's messengers--state the demand (5:1). Then Pharaoh denies knowledge of Yahweh and refuses the request (5:2). The request is repeated, describing the consequences for Israel if they do not obey Yahweh; the demand includes freedom to worship Yahweh (5:3). After this, Pharaoh accuses the Hebrew leaders of a work slowdown and commands the Egyptian taskmasters and the Hebrew overseers to increase the people's workload (5:6-9). The Hebrew overseers, caught in the middle, are flogged when the people fail to achieve their quota (5:10-14). When the Hebrews appeal to Pharaoh for redress, he repeats his accusations and maintains the quota (5:15-

18). Recognizing their evil plight, the Hebrew overseers turn on their leaders--
Aaron and Moses--who accuse Yahweh of worsening the plight of the people,
and not delivering them at all (5:22-23).

This intimate knowledge of the pattern of nonviolent resistance raises a
question as to the nature of Israel's occupation of Canaan. Three theories of
the occupation are: a conquest, a rather peaceful settlement or a people's
revolution. If one is to take the Bible seriously, there may have been aspects of
all three, with revolution (essentially nonviolent) dominant. The people of the
Canaanite city-states as a part of the Egyptian empire could easily have
identified with the escapees from Egypt, and the pattern of Exodus 5 may have
had meaning for more than a one-time strategy.

If this is true, it explains the missionary character of the young Yahwistic
movement and the early concern of Yahweh for the world's peoples--and why
the earliest literary tradition of the Pentateuch saw the election of the
Abraham people as Yahweh's alternative to the city-state society to express the
universal concern: "Where are you?" "Where is your sibling?" If this is true,
the missionary concern has its roots in the very beginnings of the biblical faith,
and this concern deals centrally with the question of the legitimate nature and
use of political power. Thus the narratives of the Exodus are of central value
to the matter of the church's task of contextualizing the world in the rule of
Yahweh.

The Sinai Theme: Exodus 10-Numbers 10

Like its contemporary NE states, early Israel had law collections (Ex.
20:22-23:19; Lev. 17-26; Deut. 12-26; 28; Ex. 20:1-17; Deut. 27:11-26). The missionary significance of this law is stated in the preamble of Israel's most ancient
law, Exodus 19:4-6; by keeping covenant law, Israel is to be Yahweh's elite
community, different from all peoples. Because the entire earth belongs to
Yahweh, Israel is to be God's holy nation; as a kingdom of priests it is to teach
the nations the way of Yahweh.

Unlike the NE codes, Israel's law was immediately linked to Yahweh, its
only king. This meant that law in the Bible was linked to the prophet as
speaker for Yahweh and guardian of law. The New Testament correctly
reflects this by the phrase, "the law and the prophets" (Matt. 7:12; 22:40; Acts
24:;18, etc.). In contrast, ancient NE collections link law to the gods through
kingship. Also, law in the Bible is within the context of its covenant structure,
God and people. Again, while law collections in the NE are strictly secular,
those in the Bible include both "religious" and "secular" law (see the Ten Commandments). Even more important, the foundation of law in the OT is God's
act of grace in delivering his people from Egypt: "I am the Lord your God who
brought you out of the land of Egypt, out of the house of bondage" (Ex. 20:2).
This is the first and most important of the ten Words, according to the Jewish
enumeration, the word which unfortunately Christian enumerations have cus-
tomarily omitted.

This act of Yahweh for his people has also invaded the law collections, a characteristic not found in NE law. The "motive clause" (or "model clause"), is found in the earliest law collection in relation to 17% of the laws. In later law collections, the percentage is as high as 60% and 63%.[3] This clause propels Israelite law forward, away from NE law. For example, the law of slavery in Exodus 21:2-6 has no motive clause. The revision of this law in Deuteronomy 15:12-18 is both liberalized and profoundly penetrated with the motive clause, salvation from Egypt. The most liberal law regarding slavery is the law that a runaway slave may not be returned to a previous owner (23:15-16). If this law had been taken seriously, slavery would have become entirely voluntary in Israel. The motive clause had the effect of making law inward, to "write it upon the heart." From this perspective, the law collections of Israel are the antecedents of the Sermon on the Mount.

If the ecclesia takes seriously the fact that God has given a new kind of law, it will take up the vocation of guardian and witness to Yahweh's justice and by teaching, preaching and example will propel state law forward by bringing it into tension with the gospel.

Israel's Society: Covenant Egalitarianism

Biblical Israelite law mirrors a covenant egalitarian structure of society rather than the pyramid structure of the NE states. Contrary to those of the NE, Israel's collections did not recognize different social classes. Their laws of land tenure gave to every household the inalienable right to the use of a plot of land--in ancient times the most important of capital goods. The law of Jubilee, sabbatical year and lending money without interest were mutual aid laws to help maintain a basic economic equality. The law of the tithe recognized the right of the Levite and of the poor who had no land. Instead of the pyramidal state structure of its environment, Israel moved forward into its contemporary world trying to maintain an intertribal covenant egalitarian structure--which is at least somewhat reflected in the structures of the NT church. This economic and egalitarian principle is fundamentally important in the ecclesia's task of contextualizing the world to the rule of Yahweh.

Deuteronomic History

The great historical work extending from Deuteronomy to 2 Kings was probably compiled shortly after the finding of the book of the law in Josiah's reign. Its universal message is somewhat restricted but nevertheless present. Deuteronomy 4:19 states that Yahweh has given the stars and all the host of heaven to the nations for their worship, but has reserved Israel to himself. In Solomon's prayer of dedicating the temple he asks Yahweh to hear the prayer of the foreigner who comes from afar to pray in the temple "in order that the peoples of the earth may know thy name and fear thee, as do thy people Israel, and that they may know that this house which I have built is called by thy name" (1 Kings 8:41-43). It is significant that the temple rather than the palace is seen as the center for Yahweh's universal rule (cf. Isa. 2:1-4).

The emphasis of the Deuteronomic historian on the failure of Israel and how the events of 722 and 587 happened or threatened to happen is summed up in the editorializing of Judges 2 and 3, and 2 Kings 17:7-41. Criticizing Israel, the historian says the kings drove Israel from following Yahweh who "removed Israel out of his sight, as he had spoken by all his servants the prophets" (2 Kings 17:21-23). This criticism concerned not only "religious matters" but also structural concern. The historian was positive toward Israel's prophets and negative toward the kings. Ancient Israel had demanded kingship and was granted kingship, but only if kingship were to be reoriented from a foundation of economics and military power to the foundation of obedience to Yahweh's torah (Deut. 17:14-20). The two Judean kings who receive unqualified endorsement, Hezekiah and Josiah, had made this reorientation at least at certain critical moments.[4] Israel and Judah fell because they were essentially Baalistic, following kings who insisted on NE concepts of economics and power politics rather than the spiritual and moral leadership of the God of Sinai. This entire history is important for the proper understanding of the ecclesia's task of contextualizing the power-oriented societies of our world to the gracious rule of Yahweh.

Prophetic Books

These books in the Hebrew classification include the historical books mentioned above. While there are obvious differences between the two, it seems that the Hebrew classification is correct since both historical and prophetic works agree that the foundation for Israel's social and political life was to be torah and prophetic oracle.

The eighth century prophets, Amos and Isaiah, directed oracles against the nations. Amos charged them with rebellion against Yahweh as evidenced by the war crimes which they perpetrated against each other (ch. 1). The collections of Isaiah and Micah both include an ancient oracle which foresees all the nations ascending the holy hill of Jerusalem (Isa. 2:1-4; Mic. 4:1-4). The issue is not sword vs. plowshare, as is often exegeted, but the torah and way of Yahweh which the nations accept for international relations instead of the balance of power (or terror) as represented by the sword. When nations accept Yahweh's torah for international relations, the sword becomes irrelevant and can therefore be beaten into instruments for the mastery of nature rather than for subjugation of other people.

Micah includes in this international picture the Yahwistic demand not only for peace among nations but for economic equality and security for every household: "But they shall sit everyone under their vine and under their fig tree, and none shall make them afraid." Fundamentally, the message of all these prophets was that Israel had rejected Yahweh's worship and way of justice, substituting power-oriented Baalism instead.

Hosea illustrates how the prophets communicated with a people who essentially did not understand Yahwism. He lay hold of the very heart of Baalism, the fertility male-female principle, translating it in terms of covenant, the relationship of Yahweh to his people. (The Psalms, omitted in this discussion, are classic examples of borrowing and translation.)

The eighth century prophets were traumatized by 722; the seventh and sixth century prophets were similarly polarized toward the event of 587. Jeremiah felt called as a messenger of Yahweh's word to the nations. He proclaimed to the foreign council of ministers gathered at Jerusalem that they were not to listen to their prophets by rebelling against Nebuchadnezzar, but that along with Judah they were to obey the God of Israel who had chosen Nebuchadnezzar as a servant to rule over the nations (ch. 27).

Jeremiah did not mean that Babylon had replaced Israel to do Yahweh's work for the nations, for it also would be destroyed when the time came. Yahweh would form a new community through Israel, but only by a new act of grace, a new covenant, which would place Yahweh's law in each person's heart. This is not to be interpreted as individualism and privatizing of religion as Wellhausen would have it--a notion of the Western church--but rather an individualization of loyalty to Yahweh's way which would produce the new community of God's people, the goal toward which the entire Bible has pointed.

The book of Habakkuk treats the problem of God's justice, recognizing that the injustice of Judah demands Yahweh's judgment. But the Chaldeans whom God used as instruments of justice were more unjust than Israel. The prophet received from Yahweh not mere theory but a practical answer: "The just shall live by faithfulness"--by keeping on. He dared to say in face of the imperialistic injustice of Babylon, "Yahweh is in his holy temple, Let all the earth be silent before him" (2:20).

Deutero-Isaiah has long been recognized as the climax to the biblical emphasis on monotheism, but this means here far more than merely confessing that there is one God. Hans Wildenberger defines it:

> To the concept of monotheism belongs the clear consciousness of the unity of the cosmos and history and the dependence of both upon the power of the one Lord, with all the consequences which such a world view brings with it for faith in one God (1977:509).

Deutero-Isaiah's monotheism speaks also to the *quality* of the unity of God, removing the argument from the battlefield to the courtroom. Three trial speeches of Yahweh against the gods (41:21-29; 43:8-13; 45:1; 18-25) set forth the either-or option of the divinity of Yahweh against polytheism. The issue is not the mere existence of the one over against the many, but the effectiveness of only the one to present an understanding of history in terms of promise/threat and fulfillment and to control the future in continuity with the historical past (41:22-23,25-27; 43:9,10; 45:21). Obviously the effectiveness of the gods in the political arena, not just to project or control a specific event but to control the present in continuity with the past so as to insure communal life is an argument which deals with the issue of power.

The Jews had their problems with Deutero-Isaiah but had no difficulty understanding this argument. They had known about Yahweh's promise-fulfillment from their oldest writings. Above all, they had experienced Yah-weh's fulfillment of two centuries of prophetic threats by their exile in the Babylonian empire--Amos, Isaiah and Micah; Jeremiah, Zephaniah and Ezekiel.

But how could the Babylonians--steeped in the concept that divinity is expressed by the supremacy of violent political power--understand the prophet's argument? In the third trial speech the prophet's answer is given to Babylon not in victory but in defeat--in the same situation as the Jewish exiles. This new situation of defeat provided a new opportunity for the prophet's oracle appealing to the nations to look to Yahweh for their continuity:

> Turn to me and be saved,
>   all the ends of the earth
>   For I am God, and there is no other.
> By myself I have sworn,
>   from my mouth has gone forth in righteousness
>   a word that shall not return:
> "To me every knee shall bow,
>   every tongue shall swear" (45:22f).

How would Yahweh achieve this voluntaristic rule over the nations? Not by means of the Persian Cyrus who is called Yahweh's anointed, his shepherd king (45:1; 44:28). Cyrus might be Yahweh's agent to exercise violent political power to achieve Yahweh's purpose, but after his victory Cyrus never becomes Yahweh's representative ruler over the nations--which was what every kingly representative of the NE gods was expected to do. Cyrus was chosen by Yah-weh for a negative purpose although he did not know Yahweh (45:4f) and received the apt title, "a bird of prey from the East" (46:11). By defeating the nations, Cyrus would return Israel to its land (45:4,13).

Yahweh achieves this rule over the nations not by Cyrus but by the ser-vant Israel whose task is to bring justice to the nations (42:1-4). Cyrus thought he was doing so by conquests, but from the perspective of Yahwism, the justice of Cyrus was the epitome of injustice. The instrument of Yahweh's servant was not to be violent political power but the word of Yahweh (42:2-3; 49:2; 50:4-5). The servant would experience opposition, persecution and death (42:4; 49:4; 50:6-9; 52:13-53:12); justice to the nations would come only by Yahweh's inter-vention, reversing the negative judgment of the nations and elevating the ser-vant to a place of rule (49:4; 52:13-15; 53:11-12). Then the nations would con-fess their rebellion and acknowledge that the suffering of the servant was on their behalf, that by his stripes they are healed (53:1-10). Yahweh's oath of monotheism in his trial speech (45:22f) is fulfilled then, not through Cyrus, who as a bird of prey had his function, but by Yahweh's intervention on behalf of Israel. This is the fantastic claim as to what the people of God are about in contextualizing the nations to Yahweh's rule as seen from Genesis to Deutero-Isaiah.

The Apocalyptic Writings: Daniel

The apocalyptic writings of Daniel should not be overlooked since along with Deutero-Isaiah they form an important bridge to the NT and the present. In this book Israel finds itself, like the servant, powerless among the nations. Apocalyptic literature is not entirely oriented to the future which Daniel demonstrates since it is composed of two parts--six narratives (1-6) and four visions (7-12). These two sections form a close unity, uniting the present situation of Israel in exile and the future victory of Yahweh's kingdom. I will demonstrate this unity by examining Daniel 6 and 7.

A unique aspect of Daniel 6 is that the king of Persia was on Daniel's side. In contrast to the enraged Nebuchadnezzar who commanded that the Hebrews be cast into the furnace (ch. 3), Darius "labored till the sun went down" to rescue Daniel (6:14). But the king, caught in the impersonality of his own state law, could not save Daniel. Who then is savior? The king must place his hope for Daniel's salvation in Daniel's God (6:16). In the end, Darius acknowledges this one as savior:

> His kingdom shall never be destroyed,
>   and his dominion shall be to the end.
> He delivers and rescues,
>   he works signs and wonders
>   in heaven and on earth (6:26f).

Israel's task among the nations was to bring the rulers of this world to at least a momentary recognition of Yahweh, his law and power (Dan. 1:17-21; 2:46f; 4:34f).

The vision of Daniel 7 sets forth the final (rather than momentary) victory of the kingdom of God, represented by his saints, over the four world kingdoms. In contrast to the four beasts which rise from the sea (7:3), the Son of Man comes "with the clouds of heaven" (7:4). The fourth kingdom, being the worst, is sentenced to death by the "ancient of days"; the lives of the rest were prolonged for a time (7:12). Then the kingdom is given to "one like a son of man" (7:13f).

Who is this "one like a son of man"? The interpretation says that it is "the saints of the Most High" (7:18). Jesus before the Sanhedrin claimed this title for himself (or perhaps for himself and his disciples? Matt. 26:64). The recognition of the final kingdom here is like that of the momentary recognition by the world powers of Daniel 6: "their kingdom shall be an everlasting kingdom, and all dominions shall serve and obey them" (7:27). The momentary victories of the church within the context of the nations partakes of the character of the final victory of the Son of Man.

Summary

This survey suggests that the entire OT is profitable for the church in

order to understand its place in Yahweh's mission and its task of contextualization. The primeval history orients the entire Bible to Yahweh's worldwide
task. The rest of the OT is largely particular with a universal goal as its vision.
This particularity has to do with a certain quality of community toward which
Yahweh is leading the nations. The church should be conscious of its political
legitimacy in this leadership of the nations. Its new experience of liberation, its
new experience of law and order are central to the needs of the nations.

The story of Israel's failure to follow the way of Yahweh and the subsequent judgments are also instructive for the church. The message of the
prophets that the power-gods of the nations are ineffective for the continuity of
their community, that Yahweh alone is effective and establishes his justice not
through violent power but by the patient proclamation of his suffering one, is
certainly central to the church's contextualizing. Finally the message of
apocalyptic, that the small and momentary victories of the people of God in
insisting upon his sovereignty partake of the victory of Yahweh's final triumph,
is again of central importance.

What is the direction of contextualization as found within these biblical
materials? Obviously contextualization moves in both directions. The
revelatory event is contextualized to the people and cultures of the world, but
the most profound movement is in the other direction. The cultures and
peoples of the world and Israel itself are contextualized by the revelatory event.
The biblical doctrine of monotheism brings all peoples under the rule of Yahweh's servant. The apocalypse of Daniel brings all peoples under the rule of
the saints of the Most High, a prophecy which the early church saw as fulfilled
in Jesus.

NOTES

1. This illustration comes from a written statement by Wilbert Shenk, Secretary of Overseas Missions, Mennonite Board ofMissions, 500 S. Main Street, Elkhart, IN, February 26, 1981.

2. Glasser points out that many evangelicals posit such limitations to any contextualizing process that they cannot see ways that the Gospel impinges on the culture, while some liberals so contextualize the Gospel that it loses its specificity (1979:404). My question is whether biblical exegesis may reveal that the biblical way of doing theology speaks to this dilemma.

3. As an example of the motive clause, see Lev. 25:42. For a discussion see B. Gemser, "The Importance of the Motive Clause in Old Testament Law," *Congress Vol.*, Supplement to *Vetus Testamentum* (Leiden: E. J. Brill, 1953), pp. 50-66.

4. For a discussion of this reorientation, see Gerald Eddie Gerbrandt, "Kingship According to the Deuteronomistic History" (Disssertation, Union Theological Seminary, Virginia, 1979).

REFERENCES CITED

Childs, Brevard
1979 *Introduction to the Old Testament as Scripture*, Philadelphia: Fortress Press.

Glasser, Arthur F.
1979 "Help from an Unexpected Quarter, or the Old Testament and Contextualization," *Missiology*, Vol. 7, October.

Harms, Jean-Michael
1980 *It is Not Lawful for for Me to Fight*, Scottdale, PA: Herald Press.

Hiebert, Paul G.
1981 "Contextualization's Challenge to Theological Education," *Occasional Papers of the Council of Mennonite Seminaries and Institute of Mennonite Studies*, No. 2.

Jacobsen, Thorkild
1946 "Mesopotamia: The Cosmos as a State," in Frankfort, et al, *The Intellectual Adventure of Ancient Man*, Chicago: University of Chicago Press.

Margulis, B.
1970 "A Ugaritic Psalm (RS 24.252)," *Journal of Biblical Literature*, 89.

North, Christopher
1964 *The Second Isaiah*, Oxford: Clarendon Press.

Pritchard, James B.
1969 *Ancient Near Eastern Texts*, 3rd Edition. Princeton: Princeton University Press.

Wildenberger, Hans
1977 "Der Monotheismus Deuterjesajas" *Beiträge Zur Alttestamentlichen Theologie*, Festschrift für Walther Zimmerli zum 70 Gesburtstag, hrsg. Herbert Donner, et al. Göttingen: Vandenhoeck und Ruprecht.

Wolff, Hans Walter
1966 "The Kerygma of the Yahwist," *Interpretation*, 20.

CHAPTER 5

TRADITIONAL AND NOT-SO-TRADITIONAL VALUES

To celebrate this Christmas season, I am lifting out of this not so traditional Bible of ours three texts which document the surprises often found within narratives that deal with traditional themes:

> a text from the story of the birth of Samuel;
> a text from the story of the birth of Obed; and
> a text from the story of the boy Jesus.

First, from the story of Elkanah and Hannah and the birth of Samuel: "And Elkanah her husband said to her, 'Hannah, why do you weep? And why do you not eat? And why is your heart sad? Am I not more to you than ten sons?'...and Elkanah knew Hannah his wife, and the Lord remembered her; and in due time Hannah conceived and bore a son, and she called his name Samuel..." (1 Samuel 1:8, 19, 20).

This text suggests that there are values in marriage more important than being fruitful and multiplying and filling the earth. Elkanah said to childless Hannah, "Am I not more to you than ten sons?"

There are societies where the institution of marriage centers mainly on fertility, where women are little more than baby machines. But in the pressure of Hannah's desire for traditional values, she is reminded that her relationship with her husband is even more important.

We are not chickens in separate cages. Marriage is made to enjoy the mutuality of relationship, a partnership as described in Genesis 2. As we become involved in the traditional values of utility and continuity, we need to remember the more ultimate value, to enjoy the companionship that we give to each other.

But perhaps we should not be too critical of Hannah's concern for traditional values. For she transformed even the traditional into the unusual. When she had finished nursing Samuel, she "lent him to the Lord for as long as the child might live." As the ingenious mother of Moses entrusted her child to the crocodile infested Nile, so this self-giving Hannah entrusted little Samuel to

From *Gospel Herald*, December 15, 1987.

a corrupt priestly center, setting in motion the development of a second great leader who would save God's people.

Hannah accepted the traditional, but in doing so she transcended mere family concerns. Both traditional and not-so-traditional values were necessary to prepare this savior of Israel.

Our second text we lift from the story of the birth of Obed to Ruth and Boaz: "So Boaz took Ruth and she became his wife; and he went in to her, and the Lord gave her conception, and she bore a son. Then the women said to Naomi (Ruth's mother-in-law)...., 'He shall be to you a restorer of life and a nourisher of your old age; for your daughter-in-law who loves you, who is more to you than seven sons, has borne him.'" (Ruth 4:13-15).

The book of Ruth is an unconventional story of how Israel's mutual aid system had worked to save the family of Elimelech and Naomi, and to integrate the foreign woman Ruth into Israelite society. To escape a famine in Bethlehem, Naomi and Elimelech had journeyed to Moab. There the family was nearly lost to Israel when the two sons integrated into this foreign society by marrying Moabite women. But the tragic death of the men of the household made Naomi decide to leave her daughters-in-law and to return to her homeland. Ruth the Moabite woman refused to part from her mother-in-law: "Your people, my people; your God, my God; where you die, I die, and there I will be buried."

In the Bethlehem barley field Ruth attracted the attention of Boaz. And by a daring, unconventional act one night, Ruth received Boaz's promise that he would act for her and her mother-in-law.

Boaz did this, and as a result married Ruth. To this union a son was born, a son who in Israelite society would be counted as the grandson of Elimelech and Naomi, thus saving both their family and their property in Bethlehem. Israel's system of mutual aid had worked even in this unusual case.

Although this story is unconventional throughout, its entire plot hinges upon the traditional value of a male heir. The tragedy of the family was the lack of a male heir to carry on the family name and responsibilities in Israel. Ruth the Moabite woman, by her conversion to Israelite faith and way of life, and by the faithful response of Boaz as go'el (savior) within Israel's mutual aid structures, gave to Naomi a male child. The family was saved for Israel.

The usual story teller would have been satisfied with the unconventional character of the story from beginning to end, even though the plot revolves around the traditional value of a male heir. Our story teller, however, was sensitized to the oppressive character even of this traditional value, so important to the story's plot, and so important to Israel's structured life. The teller reminds the hearer of another value more important even than this. In the story's resolution the Bethlehem women, even while congratulating Naomi on the birth of the son, say to her, "Your daughter-in-law who loves you, who is more to you than seven sons...."

Let me tell you a little of my personal history with this verse. I belong to a family which had seven sons, no daughters. As a boy reading the Bible, this verse offended me. "How," I wondered, "could one woman be worth more than seven sons?" Though as a boy I was unable to resolve my problem, I did perceive the story's challenge of my own traditional values. While the traditional value of a male heir was indispensable to the plot of the story, the love and loyalty of Ruth which had made the resolution possible, was worth even more than the continuity of the family.

But this not-so-traditional value did not negate the importance of the traditional value. Rather, Ruth's unconditional love saved the traditional value from its oppressive boredom. And more than the continuity of the family was involved here. By this child, Ruth the Moabite woman would become an ancestor of David. The child who saves Naomi's family participates also in the salvation of Israel. But even then, more important than the birth of the child was Ruth's loyalty to Naomi.

Our third text we lift from the story of the boy Jesus and his parents in Jerusalem. Jesus said to anxious Mary, "How is it that you sought me? Did you not know that I must be in my Father's house?'...and he went down with them and came to Nazareth, and was obedient to them..." (Luke 2:49).

The boy Jesus had been lost to his parents at the crowded passover festival. When after three days they found him in the temple surrounded by teachers, his mother said, "My son, why have you treated us like this? My father and I have been searching for you with great anxiety." Jesus replied without apology, "What made you search? Didn't you know that I was certain to be in my Father's house?" Joseph and Mary needed to learn that there was a Parent to whose business they would lose this son of theirs. Years later when Mary and his brothers came to take Jesus home, thinking that he had lost his sanity, Jesus disowned them by looking around and replying, "Here are my mother and my brothers. Whoever does the will of God is my brother, my sister, my mother" (Mark 12:35).

But that time was not yet. The boy Jesus returned with his parents to Nazareth where he grew up under their authority. If it was necessary for him to break the bond of family life to be about the business of the Heavenly Father, so it was essential that he learn obedience by subjecting himself to the demands of Nazareth family life. The routines of family life may also be heavenly business. Nevertheless, the felicity of family life can be rightly nurtured only as the family recognizes a higher business, a business which prompted Jesus like Jeremiah before him to give himself to a single ministry.

There is a unity in these birth stories of Samuel, Obed and Jesus though the stories are separated by more than a millennium. The unity of the first and last was apparent to the writer of Luke's Gospel, who paralleled the development of Jesus with that of Samuel:

> "Now the boy Samuel continued to grow both in stature and in favor with the Lord and with men" (1 Samuel 2:26).
> "And Jesus increased in wisdom and in stature, and in favor with God and man" (Luke 2:52).

Though unrecognized by the author of the book of Luke, the birth story of Obed also has unity with that of Jesus, the one as ancestor, the other as descendant of David.

As we ponder these stories in our hearts, we too will discern their unity with the traditional and not-so-traditional aspects of our life, millennia later.

II. LAW, JUSTICE AND POWER

CHAPTER 6

LAW IN THE OLD TESTAMENT

We are witnessing today a revival of the church's interest in justice and law. This is evident by the activity of organizations such as MCC Prison Ministries, VORP, the Christian Legal Society, and by the many articles appearing in legal magazines on the subject of the Christian and law. At the same time there has been a renewed interest in the Bible and law as evidenced by the many books and articles which have recently been published on this subject. The discovery of the code of Hammurabi[1] in 1901 by the French expedition at Susa (18-17th c. B.C.), the later discoveries of the Ur-Nammu code (21st c. B.C.), the Lipit-Ishtar code (19th c. B.C.), the Eshnunna code (18th c. B.C.), the Middle Assyrian laws (12th c. B.C.), the Hittite laws (date?), the Neo-Babylonian laws (7th c. B.C.), as well as many royal edicts, documents and letters referring to ancient business and legal transactions, have stimulated interest in the study of law in the Old Testament. This study of law in the Bible, however, is seldom drawn upon as a resource by those interested in the practical questions of Christianity and law. Many articles and books on Christianity and law promote a return to a revised classical medieval position, often including a revival of the doctrine of natural law, with a minimal reference to what has developed in biblical studies.[2]

It is the purpose of this paper to call attention to the new understanding in justice and law as discovered by recent studies in the Bible and to challenge the church to build its approach to modern problems of law and order upon the biblical foundation of this understanding.

The Bible is so saturated by the concept of law that it is scarcely possible to understand its narratives, prophetic oracles, prayers, songs, proverbs, even its understanding of God and his relation to Israel without understanding something of its legal concepts.[3] This legal orientation is further emphasized by the fact that the Pentateuch contains no fewer than three law codes:[4] the Covenant code (Ex. 20:22--23:33),[5] the Deuteronomic code (Deut. 12--26; 28) and the Holiness code (Lev. 17--26), besides the laws usually designated as P, and a number of smaller collections such as the Decalogue (Ex. 20:1-17; Deut.

From *The Bible and Law*, Willard Swartley, ed., *Occasional Papers*, No. 3, 1982.

5:6-22), the Cultic Decalogue (Ex. 34:10-26), and the Dodecalogue (Deut. 27:11-26).

To simplify my task, I will base this paper mainly upon the text that is generally regarded as the oldest biblical code, the Covenant code, especially Exodus 20:22--23:19.[6] I will take account of critical studies in this paper. The tentative and fragmenting tendency of such studies may be overcome to a considerable extent by canon criticism, the insistence that critical studies must contribute to an understanding of the present text.[7] I will gather up my remarks on the Covenant code under four statements: (1) The Covenant code deals with "secular matters" comparable to the concerns of Near Eastern codes, the kind of societal problems which arise in the daily life of an ancient community. (2) In the structure of the code the laws begin and end with "religious law," and the code is interspersed with that law, laws which have to do with the relationship between God and Israel. (3) The law is given in the form of *parenesis*, teaching-preaching, the radical motive and model for law being God's liberation of Israel from Egypt. (4) The purpose of the Covenant code in terms of the ancient Near East is radical and revolutionary. Following a discussion of these four points, I will comment on what I think this may mean for the church today.

I. REMARKS ON THE COVENANT CODE

1. *The Covenant code deals with "secular matters" comparable to those of the Near Eastern codes, the kind of societal relationships and problems which arose in the daily life of an ancient community.*

This point is illustrated by the following laws from the Covenant code and their parallels in the Near Eastern codes:[8]

LAW OF THE GORING OX:

Exodus 21:28f., 35,36(RSV): When an ox gores a man or a woman to death, the ox shall be stoned, and its flesh shall not be eaten; but the owner of the ox shall be clear. But if the ox has been accustomed to gore in the past, and its owner has been warned but has not kept it in, and it kills a man or a woman, the ox shall be stoned, and its owner also shall be put to death. If a ransom is laid on him, then he shall give for the redemption of his life whatever is laid upon him. If it gores a man's son or daughter, he shall be dealt with according to this same rule. If the ox gores a slave, male or female, the owner shall give to their master thirty shekels of silver, and the ox shall be stoned.

Eshunna code:[9] If an ox gores a[nother] ox and causes its death, both ox owners shall divide [between them] the price of the dead ox.

If an ox is known to gore habitually and the ward authorities have had [the fact] made known to its owner, but he does not have his ox dehorned [?], it gores a man and causes [his] death, then the owner of the ox shall pay two-thirds of a mina of silver.

If it gores a slave and causes [his] death, he shall pay 15 shekels of silver.

LEX TALION:

Exodus 21:23-25 (RSV):[10] If any harm follows [a miscarriage], then you shall give life for life, tooth for tooth, hand for hand, foot for foot, burn for burn, wound for wound, stripe for stripe.

Hammurabi code, 196ff.:[11] If a seignior has destroyed the eye of a member of the aristocracy, they shall destroy his eye. If he has broken a(nother) seignior's bone, they shall break his bone. If he has destroyed the eye of a commoner, or broken the bone of a commoner, he shall pay one mina of silver. If he has destroyed the eye of a seignior's slave...he shall pay one-half his value. If a seignior has knocked out a tooth of a seignior of his own rank, they shall knock out his tooth. If he has knocked out a commoner's tooth, he shall pay one-third mina of silver.

RAPE OF AN UNMARRIED GIRL:

Exodus 22:16-17 (RSV):[12] If a man seduces a virgin who is not betrothed, and lies with her, he shall give the marriage present for her, and make her his wife. If her father utterly refuses to give her to him, he shall pay money equivalent to the marriage present for virgins.

Middle Assyrian laws:[13] ...if a seignior took the virgin by force and ravished her, either in the midst of the city or in the open country or at night in the street or in a granary or at a city festival, the father of the virgin shall take the wife of the virgin's ravisher and give her to be ravished; he shall not return her to her husband (but) take her; the father may give his daughter who was ravished to her ravisher in marriage. If he has no wife, the ravisher shall give the (extra) third in silver to her father as the value of a virgin (and) her ravisher shall marry her.... If the father does not (so) wish, he shall receive the (extra) third for the virgin in silver (and) give his daughter to whom he wishes.

The form of the laws illustrated above is casuistic or conditional law, a type of case law which probably originated in the local courts at the city gate.[14] Presumably the legislative agency (in NE law the king; in biblical law, Yahweh as represented by specialists assembled before God) gathered up these local laws to present them as examples of how court cases should be judged. Other forms from everyday life were used also which we have not illustrated, such as proverbs and ethical statements, which some jurists would not describe as law (22:28; 23:7).

We conclude this point with the generalization that biblical law deals with the practical matters of an ancient society: rape, retribution, problems with animals, slavery (Ex. 21:2-11), business relations, etc. In this respect biblical law is secular; it deals with matters of everyday life, matters which are ordinarily taken up by secular courts.

2. *In the structure of the Covenant code the laws begin and end with "religious law," and the code is interspersed with that law, laws which have to do with relations between God and Israel.*

The laws in the Covenant code begin with a law which prohibits making an image of God, and a law in regard to the altar (Ex. 20:23-26). They end with the laws of the religious feasts and sacrifice (23:14-19). That this was done deliberately is suggested by the fact that the Holiness code (Lev. 17:3-7; 25:55-26:2), the Deuteronomic code (Deut. 12:2-7; 26:12-15), and the Dodecalogue (Deut. 27:15,26) similarly begin and end with religious laws.[15] Religious law is also interspersed with secular law. In this respect biblical law is not at all secular. People relationships are subjected to the immediate authority of the relationship between God and Israel.

The first commandment of the Covenant code prohibits the making of images of Yahweh (21:23). No comparable law is found in extra-biblical NE juridical texts. The law probably does not refer to the spirituality of God, but is directed rather against the manipulation of divinity.[16] The idol was a primary means by which ancient people manipulated their gods.

Underlying this law is a Hebrew concept of the freedom of God which makes it impossible to manipulate him. God is not identifiable with the life process, though he is creator of it.[17] He is therefore in charge, not prisoner, of fate and is able to move creation toward those goals which are consistent with his loving will and character. He takes humankind into partnership in this task by placing them under his command. Though he may be petitioned, he may not be manipulated to perform in accordance with the lesser goals of the human community. In Israelite law, God is sovereign.

The law of the altar (20:24-26) is not to be understood merely as a primitive characteristic of Israelite religion.[18] The probable intent of the law of the earthen altar is suggested by the use of the word "sword" (*ḥereb*) in verse 25. Early Israel was aware of the close relationship between cultural progress and the attempt of people involved in that progress to dominate their fellows.[19] The altar of Yahweh was not to be polluted by the instruments (such as the sword) closely associated with the domination of brother/sister. If this interpretation of the altar law is correct, it is a fitting introduction to this body of law which has to do with justice in Israel.

The prohibition of the stepped altar is related to the practice of sexual relationships in worship, a widespread practice in the ancient NE world. The ritual of sexual relations was used as a magical means whereby the worshiper might gain the fertility of the gods for family, herd, and crop. This central concept of worship was replaced in Israel by the more rational experience of the worshiper confronted by the word of God, especially his word of command. These introductory laws are polemical in their intent, set against the practices of the Canaanites among whom Israel lived. The polemical was not a superficial one, but pointed to the heart of the differences between the Canaanite and

Israelite experience of divinity and their resultant ways of life.

In contrast to Hebrew law, the laws of the NE law codes are entirely secular, that is, they deal only with people relationships. The early Mesopotamian codes are kingship law. This does not mean that the gods had nothing to do with law. In Mesopotamia the sun God, Shamash, was the god of justice.[20] Though the gods authorized the law (a few scholars have held that they even gave the law), the king was the central figure who as servant of the gods dominated the legislative process. Hammurabi is designated in the prologue of his code as "the king of justice." The coercive elements of his office provided the setting for effecting the law:[21]

> The king who made the four quarters of the world subservient; the favorite of Inanna am I.
> When Marduk commissioned me to guide the people aright, to direct the land I established law and justice in the language of the land....

The pronoun referring to the king dominates the prologue and epilogue of his code, just as it dominates the NE war literature.[22] In biblical law, as well as war literature, the first person singular pronoun of Yahweh is dominant.[23] From the Israelite point of view, this contrast was the essential difference between the word of man and the word of God.

This characteristic of the biblical law codes makes pertinent the question of the relationship of the later office of Israelite kingship to biblical law. It is obvious from the Old Testament that Israelite kingship had something to do with Israelite law and justice.[24] The most decisive and characteristic fact of Israelite law and justice, however, is that although Israel adopted (and adapted) kingship, the Israelite law codes were never reoriented to the office of kingship.[25] In this fundamental respect, kingship in Israel never became like kingship of the NE.

The administration of law in Israel was primarily the task of local courts and the clan.[26] While local justice was aided by a common cult which helped to develop and promulgate a law code comparable in some respects to the codes of other NE states, Israel's common cult was not coercive as were the centralized legislative offices (kingship) of other states. The standardization of Israel's inter-tribal justice was dependent upon the devotion of every clan and family to Yahweh, whose will was made known in Covenant law, as developed and proclaimed at the common worship center (See Deut. 31:9-13; Josh. 24) and elsewhere.

3. *The law is given in the form of teaching/preaching (parenesis), direct address which exhorts Israel to obey law for various reasons. The most radical and fundamental of these reasons is Yahweh's liberation of Israel from Egypt.*

The law is introduced by the statement that God commanded Moses to speak the words of the law to Israel. What follows then is given in prophetic speech: "You have seen that from heaven I spoke with you."[27] This speech of Yahweh is characteristic of the Covenant code throughout, though casuistic laws are set within this structure (see 21:1-22:18), laws referring to Yahweh in the third person (21:6). *Parenesis* is not characteristic of the extra-biblical NE law codes.

Moses in this law code proclaims law as the word of Yahweh not to a local meeting, to a clan, or a tribe, but to all Israel. It is an inter-tribal occasion. If this Covenant code is pre-kingship, this is evidence of some kind of pre-kingship structure to make such an occasion possible.[28]

The characteristic form of Israelite law in the Covenant code is a type of apodictic law which addresses Israel in the second person: "you shall..."; "you shall not" (see 20:23,24). This type of law (in the second person) is not found in other NE law codes. Elsewhere in the Bible this type of command is used by persons in authority such as kings or political leaders.[29] It was therefore well adapted to express the unconditional demand of Yahweh in direct address to his people. Shalom M. Paul says that this unique type of law in the Bible "is explicable only in terms of Israel's total covenant structure. God's expressed demands in covenant law were declared publicly to the total community. By making his will directly and personally known to man, an I-thou relationship is established which characterizes the unique feature of this newly founded nation. Moral and religious prescriptions are directed to each and every member of this nation in categorical imperatives."[30]

A related characteristic of Israelite law is the motive clause, a dependent clause attached to the law which gives a reason or purpose for the law. Although there are motive clauses in the NE law codes, the codes include none which refer to history, to the divine will or promise. Rifat Sonsino says of the motive clause:

> It is noteworthy that, unlike biblical laws, no cuneiform law is ever motivated by reference to an historic event, a promise of well-being or, for that matter, a divine will. In fact, in these laws the deity is completely silent, yielding its place to a human lawgiver whose main concern is ecomomic rather than religious. Biblical law on the other hand, ascribed in its totality to God both in terms of source and authorship displays a concern that goes beyond the economic enveloping all aspects of community life, whether past, present and future, and incorporating both the strictly cultic/sacral and that which remains outside of it.[31]

An example of a motive clause is found in Exodus 22:21 (RSV): "You shall not wrong a stranger or oppress him, for you were strangers in the land of Egypt." About 16 percent or 17 percent of the laws in the Covenant code are joined with a motive clause. Laws with motive clauses in the Deuteronomic and Holiness codes run as high as 50 to 65 percent.[32] The character of the motive clauses is summed up by B. Gemser:

> ...the motive clauses constitute an instructive compendium of the religion, theology, ethics, and democratic, humanitarian outlook of the

people of Israel as represented in the Old Testament laws.[33]

The purpose of the motive clause is obviously to make law inward, to write law upon the heart (see Deut. 6:6; Jer. 31:33).

Some of the most unique of motive clauses are those which allude to redemptive history, especially to liberation from Egypt. These are scattered through out the various law collections (see Ex. 22:20; 23:9,15). It is obvious that the motive attached to the law of the resident alien not only provides motivation for being kind to the alien, but provides the model for the behavior itself. This is especially significant when one realizes that NE law does not give special consideration to the alien (though it does to the widow and orphan).

Yahweh's liberation as a model for social law may also be reflected by the fact that the first societal law in the Covenant code is a law protecting the slave, an unusual fact in contrast to all other codes, except for the Decalogue which also begins with slavery.[34]

This use of Yahweh's liberative act in effect transforms law. This is suggested by the structure of the book of the Covenant. Exodus 21:1-22:18 is made up entirely of casuistic law, case law, presumably originating at the court, the city gate, not greatly affected by covenant, and inserted as a block into this code. By this act the early Israelite jurists were evidently motivated by the conviction that "secular law" must be brought under the power of the covenant God as worshipped by the covenant community.[35] What happens to this body of law over the centuries is illustrated by the parallel law of slavery found in Deuteronomy 15 (see Table 1, page 68).

I am not arguing here that the Deuteronomic law is a development of the law as found in Exodus, but I do argue that they are parallel enough to suggest a relationship. It is evident that the younger law is profoundly liberalized. Now the male and female slaves are to be treated alike; concubinage is prohibited in Deuteronomy. Now, after their service they are to be released with property for it is recognized that there is no freedom without property. The motive/model clause is added: "And you shall remember that you were a slave in the land of Egypt, and Yahweh your God redeemed you; therefore I command you this today" (v. 15). Deuteronomic law makes slavery entirely voluntary when it forbids that a runaway slave be returned to his master (23:15-16). This did not do away with slavery any more than a modern person's right to own his/her own business has done away with hired labor. It did, however, give the slave a choice in the hard economic realities of existence, and forced the slave master to be careful how he treated his slave.

Commenting on Deuteronomy 15:15, Hans Boecker writes:

> Israel's existence as a people freed from slavery demanded a different view of slavery from that current elsewhere. It is particularly clear in the Deuteronomic slave law how law in the Old Testament was interpreted and understood in an increasingly theological way. The awareness that emerged in slave law also impinged on many other areas of life. An essential feature of Deuteronomy is the theologization of older legal prescriptions.[36]

TABLE 1

Exodus 21:2-11: When you buy a Hebrew slave, he shall serve six years, and in the seventh he shall go out free, for nothing. If he comes in single, he shall go out single; if he comes in married, then his wife shall go out with him. If his master gives him a wife and she bears him sons or daughters, the wife and her children shall be her master's and he shall go out alone. But if the slave plainly says, "I love my master, my wife, and my children; I will not go out free," then his master shall bring him to God, and he shall bring him to the door or the doorpost and his master shall bore his ear through with an awl; and he shall serve him for life. When a man sells his daughter as a slave, she shall not go out as the male slaves do....

Deuteronomy 15:12-18: If *your brother*, a Hebrew man, or a *Hebrew woman,* is sold to you, he shall serve you six years, and in the seventh year you shall let him go free from you. And when you let him go free from you, *you shall not let him go empty-handed; you shall furnish him liberally out of your flock, out of your threshing floor, and out of your wine press; as the Lord your God has blessed you, you shall give to him. You shall remember that you were a slave in the land of Egypt, and the Lord your God redeemed you; therefore I command you this today.* But if he says to you, "I will not go out from you," because he loves you and your household, *since he fares well with you,* then you shall take an awl, and thrust it through his ear into the door, and he shall be your bondman for ever. *And to your bondwoman you shall do likewise. It shall not seem hard to you, when you let him go free from you; for at half the cost of a hired servant he has served you six years. So the Lord your God will bless you in all that you do.*

This influence of the motive clause is further augmented by the fact that law is placed in Israel within the context of the story of God's activity for his people. Law in Israel is not universalized but particularized. As Shalom Paul suggests, in its present context the purpose of the Covenant code is stated in the preamble, Exodus 19:3-6. After stating Yahweh's act of liberation, the purpose of the forthcoming covenant is set forth: by observing the covenant laws Israel would become Yahweh's "treasured possession," a kingdom of priests, a nation dedicated to the service of Yahweh among the nations.[37] Israel would lead the nations with a new kind of law.

This particularization and purpose of law suggests the utter fallacy of the attempt of the church to find common ground with the state by a concept of "natural law." "Natural law" is a pagan doctrine of the Stoics, found also among the Babylonians in the concept of *kittum*, "truth," or the nature of things.[38] Biblical law is revolutionary, ever driving forward with dangerous risks for the redemption of the individual and society, using as the pattern for public life the risk-taking of Yahweh himself on behalf of his people. Such a concept has nothing in common with that of natural law, a pagan doctrine founded upon the fallen structures of present reality.

4. *The purpose of the Covenant code in terms of the ancient Near East is radical and revolutionary.*

What we have said of biblical law contradicts the concept still shared by many that the characteristic of biblical law is the *lex talion* (law of retaliation). We have seen that the *lex talion* is found also in the Hammurabi code. It was designed by ancient society as a control of the vendetta (see Gen. 4), to maintain equilibrium of power between two social clans or groups. Most ancient NE law codes softened the *lex talion* by providing for the substitution of compensation to the injured party.[39] In the biblical codes it appears three times (Ex. 21:22-25; Lev. 24:18,2; Deut. 19:21). In the first instance the law is qualified immediately afterward by compensating the destroyed eye or tooth of a slave with the slave's freedom (Ex. 21:26,27). In the second instance, if the guilty party killed an animal, he was to make restitution (Lev. 24:21) by giving the victim a comparable animal. Restitution was not to be made, however, in a case of murder. For that, the guilty party was to be put to death. The same law was to apply to citizen as well as to resident foreigner (Lev. 24:22). The third instance deals with a malicious witness who in court accuses another of a crime. When the truth is discovered, the court is to do to the false witness what the witness intended to do to his brother: "Show no pity: life for life, eye for eye, tooth for tooth, hand for hand, foot for foot."

In the extra-legal literature of the Bible, capital punishment was sometimes mitigated. For example, the writer of the story of the first murder did not feel it necessary that Yahweh apply the death penalty to Cain. Instead, Yahweh protected Cain from the death penalty (Gen. 4:16). In the case of David's murder of Uriah, Nathan did not feel it necessary to apply the death penalty to David, though the crime was taken very seriously. In response to the crime of adultery (not connected with *lex talion*, but for which the law codes designated capital punishment Lev. 20:10) Hosea redeemed his wife instead because of an express command of Yahweh, who included in the command a motive clause giving a reason: "The Lord said to me, 'Go, show your love to your wife again, though she is loved by another and is an adulteress. Love her as the Lord loves the Israelites, though they turn to other gods..."(NIV). Here the motive clause becomes a model clause. Instead of capital punishment for his wife as the law demands, Hosea is to follow the model clause, the example of Yahweh's love for Israel by redeeming her.

Perhaps this concept of righteousness and justice is the reason why the Gospel of Matthew says of Joseph, "...and her husband Joseph, being a just man and unwilling to put her to shame, resolved to divorce her quietly" (Matt. 1:19, RSV). Jesus follows this legal tradition when asked to judge the woman caught in the act of adultery (somehow her lover had not been caught in the act of adultery!). The Pharisees reminded Jesus, "In the Law Moses commanded us to stone such a woman. Now what do you say?" Jesus' answer was not one of acquittal, for the woman was guilty. His answer compares to that of the prophets: the Jews were all guilty of apostasy, but obviously God, though he had punished Israel, had not executed the death sentence. Could those who were guilty of a capital offense (apostasy) execute another who was guilty of a capital offense? Like Hosea, Jesus followed the example of Yahweh, in this case by pronouncing forgiveness: "Neither do I condemn you.... Go now and leave your life of sin" (John 8:3-11, NIV).

My point in giving these examples is to show that such acts as these of Jesus and Hosea are not contrary to the law codes as those have assumed who think that the mood of the codes is *lex talion*. These examples are rather a fulfillment of the law codes, codes whose characteristic mood is that of the motive clause, especially that motive clause which points to the action of Yahweh's redemption: "I am Yahweh your God who brought you out from the land of Egypt, from the house of bondage" (Ex. 20:1). The characteristic purpose of Israelite law is to redeem, not to punish. That tension within law which exists between the *lex talion* (NE law) and the motive clause is well expressed by the Law Preacher on the Mount:

> You have heard that it was said, "An eye for an eye and a tooth for a tooth." But I say to you, Do not resist an evil person. If someone strikes you on the right cheek, turn to him the other also. And if someone wants to sue you and take your tunic, let him have your cloak as well. If someone forces you to go one mile, go with him two miles" (Mt. 5:38-41, NIV).

Furthermore, the purpose of law was to redeem more than the individual. Its purpose was social redemption, to redeem the entire society. This purpose is suggested in the eschatological oracle, Micah 4:1-4.[40] The law underlying this oracle has to do with both international relations and relationships within each nation. In international relations the world's peoples choose law instead of the sword (or balance of power) to settle disputes (4:3). The law is Yahweh's torah, based not upon force but upon the people's voluntary acceptance.

It is a teaching which they choose to learn (4:2). This international law was not a figment of the prophet's imagination. It probably came from case law, the precedents coming out of inter-tribal relationships during the period of the Judges when the tribes went up to the common worship center to adjudicate their differences. What had been inter-tribal would one day be international. The law of Yahweh will give order to international disorder.

This law of Yahweh will give order also to internal economic relations, relationships within each nation:

> Every householder will sit under his own vine
> and under his own fig tree,
> and none shall make them afraid (4:4).

This is the climax of the prophet's vision: a peaceful world order ruled by the law of Yahweh, a law which inverts the social pyramid of the kingship states of the NE. And now the prophet says that what the law of Yahweh will achieve for the world in the future is what the law of Yahweh is about for Israel in the present:

> For all the peoples walk
> each in the name of its god.
> But *we* will walk
> in the name of the Lord our God, forever (4:5).

Israel was to accept the torah of Yahweh, instead of the sword, for international relations. For internal relations, the torah called for the economic freedom of each household, inverting the Canaanite feudalistic structure of the city state. Yahweh has liberated Israel from the slavery of Egypt; each household was to remain free by obedience to Yahweh's law.

The concern for economic and social equality is further reflected in Israel's special care for people rather than property, for those who did not benefit from her economic system. We have noted how concern for the alien was linked by the Covenant code to Israel's experience in Egypt (22:21). Another law protects the widow and orphan, who if mistreated would cry out for Yahweh's justice just as Israel had cried out for justice in Egypt (22:22,23). Likewise, money was to be loaned to the poor without interest. If a cloak was taken in pledge it was to be returned before evening, again that the needy man might not cry out for justice: "What else will he sleep in? When he cries out to me, I will hear, for I am compassionate" (22:27) (an interesting motive clause to include in a law code!).

The Holiness code provides for a sabbatical year, every seventh year, when the land was to lie fallow, its natural produce reserved for slaves and hired servants, the alien, livestock and wild animals (Lev. 25:1-7: cf. Ex. 21:2). The law of Jubilee, every seventh sabbatical year, provided that the land revert to its original household, from which it was never to be permanently alienated (Lev. 25:8-17). Help for the poor is explicitly linked to Yahweh's redemption of Israel from Egypt:

> If one of your countrymen becomes poor and is unable to support
> himself among you, help him as you would an alien or a temporary
> resident, so that he can continue to live among you.... You must not
> lend him money at interest or sell him food for a profit. I am the Lord
> your God, who brought you out of Egypt to give you the land of
> Canaan and to be your God (Lev. 25:35-38, NIV).

Likewise Israelites are not to be sold as slaves: "Because the Israelites are my
slaves, whom I brought out of Egypt, they must not be sold as slaves. Do not
rule over them ruthlessly, but fear your God" (Lev. 25:42, 43; cf. vs. 55).

The Deuteronomic code is the most humanitarian of all the codes. It uses
the word "brother" approximately forty times, usually of someone who is in
need of help. The brother is a poor man for whom one must cancel a loan or
other debt on the seventh year (15:1ff.). One is not to be tightfisted toward the
brother; rather he is to be loaned whatever he needs (15:7). There will always
be the poor; therefore one must always be open-handed toward the brother.
Even the king is not to think of himself as better than his brothers and turn
away from the law to the right or left (17:20). One does not give false
testimony against his brother (19:18-19). The prophet is not to be taken from a
superior social class, but is to be one from among his brothers (18:18). One
must care for and return one's brother's animals if they stray or are in trouble
(22:1ff.). The Edomite is not to be abhorred, because he also is a brother; nor
is the Egyptian, for the Israelites lived as aliens in his country (23:7). One does
not charge interest of the needy brother (23:19,20), nor take advantage of a
hired man who is poor whether he is a brother Israelite or a foreigner (24:14;
cf. v. 17). The brother is not to be degraded by excessive flogging (25:3).

The motive clause of liberation from Egypt is sometimes linked with the
command to help the disadvantaged (15:15; 24:17,18; 26:5-11). Many of these
laws of mutual aid are concerned not just to help the disadvantaged
momentarily, but to keep them from becoming indigent or to restore them to a
level where they can help themselves.

II. WHAT DOES THIS MEAN?

I will now present a short summary of what I have said and comment on
what this may mean for the present.

1. Two Types of Law

There were two types of law in the ancient Near East, the Hammurabi
type and the biblical type of law. The Hammurabi type had its beginnings in
ancient Sumer and had spread throughout the ancient NE. It was kingship or
"state" law. The laws were purely secular, impersonal, emphasizing property
rights and a pyramid type of societal structure. Law was rooted in *kittum*,

"truth," the structure of nature and society as these structures were understood by ancient man.

A new type of law appeared in the Near East in approximately the thirteenth century B.C. It included the characteristic NE casuistic type, which presumably developed in the legal court and dealt with strictly secular subjects. However, it enveloped this secular law within Covenant law or commandments dealing with the authority of Yahweh only and with his worship. This law was uniquely characterized by *parenesis*, in which the will of God was spoken directly to the people. It is uniquely characterized by the second person singular, apodictic form, "you shall not," "you shall," a form which may have been used by persons of authority such as clan fathers and kings, and was thus especially appropriate to express the authority of Yahweh. Finally, this new type of law is characterized by the motive clause, uniquely so by those clauses referring to an historic event, a promise of well-being, or to a divine will, in this way respecting human intelligence and freedom, attempting to make law compatible with the human will. This motive clause also served as model clause, the ultimate model being Yahweh's liberation of Israel from Egypt, a revolutionary model as compared to *kittum* or "natural law." The liberation model qualified slavery, poverty, and even the rights of the resident foreigner, and had as its ultimate goal a world-wide egalitarian society ruled by this law, with each household free from poverty and oppression.

2. Where Are These Two Types of Law Found Today?

It is not difficult to identify the law of today which is in continuity with the Hammurabi type of law. The essential secularity, human origin, and power orientation of extra-biblical NE law, Roman, Continental, and English law is general knowledge. If we delete the prologue and epilogue of Hammurabi's code, as the Hebrew prophets were inclined to do, we are left with purely secular laws which express little relationship to the divine. This leaves the modern state with only the human power principle to enforce law; hence the revival of various forms of *kittum,* the doctrine that positive law has its foundation in natural law.[41]

However, it is an over-simplification to say that the Bible simply rejects the prologue and epilogue of Hammurabi's code. It only rejects Shamash, Anu and Enlil as divinities, recognizing them, however, as impersonal powers. The Bible criticizes both these impersonal powers and human princes as in rebellion against Yahweh. From Yahweh's perspective they do not rule with justice in their various states (Ps. 82).[42] Likewise there is both prologue and epilogue (written or unwritten) to modern state law. Both prologue/epilogue and the laws that derive from it are regarded from a biblical perspective as rebellion against Yahweh.

It may be more difficult to discover continuity with biblical law. In the New Testament the continuity is clear. The law sermons of Jesus, both in Matthew and Luke, are in direct continuity, fulfilling the Old Testament law codes. The New Testament use of "Stoic law" in various collections of household law

(See Col. 3:18-4:1), where Stoic law is "borrowed" and corrected by bringing it into tension with the gospel, is in obvious continuity with the way the Old Testament law codes use casuistic law.[43] There is "secular" law in the New Testament, placed within the covenant structure of God and his people. It includes the motive/model clause of God's act in Christ, a radical revolutionary law when read by Roman standards, a law which placed Greek and Barbarian, male and female, in a common brother-sisterhood relationship.

Where is the setting for biblical law today? Obviously, its continuity may be found only within the structure of covenant community, whether that of the Synagogue, the Church, or the Mosque. The Synagogue and the Mosque are clear; they acknowledge that they are guardians of law, that the faith community is a legal community. It is beyond the purpose of this paper to critique their particular understanding and practice of law.

What about the Church? Augustine set the pace for medieval legal theory by personalizing the Stoic doctrine of *lex aeterna* (eternal law), insisting that "the divine wisdom is the universal law." However, for him this personalized *lex aeterna* is administered through the impersonal powers of the state: "God legislates to the whole of mankind through the mouths of emperors and kings."[44]

As we have shown above, one cannot transform the Hammurabi type of law (kingship law) into biblical law merely by changing the prologue. The impersonal power element in kingship law is the heart of the problem. The personal God revealed in the liberation from the impersonal powers (represented by Egypt), and in the liberation in Christ from the impersonal powers of this world, and who gives at Sinai and the Mount his personal law, does not now regress legislatively to be represented "to the whole of mankind through the mouths of emperors and kings." The church has not done as well as ancient Israel; for Israel never reoriented her law codes to kingship.

Augustine's paganization of the church's law is at the heart of the church's problem of holding together law and grace, social action and the gospel. When the church deliberately reorients her law from the grace principle to the power principle, she ought not complain if grace and law, worship and life, social action and the gospel seem to "fall apart." They did not just "fall apart"; rather the church separated them by a deliberate act, just as the Sumerian-Hammurabi legislators made a clean separation of their worship and legal corpus a thousand years before Moses.

It is not my task to trace the church's paganizing of law through Thomas Aquinas and the sixteenth century reformers (it seems to become progressively worse). If congregations wish to be in continuity with biblical law, they must accept law where God has placed it, within the covenant structure of God and people. They must experience the revolutionary effect of the gospel upon those rules and regulations arising out of the social and physical structures of this world.

3. The Congregational Court

One of the most obvious meanings for us in regard to biblical law is that Christians should settle their own differences instead of taking them to the secular courts. This is an injunction from the New Testament itself. In his first letter to Corinth, Paul said, "When one of you has a grievance against a brother, does he dare to go to law before the unrighteous (*ádikos*) instead of the saints" (1 Cor. 6:1)? The Jerusalem Bible translates, "How dare one of your members take up a complaint against another in the law courts of the unjust...?" The unjust here refers to the courts of the pagan society whose justice was based on Greek-Roman law, courts which rejected the motive clause of the gospel as the model for justice. Paul makes the point that it is only the saints, whose wisdom is founded upon God's act in Christ, who are capable of making a just decision.

Just decisions do not come without effort even in a Christian community. Paul says, "Can it be that there is not a single wise man among you able to give a decision in a brother-Christian's cause?" (1 Cor. 6:5, NEB). If God's people are to judge the world and even angels, as Paul says (1 Cor. 6:2,3), it is time that we give attention to biblical principles of justice so that we can make just judgments in the mundane matters of this life (1 Cor. 6:3). We dare not leave matters of justice to the unjust courts, courts which do not accept the gospel as the norm and foundation for justice.

4. Strategies for Relating Biblical Law to State Law

We have seen that we cannot be faithful if we accept state law as our rule for communal life. Nor can we be faithful if we adopt a policy of physical withdrawal from this world (our own historical temptation), for Yahweh's law and justice are aggressive. This aggressive character of biblical law is set forth by the servant poems of Isaiah 40-55. While much has been made of the suffering servant, we should know that this passage speaks of two of God's agents. Cyrus as Yahweh's "anointed one" was chosen as Yahweh's "bird of prey from the east" (46:11). His task was to return Israel to her land. But Cyrus never became, as did Hammurabi in relation to Marduk, Yahweh's "king of justice" to establish Yahweh's justice in the earth. This was to be the work of Yahweh's second agent, his servant Israel (or representative of Israel). He "will bring forth justice to the nations" (42:1), he will establish "justice in the earth," the law of Yahweh in the far-off nations (42:4) and he will do this nonviolently (42:2-3; 49:2; 50:4-11).

It is God's strategy that his law is to rule the world; that is what Jesus and the church are about.

If we cannot make state law our law nor physically withdraw from this world, how do we relate to state law?

First, there is the strategy of participation in the economic and political structures of this world. The question for the Christian in economics is not whether a Christian may be rich, but how can a Christian participate so as to promote brother/sisterhood economics. The question is not whether the Christian can participate in the political process, but where and how to participate in that process so that people can experience something of the transforming power of the gospel. When we participate in the structures of this world we do not leave covenant structure behind; we take it with us. Also, when we enter the congregational meeting we should not leave those rules and laws by which we live and do business outside; we should bring them inside for our own scrutiny before God and for the scrutiny of our brothers and sisters. Christian associations such as the Mennonite Medical Association, MEDA (Mennonite Economic Development Association), or the Mennonite lawyers organization should help in this process.

Both Moses and Jesus rejected the state for an alternate vision and their rejection of the state is central to biblical faith. Joseph and Daniel, however, held high state office, though they rejected the wisdom by which the state is operated. Their course should not be followed without a commitment to martyrdom. The nature of the problem is pointed up by the courageous words and action of William Bontrager, judge of Elkhart Superior Court II. Commenting on Judge Bontrager's statement of a head-on collision between the law of God and the law of man, *The Goshen News* in an editorial felt that Bontrager was making the right decision by bowing out as superior court judge: "Judges must set a perfect example in following man's law, which a majority of the state legislators must feel isn't contrary to God's law."[45] Unfortunately, the "majority of state legislators" are not adequately equipped to make such a decision. This "law of man" is a legal system which assumes its own authority, backed ultimately by the threat of physical coercion.

This "head-on collision" between the two types of law is what the book of Daniel is about. In the sixth chapter the issue is which law is sovereign: the law of Daniel's God (6:5) or the law of the Medes and the Persians (6:8,15). Daniel believed in the sovereignty of the law of God and continued to worship God rather than the king, just as he had been accustomed to do. It is significant that the writer saw the clash between the sovereignty of the two laws as centering in worship, the choice being not between the worship of two gods, but between *God* and the *king* (6:7). The story then focuses on who can save Daniel from the law of the Medes and Persians. The king was on the side of Daniel but, like Judge Bontrager, found himself stuck with the sovereignty of his own law. He called his lawyers and "labored till the sun went down," but was unable to find a loophole in the law. Finally, he makes his acknowledgement: the king himself is helpless and unable to save from the sovereignty of his own law. The system works! His question then is whether Daniel's God can save, a question which we must now ask in regard to the Palmer case. The answer of the book of Daniel is that God can save from capital punishment those who obey his law. God and his law are sovereign, a point which Darius at the end of the chapter acknowledges.

We know, however, that the God of Daniel does not always save from capital punishment, the most notorious case being Jesus of Nazareth (the system works). Jesus trusted in the sovereignty of God by drinking the cup. As a result of the events which followed, the apostles proclaimed that this act was God's victory over the powers.[46]

A second way the church might relate to state law is through alternate structures. This is illustrated in the arena of justice by MCC prison ministries and Mennonite cooperation with VORP. These structures must themselves be subject to covenant structure, if they are not to become coercive and ethnic.

In all its endeavors to relate to state law, the church needs to "talk it up." The church is a community which remembers. *Living More with Less*[47] is an exchange of ideas and experiences which moves the church in the right direction. *Dial 911,*[48] the story of how Reba Place Fellowship dealt with crime, is the material out of which precedent is established. These only touch the surface of the experiences which ought to be made available to our congregations.

5. Creation and Redemption

To understand the relationship of church and world we need to understand the relationship between creation and redemption. The biblical doctrine of creation was not arrived at by acceptance of the physical and social structures of this world and by fitting the gospel within them. That only results in the paganization and surrender of the gospel. Instead, the key to that which was in the beginning is found in that which is presently becoming, the gospel itself, the prism through which all worldly structures are examined (See John 1; Gen. 1; 2). Yahweh's relationship even to the rebellious peoples of the world is expressed by language taken from the categories of Israel's salvation experience. In Genesis 8:20-22, Yahweh's providential relation to the post-flood peoples is expressed in terms of *promise.*[49] In Genesis 9:1-17, Yahweh's providential relationship is expressed in the climax of the passage in terms of *covenant.* In this passage the behavioral boundaries of humankind even in the rebellious state are set by biblical law: "Whoever sheds the blood of man, by man shall his blood be shed; for God made man in his own image" (v. 6).[50] This law controls the vendetta and was commonly known throughout the NE,[51] in the motive clause the writer reasons from creation as seen from the perspective of Israel's redemption. Creation and redemption are not conceptualized as antithetical in the Bible but as parallel. The fall is seen as antithetical to both, though even in the fall, redemption-creation sets the lower boundaries of rebellious behavior by choosing a law from the common NE law itself, and by giving its own reason for that boundary, the creation of man in the divine image.

But there is a second way by which humankind is related to Yahweh in the Genesis story. It is related to Yahweh through the Abraham people, with whom Yahweh has established a special relationship of blessing: "And in you all families of the earth shall bless themselves" (Gen. 12:1-3).[52] God was not content to relate himself to humankind merely through a covenant of providential care. His concern was to lead humankind forward by special grace into the personal relationship of God and people. The purpose of Israel, according to this writer, was to mediate God's personal blessing to the nations.

The Abraham people are called to lead out for God in matters of public policy. This is what the gospel and biblical law are about. The most important question of public policy has to do with the laws of worship: who is sovereign. But the professed sovereignty of Yahweh means nothing unless it is decisive for human behavior. The church must therefore deal not only with religious law, but with casuistic or case law, the laws of the courts. We must bring these laws which deal with family, economic and international relationships, under the authority of God who has liberated his people from Egypt, whose altar is not built by instruments used for oppression. In this way we are called to be a kingdom of priests, a religious and moral elite, to mediate God's leadership of humankind out from the burden of kingship law, a law whose lower limits as announced in Genesis, since the development of the ultimate weapon, threatens the very existence of humankind.[53]

NOTES

1. These are not to be understood as codes in the modern sense. See the discussion by Richard Hasse, *Einführung in das Stadium Keilschriftlicher Rechtsquellen* (Weisbaden: Otto Harrasowitz, 1965, pp. 19f). This book is a good introduction to NE legal literature.

2. For example, see the articles by Harold J. Berman, "The Influence of Christianity upon the Development of Law," *Oklahoma Law Review*, 12 (1959), pp. 86-101, and Wilbur G. Kratz, "Christ and Law," *Ibid.*, pp. 57-66.

3. See David Daube, *Studies in Biblical Law* (Cambridge: University Press, 1947).

4. I omit here the so-called P collection of laws since they deal almost entirely with worship.

5. The Covenant code (Book of the Covenant, Ex. 24:7) is the oldest. Sonsino dates it to the thirteenth century--*Motive Clauses in Hebrew Law* (Scholars Press, 1980), p. 19. Except for 23:20-33, Paul Hanson dates it to the period of the League--"The Theological Significance of Contradiction within the Book of the Covenant," *Canon and Authority* (Fortress Press), p. 114. The Deuteronomic code is dated in its present form in the seventh century B.C.; the Holiness code, in the time of the exile.

6. See Exodus 24:7 for the term "Book of the Covenant."

7. See Brevard Childs, *Introduction to the Old Testament as Scripture* (Philadelphia: Fortress Press, 1979).

8. It is not my intention here to suggest any direct relation between these various codes. For the hazards (though importance) of comparative studies, see Hans Jochen Boecker, *Law and the Administration of Justice in the Old Testament and the Ancient East,* trans. by Jerry Moiser (Minneapolis: Augsburg Publishing House, 1980), pp. 15-19. It is obvious that biblical law is in the context of ancient Near Eastern law, but my point here is to show that biblical law deals with the same secular concerns.

9. Albert Goetze, *The Laws of Eshnunna* (New Haven Department of Antiquities of the Government of Iraq and the American Schools of Oriental Research, 1956), p. 132f.

10. See parallels, Leviticus 23:17-21; Deuteronomy 19:21.

11. James Pritchard, *Ancient Near Eastern Texts* (Princeton: Princeton University Press, 1969), p. 175. Of the four Mesopotamian codes, only CH has the law of talion. The law of Eshnunna substitutes a payment of money.

12. See the parallel, Deuteronomy 22:28-29.

13. See Pritchard, *op.cit.*, p. 185, A55. I follow here R. Yaron, "The Middle Assyrian Laws and the Bible," *Biblica* 51 (1970), p. 556.

14. See R. A. F. MacKenzie, S.J., "The Formal Aspect of Ancient Near Eastern Law," *The Seed of Wisdom*, W. E. McCullough, ed. (University of Toronto Press, 1964), pp. 33-38.

The connection of casuistic law with the actual court case was made already by Albrecht Alt, "Die Ursprünge des Israelitischen Rechts," *Klein Schriften zur Geschichte des Volkes Israel* (München: C. H. Beck'sche Verlagsbuchhandlung, 1953), pp. 278-332. Rifat Sonsino points out that this connection cannot be proven by textual evidence.

15. The Decalogue begins with religious law but does not end with it.

16. See Martin Noth, *Exodus*, OTL (Philadelphia: The Westminster Press, 1962), pp. 162f.

17. C. R. North, *The Second Isaiah* (Oxford: Clarendon Press, 1964), pp. 14f.

18. See Boecker, *op.cit.*, p. 148.

19. See Genesis 3 and 4.

20. See Pritchard, *op.cit.*, p. 163.

21. *Ibid.*, p. 165.

22. *Ibid.*, pp. 164f., 177ff. For the war literature see D. D. Luckenbill, *The Annals of Sennacherib* (Chicago: The University of Chicago Press, 1924), pp. 23ff.

23. See Exodus 20:1,2,22-26, etc.

24. See Psalm 72; Jeremiah 22:15; 1 Samuel 30:22-25, etc. Boecker deals at length with this question, giving various viewpoints on the controversy, and examining most of the relevant texts. He holds that the OT refers nowhere to legislation by the king. Where this may seem to be the case, the king is dealing with soldiery, the royal court or the royal cities, all of which essentially were non-Israelite institutions. Following a study by Malchoz he quotes, "in none of the recorded cases does the kings' jurisdiction infringe on the rights reserved to the local courts. Nor does it establish itself as a superior court to which appeal could be made against decisions by the city courts." Boecker, *op.cit.*, p. 177. For the entire argument, see pp. 40-49. An exception to the rule was Jehoshaphat's judicial reform where the king encroached on the authority of the lower courts in cases of murder (2 Chron. 19:10) but which the law again abolished (Deut. 17:8-12). Boecker, *op.cit.*, p. 49.

25. In Deuteronomy even the laws of warfare are not oriented to kingship. See Deuteronomy 20:24.

26. There is a rather wide-spread rejection today of Martin Noth's amphictyony, a model which was taken from the Greek city states. However, sociologists of pre-industrial societies suggest several possibilities of cross-cutting systems which might provide linkage for an administratively non-centralized people. In Israel it would appear that the tribe of the Levites was such a cross-cutting mechanism. They had no tribal territory of their own, but were scattered throughout the various tribes and were responsible for teaching Yahwism and perhaps for occasional meetings of "all Israel" (Deut. 33:3-11; Josh. 14). For a discussion, see Norman K. Gottwald, *The Tribes of Yahweh* (Maryknoll: Orbis Books, 1979), pp. 293-320; 345-375.

27. In Deuteronomy, Moses is the speaker, though he spoke "according to all that Yahweh commanded him" (Deut. 1:3). Deuteronomy is a different literary type from the Covenant and Holiness codes. Compare Joshua 23 and 1 Samuel 12.

28. Paul D. Hanson holds that Exodus 20:22-23:19 is a literary unit which can be attributed as a whole to the premonarchical period--Hanson, *op.cit.*, p. 114. Sonsino attributes it to before and after the conquest--Sonsino, *op.cit.*, p. 19. Various solutions to the problem of the law speaker have been suggested. Martin Noth has suggested that the law speaker was the minor judge. Others have held that there was a "Mosaic office" in ancient Israel. See H. J. Kraus, *Die prophetische Verkündigung des Rechts in Israel* (Ag. Zollikon: Evangelischer Verlag, 1957), pp. 3-38, who discusses these various viewpoints and who tries to find a link of the ancient "Mosaic office" with the later prophets. More recently, the "wise men" are favored, (whoever they may have been at that early time). See Sonsino, *op.cit.*, pp. 120-131. I would agree with this later writer that "the setting in life of the motivated laws...cannot be located exclusively in cultic preaching"--*Ibid.*, p. 128); however, I would hold that this was one of the most important places where this kind of activity went on. After all, the book of the law at the time of Josiah was found *in the temple.*

29. See Gerhard Liedke, *Gestalt und Bezeichnung alttestamentlicher Rechtssätze* (Neukirchener Verlag, 1971), pp. 120-134. Erhard Gerstenburger argues that the original setting for this kind of law was the patriarchal family--Gerstenberger, *Wesen und Herkunft des Apodiktische Recht*

(Neukirchener Verlag, 1965), pp. 110-127. This type of law is closely related to certain forms of wisdom.

30. Shalom M. Paul, *Studies in the Book of the Covenant in the Light of Cuneiform and Biblical Law*, Leiden: E. J. Brill, 1970), p. 123.

31. Sonsino, *op.cit.*, pp. 86-96. It is difficult to determine percentages because of the complexity of the material, and thus somewhat different percentages are arrived at by different researchers.

32. *Ibid.*

33. B. Gemser, "The Importance of the Motive Clause in Old Testament Law," *Vetus Testamentum*, Supp. 1, 1964, p. 63.

34. This parallel is pointed out by Paul, *op.cit.*, pp. 106, 107.

35. See Hanson, *op.cit.*, pp. 110-131.

36. Boecker, *op.cit.*, p. 183. An example of how Yahweh's action for Israel impinged on the law of capital punishment as given in Hosea 3:1.

37. See Paul, *op.cit.*, pp. 30-32.

38. See A. Leo Oppenheim, *The Assyrian Dictionary*, Vol. 8, pp. 468f.

39. This is the interpretation of the NIV translation, I think a correct one. It may be translated "a woman."

40. This oracle is paralleled in Isaiah 2:1-4. The oracle may have been earlier than either Micah or Isaiah. See A. S. Herbert, *Isaiah 1-39* (Cambridge: University Press, 1973), p. 34.

41. See John Howard Yoder, *The Politics of Jesus* (Grand Rapids: Eerdmans Publishing Company, 1972), pp. 143-147.

42. *Ibid.*

43. I so not argue necessarily for a direct borrowing here. The Haustafeln are Colossians 3:18-4:1; Ephesians 5:21-6:9. See also 1 Peter 2:13-3:7. For a discussion see Yoder, *op.cit.*, p. 163-192. He acknowledges the dissertation by David Schroeder, "Die Haustafeln des Neuen Testaments, Ihre Herkunft und ihr theologischer Sinn" (Evangelical Theological Faculty of the University of Hamburg, 1959, unpublished).

44. I am dependent for my interpretation here upon Anton-Hermann Chroust, "The Fundamental Ideas in Augustine's Philosphy of Law," *American Journal of Jurisprudence*, 18 (1973), pp. 59-78. Quote from p. 78.

45. Quoted from "Judge Bontrager Bows Out," *The Goshen News* (March 28, 1979), p. 4.

46. See note 41.

47. Doris Janzen Longacre, compiler, *More-With-Less Cookbook* (Scottdale, Pa.: Herald Press, 1976).

48. Dave Jackson, *Dial 911: Peaceful Christians and Urban Violence* (Scottdale, Pa.: Herald Press, 1981).

49. Traditionally ascribed to J.

50. Traditionally attributed to P.

51. See my discussion above.

52. Traditionally ascribed to J.

53. Philip Berrigan points out how laws expand and preserve empire. Such law protects atomic weaponry, making it virtually impossible for citizens to touch the problem which threatens us all. State law has literally become the "law of sin and death." See Berrigan, "Sin and the Bomb: Breaking the Imperial Law," *Pacificus Papers*, Vol. 2, No. 6, Fall, 1980 (Center on Law and Pacifism, Colorado Springs).

CHAPTER 7

TRANSFORMATION OF JUSTICE: FROM MOSES TO JESUS

In his book *Justice and the Social Order*, the Protestant theologian Emil Brunner wrote that the scriptural use of the word justice has nothing to do with social justice in the everyday world. To deal with the meaning of justice, therefore, he began with Aristotle, who defined justice as "rendering to every man his due." Brunner dealt with "worldly justice," the justice of the institutions of this world, rather than with the "justice of faith." He believed that "between even-handed justice, which renders to every man his due and heavenly justice, which renders good for evil and forgives the transgressor 70 times seven, there is an ultimate secret affinity," but that these two kinds of justice do not really meet.[1]

Brunner was right in seeing a distinction between the two kinds of justice. Contrary to Brunner, however, I maintain that biblical justice has everything to do with justice in this world. I will begin with justice as defined in the Bible, and will then discuss the relationship of that justice to the institutions of this world.

I define biblical justice as that norm of behavior which arises out of the relationship of God and people, and out of the interrelationships of God's people with themselves and others. Micah 6:1-8 uses the two important words, righteousness (*sĕdāqāh*) and justice (*mishpāṭ*). God's "righteous acts" are the divine saving acts for Israel (Mic. 6:4-5). Israel is to respond to these righteous acts by doing justice, loving mercy, and by walking humbly with God (Mic. 6:8; see NIV). Justice in the Bible is not the opposite of mercy, but is parallel to it. Both justice and mercy arise out of the covenant relationship of God and people. The first centers on keeping covenant relations; the second, on reestablishing covenant when it is broken. Both are informed by a humble walk with God whose righteous acts save the people.

The difference Brunner saw between the two kinds of justice--biblical justice and worldly justice--has a long history which goes back to the last half of the second millennium B.C. It was then that Moses broke with Near Eastern

From *New Perspectives on Crime and Justice*; Occasional Papers of the MCC Canada Offender Ministries Program and the MCC U.S. Office of Criminal Justice, 1986.

empire or "state justice," represented so well by Hammurabi's law code. From Moses to Jesus there was a transformation of law and justice, a transformation which is at the base of the church's difficulty to relate to state law. It is my purpose first to set forth some of the main characteristics of this new transformed justice, and then to suggest some ways that this transformation can relate to the untransformed "justice" of state law.

THE TRANSFORMATION OF JUSTICE: FROM MOSES TO JESUS

1. The First Community of Faith: A Just Community

According to Exodus 18, the community of faith was interested from its earliest beginning with just relationships. Indeed, it saw itself above all as a community of justice.[2] The goal of Exodus 18 is the establishment of Yahweh's peace, both for external and internal relationships (shālôm; translated "welfare" in RSV, verse 7 and in verse 23, "peace"). The foundation for this peace is stated in verses 1-12, Yahweh's *deliverance* from Egypt (Ex. 18:4,8-11). Jethro, the Midianite priest, heard of this deliverance (Ex. 18:8) and rejoiced in it (Ex. 18:9), blessed God for it (Ex. 18:10) and confessed that God the deliverer is greater than all gods (Ex. 18:11). There follows a covenant meal with the officers of Israel in a worship setting (Ex. 18:12). The basis for Israel's relationships with foreign peoples was to be the foreigner's recognition of God's deliverance.

The second part of this chapter of Exodus deals with community justice. The key is the word "to judge," repeated four times (Ex. 18:13,16,22,23).[3] Israel's first organization came about in order to promote community justice. For this purpose Israel was organized into clusters of thousands, hundreds, fifties and tens (Ex. 18:21). Thus, the first "small group" was instituted by Moses for handling disputes! About 1200 years later Paul tells the Church at Corinth to organize themselves so as to handle their own disputes (1 Cor. 6). When this is done on the basis of Yahweh's deliverance, then all the people "will go to their place in peace" (Ex. 18:23).

2. Law in the Context of Covenant Making

Closely related to *justice* is the concept of *law*. While justice is the norm of behavior, law is an expression of that norm--"what a community, with its religion, values, political and economic systems, and experience of living, requires of its members."[4] In the ancient Near East, including the Bible, some of these requirements were set forth in written law codes or collections.

Israel's first law was given at Sinai (Ex. 19-24). The law begins with anticipating covenant (Ex. 19:3-6) and ends with making covenant (Ex. 24:3-8). This illustrates the first important principle of biblical law and justice; both are found within the covenant structure of God and people. In the Old Testament, obedience to law was to be a response to God's redemption from Egypt (Ex. 19:4-5). This was a fundamental break from state law, a break which in the

New Testament eventuated in law as response to God's act in Christ.

In contrast to the covenant context of law, the ancient law codes of the Near East are set within the context of coercive power--the coercive power of kingship. Hammurabi's Babylonian law code, dated to the first half of the second millennium B.C., is sometimes compared in importance to the Justinian code of the Roman Empire (seventh century A.D.). It speaks of Hammurabi as "the king of justice."⁵ Marduk, god of Babylon, was given the "Enlil function," the coercive power function over all humanity; Hammurabi as servant of Marduk has "pacified" the surrounding city states with his army. Then, as servant of his god, Hammurabi gave to his kingdom a code of law which was to function as a teaching instrument to achieve justice. Law codes such as Hammurabi's represented state law.

While state law such as that of Hammurabi may be better than none, Christians should remember that Paul called the Greek-Roman law courts unjust (1 Cor. 6:1). The bursting penitentiaries and prisons dotting the landscapes of the United States and Canada should alert even the unthinking that little has changed in regard to state justice today. Contrary to Brunner, "to every man his due" does not define justice for the Christian. Rather, justice is that norm which arises out of Yahweh's saving relationship to God's people, and out of the internal covenant relationships of God's people with each other.

3. Law for Divine-Human Relationships

The Sinai law code begins and ends with laws regulating human relationships to God (Ex. 20:22-26; 23:14-19). Also, religious laws are interspersed throughout the code. In contrast, all laws of the Near Eastern law codes are purely secular. That is, these laws deal only with inter-human concerns. For some, this "secularism" may seem an advantage. For biblical law, however, divine and human relations are so interrelated that justice must deal with both.

The Sinai code begins with the law prohibiting idols (Ex. 20:23). This law compares to the first and second laws of the Ten Commandments, laws dealing with exclusive loyalty to Yahweh. In the Bible there is no such thing as "the sovereignty of law." Only Yahweh, the giver of law, is sovereign. The worship of Yahweh from the heart, as Deuteronomy expresses it, is essential to human justice.

Prohibition of idols struck at the attempt to manipulate divinity through magic, to substitute the national will for that of the divine. The second of the Ten Commandments may be translated, "Thou shalt not put thy God in a box." Yahweh is a ruler, and cannot be controlled by the worshiper. As indicated by this law, Yahweh is revered. The worshiper will attempt to follow the way of Yahweh, applying it to human relationships. Jesus has said, love to God and love to neighbor belong together (Matt. 22:37-40). Worship is essential to biblical law and justice.

4. Law and Interhuman Relations

Biblical law deals with worldly, nitty-gritty relationships: slavery (Ex. 21:2-11), assault (Ex. 21:12), murder (Ex. 21:12-14), kidnapping (Ex. 12:16), miscarriage (Ex. 21:22), a goring ox (Ex. 21:28-32), theft of cattle, etc. This part of the law is quite secular, and means that reverence for God is not expressed by mere piety, but is directed toward everyday concerns of personal and social ethics.

In contrast to Near Eastern law, biblical law is not property, but person oriented. The Sinai code protects especially the slave (Ex. 21:1-11), the resident alien (Ex. 23:9), disadvantaged women and children (Ex. 22:22), and the poor (Ex. 22:25-27). It is prejudiced in favor of the lower rather than the upper classes. Unlike Near Eastern law, it is egalitarian, giving no special rights to the elite. An example of the "earthy," egalitarian law is found in the New Testament in the book of James.

5. Law and the Motive Clause

Traditionally, it is wrongly assumed that Old Testament law is vindictive, that its justice is characterized by "an eye for an eye, and a tooth for a tooth." Already in Near Eastern law, hundreds of years before Moses, this law of retaliation (*lex talion*) was adjusted by paying money substitutes for the loss of a body member. This law--an eye for eye--eventually came to symbolize equal justice rather than vindictive justice. But this law is found in each of the biblical law codes only one time (Ex. 21:22-25; Lev. 4:19-21; Deut. 19:21). It is not the characteristic of biblical law and justice.

Characteristic of biblical law is the motive/model clause. This is a clause from history, from religion, or from some other sphere, which modifies a law, giving to it a motive or reason, or sometimes modeling it after Yahweh's behavior. About 17 percent of the laws of the Sinai code have motive clauses, while such clauses in the Holiness (Lev. 17-26) and Deuteronomic codes (Deut. 12-28) modify about 50 to 65 percent of the laws.

What did this motive/model clause do for biblical law? This is illustrated by what the slave law of Exodus 21:2-7 developed into in the later law of Deuteronomy 15:12-18:

> Exodus 21:2-7 (RSV): When you buy a Hebrew slave, he shall serve six years, and in the seventh he shall go out free, for nothing. If he comes in single, he shall go out single; if he comes in married, then his wife shall go out with him. If his master gives him a wife and she bears him sons or daughters, the wife and her children shall be her master's and he shall go out alone. But if the slave plainly says, "I love my master, my wife, and my children; I will not go out free," then his master shall bring him to God, and he shall bring him to the door or the doorpost; and his master shall bore his ear through with an awl; and he shall serve him for life.
>
> When a man sells his daughter as a slave, she shall not go out as the

male slaves do....

Deuteronomy 15:12-19 (RSV): If *your brother*, a Hebrew man, or a *Hebrew woman*, is sold to you, he shall serve you six years, and in the seventh year you shall let him go free from you. And when you let him go free from you, *you shall not let him go empty-handed: you shall furnish him liberally out of your flock, out of your threshing floor, and out of your wine press; as the Lord your God has blessed you, you shall give to him. You shall remember that you were a slave in the land of Egypt, and the Lord your God redeemed you; therefore I command you this today.* But if he says to you, "I will not go out from you," because he loves you and your household, *since he fares well with you,* then you shall take an awl, and thrust it through his ear into the door, and he shall be your bondman for ever. *And to your bondwomen you shall do likewise. It shall not seem hard to you, when you let him go free from you; for at half the cost of a hired servant he has served you six years. So the Lord your God will bless you in all that you do.*

The italicized words show how Deuteronomic law is profoundly liberalized. Now male and female are treated alike. Now released slaves are to go out with property, for there is no freedom without property. The model/motive clause is added: "And you shall remember that you were a slave in the land of Egypt, and Yahweh your God redeemed you; therefore I am commanding you this thing today" (Deut. 15:15). Deuteronomy radicalized the slave law to make it entirely voluntary (Deut. 23:15-16). This did not do away with slavery any more than a modern person's right to own his or her own business had done away with hired labor. It did, however, give the slave a choice in the hard economic realities of ancient existence and forced slave masters to be careful how they treated their slaves.

The Holiness Code says of people who because of poverty came into possession of another: "For they are my slaves, whom I brought forth out of the land of Egypt; they shall not be sold as slaves" (Lev. 25:42).

Commenting on Deuteronomy 15:15, Hans Boecker writes:

Israel's existence as a people freed from slavery demanded a different view of slavery from that current elsewhere. It is particularly clear in the Deuteronomic slave law how law in the Old Testament was interpreted and understood in an increasingly theological way. The awareness that emerged in slave law also impinged on many other areas of life. An essential feature of Deuteronomy is the theologization of older legal prescriptions.[6]

It is obvious that the motive clause provided a model for behavior which propelled law forward, and supplied to law an inner motivation. Law was "written upon the heart." This characteristic of biblical law came to full fruition in such statements of Jesus: "You, therefore, must be perfect, *as your heavenly Father is perfect*" (Matt. 5:47).

6. The Law and the Prophets

We have seen that Near Eastern law was associated with kingship. When kingship was accepted into Israel, it too had its task in relation to law (see Ps. 72). Jesus, however, correctly characterizes law in the Old Testament by associating it with the prophets: "the law and the prophets" (Matt. 7:12; 22:40). This phrase referred, in the first place, simply to the Old Testament. But more than this, there is a vital relationship between the law and the prophets. The great prophets, by their preaching, enforced especially the first commandment, loyalty to Yahweh and Yahweh's law. Naboth confronted David, Elijah confronted Ahab when these kings had broken the law (2 Sam. 12:1-15; 1 Kings 21). The prophets Amos, Hosea and Ezekiel proclaimed legal collections to their people (Amos 2:6-8; Hos. 4:1-2; Ezek. 18:5-9).

The prophets sometimes mitigated capital punishment. For adultery and murder, Nathan did not pronounce the death sentence upon David, though his crime was taken seriously (2 Sam. 12:13-14). In response to adultery, Hosea redeemed his wife at the express command of Yahweh, "Go again, love your wife loved by another, an adulteress, *just as Yahweh loves Israel, though they turn to other gods....*" (Hos. 3:1). Instead of capital punishment as law demands (Lev. 20:10), Hosea was to follow the model clause, the example of Yahweh's love for Israel (Hos. 3:1). Jesus was in this same prophetic tradition when he said to the woman caught in the act of adultery, "Neither do I condemn you, go now and leave your life of sin" (John 8:3-11, NIV).

If "an eye for an eye, and a tooth for a tooth" is the characteristic mood of the law codes, then the acts of Hosea and Jesus contradicted the law. But if their characteristic mood is denoted by the motive clause, then the acts of Hosea and Jesus were in the tradition of the codes. The characteristic purpose of the law was to redeem, not to punish: "I am Yahweh your God who brought you out of the land of Egypt, from the house of bondage" (Ex. 20:2). That tension within law which exists between the *lex talion* (Near Eastern law) and the motive clause is well expressed by the Law Preacher on the Mount. "You have heard that it was said, 'An eye for an eye and a tooth for a tooth.' But I say to you..." (Matt. 5:38-41).

The purpose of law was not merely individual but social redemption, aimed at redeeming the entire society. This wider application is suggested by the prophet Micah (Mic. 4:1-4) as he foresees the peoples of the nations one day choosing Yahweh's law to settle disputes, instead of choosing the sword (Mic. 4:3). This law would be based not upon coercion, but voluntary acceptance, teaching which the nations choose to learn (Mic. 4:2). This concept of international law was based not merely on the prophet's idealism. It had its precedent in Israel's intertribal law in the period of the judges when the tribes went up to Shilo to adjudicate their differences. Micah saw that the peace which in the time of the Judges had been intertribal would one day be international; it would be based on Yahweh's law.

The prophet also says that the law of Yahweh will give order to economic relations within each nation: "Every householder will sit under his own vine and under his own fig tree, and none shall make him afraid" (Mic. 4:4).

This oracle places its emphasis not merely on the well-being of the nations, but on every household within each nation.

A point we should not miss is that what Yahweh will achieve for the world in the future is what Israel, by following the law of Yahweh, is to achieve in the present: "For all the peoples walk every one in the name of their God. But we walk in the name of our God, forever" (Mic. 4:5).

Judah *now* was to accept the law of Yahweh instead of the law of the sword for international relations. Judah *now* was to promote the economic freedom of every household instead of the feudalistic structure of the Caananite city state. Yahweh had liberated Israel from the slavery of Egypt. Each household was to remain free in its relatedness to other households by walking in this way of Yahweh. Redemption rather than punishment was to be Judah's present goal both for the individual and for the total society.

Jesus and the early church began a new stage in this legal transformation ("the law and the prophets") when Jesus' teaching was carried from Israel to the cities and villages of the Mediterranean world. With the advent of Jesus, "to each his due" was no longer to be the measure of justice for this world. Christian missioners called humanity to a new norm of justice, a new norm which relates human behavior to the model clause of God's act in Christ.

TRANSFORMATION OF JUSTICE: FROM CHURCH TO WORLD

Emil Brunner was right in seeing a difference between biblical justice and the justice of this world. As we have seen, this justice did not rise suddenly with Jesus, but was due to a deliberate transformation of justice which extended from Moses to Jesus.

If Hammurabi's concept of justice were modernized a little, the world today could be quite at home with it. In contrast, however, the justice of the church is not easily related to the institutions of this world. Justice for the Christian, due to this long transformation from Moses to Jesus, can no longer be defined by Plato's "to every man his due," but by that norm which arises out of Yahweh's relationship with God's people, and by the interhuman relationships which develop from that experience.

This was a revolutionary model as compared to the model of natural law. This liberation model qualified slavery and poverty, gave rights even to the resident foreigner, and had as its goal an egalitarian universal society, with each household free from poverty and oppression.

How do Christians relate this new, transformed, model of justice to the justice systems of this world? The following are some options:

1. Withdrawal Strategy: Strategy of Unfaithfulness?

One possible response is withdrawal from worldly structures, a procedure which in some cases may be valid. But any strategy of withdrawal from the justice systems of this world must be partial, because Yahweh's justice is aggressive. The objective of this new justice is to take over the entire world.

I cite two texts. The first is Psalms 82, a legal form. In this Psalm the God of Israel calls into court the gods of the nations. God indicts them because of their failure to dispense justice:

> How long will you judge unjustly
> and show partiality to the wicked?
> Give justice to the weak and the fatherless;
> maintain the right of the afflicted and the destitute.
> Rescue the weak and the needy;
> deliver them from the hand of the wicked (Ps. 82:2-4).

Because these gods of the nations were unjust, God sentenced them to die like the princes through whom they dispensed their justice on the human scene (Ps. 82:6-7). The God of Israel is then called upon to dispense justice to the earth, for all nations belong to Yahweh (Ps. 82:8).

This Psalm is an expression of more than mere nationalism--"my God is better than your god." Israel's main dispute with the nations, according to this Psalmist, had to do with the matter of justice, the way of Yahweh versus the way of the nations. Since all nations belong to Yahweh, the establishment of God's justice in Israel was the beginning of a process in which this justice would be established in the earth. Israel is God's bridgehead for a just society; the long range objective is "all the earth."

How will this objective be reached, since Yahweh has chosen a militarily weak and insignificant people as a bridgehead? Did Yahweh make a mistake in this choice? Should God have chosen a mighty nation such as Egypt, Assyria or Persia? Our second text, Isaiah 42, speaks to this question.

The first of the traditional Servant Songs, Isaiah 42 sets forth the call of the servant. The servant's task is stated in three verses:

> "He will bring forth justice to the nations" (Is. 42:1).
> "He will faithfully bring forth justice" (Is. 42:3).
> He will establish "justice in the earth" (Is. 42:4).

Each time, the word for justice is *mishpāṭ*, the same word as that translated "to do justice" in Micah 6:8. The Song closes by saying that the far-off nations are waiting for Yahweh's law (*tōrāh*, v. 4).

Our usual preoccupation with these Songs has been with the Servant's suffering. Indeed the Servant does suffer, as the later Songs, especially Isaiah 53, indicate. But we must begin our study with this first Song to see *why* the Servant suffers. Why do the nations pull his beard, beat him and finally lead him "like a lamb to the slaughter?" (Is. 50:6; 53:7). Because he dares to challenge the unjust legal systems of the nations, and to replace them by the justice and law of Israel's God! What God is about in the Bible is not a vocation for playboys and playgirls. God has a bold and daring plan to take over the world with a new system of justice.

The Servant suffers not only because of this vocation to establish God's justice in the nations.The Servant suffers because of daring to enlarge God's bridgehead by a nonviolent method:

> He will not call or lift his voice high, or make
> himself heard in the open street.
> He will not break a bruised reed,
> or snuff out a smouldering wick;
> he will make justice shine on every race,
> never faltering, never breaking down (Is. 42:2-4, NEB).

Some interpreters think the word "call" at the beginning of this statement refers to calling up the militia, an act which the Servant will not do. This nonviolent method is the vocation of a prophet, the proclamation of Word:

> The Lord God has given me
>   the tongue of those who are taught,
> that I may know how to sustain with a word
>   him that is weary (Is. 50:4, RSV).

This word by which the Servant establishes justice is expressed here for the first time in the Bible in terms of a transformed sword; God "made my mouth like a sharp sword" (Is. 49:2). This figure is used also of the triumph of Jesus in the book of Revelation: "From his mouth issues a sharp sword..." (Rev. 19:15).

To understand this Servant, we must see him as the transformation of the Near Eastern war hero and empire builder. Sennacharib rode forth at the head of his armies to establish Assur's justice over the nations. Hammurabi by means of his armies subjugated the city states of Mesopotamia to establish Marduk's justice. In these very poems of Isaiah 40-45, Yahweh anoints Cyrus, king of Persia, to be God's "bird of prey" to subjugate the nations (Is. 46:11), to build Yahweh's city and to set the exiles free (Is. 45:13). Cyrus however, did not become God's "king of justice" as did Hammurabi in relation to the god Marduk. As Servant of justice, God chose a prophetic personality, one whose mouth was made "like a sharp sword," to win the nations to a new legal order.

We have noted that Jesus' reference to the Old Testament as "the law and the prophets" had deeper meaning than just the first five books of Moses followed by the prophetic books. As the Hammurabi style of law is associated with kings and the police force, so Yahwistic law is associated with the prophet and the word of God. It is significant that even when Jesus rode into Jerusalem as the *Son of David*, the crowds still identified him as "the *prophet* Jesus from Nazareth of Galilee" (Matt. 21:9-11). This prophet Jesus, without honor in his own city, set forth Yahweh's program of justice in the synagogue at Nazareth,

> He has anointed me to preach good news to the poor. He has sent me to proclaim release of the captives and recovering of the sight to the blind, to set at liberty those who are oppressed..." (Luke 4:18).

This proclamation of justice, like the story line of the Servant in Isaiah 40-55, meant for Jesus a ministry of suffering and death. That death, however, was interpreted by his followers as the triumph of Yahweh's justice over the impersonal powers and gods of this world (Col. 2:14,15).

We have seen from our two texts that the character of Yahweh's justice is aggressive. In the prophetic servant Jesus, God moved out from the bridgehead of Israel to establish communities of divine justice throughout the world. A strategy of justice which primarily withdraws into isolated communities denies this aggressive character of Yahweh's justice.

2. The Constantinian Strategy: Strategy of Capitulation

According to Harold J. Berman, former professor of law at Harvard University, modern law began in the 11th and 12th centuries A.D. under the guidance of the church.[7] It was motivated by the struggle for supremacy between the pope and the emperor, a struggle which resulted in a counterbalancing between secular and religious authorities. This struggle resulted in the codification of canon and civil law, the establishing of both church and civil courts. What both authorities shared in common was "the integration of law with religion, of order and justice with faith and morals, in an integrated community which transcended both."[8]

In some ways this solution resembled that of Old Testament law in which laws of worship and conduct were intermingled. An advantage was that all courts were not under the jurisdiction of the emperor; there were also church courts. Law and "state" were not synonymous. The crucial factor, however, had to do with the motive clause. Was law "written upon the heart" and enforced by preaching and exhortation or was church law enforced upon those who rejected covenant law? Was even baptism backed by violent force, along with laws against theft and murder?

My point is illustrated by the history of the word "pastor." Today we use the word *pastor* or *shepherd* of persons who are servants in our congregations (voluntary, covenant societies). In the ancient Near East *pastor* (*shepherd*) was used in the political sphere almost exclusively for the king. For example, Sennacherib called himself pastor. How is it that congregational servants have inherited a favorite term of Near Eastern kingship, a term used of Sennacherib? This has happened because of the transformation made by the biblical faith community. According to the Bible, early Israel by conviction had no king. When Israel demanded kingship, the prophets insisted that it be different from that of the Near East. For example, Ezekiel criticized Israel's pastors (shepherds) because they fed themselves on the sheep instead of feeding the sheep (Ezek. 34). Ezekiel predicted a new community with a "new heart" and "new spirit," which would cause Israel to walk in God's statutes (Ezek. 36:26-27). In the New Testament, Jesus is seen as the transformed king, the "good shepherd," who gives his life for the sheep; and the faith community is a transformed community of those who "follow him, for they know his voice" (John 1).

In this tradition of transformation, Peter exhorts the elders to "be pastors of God's flock," not domineering over them, but remembering the example of the Chief Shepherd (1 Pet. 5:2-4). This tradition of the Bible, begun in the Old Testament community and fulfilled in the New Testament, makes untenable the Constantinian solution to the question of law. That solution is a flight backward toward Hammurabi's law. In some ways it is worse than his law.

Lutherans of the Reformation period did not reject Constantinianism but heightened the problem by making the law more exclusively the domain of the state. Luther rejected canon law, rejecting the validity of the church's jurisdiction of law altogether. Luther held a doctrine of two kingdoms but, contrary to Scripture, saw the Christian as citizen of both. The Christian in private life was to follow the Sermon on the Mount. In public life the Christian must engage in vocations such as those of the soldier and executioner.

Unlike Luther's contemporary, Machiavelli, Luther's prince was not to act solely from considerations of power politics, but was to do justice, to use both reason and will to serve God. The pastor was to preach the gospel to the prince, to inspire him to fulfill his calling. The prince became the head of the churches of his principality and determined to what confession his subjects would belong.

Calvinists accepted many teachings of Luther but modified his doctrine of the two kingdoms. For them the church was an institution consisting of politically independent, local congregations, each with its own elected leadership and legal authority. This congregational legal authority was balanced against the civil polity, and like the older Catholic vision, might even dominate it. These congregations had their own law regulating worship, theological doctrine and morals of the civil society, including aspects of social, economic and political life.

Most English Calvinists, the Puritans, did not challenge the authority of the king over the church as Calvin would have done, but tried to reform the Church of England from within. They were great patriots, entering public life as members of Parliament and justices of the peace. Toward the mid-17th century, they took over the leadership of parliament, believing that God had destined England as an elect nation to incarnate the divine purpose for humanity. Both in England and America they believed in the reformation of the world and emphasized law as a means to that reformation. They believed that the principle use of the moral (natural) and civil law was to teach humanity to walk in the way which God had laid out. This was a way not only for the individual, but also for the corporate body, the family, church and nation.

The left wing of the Reformation, the Anabaptists, should also be understood from the viewpoint of the legal revolution begun in the 11th and

12th centuries. We have noted that this legal revolution was begun by the church, splitting German Christianity into two parts, the church and the secular order. The church was an independent, visible, corporate legal structure. The secular order was divided among various polities.

Like Luther, the Anabaptists emphasized the doctrine of the two kingdoms, but instead of the prince defining the confession of his principality, they defined the congregation as all those and only those who were voluntarily baptized as adults. The order of the congregation was a covenant order which demanded a personal decision of life-long commitment for those who wished to be members. Anabaptists held that the just community of Yahweh cannot be created by coercion.

A second demand of this covenant order, shocking to the orders of Reformation society, was the acceptance of Christ's demand to love the enemy, even the enemy of the state (Schleitheim Confession, 1527). In contrast to Luther's prince who was head of the church, Anabaptists believed that Christians could not be magistrates, since magistrates were expected to enforce the law against the principality's internal enemies by police force and to protect the principality against external enemies by force of arms. They insisted that Christians were not to serve as soldiers nor as executioners.[9]

Besides emphasizing the legal autonomy of the congregation (as did also Catholics and Calvinists in their own way), Anabaptists denied and limited the legal sovereignty of the states. Quoting Paul, they noted that the powers are "to do that which is good." These powers were to refrain from persecution and from otherwise interfering with the legal polity of the church. This limitation would ultimately influence the writing of the United States' constitution.[10]

The United States' constitution was influenced by another major revolution in law, the Enlightenment and the French Revolution.

3. Enlightenment Strategy: Strategy of Denial

The Enlightenment was the first European system of belief formulated by people who were not Christians. Its religion was deism, a belief in a God as creator in the remote past, but who does not subsequently interfere in this creation. While God was essential to the Enlightenment's belief system, the church was not. Nature operates harmoniously for human benefit and "the laws of nature and nature's God" (Jefferson) are the important guides for human conduct. While the congregation was denied as an independent, visible, corporate legal structure, individualism and nationalism were emphasized. The nation-state was sovereign and public opinion was its ultimate authority. Criminal law was made an instrument of the state. These ideas influenced nearly all Western governments; they undergirded the French Revolution beginning in 1789 and were influential in the American revolution of approximately the same period.

In the conflict occasioned by the German split between church law and the law of secular states discussed above, the secular arm of government won out under this deistic influence. In deism secular government was represented not by the princes as in Lutheranism but by the people; it was nevertheless a democratic totalitarianism. The congregation was not recognized as a legal entity, independent of the state. In terms of the ancient Near Eastern situation, the secular Hammurabi style of law had won out over the Moses-Jesus sovereignty in corporate human affairs, except insofar as the congregations are ready to back their convictions with imprisonment and martyrdom. In terms of the demands of biblical law, the clash between the two public legalities of church and state is not essentially different from what it has always been. But the clash need not come to martyrdom. If there is mutual recognition, there may be interaction, at times cooperation and at times a standoff.

4. Strategies for Faithfulness

A requirement for faithfulness is that congregations recognize above all their own legal autonomy. The law of God in Christ is found only within the structure of covenant. This certainly means that congregations must establish their own structures to reconcile internal disputes. We have noted that the first organized structure of God's people in the book of Exodus was for handling disputes, the smallest group being made up of ten people. Why has this Bible vision become lost? Why does Paul still have to say to us, "How dare one of your members take up a complaint against another in the courts of the unjust..." (1 Cor. 6:1, JB)?

Just decisions do not come without effort in a Christian community. Paul says, "Can it be that there is not a single wise man among you able to give a just decision in a brother-Christian's cause" (1 Cor. 6:5, NEB)? If God's people are to judge the world, and even angels (1 Cor. 6:2-3), it is time to give attention to biblical principles of justice so that we can give just judgments at least in the mundane matters of this life (1 Cor. 6:3). We dare not leave matters of justice to unjust courts, courts which do not accept the gospel as norm for justice. One strategy for recognizing the congregation's legal autonomy, then, is to establish methods for dealing with internal issues of justice and conflict.

A second strategy is to relate to the legal, economic and political structures of this world from the perspective of the congregation. The question for the Christian in economics is not whether a Christian may be rich, but how one may participate so as to promote sister/brotherhood economics. The question is not whether the Christian may participate in the legal or political process, but where and how to participate in that process so that persons can experience something of the transforming power of the gospel.

When we participate in secular structures we do not leave covenant structure behind, but take it with us. When we enter the congregational meeting we should not leave outside those rules and laws by which we do business. We should bring them inside for our own scrutiny before God and for the scrutiny of brothers and sisters. Associations of Christian medical, legal and business people should help us in this process.

A third strategy for recognizing the congregation's legal autonomy is the devising of alternative structures to the state system, structures more compatible with covenant structure. This is illustrated by prison ministries and by the Victim Offender Reconciliation Program. These structures must themselves submit to the congregation's renewal and critique from the viewpoint of covenant structure, if they are not to become coercive and ethnic.

In all its efforts to participate in the justice process, the church needs to "talk it up." The church is a community which shares and remembers. The *More With Less* books are examples of the exchange of ideas and experiences which point the church in the right direction.[11] *Dial 911*, the story of how Reba Place Fellowship dealt with crime in Chicago, is the sort of material out of which precedent is established.[12] These only touch the surface of the wealth of Christian experience which ought to be shared among our congregations.

CREATION AND REDEMPTION

To understand the relationship of church and world, we need to understand the relationship of creation to redemption. God relates to humanity through creation. The biblical doctrine of creation was not arrived at by acceptance of the physical and social structures of this world and by fitting the gospel within them. That results in the surrender of the gospel. The key to "that which was in the beginning" is "that which is presently becoming," the gospel itself, the prism through which all worldly structures are examined (John 1; Gen. 1). Not only the church but also the world is included in God's promise, in God's covenant of providential care (Gen. 8:20-22; 9:1-17). The Jesus of the gospels is elevated to a place of rule over "every authority and power and dominion...not only in this age but also in that which is to come" (Eph. 1:21-22). To understand the biblical doctrine of creation we must begin with the gospel.

God also relates to humanity through redemption, a special relationship by which blessing may come to the world through Abraham's people: "And in you all families of the earth shall bless themselves" (Gen. 12:1-3). God's concern is not merely for providential care, but by special grace to lead humanity into a personal relation of God and people. The purpose of the church is to mediate personal blessing to the earth's families.

I began this address with Emil Brunner's statement that if we start from the Scriptural use of the word "justice," we are speaking of something which has nothing to do with social justice. What Brunner did not seem to understand is that biblical justice speaks to the world's problem of justice, and it speaks so radically (to "the root" of the matter) that it changes the definition of justice. Worldly justice is defined as "to everyone his due," and is centered on the state. Biblical or covenant justice is defined "to each according to the norm of Yahweh's relation to God's people, and the relationship of these people to each other in the light of that norm," and is centered in the congregation.

The road from worldly justice to biblical justice is the long way of the transforming biblical story which we have tried to trace. If we find the connection from biblical justice back to state "justice" difficult to make, let us rejoice in the transforming power of the story which created the chasm in the first place. And let us have faith that the same transforming power is at work today in us, through us, beyond us and in spite of us. By this transforming power, we can annul secular law when necessary, and whenever possible, bring it into tension with the gospel.

NOTES

1. Emil Brunner, *Justice and the Social Order*, trans. by Mary Hottinger (New York, London: Harper and Brothers, 1945), p. 13.

2. The events of Exodus 18 are evidently placed here, before Sinai, to sum up two parts of the book of Exodus, deliverance from Egypt and justice associated with Sinai. See Deuteronomy 1 where these events are associated with Israel's leaving Sinai.

3. Shāphaṭ, translated by RSV, "to judge" and "decide."

4. Dale Patrick, *Old Testament Law* (Atlanta: John Knox Press, 1985), p. 6.

5. James B. Pritchard, *Ancient Near Eastern Texts* (Princeton, N.J.: Princeton University Press, 3rd ed., 1969), p. 178.

6. Jochen Boecker, *Law and the Administration of Justice in the Old Testament and the Ancient Near East*, trans. by Jerry Moiser (1980), pp. 15-19, 183.

7. Harold J. Berman, *Law and Revolution: The Formation of the Western Legal Tradition* (Cambridge, Mass; London, England: Harvard University Press, 1983). I am indebted to Berman for the following analysis of law in the Middle Ages, Reformation and Enlightenment, except for the Anabaptists.

8. William J. Hawke, "The History of Law During the Protestant Reformation," in *The Bible and Law*, edited by Willard Swartley (Occasional Paper No. 3, Associated Mennonite Biblical Seminaries, 1982), p. 98.

9. For an analysis of Anabaptism in relation to the Reformers, see John Howard Yoder, "The Hermeneutics of Peoplehood: A Protestant Perspective," *The Priestly Kingdom* (Notre Dame, Ind.: University of Notre Dame Press, 1984), pp. 15-45. For an original Anabaptist statement on law, see Hans Schnell ca. 1575, translated by Elizabeth Bender and Leonard Gross, edited by Leonard Gross (unpublished copy).

10. For part of the story of this influence, see W. R. Estep, "Baptists: Exponents of Religious Liberty," paper read at Jurisprudential Working Meeting, Pheasant Run, Ill., April 8-9, 1984.

11. Doris Janzen Longacre, compiler, *More-With-Less Cookbook* (Scottdale, Pa.: Herald Press, 1976).

12. Dave Jackson, *Dial 911: Peaceful Christians and Urban Violence* (Scottdale, Pa.: Herald Press, 1981).

CHAPTER 8

THEOLOGY OF LAW

Law may be defined as "the order of justice and right to which individuals and groups should conform and which judicial authority should enforce" (Patrick, 4). Moral law is what a person or groups are obligated to do regardless of legal consequences; judicial law is what sovereign authority is obligated to enforce. Both are part of a legal system. "Theology of law" is then the relation of God to "the order of justice and right," a relationship which profoundly affects the definition of law itself.

Harold Berman maintains that modern western law began in the eleventh/twelfth centuries A.D., under church guidance. Motivated by a struggle for supremacy between pope and emperor, it resulted in a counterbalancing between secular and religious authorities, the codification of Canon and civil law and the establishment of both church and civil courts. Both authorities shared in a common "integration of law with religion, of order and justice with faith and morals, in an integrated community which transcended both" (Hawke 98). An advantage of this system was that law and "state" were not synonymous, since there were both church and civil courts. The integration meant, however, that the laws of both were backed by coercive force.

Early Lutheranism accepted this Constantinian solution, but rejected the church's jurisdiction of law, making law the exclusive domain of the state. Lutheran doctrine of the two kingdoms maintained that the Christian, citizen of both, was to follow the Sermon on the Mount in private life, but in public life was to uphold law by engaging in vocations such as executioner and soldier.

Though Calvinists accepted many of Luther's teachings, they modified his doctrine of two kingdoms. For them the church consisted of congregations, each with its own elected leadership and legal authority. This legal authority, like the older Catholic vision, was balanced against the civil polity and might dominate it. Congregations had their own laws regulating worship, theological doctrine and morals, including aspects of economic and political life.

Most English Calvinists (Puritans) did not challenge the king's authority over the church as Calvin would have done, but attempted to reform the English church from within. They took over leadership of Parliament in the

From *Mennonite Encyclopedia*, Vol. 5, 1990.

seventeenth century, believing that God had destined England an elect nation to incarnate the divine purpose for humanity. In England and America they believed that the principle use of moral and judicial law was to teach humanity the way of God, a way for individual and corporate life.

Varied in their beliefs, Anabaptists like Hubmaier held that the Christian may be a judge, and "bear the sword in God's stead against the evil doer"; others such as the apocalyptic Münsterites maintained that God had established the final kingdom at Münster and that the elect were to execute vengeance on oppressors of the poor.

This essay will deal with those southern Anabaptists represented by the Schleitheim Confession (1527), Hans Schnell's statement on law (ca. 1575) which breathes the spirit of Schleitheim, the view of the Hutterite leader, Peter Rideman, and the writings of Menno Simons, leader of the Northern wing.

The Anabaptist theology of law should be understood against the background of the legal revolution begun in the eleventh/twelfth centuries and the sixteenth century reformers. It was based upon a doctrine of two kingdoms which, unlike that of Luther, defined the congregation as voluntarily baptized adults, and argued for a strict separation of church and state. Accepting Christ's demand to love the enemy, Anabaptists rejected Luther's concept that the prince was head of the church, maintaining that Christians should not be magistrates since magistrates were expected to enforce law by use of arms against the principality's internal and external enemies. They insisted that Christians were to serve neither as executioners or soldiers, and that the state on the other hand was not to interfere with or persecute the church.

Hans Schnell, naming three types of law, argued that government is based upon the Noahic law of vengeance (Gen. 9:6), "natural law" which he identified with Paul's admonition in Romans 13. A positive institution in a fallen world, government's power is limited to punishing the evil and protecting the good, for which Christians pay taxes. Although Paul called government a "minister of God," Schnell pointed out that he thus spoke of Nero, persecutor of Christians, of Pharaoh, a "vessel of wrath fitted for destruction," of the Babylonian king who was God's rod to punish Israel, and of Pilate who crucified Jesus. Whether it performs well or badly, government performs as a slave rather than as an heir, and will be rewarded or punished according to its performance.

Schnell's second type of law which God gave through Moses that Israel might know sin until Christ comes, is equated with the O.T. which includes a physical kingdom with a ruler, power of the sword, a priesthood and literal law. Though this law included the law of vengeance (body for body), the O.T. differed from Gentile law in that it "foreshadowed the true essence in Christ and his kingdom."

Schnell's third type of law, the law of Christ, annuls the law of vengeance: "For Christ is the end of the law. We become dead to the law through the body of Christ, so that we have another law. There it is no longer a matter of body for body but only love and mercy, repentance and forgiveness of sins, loving the foe and praying for him" (Schnell).

Schnell tends to equate the O.T. law of vengeance with state law which, in the new order represented by the church, is annulled in Christ. He maintains that the law of vengeance and the law of Christ should not be mixed as when Constantine assumed the name Christian, "which is indeed itself a cause for lamenting...." Schnell cites Mark 10:42 to contend that if any ruler wishes to be a Christian he must be born again by the Spirit, dare no longer execute vengeance with the sword, "but must love his enemy and in suffering with Christ must pray" for him, bearing the cross of Christ.

The Hutterite leader, Peter Rideman, admonished Christians to neither go to law with their own case nor be judges (1 Cor. 6).

Menno Simons, taking on the task of transforming the remnants of the Münsterite Anabaptists into the peaceable kingdom, had a more positive attitude toward government than did the Schleitheim Confession though he says little about law. Addressing princes, he admonished: "...believe Christ's word, fear God's wrath, love righteousness, do justice to widow and orphans, judge rightly between a man and his neighbor, fear no man's highness, despise no man's littleness, hate all avarice, punish with reason...." He condemns rulers who accept bribes, pervert justice, and who persecute Christians.

Ernst Troeltsch assessed that the Protestant reformers added nothing new to medieval jurisprudence: "The Protestant theory of the state is in both [Lutheranism and Calvinism] based on that very same Christian 'Law of Nature' which, in the Middle Ages, was compounded out of Stoicism, Aristotle and the Bible..." (Troeltsch, 107). He maintained that the parent of modern human rights was not church Protestantism but Anabaptism and Spiritualism which the Reformation hated and drove forth into the new world. It is generally recognized that in this area Anabaptism has made a major contribution to modern jurisprudence.

Because of persecution the strategy of nonresistant Mennonites since the Reformation has been largely one of withdrawal, by which they maintained the Anabaptist attitude toward state law. Communities in Russia accepted some state characteristics, but never lost the tension between coercion and biblical pacifism. Communities in Colonial America became somewhat more positive to state law because of William Penn's "Holy Experiment." Canadian communities are more active in a government sympathetic to minorities, though not without some tensions of faith.

Influenced by the Great Awakening, two world wars, urbanization, education, world mission, relief service, health, reconciliation and prisoner rehabilitation programs, Mennonites have largely ended their strategy of withdrawal, reviving an interest in justice and law.

Writing in mid-century, Guy Hershberger attempted to apply the Schleitheim position to the modern world. He maintained that Christians may use state law for purposes of justice, may defend themselves in court but should work for a just and peaceful settlement outside the courts, and should settle their own disputes among themselves. He recognized a need for Christian attorneys who walk in the way of the cross, whose services do not include aggressive litigation, and who assist fellow Christians in this way. More recently there is renewed interest in reconciliation programs for justice alongside of and outside of state legal structures.

Theology of law is being clarified further among Mennonites by modern biblical studies. Modern O.T. study of law began with the discovery of an extensive body of Near Eastern law, dramatized especially by the Hammurabi Code. O.T. law deals with secular concerns comparable to Near Eastern law, but is oriented from violent kingship power to the structures of covenant and worship. Its dominant characteristic is not vengeance but the motive/model clause, especially Yahweh's liberation of Israel from Egypt. Though O.T. law codes provide for capital punishment, some O.T. texts emphasize forgiveness and reconciliation even for capital crimes (Gen. 4; Hos. 1-3; 11; Jer. 3). O.T. law is especially concerned for the slave, the poor and politically weak. Its goal is an egalitarian society, each household an economic unit free from tyranny. From a Near Eastern perspective, O.T. law represents a major break from state law, a turning toward Jesus and the N.T.

New Testament studies reveal that Jesus affirms covenant law in the synoptic Gospels. In the Sermon, household laws, and Apostolic admonitions, Jesus and early church deepened and widened covenant law for all nations by orienting it about the authority and example of Christ's person.

In summary then, biblical theology of law represents a new "order of justice and right," which creates a tension with, and occasionally provides an alternative to state law.

BIBLIOGRAPHY

Berman, Harold J. *Law and Revolution, The Formation of the Western Legal Tradition*, Harvard University Press, 1983.

Gross, Leonard. "Jurisprudential Perspectives in the Light of Anabaptist-Mennonite Tradition: Bibliography with an Interpretive Introduction." *Quarterly Christian Legal Society*, Vol. V, No. 2, 1984.

Gross, Leonard. "The Anabaptists and Law," Unpublished Paper, 1986.

Hawke, William J. "The History of Law during the Protestant Reformation," in *The Bible and Law*, op. cit.

Hershberger, Guy Franklin. *The Way of the Cross in Human Relations*, Herald Press, 1958.

Juhnke, James C. "Mennonites in Militarist America: Some Consequences of World War I." John Richard Burkholder and Calvin Redekop, eds., *Kingdom, Cross and Community*. Herald Press, 1976.

Klaassen, Walter, ed. *Anabaptism in Outline, Selected Primary Sources*. Herald Press, 1981.

Lind, Millard C. "Law in the Old Testament" in *The Bible and Law*, Occasional Papers No. 3, Council of Mennonite Seminaries/Institute of Mennonite Studies, 1982.

Lind, Millard C. *Transformation of Justice: From Moses to Jesus*. New Perspectives on Crime and Justice: Occasional Papers of the MCC Canada Victim Offender Ministries Program and the MCC U.S. Office of Criminal Justice, Dec. 1986, Issue no. 5.

Patrick, Dale. *Old Testament Law*. John Knox Press, 1985.

Rideman, Peter. Trans. by Kathleen E. Hasenburg. *Account of Our Religion, Doctrine and Faith*. Hodder and Stoughton and the Plough Publishing House, 1950.

Schnell, Hans. "Thorough Account from God's Word, How to Distinguish Between the Temporal and Spiritual Regimes...," edited by Leonard Gross, trans. by Elizabeth Bender, unpublished.

Toews, John E. "Some Theses Toward a Theology of Law in the New Testament," in *The Bible and Law*, op. cit.

Troeltsch, Ernst. *Protestantism and Progress, A Historical Study of the Relation of Protestantism to the Modern World,* trans. by W. Montgomery. Beacon Press, 1958.

CHAPTER 9

OLD TESTAMENT LAW: REVIEW ESSAY

OLD TESTAMENT LAW. By Dale Patrick. Atlanta: John Knox Press, 1985.

A revival of interest in the study of law in the Bible has coexisted with the revival of interest in the relationship between law and faith. These two interests need to find each other. It is not sufficient for lawyers merely to return to the old confessional answers of the relation between church and law, whether Catholic, Reformed, Lutheran, or Anabaptist. We have new needs, new problems which a return to the Biblical sources will help us to answer. And Biblical scholars should not be satisfied to have their tomes merely sit on the shelves of libraries without entering the arena of public usefulness.

This new book by Dale Patrick will help these interests come together. *Old Testament Law* is a thorough work designed to introduce the layman to the results of the new Biblical studies on law. It is informed by Patrick's chairship of the Group on Biblical Law and Comparative Studies, a program unit of the Society of Biblical Literature which has been studying the Old Testament and law for the past decade (p. iii).

The book is an accessible introduction written in simple, nontechnical language. It includes a chapter on how biblical law is studied by critical scholars, introducing the reader to literary criticism, form criticism, history of tradition, and study of the legal tradition of the ancient Near East. Each chapter includes a bibliography for those who wish to do further study in the various areas discussed by the book.

The first chapter is an introduction which includes a definition of law; it carefully distinguishes between moral and judicial law, and discusses the relationship between law and community. This definition is essential to a study of law in the Bible, but is nevertheless hazardous in that it may exclude from the study aspects of biblical law which may be different from the usual concepts of law. For the most part, Patrick guards against this by his descriptive approach. This may explain, however, his lack of a satisfactory discussion of biblical law's characteristic feature of the motive clause, a feature all but totally lacking in ancient Near Eastern and Roman law, and to my knowledge, in modern law. While a discussion of the motive clause is omitted, the author does cite the im-

From *Journal of Law and Religion,* IV, 1986.

portant literature: Gemser (p. 32), Sonsino (p. 33), and Beyerlin (p. 95).

Patrick deals further with the unique characteristic of biblical law in his chapter on "Law and Covenant" (pp. 223-48). Here he sees the term *covenant* as the biblical term for Israel's constitution. Patrick is careful to distance himself from those biblical scholars who have found significant formal parallels between Yahweh's covenant with Israel and the international treaties of the Near East. He is rightly cautious, though he might have discussed a number of insights which these comparisons may give to the character of biblical covenant. Here again, Patrick includes suggested reading for those who wish to pursue this topic (p. 247).

The heart of Patrick's work is made up of four chapters, a chapter each on the various complexes of Old Testament law: "The Ten Commandments" (pp. 35-61); "The Book of the Covenant" (Ex. 20:23-23:19, pp. 63-96); "The Deuteronomic Law" (Deut. 12:1-26:19, pp. 97-144); "The Holiness Code and Priestly Law" (Ex. 25-31; 35-40; Lev. 1-27; Num. 1-10, pp. 145-88). These chapters include helpful tables which compare the content of the various complexes of law with each other and comparable material in the Pentateuch (pp. 39, 91, 97, 162). They also include complete outlines of the various complexes (pp. 39, 66-67, 104, 155), except for priestly law. Most important, each chapter has a rather detailed commentary on the respective complexes.

Patrick is legitimately critical of the scholarly urge to simplify the "original statement" of the Ten Commandments (pp. 39-40). He recognizes the Ten Commandments as a high level of abstraction and "a highly sophisticated attempt to summarize the basic postulates of Israelite law" (p. 40). Because of this, he hesitates to credit them to Moses, though he regards them as part of "the classical development of the movement he inaugurated." Patrick may be right in this, but if some of the most sophisticated poetry of the Bible (Ex. 15:1-18; Judges 4:2-34) can be credited to Israel's earliest period, it is perhaps not too unreasonable to accept the judgment of the growing number of scholars who regard the Ten Commandments as from this period also.

It is a considerable gain that Patrick concludes that the Book of the Covenant "once had a narrative framework consisting of the initial negotiation of the covenant (19:3-8), the revelation of covenant law (20:23-23:19), and the ceremonial ratification of the covenant (24:3-8)" (p. 64). It is necessary to break the tyranny of form criticism's tendency to reduce this material to small snippets, if one is to get the full impact of the biblical message. Patrick is probably correct in dating this code to the period of the Judges (p. 65). He sees the *whole* of this covenant book as it now stands as "an oral proclamation of law to the community under its authority" (p. 66). This view gives us an important glimpse into the character of the theopolitical structure of early Israel. The "rule of Yahweh" was not a mere spiritual concept but was a reality which took on sociological and political form by the proclamation of a law which had a radically different concept of justice from that reflected in the other law collections of the ancient Near East.

This radically different concept of justice is expressed especially in relation to the slave, the person on the lowest rung of the socio-economic order.

As Patrick says, these laws do not assail the institution of slavery, "but attempt to regulate it and to protect the slaves from their masters. In the initial address (21:2) and various admonitions in the law, one can hear the appeal of the law-giver to the master to honor the rights of his slave. The very act of enunciating slave rights laid the foundation for a more radical critique of the institution in later law" (p. 72). This radical concern for the slave was founded upon Yahweh's deliverance of Israel from state slavery, as stated in the introductory "motive clause" of the Ten Commandments. As Patrick points out elsewhere (pp. 41, 47), the first two commandments are a distinct unit of I-Thou address which are placed within two motive clauses (Ex. 20:2, 5-6), forming an inclusio. These motive clauses, sometimes used as model clauses for Israel's own behavior, qualify the character of Yahweh, the God who alone is to be worshiped. Israel is to worship only that God who frees from state oppression (20:2) and whose holy zeal rules with limited retribution (wrath to three or four generations) and with love to infinity (to a thousand generations, as interpreted by Deut. 7:9).

The radical forward propulsion which these motive clauses provide in Israel's law is suggested by the developments in Deuteronomic law and the holiness code. Patrick lists five ways in which Deuteronomic law qualifies the slave law of the Book of the Covenant (Deut. 15:12-18, pp. 112-113). His fifth point is a correct summary statement: "Overall, servitude has been reduced to ownership of a person's labor, not of the person." This radical circumscription of the slave law is matched by the law in Deuteronomy 23:15-16 which, as Patrick points out, made slavery voluntary. Unfortunately, Patrick regards this legal prescription (or is it homily? cf. pp. 101-103) as "utopian": "Obviously such an institution is utopian. For slavery to operate, a slave must be compelled to work and not allowed to break the relationship at will" (p. 133).

This "utopian" character of the Scripture is due to the fact that justice is a norm arising not merely out of inter-human relationships, but also out of the relationship between Yahweh and Israel. In the case of slavery, that relationship was grounded in the deliverance from Egypt. Thus, the term "utopian" as used of Scripture should not be regarded as too "idealistic" to be workable. Voluntary slavery in ancient times should have been workable. Economic necessity made it so. Although American law permits everyone to own their own business, most of us prefer to work for somebody else. The runaway slave risked starvation and would escape from the master only if he/she thought that a better deal was to be had elsewhere. Competition would force the master to treat the slave with care. Economic necessity, on the other hand, would cause the slave to think twice before running away. Biblical law pushed the institution of slavery to the utmost limits of economic necessity, but did not fly off into utopian impracticality.

The experience of the divine-human relationship in history qualified Israel's legal concept of justice in many other areas (cf. Lev. 25, pp. 181-185). It is the fundamental reason for the difference between biblical and state (or kingship) law, both ancient and modern.

Patrick rejects the concept that the book of Deuteronomy was a "pious fraud" instigated by priests in the time of Josiah to further their reform (p. 99). He holds that it was written a century earlier from northern Shechemite oral traditions brought south after the fall of Samaria, 721 B.C. This recognition of the place of oral tradition challenges Wellhausen's concept that law originated after prophecy. Law preceded prophecy, and much that the prophets said was based upon it.

Although Patrick acknowledges that the "substance of Priestly theology existed in Israel's early days," he regards P as written in exilic or post-exilic times (pp. 146-147), envisaging the community "not as a political entity but a religious one." He tends to depreciate the P legislation as "of historical interest" while he regards the Holiness Code as continuing "to instruct all those who recognize the Biblical God as God indeed."

This analysis is unfortunate. It obscures the fact that all sources of the Sinai pericope depict Israel as a religious-political community. Israel was given law and government in the wilderness, before it had a land. While P emphasizes worship legislation, all the law codes correspond with this by beginning with laws regulating worship; all have laws relating to God interspersed throughout the code. The fact that P has gathered within itself the Holiness Code suggests that P recognized that the law of Yahweh who rules from the temple includes also economic and political concern. Israel was like other Near Eastern communities in that it was both religious and political. It differed from other Near Eastern communities, however, in that the word of Yahweh rather than the power base represented by kingship was central to its governance. As Patrick acknowledges, none of the Israelite law codes are oriented to kingship. This difference meant that both Israel's religion and its politics (including its law) were fundamentally different from religion and politics of the Near East. The conceptualization of the cultic community of early Israel in the P tradition was essentially correct, though it was no longer possible to distinguish the early wilderness tent from the evolution to tabernacle of the pre-kingship settlement period.

The cutting edge of biblical scholarship may be moving towards accepting a pre-exilic origin of P. If this dating is correct, then P may have been written down more or less parallel to the time of Deuteronomy as a powerful testimony to ancient tradition against Israel's paganization by a power-oriented king such as Manasseh. Fortunately, Patrick has given us a good statement of P's religious-political structure, no matter when P is dated.

In chapter seven, "The Written and Unwritten Law," Patrick correctly emphasizes that the purpose of the biblical law codes was educational. Their intent was "to inculcate the values, principles, concepts, and procedures of Israel's legal tradition, not to decree specific rulings of specific cases" (p. 190). Patrick sees a change from this emphasis on "the spirit of the law" to an emphasis on "the letter" in a few verses of Deuteronomy, representing the changed attitude toward law which began with Josiah's reform. He sees this as part of the development of normative Judaism between 70 A.D. and 500 A.D., a position with which Jesus and then Paul clashed in the earlier part of the first century. While there may be something to this argument, it must be fundamentally qualified, as recent studies on law and the New Testament have shown. I find objectionable the statement "love stands in tension with the principles of justice and right forming the basis of Old Testament law" (p. 213). This evidently omits from consideration the historic motive clause which is fundamental to Old Testament law and which is considered by Hosea as the expression of Yahweh's love for Israel (Hos. 11:1).

Fortunately, Patrick goes on to say that the kingdom of God is present as well as future and that "the law of love which belongs to the order of the kingdom can make claims upon those living in history" (p. 214). He also notes: "Since life in historical communities is under the sway of a perverted and tenuous justice, those who practice love now are bound to suffer." My quarrel with Patrick is his individualism; he does not take the church seriously as the historical community which is heir to the Old Testament law codes as qualified by the historical motive clause. This community, whose motive clause is the life, death, resurrection and present rule of Christ, does not vaporize the law of love into a meaningless utopia, and then fall back upon state law for the ordering of its life, but restates in rules and laws for educative purposes what love means in specific situations (witness the household rules of 1 Peter 2:11-3:12 and Paul's exhortation at the end of his typical letter).

The book ends with a postscript, "What is the Meaning of this Law," dealing with the value of biblical law for today. As a person of faith, Patrick rejects the humanistic, historical interpretation of a J. J. Finkelstein, maintaining rather that "the theology informing biblical law grew out of Israel's encounter with the holy" (p. 252). Because of this, Patrick sees the principle and values informing Old Testament law as binding for today (pp. 253-254). He then reviews each of the bodies of Old Testament law to state some of their significance for the believing Jew and Christian.

It is significant that Patrick does not discuss Paul's exhortation to the Church at Corinth that they should not resolve their disputes according to pagan Roman law, but should establish their own congregational courts where their wise can make just decisions according to the gospel (1 Cor. 6:1-8). As Patrick so well states, the Creator's identity is "revealed in the encounter with the sacred order of justice and right embedded in the community's law" (p. 252). This legal independence of the congregation from the state also gives to the Christian lawyer a divinely authorized basis for evaluating state law, for transforming it, and for rejecting that which cannot be at least partially transformed by the gospel.

My criticisms of this book are not to be interpreted as a negative evaluation of the book as a whole. This is by far the best introduction to be published on Old Testament Law. The author sees his own faith as joined to that of Israel, and the Bible as the Word of God with authority for today. This book should be on the shelf of every lawyer who is interested in taking Christian faith seriously in the practice of law.

CHAPTER 10

THE ANOMALY OF THE PROPHET

In the call of Jeremiah, there is an anomaly characteristic of the great prophets in Israel:

> "There! I have put my words in your mouth.
> See! I have made you an overseer this day
> over nations and kingdoms..." (Jer. 1:9-10).[1]

In the history of the Near East (indeed in the history of the world) the warrior-king is placed over the nations.[2] How are we to understand that a prophet is placed over the nations, a man whose claim to political power is only that he speaks the word of God?

It is my thesis that this anomaly is to be taken seriously from the standpoint of the theopolitical view of ancient Israel. My method is to examine the call of Jeremiah in relation to other relevant materials of his book. We will then examine the calls of Gideon and of Moses to see if this anomaly can be understood in terms of pre-kingship roots in the history of Israel. This paper only opens up the question, since an adequate treatment demands much more than the allotted space. The relevance of this subject to an understanding of the style of leadership of Jesus and his disciples should be self-evident. It is hoped that the subject is an appropriate one for the event which this book celebrates.

The Call of Jeremiah

The difficulty created by this anomaly is reflected in the history of exegesis. Bernhard Duhm regarded this feature of the call as apocryphal.[3] According to him it was "only the imagination of later Judaism which transformed the modest young priest of Anathoth into the colossal figure who pulls down and builds up nations and kingdoms, and pours out vials of wrath on the whole world."[4] Since this is regarded by most modern commentators as au-

---

From *The New Way of Jesus, Essays Presented to Howard Charles*, William Klassen, editor, 1980.

thentic to the experience of Jeremiah, is it megalomania?[5] Or does it suggest a
new kind of political structure in Israel as compared to the Middle East, a
structure in which the prophet rather than the warrior-king is the chief political
officer? Is it the prophet's abnormal psychology or is it Israel's unique sociology, specifically her politics, which is responsible for the anomaly?

The causative form of *pāqad* ("make...an overseer," J. Bright;
"give...authority," NEB; "have set...over," RSV; "am setting...over," JB) occurs
approximately twenty-nine times in the Old Testament. Of the twenty-three
times the verb is used of people, it is used fifteen times in a "secular" sense of a
political or military appointment. Of these occurrences the verb is united with
the preposition *al* (over) comparable to Jeremiah 1:10, in the following passages:

> Jeremiah 40:11: had appointed (causative of *pāqad*) Gedaliah....
> governor over (*al*--Heb.) them (RSV)
> 2 Kings 25:22: and over (*al*) the people...he appointed (causative
> of *pāqad*) Gedalih...governor (RSV)
> Genesis 41:34: Let Pharaoh proceed to appoint (causative of *pāqad*)
> overseers (noun form from the verbal root, *pāqad*) over
> (*al*) the land (RSV)
> Genesis 39:4: and he made him overseer (causative of *pāqad*) of
> (over, *al*) his house (RSV)
> 1 Chronicles 26:32: King David appointed (causative of *pāqad*)
> him and his brethren...to have the oversight of (over, *al*)
> the Reubenites (RSV)
> Joshua 10:18: and set (causative of *pāqad*) men by (over, *al*)
> it to guard them (RSV)[6]

In light of this usage and of its context in Jeremiah 1:10, the term in this
passage can hardly mean other than official appointment, an appointment to an
office over the nations. This great prophet in Israel, unique to the Near East
so far as we know, was regarded by Israel as Yahweh's chief political officer.[7]
As Yahweh's official, he is placed over the nations to destroy and to build.

While the prophet is Yahweh's political officer, set over the nations of the
world, we dare not forget the anomaly. The basis of his power is not military
force (he has none), but the word of Yahweh: "There! I have put my word in
your mouth. See! I have made you an overseer this day over nations and kingdoms." It is this anomaly which is strange to the history of the Near East, and
indeed of the world. Political power is here ultimately based not on an office
representing violent power, but on an office whose only power is Yahweh's
word.

Jeremiah recognized that Yahweh also had other political officers. The
place of violent political power was seen early in his ministry.[8] Identified first
with "all the kings of the North" (Jer. 1:15),[9] this officer was later identified as
Nebuchadnezzar of Babylon, the "servant of Yahweh" (Jer. 27:6, *abdî*, *"my ser-*

vant").[10]

Three times Jeremiah represents Yahweh as calling Nebuchadnezzar "my servant" (*abdî*).[11] One of the most dramatic, and perhaps authentic of these is his oracle to the council of nations gathered at Jerusalem: "Now I have given all these lands into the hand of Nebuchadnezzar, the king of Babylon, my servant,...." (*abdî*, 27:6, RSV). If Jeremiah had had the usual Near Eastern understanding of the relationship of political power to deity, he need only have heard Yahweh say in his call, "See, I have made Nebuchadnezzar overseer this day over nations and kingdoms...." This avoidance of the anomaly would have made Yahweh's choice of Nebuchadnezzar analogous to Marduk's choice of Cyrus.[12]

Congruent with the anomaly, however, is Jeremiah's dramatic oracle of the destruction of Babylon (51:59-64), likely spoken in the very year of his oracle to the nations.[13] The kingdom of Babylon, whose violent political power as wielded by Nebuchadnezzar was Yahweh's servant to subject the nations, would itself be brought to an end by violent political power. It is an illustration of what was later formulated, "He who takes the sword shall perish by the sword." While Jeremiah saw Nebuchadnezzar as an officer of Yahweh, Nebuchadnezzar did not represent the central office in Yahweh's kingdom, and the choice is therefore not parallel to Marduk's election of Cyrus.[14] Jeremiah's positive oracles concerning Nebuchadnezzar are not in conflict with the oracle in regard to his own office.[15]

Another political officer of Yahweh recognized by Jeremiah was King Josiah. Had Jeremiah envisioned with Josiah that the way to the future was via the revival of the Davidic empire, he might have shared the enthusiasm of the Deuteronomic historian for Josiah's reform (2 Kings 23:1-25). The oracle of his call would have fit the spirit of the times at the beginning of Jeremiah's ministry,[16] had he stated, "See! I have made Josiah an overseer this day over nations and kingdoms...."

Since Jeremiah thought well of Josiah (22:15-16) his criticism of Josiah's reform is all the more striking (3:6-10). The messianic theme is shrunken down by Jeremiah (23:5-6, 33:14-18) and the martial character of the future ruler is not his point. It is evident that the king as known to Near Eastern states is not central to his thought of the future.[17]

While the messianic theme is not emphasized by Jeremiah, the positive oracles of the future of Israel and the surrounding nations are in keeping with the prophet's anomalous office. Israel is called to return to Yahweh so that the patriarchal promise might be fulfilled: "Then nations shall bless themselves in him, and in him shall they glory" (4:1-2, RSV).[18] The planting of the nations again in their land is dependent not upon their military prowess but upon their learning the ways of Yahweh's people: "...if they will diligently learn the ways of my people,...then they shall be built up in the midst of my people" (12:14-17).[19]

One of the most quoted of Jeremiah's oracles is the promise of the new covenant (31:31-34).[20] While it deals only with Israel, it sets forth in a striking way the goal of the Old Testament. Contrary to the view of Wellhausen,

Jeremiah does not here break out of the confines of a "state religion" to a religion of the heart of the individual.[21] The passage deals not merely with the
individual but with God and people. As in the life of any community, law is
still necessary. The point is, however, that violent power for the enforcement
of law is replaced by voluntary response to the word of Yahweh. Law is "written upon the heart." Thus this great passage corresponds to the anomalous
character of the prophetic call in chapter 1. In chapter 1 the prophet is placed
over the nations, ruling not as a representative of violent power, but by the
word of Yahweh; in chapter 31 the people respond to law not as enforced by
police power, but as a response to an inner reconciliation to that law, with an
inner motivation to obey it.

This anomaly of Jeremiah was an accepted reality not by Jeremiah alone,
but was acknowledged by Israel's structured institutions. This is evident from
Jeremiah's court trial in the accession year of King Jehoiakim (Jer. 26).[22]
Saved by the princes from a lynching, Jeremiah was brought by them into
court. His defense against the charge that he had "contradicted a cardinal
dogma of the official state religion"[23] was not to deny that he had contradicted
it, but simply to rest his case on the claim that Yahweh had sent him to speak
these words. Jeremiah made this claim both at the beginning and at the end of
his defense: "Yahweh sent me to prophesy...all the words you have heard"
(26:12); "Yahweh sent me to you to speak all these words..." (26:15). The
princes and "all the people" gave the verdict of "not guilty," a verdict which they
based upon this very defense (v. 16).

This anomaly of the prophet was a fact not merely of Jeremiah's time but
was a structure which his generation had inherited from the past. This is made
clear by the decision of the court, a decision in line with the legal precedent of
the prophecy of Micah of the eighth century B.C. (26:17-18). The statement of
this precedent makes clear the place of the prophet in the political structure of
Israel. Micah had spoken to all the people of Judah as messenger of their ruler,
Yahweh (26:18). The prophet was not put to death by the community. Rather,
the representatives of the community's political structures feared Yahweh, and
brought their policy in line with Yahweh's demand. The prophet addressed
himself to all the people in opposition to national policy. This right was
acknowledged by both the judiciary (seventh century) and by the king (eighth
century), to the extent that, in the latter case, national policy was changed.
Consequently, it was not merely the psychology of the prophet which distinguished him from the prophets of the Near East, but more importantly the
unique role he played within the structure of Israel's government.[24]

This tie with Israel's ancient past was a strong element in the consciousness of Jeremiah and was clearly stated in his opposition to Hananiah, the self-
styled prophet: "The prophets who preceded you and me from ancient times
prophesied war, famine, and pestilence against many countries and great kingdoms" (28:8, RSV). The close resemblance to his call to the call of Moses suggests that he saw himself in the tradition of Moses.[25] We will now look at that
ancient past to see if this anomalous character of the prophetic office is found
there.

The Call of Gideon

The call of Gideon forms a common literary pattern with the call of Moses and with the later prophets.[26] The similarity of the form of the call of Gideon to that of Moses suggests the probability of a preliterary (or literary) form of the call in prekingship times.[27] The outstanding difference of this call from the prophetic call has to do not with the form, but with the content. For this call presents no anomaly whatsoever. It is the call of a môšîa ("deliverer," cf. Judg. 6:14,15, a gibbôr heḥāyil "mighty warrior," 6:12). The logical outcome of such a call is kingship, which is precisely what is stated in the subsequent material: "Then the men of Israel said to Gideon, 'Rule over us, you and your son and your grandson also; for you have delivered (hôšaʻtānû) us out of the hand of Midian'" (8:22).[28]

Wolfgang Richter proposes that this prophetic call (Judg. 6:11b-17) was adapted to the môšîa and inserted into the segment on Gideon after the time of kingship. The writer was interested in promoting royal, coercive authority by originating it already in the prekingship confederation, and derived directly from Yahweh. Elsewhere this authority is always communicated through the prophet, as indicated by the narrative of Samuel's anointing of Saul (1 Sam. 9:10-16), which follows the same schema as the prophetic call. This suggests that the prophet or seer in the Israelite League had full authority to call a deliverer, who might then be anointed as nagid (military leader). The prophet was thus important to the institution of warfare for whose execution the nagid was installed. The latter office developed into kingship, in which the rite of the prophet's calling of the nāgîd was replaced by the rite of the enthronement of the king, a development with which the Northern Kingdom did not go along. The later insertion by the writer of a direct prophetic call, instead of a call through a prophet, into the story of a môšîa (according to Richter) was a part of the tendency to make the king independent of prophetic authority.[29]

The advantage of Richter's hypothesis is that it shows the call of Gideon to be a part of the same tendency in early Israel as the demand for kingship (1 Sam. 8:4-22).[30] Contrary to Richter, however, there is the probability that the text reflects an historical memory, and was due to the mixing of the Israelite and Canaanite traditions. As in the story of Abimelech (Judg. 9:1-57), the Gideon pericope evidences a process of "Israelizing" of the mixed Canaanite population in the tribal territories of Ephraim and Manasseh.[31] That the process did not go in one direction only is apparent by the fact that Gideon's father had erected an altar to Baal (Judg. 6:25-32). It is unnecessary to posit with Richter that a later writer from the time of kingship made a literary transfer of the prophetic call from the prophet to the môšîa, for such pressures to "Canaanize" Israel's tradition were already present in the time of Gideon himself.

The relationship of the call of a military deliverer to the office of kingship is evident in the literature of the ancient Near East. In the *Enuma Elish* the father of the gods, Anshar, named Marduk "the hero" as the one who would be able to meet the threat of Tiamat:

> He whose [strength] is potent shall be [our] avenger,
> He who is *keen* in battle, Marduk, the hero![32]

Called by the gods to meet this threat, Marduk demanded and was given the powers of kingship in order to perform his task.[33]

> Hammurabi tells of his call by Anu and Enlil:
> ...to cause justice to prevail in the land, to destroy the wicked
> and the evil, that the strong might not oppress the weak, to rise
> like the sun over the black-headed (people), and to light up the land.[34]

In relation to external powers he was to make "the four quarters of the world subservient...."

A parallel to the predestination of Jeremiah is stated in an ancient Sumerian royal hymn, "King am I; from the womb a hero am I."[35]

In the Egyptian texts there is a stele of King Pianchi (25th dynasty, c. 751-730 B.C.) in which the god Amon speaks to the king:

> It was in the belly of your mother that I said concerning you that
> you were to be ruler of Egypt; it was as seed and while you were
> in the egg, that I knew you, that (I knew) you were to be Lord.[36]

When there was no question as to the succession, a "call" may not have been necessary; but when a new dynasty was founded (as in the case of Gideon's temptation), or some irregularity occurred, the king's authority needed augmentation by a special manifestation of divine authority. Perhaps because of an irregularity, Thut-Moses III gave at length his call to kingship:

> ...(The god Amon)--he is my father, and I am his son. He commanded
> to me that I should be upon his throne, while I was (still) a nestling.
> He begot me from the (very) *middle* of [his] heart *[and chose me for
> the kingship*...There is no lie], there is no equivocation therein--when
> my majesty was (only) a puppy, when I was (only a newly) weaned
> child who was in his temple, before my installation as prophet had
> taken place....[37]

From these comparisons, it is apparent that the call of Gideon as a *môšîʿ-a* represented no anomaly whatsoever. The pressures of such ideas pushed into Israel from every side. The anomaly of Gideon was that even as warrior he relied mainly upon the miracle of Yahweh (Judg. 9-23), and that, though called of Yahweh, he rejected the logical eventuation of that call--kingship (8:22-23). In a negative way, the narratives of Gideon confirm the anomaly of the prophet, that is, that the *môšîʿ-a* was not to be placed over the nation. The interpretation of a later demand for a change to kingship might be instructive here: "And the Lord said to Samuel, 'Hearken to the voice of the people in all that they say to you; for they have not rejected you, but they have rejected me from being king over them'" (1 Sam. 8:7).[38] By rejecting the seer or prophet and by substituting a king as Yahweh's chief political officer, Israel was rejecting the kingship of Yahweh himself. Later conflict between king and prophet had to do with this issue.[39]

The Call of Moses

The anomaly of the call of Jeremiah is evident in the call of Moses, especially as presented by what is traditionally known as the J narrative.[40] In the call as set forth by J,[41] Yahweh announces to Moses that he has seen and heard the plight of his people in Egypt[42] and has come down to deliver them from the hand of the Egyptians (Ex. 3:8). Moses is then commissioned to go, assemble the elders of Israel and to tell them Yahweh's resolve to bring them out of their slavery in Egypt (3:16-17). Moses' first objection, according to J, had to do with his rejection by his people as their political leader (4:1), an objection which Yahweh promised would be overcome by signs (4:2-9). His second objection had to do with his problem of speech (4:10-12) while the third objection was an outright refusal of the task (4:13). Moses did not have the eloquence necessary to accomplish the warrior's task!

It is evident that for J, Yahweh was the deliverer and that Moses was simply Yahweh's messenger to convey his word to his people and to Pharaoh. For J, Yahweh did not deliver his people by means of a warrior, but by a messenger who merely spoke Yahweh's word.

The traditional E narrative is essentially no different, though Moses is given a more prominent role as deliverer. Yahweh announces to Moses that he has heard the outcry of the people of Israel and has seen the oppression of the Egyptians (3:9). Unlike J, E says that Moses was commissioned to go not to Israel (see 3:16) but to Pharaoh (3:10). Also unlike J who says that Yahweh will bring up his people from Egypt (3:17), E ascribes this function to Moses (3:10). Too much should not be made of this difference, however, as it is evident that for E, as well as for J, Moses was not a warrior, but simply a messenger who spoke Yahweh's word.[43] Yahweh alone performed the warrior's function.

Moses' objection, according to E, had to do with the credibility of his task in regard to Pharaoh: "Who am I that I should go to Pharaoh, and bring the sons of Israel out of Egypt?" (3:11). This is a similar type of objection to the one found in the call of Gideon and of Jeremiah (Judg. 6:15; Jer. 1:6). God's answer to the objection is also similar: "But I will be with you..." (Ex. 3:12). This formula expresses the fundamental structure of Israel's thought and piety.[44] While it does not belong exclusively to the life situation of warfare, this was nevertheless one concretization of the presence of God with one whom he accompanies. A study of the prophet's relation to warfare overlooks Israel's most unique and fundamental relationship if it overlooks this anomaly of the call of Moses.[45] Armed only with the word of Yahweh, Moses went forth simply as Yahweh's envoy to proclaim freedom both to his people and to Egypt. This act of Israel's history is foundational to Israel's confession of her history: "I am the Lord your God who brought you out of the land of Egypt." Yahweh, not man, is the warrior God who saves his people. The prophet is only the herald of that which God is about to do. This is what both J and E have to say in the narrative of the exodus.

Is this prophetic anomaly an event of history? One can only point out that this is Israel's unanimous testimony, including her very oldest testimony. Martin Noth writes, "J formulated the commission to Moses long before the appearance of 'classical' prophecy; thus at this early stage the arrival of a messenger of God who was sent to precede an imminent divine action was not unknown to Israel."[46] Since both J and E are in agreement in regard to this anomaly, one might assume that this was the testimony of G (the foundation document behind J and E), and that this was Israel's tradition before the fall of Shiloh.[47]

The importance of this anomaly of the prophet is evident when one compares Exodus 1-24 with the *Enuma Elish*, both of which have approximately the same value for understanding the structures of their respective societies.[48] Both see divinity as warrior fighting against the enemy. Both emphasize the kingship of the divinity in connection with the victory. Both eventuate in an ordered society. In the Exodus story, however, the action of Yahweh is not against other cosmic powers, but is immediate upon the human scene against the historical enemy of Israel, without the human correspondent of warrior and king. The only herald to Israel and to the foreign power of what Yahweh is about to do is the prophet. Not Yahweh's action in history, but the quality of his act expressed in this new structure is the uniqueness of Israel, both in the ancient and modern world. The figure of the prophet is essential to that uniqueness.

Years ago, Howard Charles pointed out to me that the leadership of Jesus' disciples is to be in contrast to leadership as it was known by politicians among the nations: Jesus said, "You know that those who are supposed to rule over the Gentiles (nations) lord it over them, and their great men exercise authority over them. But it shall not be so among you; but whoever would be great among you must be your servant, and whoever would be first among you must be slave of all" (Mk. 10:42-45; cf. Mt. 20:25-28; Lk. 22-25-27). It is a long journey from Moses to this statement of Jesus, a journey beyond the scope of this paper. That the journey is via the anomaly of the prophet Jeremiah, however (as representing the anomaly of all the prophets),[49] I have no doubt.

NOTES

1. This translation is that of John Bright, *Jeremiah* (*Anchor Bible*, New York: Doubleday, 1956), p. 3.

2. *Enuma Elish*; also the introduction to the law code of Hammurabi. These are discussed below.

3. Discussed by John Skinner, *Prophecy and Religion: Studies in the Life of Jeremiah* (Cambridge: University Press, 1951), p. 29.

4. *Ibid.*

5. Walter Harrelson in *Jeremiah, Prophet to the Nations* (Philadelphia: Judson Press) admits that "this may sound like megalomania..." (p. 18).

6. This usage is not really parallel with the others, as it has to do with a temporary military assignment rather than an appointment to an office.

7. G. Ernest Wright, "The Nations in Hebrew Prophecy," *Encounter* 26 (1965): 225-237.

8. Jeremiah 1:13ff., cf.John Bright, *op.cit.*, pp. 7f.

9. *Ibid.*, p. 6.

10. For a discussion of this term, see David Noel Freedman, "The Slave of Yahweh," *Western Watch* (1959), 1-19.

11. Jeremiah 25:9; 27:6; 43:10. Could it be that later Jewish resistance to this designation of Nebuchadnezzar is represented by the fact that the LXX avoids it in every case?

12. ANET (1969), p. 315.

13. For a discussion of these dates, see John Bright, *op.cit.*, pp. 201, 210-212.

14. For a Babylonian concept of the king as the gods' chief political servant, see the introduction to Hammurabi's law code, Pritchard, *Ancient Near Eastern Texts*, 1969, p. 164.

15. For the disharmony of prophet and kingship in Israel see Baltzer, note 39 below. This disharmony is even more pronounced in regard to kingship outside of Israel.

16. Usually set about 627. Bright, *op.cit.*, p. 84.

17. *Ibid.*, p. 115.

18. John Bright regards this as authentic to Jeremiah and places it before 622. See *ibid.*, pp. 25f.

19. Wilhelm Rudolph regards verses 15-17 as not from Jeremiah, but as a later addition--*Jeremia* (HAT), 3rd ed., p. 90. But see Weiser, *Das Buch des Propheten Jeremia* (ATD), 1960, p. 107.

20. For comment on its authenticity, see Bright, *op.cit.*, p. 287.

21. Wellhausen, *Prolegomena to the History of Ancient Israel* (Meridian Books, N.Y., 1957), p. 491.

22. John Bright, *op.cit.*, pp. 167ff.

23. *Ibid.*, p. 172.

24. James G. Williams, "The Social Location of Israelite Prophecy," *Journal of the American Academy of Religion* 37(1969), 153-165.

25. William Holladay, "The Background of Jeremiah's Self-Understanding, Moses,Samuel, and Psalm 72," *JBL* 83 (1964), 153-164; Rolf Rendtorff,"Erwägungen zur Frühgeschichte des Prophetentums in Israel,: *Zeitschrift für Theologie und Kirche* 59 (1962), 145-167; especially N. Habel, "The Form and Significance of the Call Narrative," *ZAW* 77 (1965), 305ff.

26. Ernst Kutsch, "Gideons Berufung und Altarbau, Jdc. 6, 11-24," *Theologische Litera-turzeitung* 81 (1956), 79.

27. Habel, "Call Narrative," p. 305.

28. For a review of the history of the exegesis of Judges 6-8, see Wolfgang Richter, *Traditionsgeschichtliche Untersuchungen zum Richterbuch* (Bonn: Peter Hanstein, Verlag GMBH, 1966), pp. 112-114. For Richter's own analysis, see *ibid.*, pp. 114-121. Richter is too negative in his analysis. (See Jacob M. Myers, "The Book of Judges," IB 2:678ff., 729, 731). For a treatment of the tradition in 8:22, 23 see Richter, *op.cit.*, pp. 235f. Such scholars as Martin Buber and H. J. Kraus regard this tradition as a genuine memory. Martin Noth argues that some such prejudice must have existed to keep Israel from accepting kingship for two full centuries after the tribes had settled down, (*The History of Israel*, 1958, p. 165).

29. Richter, *op.cit.*, pp. 153ff.

30. We have already suggested such a tie above.

31. Jacob M. Myers, *op.cit.*, p. 751.

32. 2:94f. Translation by E. A. Speiser, ANET (1969), p. 64.

33. 2:122-129; 4:1-30, ANET (1969), pp. 64, 66.

34. From the introduction to the code of Hammurabi. See ANET (1969), pp. 164-165. We cannot know whether the call came "direct" or through a cultic medium, though the latter possibility is not mentioned.

35. Samuel N. Kramer, "The Oldest Literary Catalogue," BASOR no. 88 (December 1942), p. 14. Cited by Hyatt, "The Book of Jeremiah," IB (1956), p. 800.

36. Translated by M. Gilula, "An Egyptian Parallel to Jeremiah 1:4-5," VT 17 (167), p. 114.

37. ANET, pp. 446f. The word translated "prophet" in the quote, *hem-netjer* "Servant of the god," was a high temple officiant. See ANET, Note 1.

38. This account is usually regarded as a late source. See George B. Caird, "The First and Second Books of Samuel," IB 2:917. That it reflects an ancient criticism of the kingship, however, is suggested by I. Mendelsohn, "Samuel's Denunciation of Kingship in the Light of the Akkadian Documents from Ugarit," BASOR, no 143 (October 1956), 17-22.

39. Klaus Baltzer has suggested that the offices of prophet and priest and king are not so harmonious as often supposed. "Especially the origin, tradition, historical development, and theological implications of the office of the prophet and of the king necessitate competition. It is of fundamental importance to recognize that the concept of the kingship of Yahweh by no means has its presupposition in the earthly Davidic kingdom, but rather is linked with the prophet as his vizier"-- "Considerations Regarding the Office and Calling of the Prophet," *Harvard Theological Review* 61 (1968), 581. While prophet as vizier might be debatable (see James F. Ross, "The Prophet as Yahweh's Messenger," *Israel's Prophetic Heritage*, ed. by Bernhard W. Anderson and Walter Harrelson [1962], pp. 98-107, the rest of the statement is nevertheless correct.

40. M. Noth sees two sources in this call, as follows: J: 3:1-4a, 5, 7, 8 ad, (8abd), 16, 17ad, (17abb), (18-22); 4:1-4,(5), 6, 7, (8,9), 10-12, (13-16). E: 3:4b, 6,9-14, (15)...; 4:17, 18 (*A History of Pentateuchal Traditions*, trans. by Bernhard W. Anderson [Englewood Cliffs, N.J., 1972], pp. 30,36). M. Habel disagrees with Noth, arguing for the unity of 3:1-6,E. Even if one is to accept Noth's analysis, however, E has all the major features of Gideon's call. See M. Habel, "The Form and Significance of the Call Narratives," ZAW 77 (1965), 301ff.

41. Habel's analysis of what he calls the "Yahwist Expansion" is as follows: (1) Intro-ductory Word, 3:7, 8; (2) Commission, 3:16, 17 (18-22); (3) First Objection, 4:1; (4) Signs, 4:2-9; (5) Second Objection, 4:10; (6) Reassurance, 4:11-16; (7) Signs? 4:17 (*Ibid.*, p. 303, note 18).

42. Noth regards the theophany as also belonging to J. See above, note 40. For a discussion of the theophany, see D. N. Freedman, "The Burning Bush (Ex. 3:2-3)," *Biblica* 50 (1969), 245-246.

43. While the various sources set forth different details in regard to the escape from Egypt, all agree on the essential point that the escape was due not to an act of war on the part of Israel but on the part of God. For both J and E, Moses was simply an envoy. See Martin Noth, *Exodus* (Philadelphia: Westminster Press, 1962), pp. 40, 41. Also see page 119 where Noth speaks of the consensus of the sources in regard to the escape at the sea. See M. Lind, "Paradigm of Holy War in the Old Testament," *Biblical Research* 16 (1971), 16-31.

44. Horst Dietrich Preuss, "...ich will mit dir sein" ZAW 80 (1968), 154.

45. Von Rad's study of holy war (*Der heilige Krieg im alten Israel*) ignores this most fundamental relationship of the prophet to holy war. He does not deal with this obvious connection because of his presuppositions regarding Israel's early testimony: *Old Testament Theology* 1:107. Quoting Tröltsch sympathetically, he says, "The means by which criticism is at all possible is the application of analogy...but the omnicompetence of analogy implies that all historical events are identical in principle."

46. Martin Noth, *op.cit.*, p. 40.

47. Noth, *A History of Pentateuchal Traditions*, p. 39: "Everything in which J and E concur can be attributed withsome certainty to G."

48. The question of the original unity of this material is not the point here.

49. For example, see Hosea 12:13: "By a prophet the Lord brought Israel up from Egypt, and by a prophet he was preserved."

CHAPTER 11

IS THERE A BIBLICAL CASE FOR CIVIL DISOBEDIENCE?

The purpose of this paper, as the title suggests, is to discover whether there is a biblical (Old Testament) case for civil disobedience. In order to proceed we need first to define civil disobedience. Since at the time of this writing I do not have access to conference papers which may define this concept, I will use the following definition provided by the *Random House Collegiate Dictionary*, Revised Edition, 1975:

> The refusal to obey certain governmental laws or demands for the purpose of influencing legislation or government policy, characterized by such non-violent techniques as boycotting, picketing and non-payment of taxes.

A second clarification should be made regarding the extent of the Old Testament. For our purposes this will be defined as the 39 books of the Jewish and Protestant canon. Since it is impossible to make a survey of all the relevant material in this corpus, I will examine only selected relevant texts, texts which will hopefully be diverse enough to give a fair sampling of the Old Testament view of the relationship of the covenant people to state authority and power.

I have some reservations about using the title: "Is there a biblical case for civil disobedience?" This way of stating the question fits the ideology of ancient Near Eastern governments (provided "biblical" were replaced by "religious") better than it fits the biblical understanding. *It assumes that the civil government provides the norm for the person of faith and asks whether there may be a religious basis for sometimes disobeying it.* This presupposition is not radical enough for the Bible. The Biblical message is that not only individuals, but above all the city-state, with its self-interest and empire-building propensities, is in rebellion against the rule and order of Yahweh. For example one of the oldest Pentateuchal recensions sees the city-state as formed by an intimate bond between a societal order and land (blood and soil), ruled by the word and wisdom of man (Gen. 11:1-9). It was from such an order that Abraham was

---

Paper read at Consultation on Civil Responsibility, AMBS, 1978.

called by the word of Yahweh: "from (1) your country (or land) and (2) your kindred and your father's house" (the societal structure built thereupon, Gen. 12:1). The order to which Abraham was called was that of Yahweh and people. Here the relation to land was based upon Yahweh's promise: "to the land that I will show you" (11:1).

This radical reordering of life as stated by the above text concerned Israel's total existence. In the Old Testament there is no concept of separation between "church" and "state," between faith and politics. Yahweh, through his Torah ("law") and the prophetic word, was regarded as ruler of Israel's total life, both internal affairs and Israel's relations to the nations. The separation as set forth in the Bible is not between worship and politics but between two kinds of theopolitical systems; for example, between the Yahweh-Moses system and the Marduk-Hammurabi system. The latter Israel regarded as false, both in regard to worship (no-gods) and in regard to politics (rebellion). The gods of the nations are considered in Psalm 82 as upholders of unjust systems, whom Yahweh had placed under sentence of death.

These mutually exclusive systems, the kingdom of Yahweh vs. the rebellious kingdoms of man, could co-exist only in an uneasy, competing relationship, each denying the sovereignty of the other, repudiating one another's methods and ultimate goals. In this relationship, a topic such as "The Biblical Case for Civil Disobedience" would sound foreign to the biblical ear. *The problem is of the opposite sort, how the people of Yahweh can possibly relate in a positive way to the rebellious kingdoms of man.* The issue of the relation of church and state thus finds its Old Testament paradigm not between presumably conflicting institutions within Israel (the prophets and kingship, the "charismatic" and "institutional" offices, etc.), nor between Israel's worship and political life, but between Israel and the nations, or between a faithful remnant and an Israel who insisted on becoming like the nations.

The method of this paper will be to examine a few biblical texts which set forth the clash between these two mutually exclusive political systems. (The choice of texts is somewhat arbitrary, as a complete treatment would demand an exegesis of the entire Bible.) We will examine the story of the exodus (Ex. 1-15), Jeremiah's trial and message to the diplomats gathered at Jerusalem (Jer. 26; 27), the Servant Songs (Isa. 40-55), and the narrative of Daniel in the lion's den (Dan. 6).

I. THE EXODUS (Ex. 1-15)

A. How five women frustrated the decree of an absolute monarchy.

The story of the exodus begins by telling how five women were involved in frustrating the decree of Pharaoh (Ex. 1:15-2:10). The first of these women were two midwives, Shiphrah and Puah. The decree was: "When you serve as midwife to the Hebrew women, and see them upon the birthstool, if it is a son, you shall kill him; but if it is a daughter, she shall live (1:16). In theory the Egyptians regarded Pharaoh as one of the great gods and his authority was absolute. There was no concept of personal freedom in ancient Egypt. While it was sometimes difficult to execute this absolutism in an actual situation, the point of this narrative is that the midwives rejected the *theory* of Pharaoh's absolute authority because they had given their allegiance to another theopolitical system: "But the midwives feared God, and did not do as the king of Egypt commanded them, but let the male children live" (1:17). There is no concept of anarchy here on the part of the Hebrew midwives. The issue lay in the conflict between two mutually exclusive political systems. The political system of Egypt postulated the sovereignty of Pharaoh. The political system to which the midwives belonged postulated the sovereignty of the God of the Hebrews: "But the midwives feared God..." (v. 17). Each system assumed an accounting, including the concept of punishment or reward for disobedience or obedience:

> So the king of Egypt called the midwives, and said to them, "Why have you done this, and let the male children live?" (v. 18)
> So God dealt well with the midwives; and the people multiplied and grew very strong. And because the midwives feared God he gave them families (vss. 21-22).

The difference in the two systems was that Pharaoh had a police force to implement the punishment, while the God of the Hebrews did not. An element of daring faith was required on the part of the midwives in order to discount the power of Pharaoh's police force, and to believe in the power of the God of the Hebrews to protect them.

It is at this point of the narrative that the element of wisdom is involved, wisdom which is the ability to give an answer for one's actions. Whatever one may think of the ethics of the midwives' answer to Pharaoh (vs. 19), it should finally be judged in the context of the two mutually exclusive political systems, with their respective concepts of sovereignty and their mutual rejection of the other. There can be little doubt where the narrator(s) stood on this question, as is indicated by the element of humor introduced into the grim situation. Our own ethics will be informed by the political system we identify with, and by our ability or inability to see humor as a legitimate part of ethics.

The women involved in frustrating the second decree of Pharaoh ("Every son that is born to the Hebrews you shall cast into the Nile, but you shall let every daughter live," 1:22) are the mother of Moses, his sister, and the daughter of Pharaoh (with her maidens). Moses' mother hid her child for three months, then complied with Pharaoh's decree by placing the child "among the reeds at the river's brink," albeit in a watertight basket. The baby is saved by a member of Pharaoh's own court (his daughter), the only one of the women to whom the decree applied, since it was directed not to the Hebrews but to Pharaoh's own people (1:22). The climax is achieved when, through the request of the child's sister, the child's mother becomes his nurse (2:7-9). Here, even the enemy is enlisted in the cause of Yahweh, and to involve the enemy to the extent of owning and naming the boy caused no difficulty (2:10). In this way the child is reared as the son of two cultures.

B. The flight and call of Moses (2:11-4:17).

The fundamental point of the call of Moses (as with all later prophetic calls) had to do with the problem of political legitimacy. The ancient Near Eastern concern for political legitimacy is demonstrated in the introduction to the law code of Hammurabi, in the introductions to the Annals of various kings, in Thutmose III's recounting of his call by the gods, and in a treatise written by a Hittite king who came to power other than by dynastic succession, and who thus felt it necessary to defend his right to the throne. This is not only an ancient problem but also a modern one, especially acute for those who believe in order and yet must challenge the decisions of the various states. By what authority do they make such a challenge?

The question of political legitimacy was put to Moses by one of the Hebrews in whose quarrel Moses had presumed to interfere: "Who made you a prince and a judge over us? Do you mean to kill me as you killed the Egyptian?" (2:14). In most societies both ancient and modern, to kill a man without political legitimacy is murder. The question seems to be asked from the perspective of the government of Egypt, by a Hebrew who perhaps was a collaborator with that government. At any rate, Moses had no answer and thus became a fugitive from Pharaoh.

The call of Moses spoke directly to the question of political legitimacy. The task in which he was to be involved was a political task, to "bring forth...the sons of Israel, out of Egypt" (3:10). Again and again Moses poses the question of legitimacy:

> Who am I that I should go to Pharaoh, and bring the sons of Israel out of Egypt (3:11)?
> If I come to the people of Israel and say to them, "The God of your fathers has sent me to you," and they ask me "What is his name?" what shall I say to them (3:13)?
> But behold, they will not believe me or listen to my voice, for they will say, "Yahweh did not appear to you" (4:1).

The answer to the question of legitimacy is also repeated throughout the call:

> Come, I will send you to Pharaoh... (3:10).
> But I will be with you... (3:12).
> Say this to the people of Israel, "Yahweh, the God of your fathers...has sent me to you" (3:15).
> ...you and the elders of Israel shall go to the king of Egypt and say to him, "Yahweh, the God of the Hebrews, has met with us; and now, we pray you, let us go..." (3:18).

The question of political legitimacy was important to Moses' own people as well as to Pharaoh. It is significant that in Moses' mission he must first gain the political confidence of his own people by convincing them that he is indeed the messenger of the God of the Hebrews, and that this God had given the command that they leave Egypt. The conflict between Yahweh and Pharaoh was a conflict not merely in the realm of ideas, but involved a competition for the allegiance of a people. The message demanded that the people respond by reaffirming allegiance to Yahweh and Moses and by rejecting as illegitimate the political sovereignty of Pharaoh.

For Pharaoh, the question of political legitimacy could be resolved only by a display of force. Though Moses was to be merely Yahweh's messenger or ambassador (3:18), Moses was left with no illusions on this issue:

> I know that the king of Egypt will not let you go unless compelled by a mighty hand (not by a mighty hand, Heb.). So I will stretch out my hand and smite Egypt with all the wonders which I will do in it; after that he will let you go (3:19-20).

Here one political system was set against another, and the usual questions of political legitimation and power were involved. The obvious difference in the two systems was that Moses was not a warrior and led no army. He was sent forth only as a messenger, an ambassador or politician of faith, who like the two mid-wives must fear God rather than the military power of Pharaoh.

C. The plague narratives and the account of the sea crossing.

The narrative of the plagues and account of the sea crossing portray the clash of the two political systems. The kingship of Yahweh is celebrated at the end in the tradition of the sea crossing, a tradition which is both the climax of the plague narratives and the beginning of the wilderness narratives which follow.

The introduction to the plagues (5:1-6:1) presents the main issues involved in the clash between Pharaoh and Yahweh. We will deal with these issues under four headings: (1) The political vocation and legitimacy of Moses as messenger of Yahweh; (2) Yahweh's purpose of making himself known through the clash; (3) Punishment for disobedience to the respective political systems; (4) The recognition of Pharaoh's political system as being under the order of Yahweh.

(1) Since we have already dealt with the issue of the political vocation and legitimacy of Moses as messenger of Yahweh in our discussion of the call of Moses, it need not detain us long here. The plague narratives agree with the call of Moses regarding his vocation. The messenger formula reoccurs throughout this material: "Thus says Yahweh" (5:1; 7:17; 8:1,20; 9:1,13; 10:3; 11:4). Congruent with this messenger formula, the entire plague statement indicates that this clash of Yahweh against Pharaoh is not a usual clash in which Israel fights or is represented by a warrior leader, but rather one in which Israel is represented by a prophetic messenger who speaks Yahweh's

word, and who has faith in Yahweh's act of deliverance.

(2) The ultimate purpose of the clash is that Israel, Egypt, and the world might know Yahweh (5:2; 7:5,17; 8:10,22; 10:2). The narrative of the sea crossing makes the same point (14:4,18). This point is a major issue of the clash. For Pharaoh, to know Yahweh was to recognize Yahweh's authority and power, to "heed his voice and let Israel go" (5:2). For the Egyptians, to know Yahweh was to experience Yahweh's judgments and his bringing "out the people of Israel from among them" (7:5). Pharaoh would know Yahweh by his turning the Nile water to blood (7:17). Pharaoh would know that there is no one like Yahweh when the frogs would depart from Pharaoh and his houses (8:10-11). He would know Yahweh "in the midst of the earth" when Yahweh would "set apart the land of Goshen...so that no swarms of flies shall be there" (8:22). Pharaoh would know that there is none like Yahweh "in all the earth" when Yahweh would send his plagues upon Pharaoh's heart, and upon his servants and people (9:14). Yahweh had not cut off Pharaoh and his people but "for this purpose" had let him live, to show Pharaoh his power, so that Yahweh's "name may be declared throughout all the earth" (9:15). Moses would stretch out his hands to Yahweh and the thunder and hail would cease, that Pharaoh might "know that the earth is Yahweh's" (9:29). Yahweh had shown his signs among the Egyptians that Israel might tell in the hearing of their sons and grandsons what signs Yahweh had done among them, that Israel may know that he is Yahweh (10:1-2). In the Sea narrative it is stated that Yahweh would be victorious over Pharaoh, that the Egyptians might know that he is Yahweh (14:4,17-18).

What is means to know Yahweh is closely connected here with the fact that Moses was Yahweh's messenger. It was for Pharaoh an introduction to a new kind of political reality. For the Yahweh whom Pharaoh was to know was the God of a slave people, one who would lead his slave people out of Egypt without an army, indeed with only a messenger. As Hosea was later to state it, "By a prophet Yahweh brought Israel up from Egypt, and by a prophet he was preserved" (12:13).

(3) Punishment is designated for disobedience to the two political systems. The punitive character of Pharaoh's administration is described at some length in 5:4-19, where Pharaoh does not supply straw yet demands that the Hebrews produce their quota of brick. At the end of the 9th plague he threatens Moses with death (10:28). On the Yahwistic side, the judgments of Yahweh are the main point of the plague tradition.

(4) The point of the narrative throughout is not that Pharoah's political system is to be liquidated or even unrecognized by the Hebrews. On the contrary, the sending of a messenger to Pharaoh is a recognition of Pharaoh's government, an appeal to the rationality of that government. The Hebrews deny only the sovereignty of Pharaoh's government, and assert that Pharaoh must acknowledge the sovereignty of Yahweh, his word of command through his messenger.

The insistence upon Yahweh's sovereignty is so strong that Pharaoh's ill treatment of Israel is seen as the responsibility of Yahweh (5:22,23). Also,

Pharaoh's rebellions are regarded by Israel as Yahweh's hardening of Pharaoh's heart (7:3; 9:12; 10:20,27; 11:10; 14:4,8; cf. 14:17; 10:1). The entire emphasis is that Yahweh is in charge even though Pharaoh has rebelled.

Instead of being liquidated, Pharaoh's political order is the object of Moses' intercession before God. When Pharaoh requested intercession, "Moses went out from Pharaoh and prayed to Yahweh. And Yahweh did as Moses asked," removing from Egypt the plague (8:28-31; 8:8,9; 9:28-33). At the death of the first born, when Pharaoh relented and sent forth the people from Egypt, Pharaoh requested the blessing of Moses and Aaron (12:30-32). This activity of intercession, in which the prophet argues with God that the judgment prophesied should not come to pass or should be abated, was an important part of the prophetic activity (cf. Gen. 20:7; Jer. 14:11-13; 15:1). If the prophet fails to do this, he is guilty before God (Jer. 15:11). One of the oldest pentateuchal narratives portrays Abraham as withstanding Yahweh's judgment upon Sodom (Gen. 18:22-33). This is Israel's proper vocation in their relation to the Caananite city states.

II. THE TRIAL OF JEREMIAH (Jer. 26:1-19)

The trial of Jeremiah was a conflict between the institutions within Judah, and is therefore not a paradigm for relations between "church and state." However, the clash clearly challenges the autonomy of kingship, and sets forth torah and prophetic word as ultimate authority in the arena of Judah's domestic and international relationships.

> The narrative of the trial is as follows:
> 1. Jeremiah proclaims in the temple precincts that if the people do not walk in Yahweh's law Jerusalem would be destroyed, just as Shilo had been destroyed before it (vss. 2-6).
> 2. The priests, prophets and people lay hold of him and declare that because of these words the prophet is guilty of treason and should die (vss. 7-9).
> 3. The princes overhear this conflict from the palace precincts and set up court at the temple gate (vs. 10).
> 4. The priests and prophets present their case, arguing that the prophet deserves the death sentence because he had prophesied against Jerusalem (vss. 11-12).
> 5. Jeremiah presents his defense. His defense is based not on a denial that he had said these words, but that Yahweh had sent him "to prophesy against this house and this city all the words you have heard (vs. 12; cf. vs. 15b). It is the duty of Judah therefore, to change their direction that they might escape punishment. *Unlike Socrates who recognized the authority of the state even when it was wrong by cooperating in his execution, Jeremiah says that the court would be guilty of murder if it takes his life* (vss. 14-15).
> 6. The court recognizes as valid Jeremiah's plea that Yahweh had sent

him, and therefore declares him not guilty (vs. 16).
7. Certain elders justify the courts verdict by citing a precedent. As repositors of Judah's tradition, they reminded the assembled people of Micah's prophecy against Jerusalem a century earlier, that instead of executing Micah, King Hezekiah and Judah changed their domestic policy, so that Yahweh did not enforce his own pronouncement against them (vss. 17-19).

This trial is important for the clear way in which it shows that the authority of the prophet, Yahweh's messenger for the political direction of Israel, was not a prophetic idiosyncrasy but was recognized by the legal court, recognition established on the basis of a political precedent of a century earlier. The political authority of the prophet's word, based only upon his call by Yahweh and his spiritual succession with Moses, was quite different from political authority in a Hammurabi state where the king as leader of army and police force was chosen by the gods as their chief servant to promote justice and order. This prophetic political authority is a venerable tradition, a precedent not only for Jeremiah but for many others since, who together form the political precedents upon which we stand.

III. JEREMIAH'S MESSAGE TO THE NATIONS

Most of the great writing prophets include in their works a series of prophecies directed against the nations. Just what the function of this prophecy might have been is debated. The function of the prophecy of Jeremiah to the representatives of the nations gathered at Jerusalem in about 592 B.C., however, was clearly to challenge the international political policy of the nations, nations who were devising rebellion against Nebuchadnezzar. The account may be analyzed as follows:

(1) Jeremiah addresses those envoys in the name of Yahweh of hosts, the God of Israel. He in no way recognizes the gods of these nations, though he recognizes their institutions, such as their prophets (vs. 9).
(2) Jeremiah sets forth the claim of this God of Israel upon the nations as based upon his creative power as maker of the earth with its people and animals.
(3) This creator God of Israel, according to Jeremiah, is also ruler of the earth, giving it to whomever it seems right, now specifically to Nebuchadnezzar, his servant. This kind of language was certainly familiar to these envoys, since according to the introduction to Hammurabi's law code, the great gods of the Akkadian pantheon had chosen Hammurabi as their servant to establish justice on the earth. Slightly later than Jeremiah, the Cyrus stele records that Marduk, god of Babylon, had chosen the foreigner Cyrus to give freedom to the people of Babylon. Since Yahweh had chosen Nebuchadnezzsar, Jeremiah says that now all nations were to quit their plans of rebellion

on penalty of deportation and death.

(4) While Jeremiah's concept of Yahweh's appointment of Nebuchadnezzar over the nations had its analogies to the concept of Marduk's
appointment of Cyrus, Jeremiah's concept was nevertheless different
in that it was Yahweh the God of Israel, represented through Israel's
peculiar institutions, who had made the appointment. Central to these
institutions was the prophet Jeremiah himself who only as bearer of
Yahweh's word was placed over the nations (chap. 1). After three
generations Babylon's own time would come, and it would become the
slave of the nations.

Jeremiah thus regarded the prophetic word as having political authority
not only over Israel, but also over the nations. Nebuchadnezzar as Yahweh's
servant was only a stage hand whose kingdom would itself perish in three generations. Jeremiah saw the kingdom of Babylon not as independent of Yahweh, but as part of Yahweh's system. This was not an entirely new idea, as we
have seen that in the oldest documents Pharaoh of Egypt was related to Yahweh's government. What is new in Jeremiah is that since Yahweh had given all
lands into the hand of Nebuchadnezzar, all nations, including Israel were to
bring their "necks under the yoke of the king Babylon, and serve him and his
people, and live" (27:12). As in the case of Paul in Romans 13, from the perspective of the Biblical faith it was not at all necessary to make a case for civil
disobedience, that is, a case for obedience to Yahweh instead of Nebuchadnezzar. That was understood. The problem was how to fit service to Nebuchadnezzar and the succeeding Near Eastern emperors under the service of Yahweh. This was the intent of Jeremiah, and I think also the intent of Paul in
regard to Caesar.

Yahweh was not just another Marduk who ruled the world through
Nebuchadnezzar. He was the God of *Israel* who ruled the world through
Nebuchadnezzar. He was the God of *Israel* whose political system was different: who ruled the world not centrally through a representative of military
power but by Torah and prophetic word. Yahweh's goal for Israel was not a
nation ruled by a law backed by a representative of violent power, but by a law
written upon each individual heart (31:31-34). Jeremiah suggests that all
nations are to bless themselves in Yahweh's rule of Israel (4:1-2). For the best
statement of this concept in the Old Testament we will examine the Servant
Songs of Isaiah.

IV. THE SERVANT SONGS OF THE BOOK OF ISAIAH (Isa. 40-55)

Since the rise of critical biblical studies, the Servant Songs of Isaiah have
traditionally been regarded as these four: Isaiah 42:1-4; 49:1-6; 50:4-11; 52:13-
53:12. The question which we ask these Songs is not who the Servant is, but
what is his vocation, his method, and his politically legitimacy.

The first Song sets forth the political character of the Servant's vocation.
His vocation is "to bring forth justice to the nations" (42:1), to "faithfully bring

forth justice" (42:3), to establish "justice in the earth" (42:4). This vocation of the servant is not particularly different from that of Hammurabi as stated in the introduction to his law-code, except of course in the radically divergent perception of what justice is and how it is achieved. Hammurabi was chosen by the gods Anu and Enlil "to cause justice to prevail in the land, to destroy the wicked and the evil, that the strong might not oppress the weak..." (ANET, p. 164). The analogies of the ancient Near East which would compare with the servant of the Songs were kings and emperors, the purpose of whose armies and police force was to establish the justice of their god upon the earth.

Contrary to these rulers, however, the method of the Servant is to be nonviolent:

> He will not cry or lift up his voice,
>   or make it heard in the street;
> a bruised reed he will not break,
>   and a dimly burning wick he will not quench (42:3).

He is nevertheless to have a certain power. Yahweh would put his "Spirit upon him" (42:1). Thus he will not fail or be discouraged until he has accomplished his task (42:4). The nature of this power is further illustrated in 49:2, 50:4-11, and in 52:13-53:12. In 49:2 the Servant announces:

> He (Yahweh) made my mouth like a sharp sword.

In 50:4,5 the Servant says:

> Yahweh God has given me
>   the tongue of those who are taught,
> that I may know how to sustain with a word
>   him that is weary.
> Morning by morning he wakens, he wakens my ear
>   to hear as those who are taught.
> Yahweh God has opened my ear,
>   I was not rebellious,
> and I turned not backward.

It is evident that the servant's method of establishing Yahweh's justice in the earth was simply to go to the nations with a proclamation of Yahweh's kingdom. His success was to be entirely dependent upon Yahweh's help (50:7-9). Even the suffering and death of the Servant would not defeat his cause, for suffering and death would become the incarnation of his message, and beyond death he was to be raised to kingly rule. Yahweh will establish his justice in the earth by means of the Servant's proclamation and the incarnation of the proclamation in his suffering, death and resurrection.

The political legitimacy of the servant is established by his call and appointment by Yahweh. When the Servant goes out among the nations, he sets forth his political legitimacy simply by telling them of his call:

> Listen to me, O coast lands,
>   and hearken, you peoples from afar.
> Yahweh called me from the womb,
>   from the body of my mother he named my name (49:1).

This call is similar to other prophetic calls throughout the Bible, but it is broader in its scope. Other such calls generally relate to the work of the prophet to Israel, while here the Servant is sent to the ends of the earth. This difference is expressly stated in the call narrative.

The nations of the Near East probably would have recognized the significance of such a call, and would have associated it with the call to kingship. What they would not have understood nor have accepted however, was the servant's method, and ultimately, of course, the type of justice which he sought to establish. Like Pharaoh in the time of Moses, they did not know Yahweh, his ways, and his justice. This unbelievable knowledge of Yahweh and his justice is what the kings and nations finally confess in Isaiah 53. Despite its unheard-of character, Yahweh's rule will be established on the earth.

V. DANIEL IN THE LION'S DEN (Dan. 6)

I regard the apocalyptic book of Daniel to be in the succession of the prophetic movement rather than in the succession of wisdom, though wisdom has certainly contributed to its message. The book is an expression of the adjustment to the new situation in which Yahweh had made the successive emperors of the Near East his servants, while advancing his kingly rule through Israel as represented by Daniel and his friends, the Wise. The book probably achieved its present form in 164 B.C.; it propounds a nonviolent opposition to the persecution of Antiochus Epiphanes, in contrast to the violent strategy of the books of Maccabees.

The conflict of chapter 6 centers about the law of Daniel's God and the law of the Medes and Persians. Daniel's jealous competitors could find no fault in him, and therefore prepared their trap around the issue of the authority of the two laws. Daniel gave allegiance to "the law of his God" (6:5) which he continued to obey regardless of the law of the Medes and Persians (6:8,12,15).

This narrative of Daniel in the lion's den has many similarities with chapter 3, the narrative of the three men who were thrown in the fiery furnace. The main point of difference has to do with the different character of the emperor's authority. In chapter 3, the emperor is represented as a brutal, unreflective political power. When the three men do not obey, Nebuchadnezzar, "full of fury" (3:19), heats the furnace seven times more than usual, and orders the mighty men of his army to throw them into the furnace.

In contrast, chapter 6 sets forth the issue not in terms of raw, unreflective authority, but in terms of sovereignty in Medo-Persian law to which the kingly authority itself must submit. The point of the chapter throughout is that the king, while on the side of Daniel, is himself a captive of the sovereignty of Medo-Persian law. Confronted by Daniel's disobedience the king "was much distressed, and set his mind to deliver Daniel; and he labored till the sun went down to rescue him" (6:14). Unsuccessful and forced to give the command of execution, the king expresses hope that the God whose law Daniel serves would deliver him (6:16). That night the king has no sleep and the next morning he hastens to the place of execution and cries out "in a tone of anguish,...O Daniel, servant of the living God, has your God, whom you serve continually, been able to deliver you from the lions?" (6:19-20).

The response of Daniel to Darius is very important for an understanding of the Biblical concept of political authority. Daniel replied, "My God sent his angel and shut the lions' mouths, and they have not hurt me, because I was found blameless before him; and *also before you, O king*, I have done no wrong" (6:22). Daniel had disobeyed the law of the Medes and Persians. Because of this refusal to recognize the law's sovereignty Daniel is subject to the sentence of capital punishment. But Daniel proclaims himself guiltless not only before Yahweh's court ("before him"), the sovereignty of whose law he had recognized, but also before the court of the king ("and before you, O king, I have done no wrong,"), the sovereignty of whose law he had rejected.

One might speculate that the members of the movement which the author of the book of Daniel represented would have been forced to a different conclusion had Yahweh not delivered Daniel. But they lived in a situation where martyrdom certainly did occur, and that eventuality is suggested in chapter 3: "O Nebuchadnezzar, we have no need to answer you in this matter. If it be so, our God whom we serve is able to deliver us from the burning fiery furnace; and he will deliver us out of your hand, O king. But if not, be it known to you, O king, that we will not serve your gods or worship the golden image which you have set up" (3:17-18).

While chapters 3 and 6 resolve the issue of sovereignty through confrontation between Israel's God and the human empires, chapter 1 resolves this issue through negotiation between Daniel and his "superiors." This type of negotiation, as well as confrontation, is quite typical of the way the issue of conflicting sovereignties was handled throughout Jewish history. The book of Daniel represents a non-violent approach to the conflict of sovereignty, an approach which is in continuity with the suffering servant concept of Deutero-Isaiah. Victory is not achieved by the violence of the saints but by patient faithfulness and the suffering entailed by it, patience which will finally be rewarded by the direct action of Yahweh's court on the day of judgment:

> But the court (of Yahweh) shall sit in judgment,
>> and his dominion (Antiochus Epiphanes) shall be taken away,
>> to be consumed and destroyed to the end.
> And the kingdom and the dominion
>> and the greatness of the kingdoms under the whole heaven
>> shall be given to the people of the saints of the Most High;
> their kingdom shall be an everlasting kingdom,

and all kingdoms shall serve and obey them (7:26).

Yet another method of how the issue of sovereignty was handled in Jewish history is set forth in the first book of Maccabees. Here the problem is resolved by violence. This resolution is not too different from that of the Hammurabi type of state, and resulted in a later Hasmonean rule of injustice characteristic of the nations.

The revolt of the Maccabees found its continuity in the Zealot movement of the first century A.D. The nonviolent way of Daniel found its continuity in the movement of Jesus and his disciples (note Jesus' emphasis on the "Son of Man," Dan. 7). It is significant that the Jewish community itself established its 2000 years of continuity under the leadership of Yohanan ben Zakkai who, turning his back upon the violent way of the Maccabees and Zealots, founded the Jewish community upon the study of Torah. The tragedy of our own century is that under the hammer blows of Gentile violence and contempt, the Jewish community has deserted this leadership to take up again the way of a violent state.

Summary and Conclusion

Following is a brief summary of the texts discussed above:

The midwives disobeyed Pharaoh's edict because they rejected the theory of Pharaoh's absolute authority. They feared Yahweh instead, and thus were not anarchists. They believed in his power and discounted the power of Pharaoh's police force.

The call of Moses was the basis of his political legitimacy. It was necessary for him to first convince his own people of this legitimacy, and secondly, to convince Pharaoh. Pharaoh could not be convinced without Yahweh's miraculous show of force. The purpose of the conflict was that Israel, Egypt, and the world might "know Yahweh," that they might know the unique character of his government, by which Yahweh could bring his slave people out of Egypt with only his messenger as his representative. It was not the purpose of Yahweh's government to liquidate Pharaoh's system, but to bring it into relationship with Yahweh's authority and purpose. Moses interceded for Pharaoh and Egypt, and Pharaoh asked for Moses' blessing.

In the trial of Jeremiah, it was decided that the prophet as Yahweh's messenger had the right and duty to address the entire people, challenging the political policy of the king, who was then to bring his policy in line with the prophet's message. Political policy was to be based upon Torah and upon prophetic decision.

Jeremiah regarded the prophetic word as having authority also over the nations. The emperor of Babylon was accepted as the servant of the God of Israel, to whom Israel itself was to be subject. This does not mean that Jeremiah had now made Yahwism over into a Marduk-Hammurabi (or Marduk-Nebuchadnezzar) type of government. Nebuchadnezzar as servant of the God of Israel was only a temporary and marginal feature of Yahweh's rule.

The concept of Yahweh's future rule of the nations through torah and oracle (Moses and the prophets) is set forth in the Servant Songs. The servant is "imperialistic;" he is to establish Yahweh's justice in the earth. In contrast to the empire builders of his day, however, his method is non-violent, the quiet and assured proclamation of Yahweh's word. When this word results in violence against himself, his suffering and death become the incarnation of his message. In the end, Yahweh raises him to kingly rule. The justice of Yahweh is acknowledged by the kings and peoples of the earth.

The book of Daniel recognizes more than one type of state sovereignty which Yahweh's rule must challenge: the brutal unreflective power of Babylon (chap. 3) and the sovereignty of law of Medo-Persia (chap. 6), law to which the king himself must submit and from which he cannot deliver. In his challenge, Daniel regarded himself as innocent not only in Yahweh's court, the sovereignty of whose law he had recognized, but also before the king's court, the sovereignty of whose law he had rejected. The non-violent method of the book of Daniel is in continuity with the emphasis of the Servant Songs and flowers in the ministry of Jesus with his emphasis on the Son of Man. This is in contrast to the violence of I Maccabees, a movement which had its continuity with the revolutionary zealots. The Zealot movement was repudiated by Yohanan ben Zakkai, but has been revived in the modern state of Israel.

It should be evident from this study that one cannot do justice to the teaching of the Bible under the title, "The Biblical Case for Civil Disobedience." Such a title is liable to be understood as a denial of the main point of the Biblical emphasis: the absolute sovereignty of the God of Israel, and the rejection of all other sovereignties. In Biblical thought the *civitas* cannot be considered as the normative sovereignty from which there may be occasional deviations. Biblical thought challenges the sovereignty of the *civitas* itself, calling it rebellion, and proclaims the sovereignty of the God of Israel alone. All other authorities are related to this sovereignty. Ultimately all dominions shall serve and obey "the people of the saints of the Most High." "Here is the end of the matter" (Dan. 7:28).

Practical considerations for those who regard the rule of God as normative:

1. The guide for their life is the Torah of Yahweh, including both grace and law. This Torah, and prophetic decisions based upon it, gives political legitimacy to their actions.
2. They are active promoters of Yahweh's Torah and justice in the earth, and thereby undermine the sovereignty of earthly governments.
3. They do not hesitate to disobey a demand of a state which challenges the sovereignty of Yahweh's law. They regard such a state as in rebellion against Yahweh, and thus as guilty of anarchy.
4. They recognize and are subject to the governments of this world, intercede on their behalf and regard them as servants of Yahweh for

the achievement of his marginal and temporary purposes.

5. Those who regard the rule of Yahweh as normative for the present believe that they will be vindicated at the coming of the Son of Man when the kingdoms of this world will be judged. Is this Son of Man already among us, and has the judgment already taken place (according to the Gospel of John)? We leave such questions to the New Testament interpreter.

CHAPTER 12

THE CONCEPT OF POLITICAL POWER IN ANCIENT ISRAEL

Flavius Josephus coined the word "theocracy"[1] to describe the unique government of his people. Since he contrasts this form of government with monarchic, oligarchic, and republican forms, it is a misunderstanding to regard theocracy as the rule of God mediated through a monarchy,[2] or a hierocracy.[3] It is evident that Josephus used "theocracy" to describe the rule of God in an immediate sense, a rule by persuasion. "...our legislator," he says, "had no regard to any of these forms, but he ordained our government to be what, by a strained expression, may be termed a *Theocracy*, by ascribing the authority and the power to God, and by persuading all the people to have a regard to him, as the author of all the good things that were enjoyed either in common by all mankind, or by each one in particular.... He informed them, that it was impossible to escape God's observation, even in any of our outward actions, or in any of our inward thoughts."[4]

It is our purpose to examine the early form of this rule of God as it was witnessed to by ancient Israel that we might understand more clearly this strange "rule by persuasion" of which Josephus spoke. First, we will see that Yahweh was regarded as political leader both of Israel and of the world, a concept which in itself was not unique, however, as the rule of divinity was a belief held by all ancient Near Eastern peoples. Second, we will inquire as to Israel's experience of the nature of Yahweh's political leadership. Third, we will examine the institutional form of Yahweh's political leadership, the covenant form which paralleled political forms of the second and early first milleniums. In a paper of this size, we can deal with our subject only in the barest outline, hopefully giving enough documentation to see some of the main trends of Biblical thought.

I. YAHWEH AS POLITICAL LEADER OF ISRAEL AND THE NATIONS

That Yahweh was regarded as political leader both of Israel and of the nations is found pervasively throughout the Bible. It is clearly stated for example in the enthronement Psalms:

From *Annual of the Swedish Theological Institute*, Vol. VI, 1970.

> Sing praises to God, sing praises
> Sing praises to our King, sing praises!
> For God is the king of all the earth;
> Sing praises with a psalm! (Ps. 47,6,7)[5]

It is clearly implied in the story of the Exodus where Yahweh commands
Pharaoh to perform the political act of freeing His people, and where Yahweh
exercises his political leadership by his act of war and by leading Israel out of
Egypt.

This concept of the rule of divinity is hardly unique, however, as it pervades the mythological literature of the ancient Near East. For example, it is
said of Sargon, founder of the empire of Akkad (ca. 2360-2180 B.C.): "Enlil
did not let anyone oppose Sargon, the king of the country. Enlil gave him (the
region from) the Upper Sea (to) the Lower Sea."[6] The prologue to the law
code of Hammurabi (ca. 17128-1686 B.C.) provides an even clearer example:

> (i) When lofty Anum, king of the Anunnaki,
> (and) Enlil, lord of heaven and earth,
> the determiner of the destinies of the land,
> determined for Marduk, the first-born of Enki,
> the Enlil functions over all mankind,
> made him great among the Igigi,
> called Babylon by its exalted name,
> made it supreme in the world,
> established for him in its midst an enduring kingship,
> whose foundations are as firm as heaven and earth--
> at that time Anum and Enlil named me
> to promote the welfare of the people,
> me, Hammurabi, the devout, god-fearing prince,
> to cause justice to prevail in the land,
> to destroy the wicked and the evil,
> that the strong might not oppress the weak,
> to rise like the sun over the blackheaded (people),
> and to light up the land.
> Hammurabi, the shepherd, called by Enlil, am I.

> ....

> (v)...the king who has made the four quarters of the world subservient;
> the favorite of Inanna am I.
> When Marduk commissioned me to guide the people aright...[7]

This statement contains a number of parallels with biblical thought
including the rule of divinity over the world, and the divine election of a particular people and person. The two heads of the Babylonian pantheon, the gods
Anum and Enlil, lord of heaven and earth and of history, elected Babylon as

supreme in the world by giving Marduk, god of the city of Babylon, the "Enlil" or executive functions "over all mankind." They established for Marduk "an enduring kingship, whose foundations are as firm as heaven and earth." Also, these gods called Hammurabi as their human representative to rule over the earth. As the servant of Marduk, Hammurabi "made the four quarters of the world subservient." He was commissioned by Marduk "to guide the people aright."

The Assyrian mythologies contain the same fundamental concepts though differing somewhat in detail. It was the task of the Assyrian king to actualize the law and order of the state god Assur in the world. In pursuit of this purpose he subdued all enemies.[8] Anton Moortgat notes that the expansive vitality of the Assyrian people was founded upon their faith in Assur and the moral worth of his divine commission. The ability of the Assyrian king to actualize this world rulership was decisive for his own importance. His deeds against the enemy and wild animals were his justification before his god. For this reason he recorded these deeds in long inscriptions in the state annals or in a letter to his god.[9]

The mythological texts of Ugarit portray the universal kingship of the gods El and Baal. These gods also rule on the human scene chiefly through their chosen servant, the king. The KRT text "served particularly as a charter for the royal office as leader in war and priest...."[10] As a parallel to God's promise to Abraham, El appears to king KRT in a dream and promises him a descendant.[11]

The relevance to the Bible of this Near Eastern concept of the divine election of kingship is evident when one realizes that "the evidence...is rather impressive for concluding that Yahweh's choice is closely bound up with ancient concepts of legitimacy."[12] The question remains then as to the quality of Yahweh's political leadership in its particular as well as universal dimensions. Is the quality of the rule of Yahweh over Israel and the world similar to the quality of the rule of Marduk over Babylon and the world? Some passages of the Bible, both of pre-kingship and kingship vintage, would suggest that this is the case.[13] There are other passages, however, equally as old, which present a quite different picture.[14] We will now examine this fundamental issue, the essential nature of Yahweh's rule, as set forth in the Bible.

II. THE NATURE OF YAHWEH'S POLITICAL LEADERSHIP

What is the nature of the political leadership of Yahweh? To answer this, one must inquire concerning the nature of Israel, and more ultimately, the nature of God. What is Israel? and what is the nature of the kingship of God?

A. What is Israel?

This question is not an easy one, and its answer may reveal one's own presuppositions even more than the thought of the Bible.[15] We will begin with a survey of positions held by various students of the Old Testament. For

Wellhausen "the nation is more certainly created by God than the church"; "...God works more powerfully in the history of the nations than in church history."[16] For him the "state is always the presupposition of the church...." While Moses did not form a state, yet it was "the chief task of the age of Moses to bring about...the state, in the absence of which the church cannot have any subsistence either."[17] Out of this "religion of Israel...the commonwealth of Israel unfolded itself,--not a *holy* state, but *the* state."[18] After the fall of the commonwealth of Israel it was the genius of Ezekiel to "enclose the soul of prophecy in the body of a community which was not political, but founded on the temple and the cultus."[19] This creation Wellhausen regarded as an artificial product which, contradicting the viewpoint of Josephus, he regarded as the beginning of the "theocracy."[20] "The Mosaic theocracy, the residium of a ruined state, is itself not a state at all, but an unpolitical artificial product created in spite of unfavorable circumstances by the impulse of an ever-memorable energy: and foreign rule is its necessary counterpart."[21] For Wellhausen the normative form of the biblical faith is the state, towards which the Mosaic religion was unfolding, and to which it bridged over in times of political collapse.

On the other hand, the proper concern of religion for Wellhausen is the heart and individual conviction. What the prophets "were unconsciously laboring towards was that religious individualism which had its historical source in the national downfall, and manifested itself not exclusively within the prophetical sphere. With such men as Amos and Hosea the moral personality based upon an inner conviction burst through the limits of mere nationality; their mistake was in supposing that they could make their way of thinking the basis of a national life. Jeremiah saw through the mistake; the true Israel was narrowed to himself. Of the truth of his conviction he never had a moment's doubt; he knew that Jehovah was on his side, that on Him depended the eternal future. But, instead of the nation, the heart and the individual conviction were to him the subject of religion."[22] Wellhausen failed to realize that Jeremiah's concern about religion was a concern for community, that his emphasis upon the individual was a concern for the quality of community.

For Wellhausen "every formation of a religious community is a step toward the secularization of religion; the religion of the heart alone remains an inward thing."[23] He held that religion in its social expression was for the Jews a theocracy built on top of the state "as a specially spiritual feature: just as we moderns sometimes see the divine element in settled ordinances, such as marriage, not in their own nature, but in the consecration added to them by the church."[24] At the foundation of Wellhausen's thought seems to lie a Platonic dualism.[25]

The sacral kingship school of thought, represented by many Scandinavian and English writers, assumes that Israel was a state.[26] Sigmund Mowinckel, a moderate exponent of this school, attempts to trace in *He That Cometh* how the concept of Messiah developed from sacral kingship, a national, political, this-wordly figure, to a superterrestrial, universal, cosmic religious figure.

Martin Noth distinguishes between a nation and a state and defines Israel as a nation. He uses "nation" of Israel on the basis of the biblical tradition itself, saying that "whenever a definite appelative term is used at all, 'Israel' is normally described as a nation in the Old Testament tradition, and thereby reckoned among the many nations of the ancient Orient."[27] He defines a nation as a people with a common language, a common area, and a common historical experience. On the basis of this definition, Noth begins his history with the period of the Judges. He ends it with the Jewish revolts of 66-70 and 132-135 A.D.[28] However, Noth recognizes the inadequacy of this definition of Israel, not because of Israel's peripheral differences from other nations, but because of its uniqueness at the center. He writes, "...in spite of all these historical connections and possibilities for comparison, 'Israel' still appears a stranger in the world of its own time, a stranger wearing the garments and behaving in the manner of its age, yet separate from the world it lived in, not merely in the sense that every historical reality had its own individual character, and therefore an element of uniqueness, but rather that at the very center of the history of 'Israel' we encounter phenomena for which there is no parallel at all elsewhere, not because the material for comparison has not yet come to light but because, so far as we know, such things have simply never happened elsewhere."[29]

In the light of this professed uniqueness of Israel, one might ask whether it is possible to give a valid picture of its history by confining oneself so exclusively to the political institutions and by treating the nature and development of Israel's faith so incidently as does Noth in his *History of Israel*. John Bright asks, "Was not faith too central a moving force in Israel's history, even in political events, for it to be relegated to the fringes of the picture without throwing the picture out of proportion?"[30]

John Bright rejects the definition of Israel as a state or a nation, holding that it is *historically* inaccurate to treat Israel in this way. Beginning with the question, what made Israel Israel, the unique phenomenon that it was, he can only answer that it was not language nor geography nor historical experience alone nor material culture, but faith. "Israel was a people who became a people precisely because of her faith. The history of Israel, therefore, is not the history of a Twelve-Clan League, nor of a nation; *it is the history of a faith and its people.* It is for that reason, a most serious omission when the attempt is made to write a purely political history of Israel, for this is to attempt a history with the fundamental factor of that history left in the background. That is another way of saying that the history of Israel and the history of Israel's religion are one and the same topic. The historian may, for good reason, lay stress on one side or the other, but never on one to the exclusion of the other."[31]

Roland de Vaux comes out strongly on the same side, "...there never was any Israelite idea of the State. Neither the federation of the Tribes nor the post-exilic community were states. Between the two, the monarchy, in its varying forms, held its ground for three centuries over the tribes of the North, for four and a half over Judah, but it is hard to say how far it penetrated or modified the people's mentality. The post-exilic community returned to the premonarchical type of life with remarkable ease; this suggests some continuity of institutions at the level of clan and town. This municipal life is also the only aspect of public life considered by the legislative texts....

"It was religion which federated the tribes when they settled in Canaan, as it was to gather the exiles on their return from Babylon. It was religion which preserved the unity of the nation under the monarchy, in spite of the division of the kingdoms. The human rulers of this people are chosen, accepted or tolerated by God, but they remain subordinate to him and they are judged by the degree of their fidelity to the dissoluble covenant between Yahweh and his people. In this view of things the State, which in practice means the monarchy, is merely an accessory element; in actual fact Israel lived without it for the greater part of its history."[32]

And so the battle is joined. To make a judgment between these alternatives, it is important to consider the nature of the rule or kingship of God.

B. What is the Kingship of God?

Critical scholars of the end of the 19th and first part of the 20th century held that the concept of God's kingship began in Israel only after Israel herself had a human king. Underlying this conclusion was the thought regarding analogical thinking, that is, that a great part of religion was ancient man's projection into the sky of his perception of the structure of nature and of his social organization. Let us look, for example, at J. Wellhausen as an exponent of this point of view. He held that the kingship of Yahweh is "the religious expression of the fact of the foundation of the kingdom by Saul and David. The theocracy was the state of itself.... When the later Jews thought or spoke of the theocracy, they took the state for granted as already there, and so they could build the theocracy on the top of it as a specially spiritual feature...."[33] Of the prophets he says, "The theocracy as the prophets represents it to themselves is not a thing essentially different from the political community, as a spiritual differs from a secular power; rather it rests on the same foundations and is in fact the ideal of the state."[34]

The exponents of this point of view found portions of the Old Testament which were quite at odds with their thought. For example a number of references in the Old Testament claim Yahweh as king before the time of Saul and David,[35] references which were explained as anachronisms. Passages which would not bear such violent treatment, such as the book of Hosea, were explained in other ways. Wellhausen writes, "The other prophets...agree with Isaiah (Lam. iv, 20), only Hosea is peculiar in this as in other points. He appears to have regarded the kingdom as such as an evil; *in more than one expression he makes it the antithesis of the rule of Jehovah.*"[36] He then explains how it is that Hosea was out of step.

While some scholars still hold that Yahweh's kingship in Israel was conceived after the erection of the Davidic state,[37] there has been an important movement of scholarship toward the biblical representation, that Yahweh was regarded as king in Israel before the institution of the Davidic kingship.[38] In the first place, the gods outside of Israel were regarded as kings. The Creation

Epic of the time of Hammurabi celebrated the yearly enthronement of the god with the statement, "We have granted thee kingship over the universe entire." This enthronement climaxes with the shout, "Marduk is king!"[39] The Baal epic regards both El and Baal as king.[40] If kingship of the gods was a major emphasis of ancient Near Eastern mythological literature, one ought to hesitate before ascribing such a reference to Yahweh in biblical literature as necessarily late.

In the second place, Yahweh is regarded as king in early Israelite poetry. The Song of Miriam (Ex. 15,1-18) ends with the affirmation:

> The Lord will reign (yimlok)
> For ever and ever![41]

While many writers regard this hymn as post-Solomonic because of reference to the sanctuary, the Ugaritic poems speak of temple building in the sky as one of the god's chief pastimes. This very temple building is related in the Baal Epic to the reign of the god.[42] An indication of the ancient character of the hymn is suggested by antique spelling, the ancient forms of the poetry, and the reference to the pre-kingship leadership of Moab and Edom.[43] Yahweh is also called king in the Oracles of Balaam (Num. 23,21)[44] and in the Song of Moses (Deut. 33,5).[45]

A third argument is the ark which was regarded in early times as "the ark of the covenant of the Lord of hosts, who is enthroned on the cherubim" (1 Sam. 4,4). This symbolism is obviously the cultic background of the prophetic vision of the eight century prophet, where Yahweh is called king.[46]

In the fourth place, Yahweh is recognized as political leader in the ancient narratives of the books of Judges and Samuel. The first of these is Gideon's reply to the men of Gibeon who request of him, "Rule over us, you and your son and your grandson also; for you have delivered us out of the hand of Midian." Gideon answered, "I will not rule over you and my son will not rule over you; the Lord will rule over you" (Judges 8,22-23). Here then is a new element in Yahweh's kingship, that is, his kingship excludes human kingship. While the kingship of Yahweh as such is paralleled, as we have seen, in the ancient mythologies of the Near East, this exclusion and polemic against the human institution is unparalleled, and gives to Yahweh's kingship a new dimension. We will comment on the meaning of this a little later. Our interest now is to establish as a fact that prior to the rise of the Davidic monarchy Israel regarded Yahweh as her political leader, to the exclusion of the human ruler. While the historicity of Gideon's statement has been attacked by those who dogmatically hold that Yahweh's kingship could not have happened in Israel before Saul and David, it is only some such belief in Israel which could have kept it from accepting kingship for two full centuries after the tribes had settled down. Other peoples such as the Moabites and Edomites accepted kingship almost immediately after settling down. Why did Israel wait for two centuries[47] and why was kingship never really accommodated to Israel's ancient faith?

Another narrative representing this period of the Judges which specifically recognizes Yahweh as king is Samuel's response to the people who
demand "a king to govern us like all the nations." In his reply Yahweh said to
Samuel, "...they have not rejected you, but they have rejected me from being
king (mimmelok) over them" 1 Sam. 8,4-7). Here again the kingship of Yahweh meant the exclusion of the human institution. Samuel's criticism of the
human institution is that it is enslaving (1 Sam. 8,11-18), thus regarding it as a
return to the situation in Egypt. The historicity of this passage has been challenged, many regarding it as a read-back after Israel had experienced the
nature of kingship. But this argument does not adequately explain Israel's
critical attitude toward kingship both during and after the kingship period.
Every point at which Samuel levels his criticism against kingship can be documented as characteristic of Canaanite kingship from the Ugaritic texts.[48] Israel
did not need to learn about kingship by her own adoption of the institution. It
had learned its lesson well as it had experienced the institution as practiced by
others, in Egypt and in the city states of Canaan.

Another passage of this period of the Judges is Jotham's parable (Judg.
9,7-15). While this parable does not set forth the proposition that God is king,
it clearly sets forth Israel's dogmatic opposition to kingship. According to the
parable, kingship is a socially useless, even a harmful institution.

We must now say something about the pro-kingship stream of thought
which we find in Judges and Samuel (Judg. 18,1; 19,1; 21,25; 1 Sam. 9, etc.).
No canonical pro-kingship thought in the Old Testament was in favor of
accepting kingship which would be, either ideally or in practice, a mere borrowing from the nations. As Roland de Vaux has pointed out, both pro- and
anti-kingship streams of thought in the Old Testament "are inspired by the
same conception of power, one which is fundamental to Israelite thought, the
conception of theocracy. Israel is Yahweh's people and has no other master
but him."[49]

As we have noted above, it is not at all remarkable that Yahweh was
regarded as king by Israel, for kingship of divinity was characteristic of all the
Near East pantheons. The remarkable point is that the kingship of Yahweh
excluded human kingship.

To understand the radical nature of this break with the Near Eastern
background, and indeed with all ancient and primitive thinking, we will need to
understand something of the law of "mythological correspondence." It is briefly
stated by B. Meissner: "...in conformity with the law of the correspondence of
macrocosm and microcosm, the prototypes of all countries, rivers, cities, and
temples exist in heaven in the form of certain astral figures, while those on
earth are only copies of them."[50] Remnants of this kind of thought are found
within the Bible. For example, Moses is shown on Mount Sinai the form of the
sanctuary which he is to build: "According to all that I show you concerning
the pattern of the tabernacle, and of all its furniture, so you shall make it."
"...And see that you make them after the pattern for them, which is being
shown you on the mountain" (Ex. 25:9,40). To the ancient an object or act
becomes real only as it imitates or repeats an archetype. The importance of

this kind of thinking even in modern times becomes apparent when we realize that Plato was "the thinker who succeeded in giving philosophic currency and validity to the modes of life and behavior of archaic humanity."[51]

While as we have noted there are remnants of this type of thought in the Bible, yet it represents a fundamental break with this thought. In the matter of kingship for example, Yahweh is king; but there is no corresponding human king. Thus the pre-Platonic law of correspondence of mythological thought was broken at the very practical point of the exercise of political power. It therefore becomes impossible for anyone oriented toward the Platonic viewpoint of correspondences to understand what Israel was. From such an orientation, one can only understand Israel as an ancient Near Eastern state, and the prophets as transforming the state into a transcendental religion. Neither pre-exilic nor post-exilic Israel fit such Platonic archetypal presuppositions.

The fact is that we meet here at the very heart of the biblical faith a most radical affirmation and negation, not only in the area of metaphysics, but more important in the practical areas of ethics and political science. On the positive side there is affirmed a divine politics, the "politics of God" who acts immediately upon the human community in grace and judgment, having saved that community by a political act, and having given to that community law. On the negative side it regards political power, when wrested from God by the human community, as under the sign of unbelief,[52] and the state itself as an order which mistrusts God and his rule.[53] This radical faith in the immediacy of Yahweh's political leadership was more than a mere belief; it was an experience to which Israel witnesses, an experience from which Israel continually fell away in its first and especially its second adaptive periods,[54] an experience to which Israel was called back again and again by the great prophets. Only by a combination of faith and political events is Ezekiel able to lead a return toward the original vision. This response of faith and unfaith to the political leadership of Yahweh is both the glory and tragedy of Israel's history, and we might add, of the history of the church.

In our quest for the nature of Israel and of the kingship of God in Israel, we have discovered at the center of Israel's existence a radical re-orientation which broke with the usual processes of mythological thought and political practice, making it impossible to fit Israel into categories of thought of the ancient Near East. We will now examine the institutional form which this unique experience took in the history of Israel.

III. THE INSTITUTIONAL FORM OF YAHWEH'S POLITICAL LEADERSHIP

A. The Covenant, Law and History

For Wellhausen, covenant in the Old Testament was an idea which developed with the downfall of the nation. He held that Israel in the early period had a "natural divine relationship." Covenant for him was an artificial idea created for the continuity of the community when it no longer had a national existence.[55]

Since Wellhausen, it is recognized that covenant in Israel was not a mere idea, but was celebrated as a cultic act.[56] Also, covenant is accepted by many as an event of Israel's early history.[57]

An advance in our understanding of the biblical faith was made by the discovery that the form of the Sinai[58] and Shechem[59] covenants have certain parallels with the form of international treaties of the second millenium B.C.[60]

To understand the importance of this discovery one must know something about the history of form criticism. Form criticism has to do with the study of the various literary or pre-literary forms of the Bible such as law, the credos, curse and blessing formulas, etc., as well as the institutions in Israel which produced these forms. A presupposition held by many form critics was that each literary form originated in a different institution.[61] These various literary forms were then united into larger unities artificially, either by oral tradition or a literary process. While there is some value in this idea, it was carried much too far. For example, because of this theory it was assumed that the historical statement which introduces the Ten Words was originally not included with the Ten Commandments (Ex. 20:2). Also it was assumed that the credo of Joshua 24:2-13 was originally a separate unit from the covenanting of the rest of the chapter.[62]

On the analogy of the ancient international treaty form, however, the Mosaic covenant is a literary form which brings into unity such disparate literary forms as history, law, blessing and curse formulae, and the covenant formula. More important, the covenant also unified the commitment of the various institutions in which the diverse literary forms developed: the royal court,[63] the legal court,[64] the cult,[65] the institution of holy war.[66]

The discovery of the analogy between the international treaty and the Mosaic covenant adds credibility to the biblical claim that Israel began as the people of God in a covenant-making ceremony at Sinai. This covenant brought all of Israel's institutions under the authority of the covenant God. It excluded the institution of human kingship altogether,[67] and radically qualified the others.[68] Corrected by archeology, form criticism now lends support to the judgment of Henry S. Gehman, "The unifying bond (of Israel) was the name of Yahweh and the covenant sanctioned by God. Naturally there were centrifugal tendencies in the tribes, but on the other hand they had a common law, a common cult, and a common historical consciousness. With such a common basis the revelation of the divine Lord of the covenant exercised the controlling influence. In other words, the authority of the divine covenant will subordinate the whole national life to its purpose."[69]

We will now examine the Sinai and Shechem Covenants,[70] noting how Yahweh is (1) leader of history both in (2) war and as (3) giver and enforcer of law. These three points make up the peculiar characteristics of Near Eastern kingship[71] as we shall see, although spatial limitations make it impossible to enlarge upon the last two.

B. Yahweh as political leader; leader of history

Yahweh is the central I of Israelite history writing.[72] The ultimate source of this Yahweh egoism lies in the unique nature of Israel's experience with Yahweh, and was reflected in literature in the making of Covenant. This Yahweh egoism displaces the egoism of Near Eastern kingship, as can be seen by the comparison of this introduction of a Hittite treaty with the Sinai Covenant:

Hittite Treaty: "These are the words of the *Sun Mursilis,* the *great king,* the *king of the Hatti land,* the *valiant,* the *favorite* of the Storm-god, the *son* of Suppiluliumas, the *great king,* the *king of the Hitti land,* the *valiant.*" This is followed by several paragraphs of the history of the king's relationships with his vassal, in which the pronoun I of the king of Hatti is central.[73] Exodus 20:1-2: And *God* spoke all these words, saying, *I am Yahweh your God,* who brought you out of the land of Egypt, out of the house of bondage.[74]

This remarkable difference in historical writing is not a mere isolated phenomenon, but is characteristic of Biblical history as contrasted to the official Near Eastern Annals. This difference was known in Israel and was contrasted already in the 8th century B.C. in Isaiah's taunt song against Sennacherib:[75]

> Whom have you (Sennacherib) mocked and reviled?
> > Against whom have you raised your voice
> and haughtily lifted up your eyes?
> > Against the Holy One of Israel!
> By your messengers you have mocked the Lord,
> > and you have said, With *my* many chariots
> *I* have gone up the heights of the mountains,
> > to the far recesses of Lebanon;
> *I* felled its tallest cedars,
> > its choicest cypresses;
> *I* entered its farthest retreat,
> > its densest forest.
> *I* dug wells
> > and drank foreign waters,
> and *I* dried up with the sole of my foot
> > all the streams of Egypt.
> Have you not heard
> > that *I* (Yahweh) determined it long ago?
> *I* planned from days of old
> > what now *I* bring to pass,
> that you should turn fortified cities
> > into heaps of ruins,
> while their inhabitants, shorn of strength,
> > are dismayed and confounded,
> and have become like plants of the field,
> > and like tender grass,

like grass on the housetops;
    blighted before it is grown?
But *I* know your sitting down
    and your going out and coming in,
    and your raging against *me*.
Because you have raged against *me*
    and your arrogance has come into *my* ears,
I will put *my* hook in your nose
    and *my* bit in your mouth,
and *I* will turn you back on the way
    by which you came.

That Isaiah was not thundering against mere personal pride is evident from an examination of any Near Eastern official annal. An example follows from Sennacherib's Annals, telling of his advance against the cities of Palestine which were allied with Hezekiah and Judah.

(Trusting) in the aid of Assur,
my lord, *I* fought with them and
brought about their defeat. The Egyptian charioteers and princes,
together with the charioteers of the Ethiopian king,
my hands took alive in the midst of the battle.
Eltekeh (and) Timnah
I besieged, *I* captured and took away their spoil.
I drew near to Ekron and slew the governors and nobles
who had committed sin (that is rebelled), and
hung their bodies on stakes around the city.[76]

Isaiah saw the Near Eastern political systems, undergirded by pagan religion, as a human attempt to control history, an attempt founded upon self interest, and as such arrogance against Yahweh who alone controls the future and rules history.

How the oppressor has ceased,
    the insolent fury ceased!
The Lord has broken the staff of the wicked,
    the scepter of rulers,
that smote the peoples in wrath
with unceasing blows,
that ruled the nations in anger
    with unrelenting persecution.
    . . . .
How you are fallen from heaven,
    O Day Star, son of Dawn!
How you are cut down to the ground,
    you who laid the nations low!

You said in your heart,
    I will ascend to heaven;
above the stars of God
    I will set my throne on high;
I will sit on the mount of assembly
    in the far north (Baal's Mountain);
I will ascend above the heights of the clouds,
    I will make myself like the Most High
But you are brought down to Sheol,
    to the depths of the Pit....[77]

I have italicized the above colon to suggest its possible relationship to the critique of the ancient writer of Genesis 3-11 (J). In the narrative of the fall the temptation was that man might "be like God, knowing good and evil" (Gen. 3,5). The depth of this biblical writer's critique of the human situation among the nations is seldom plumbed. His critique of the society of his day is not that the nations served idols, or even foreign gods. Neither are even so much as mentioned. His criticism is that humanity in the exercise of political power try to take the leadership of history into their own hands, but are invariably frustrated in their purpose to achieve community (11:1-9). According to J's thought, paganism is a false cult which sacralizes the human attempt to control the powers of nature and society for their own advantage, to fulfill his own destiny. It is rebellion against the political leadership of God, a building of the tower and civilization of Babel which ends in the frustration of a scrambled language. Cf. also 1 Sam. 15:22f.

We have seen that in ancient Israel's experience Yahweh is leader of history, a concept rooted in covenant, which pervades the Old Testament, and which stands in contrast to ancient Near Eastern thought. While in Near Eastern mythologies the gods war chiefly with one another, in ancient Israelite thought Yahweh's conflict is with Pharaoh, with the kings of Assyria and Babylon, or even with the kings of Israel. But what practical difference does it make whether Yahweh or the human king is leader of history? To understand this difference it is essential to understand the nature of sacral kingship in the ancient Near East. The king was the chief intermediary between the human and the divine community.[78] His main function was two-fold, to protect and promote his country externally by conducting foreign wars, and to uphold law and order internally by punishing evildoers.[79] In Mesopotamia, the king exercised on earth the powers of Enlil who as storm-god represented the power of compulsion, the executive powers of sheriff and commander of the armed forces.[80] In the Canaanite city-state, the king exercised the same powers as servant of El and the storm god, Baal.[81]

It is this office of kingship which is swept aside by the Mosaic covenant, and the functions of this office are taken over by the immediate rule of Yahweh. The beginning of Israel "involved a radical rejection of Canaanite religious and political ideology, especially the divine authority underlying the political institutions, and the Canaanite concept of religion as essentially a

phenomenological cultic celebration of the economic concerns of the group--
the fertility cult. Only under the assumption that the groups involved had
actually experienced at first hand over a period of time the malfunctioning of
Canaanite kingship, can one understand the concept of God in early Israelite
religion, for the usual functions, authority, and prestige of the king and his
court are the exclusive prerogative of deity. So, land tenure, military leadership, 'glory,' the right to command, power, all are denied to human beings
and attributed to God alone. In this way, even the theological aspects of OT
religion represent a transference from the political to the religious. Not until
David is the old Canaanite legitimacy of kingship re-introduced, but con-
siderably modified at first by the entrenched Israelite system of religious
values.[82]

This denial that the human exercise of violent power is necessary to existence was not a withdrawal from political concerns, that is, concern for community, as tends to happen in some forms of mysticism. Yahweh's leadership
in history had to do with political order, both for the community's external and
internal relationships. The covenant law (Deut. 2ff.) sets forth Yahweh as
political leader in His act of warfare: "I am the Lord your God, who brought
you out of the land of Egypt..." (Ex. 20:2).[83] This law acknowledges Yahweh as
political leader also with its "Thou shalt" (Ex. 20:3ff.), proclaiming God as giver
and upholder of law.[84] A consideration of these concerns properly belongs to
this paper, but would carry us far beyond our spatial limitations. We only suggest that warfare and law within the transforming experience of Yahweh as
political leader are not incongruous with the Servant Songs of Deutero-Isaiah
nor with the transformation of the concept as proclaimed by the New Testament Church.

NOTES

1. Theokratian apedeixe to politeuma. Flavius Josephus, *Against Apion*, II, 16 165.

2. As for example Wellhausen and many since. See below.

3. G. Mensching, "Theokratie," RGG, 3rd ed., VI Band, p. 751, represents this view. He sees three historical forms: Lamanism, Islam, and Christendom of the Middle Ages.

4. Josephus, *op.cit*. This translation is that of William Whiston, ed. by D. S. Margoliouth, *The Works of Flavius Josephus*, p. 944. Josephus makes this statement despite his recognition of the fact that Israel was ruled by "judges and monarchs," by a "kingly government" and by aristocratic, oligarchic, and priestly types. Cf. *Antiquities*, Book XI, Chapter IV, Par. 8. My point is that in his statement on "theocracy" he is the bearer of a tradition which was quite at variance from these later types, though even these types were adjusted somewhat toward the ancient concept. Cf. Martin Buber, *Königtum Gottes, 1966, pp. 139ff.*

5. All translations of the Bible are from the RSV.

6. ANET, p. 267.

7. *Ibid*., pp. 164,165.

8. Cf. Scharff, Moortgat, *Ägypten und Vorderasien im Altertum*, p. 397.

9. *Ibid*., pp. 399-400. Cf./ also pp. 427-31. Shalmanezer I (ca. 1280 B.C.), wrote: "...the lord to whose feet Assur and the great gods have brought all kings and rulers in submission. When the Lord Assur chose me for his legitimate worshipper, and, for the ruling of the black-headed people, gave me scepter, sword, and staff, he presented me the diadem of legitimate rulership"--D.D. Luckenbill, *Ancient Records of Assyria* and Babylonia, *Vol. I, p. 39.*

10. John Gray, *The Legacy of Canaan* (second, revised ed.), p. 17.

11. ANET, pp. 143-144.

12. G. E. Mendenhall, "Election," *The Interpreter's Dictionary of the Bible*, II, p. 80.

13. Gen. 49:8-12; Num. 24,15-19; Ps. 2.

14. Deut. 32,7-9; Isa. 2,1-4.

15. Joachim Kraus, after surveying various viewpoints on the political message of the Old Testament prophets, states that the ideological and dogmatic presuppositions of the scholars were decisive in their various attempts to understand the prophets on this question. Kraus, *Prophetie und Politik*, pp. 16f.

16. "Israel" in *Prolegomena to the History of Ancient Israel* (Meridian Books, 1965), pp. 512f.

17. *Prolegomena*, p. 412.

18. *Prolegomena*, p. 436.

19. *Prolegomena*, p. 421.

20. Josephus regarded Moses as the legislator for the theocracy; for him the theocracy was pre-state. Cf. above.

21. *Prolegomena*, p. 422.

22. *Prolegomena*, p. 491.

23. *Prolegomena*, p. 512.

24. *Prolegomena*, p. 414.

25. See below.

26. Sigmund Mowinckel in his great work on the Psalms points up parallels between the

Psalms and the enthronement literature of Babylonia. Cf. *Psalmenstudien* II. Mowinckel drew back from the position that the king was the incarnation of Yahweh, holding that while Israelite kingship was strongly influenced by oriental practices, its main influence was Israel's rootage. Cf. *He That Cometh*, trans. by G. W. Anderson, pp. 21-95. For more radical representations see Geo. Widengren, *Sakrales Königtum im Alten Testament und im Judentum*; S. H. Hooke, ed., *Myth, Ritual and Kingship* (1958). Aubrey Johnson is less radical but in my judgment goes much too far in *Sacral Kingship in Ancient Israel*. For criticism of this position, see Martin Noth, "Gott, König, Volk im Alten Testament," *Gesammelte Studien zum AltenTestament*, pp.188-229. Roland de Vaux in *Ancient Israel, Its Life and Institutions*, trans. by John McHugh (1961), p. 99, warns against their preoccupation with Israel as a state.

27. Martin Noth, *The History of Israel*, (revised translation, 1960), pp. 4-5.

28. *Ibid.*, pp. 5-7.

29. *Ibid.*, pp. 2-3.

30. John Bright, *Early Israel in Recent Historical Writing*, p. 35.

31. *Ibid.*, p. 114.

32. De Vaux, *op.cit.*, pp. 98f.

33. *Prolegomena*, p. 414.

34. *Ibid.*

35. Judges 8,23, etc. See below where these passages are treated.

36. *Prolegomena*, p. 417. Underlining mine.

37. Those who hold that ancient Israel was primarily a state would be inclined to subscribe to such a view. See for example John Gray, "The Kingship of God in the Prophets and Psalms," V.T., Vol. XI (1961), pp. 1-29.

38. Reference is made to some of the scholars in the argument that follows.

39. Cf. ANET, p. 66.

40. *Ym lmt b'lm yml [k?]*--Cyrus Gordon, Ugaritic Manual (1955), p. 150, Text 68:32. Cf. Arvid S. Kapelrud, *Baal in the Ras Shamra Texts*; Marvin H. Pope, *El in the Ugaritic Texts*; Werner Schmidt, *Königtum Gottes in Ugarit und Israel*.

41. Ex. 15,18.

42. ANET, pp. 131ff.

43. Among older writers Ewald and Dillman regarded the hymn as having a genuine Mosaic kernel. But Bruno Baentsch held that it was hardly written before Deuteronomic times since it refers to the temple. Cf. Exodus, Leviticus, Numeri in HAT (1903). Martin Noth also sees it as relatively late (*Das Zweite Buch Mose, Exodus*, ATD (1959), pp. 96-97, but makes no reference to the new evidence of the Ugaritic literature. For an early dating, see Frank M. Cross Jr. and David Noel Freedman, "The Song of Miriam," JNES XIV (1955), p. 237ff.

44. An argument for early dating will be found in W. F. Albright, "The Oracles of Balaam," JBL, LXIII (1944), pp. 207-233.

45. The main argument for dating this poetry late is that the ideas are too advanced for an early time. This argument no longer holds, however, if we see the Israelite contribution within the context of the literature of the Near East. For a discussion of this, see Otto Eissfeldt, *Das Lied Moses Deuteronomium 32, 1-43 und das Lehrgedicht Asaphs Psalm 78 samt einer Analyse der Umgebund des Mose-Liedes*.

46. Isa. 6,1-5. Albrecht Alt makes this connection in "Gedanken über des Königtum Yahwes," 1945, KS, I, pp. 345-357. He also sees in this "divine court" the possibility of the source of Yahweh's kingship rather than in that of the Davidic kingship.

47. This is Martin Noth's argument. Cf. Noth, *The History...*, p. 165.

48. *The Institutions...*, p. 99.

49. *The Institutions...*, p. 99.

50. Quoted from Von Rad, "Typological Interpretation of the Old Testament" in *Essays on Old Testament Hermeneutics*, 1963, ed. by Claus Westermann, p. 18. Cf. James Barr, "The Meaning of 'Mythology' in Relation to the Old Testament," VT, IX (1959), pp. 1-10.

51. Mircea Eliade, *Cosmos and History*, p. 34.

52. 1 Sam. 8,7. See the above discussion.

53. Hans-Joachim Kraus, *Prophetie und Politik*, p. 30: "'Politik' steht im Alten Testament unter dem Zeichen des Unglaubens, sofern der Staat selbst nichts anderes ist als eine Ordnung derer, die Gott und seiner Herrschaft misstrauen."

54. I regard the creative period as that of Moses, the first adaptive period as that of the Judges, and the second as that of the kings. Cf. George Mendenhall, "Bible History in Transition," *The Bible and the Ancient Near East*, ed. by G. Ernest Wright.

55. *Prolegomena*, p. 440.

56. Kraetzschmar, *Die Bundesvorstellung im Alten Testament in ihrer geschichtlichen Entwicklung*. For a short review of the history of scholarly opinion on this question, see Klaus Baltzer, *Das Bundesformular*, pp. 11ff.

57. Cf. Johs. Pedersen, *Israel*, Vol. III, IV, pp. 657ff.

58. Ex. 20,1-17; Deut. 5,6-21.

59. Josh. 24.

60. George Mendenhall ws the first to discover this relationship on the basis of the work of Viktor Korosec, *Hethitische Staatsverträge*. Cf. *Law and Covenant in Israel and the Ancient Near East*. Klaus Baltzer, a student of von Rad, published five years later *Das Bundesformular*, a work which comes to similar conclusions. For a discussion and example of how this discovery is revolutionizing Old Testament studies, see Delbert R. Hillers, *Treaty-Curses and the Old Testament Prophets*. While these parallels are obvious, one must be careful that this does not become another "Pan-Babylonianism." Parallels as well as differences should be noted.

61. Cf. Mendenhall, *op.cit.*, p. 44; Gerhard von Rad, *Der Heilige Krieg im Alten Israel*, p. 5.

62. Von Rad sees J as a great theologian who after the time of Solomon was the first to unite law and gospel--von Rad, *Das erste Buch Mose, Genesis* (1949), pp. 13f.

63. Yahweh is the suzerain or political leader of his people.

64. The covenant itself is a legal document. Also, it contains stipulations or "law."

65. The international treaties were sealed before the gods who were witnesses. Since the Mosaic covenant was between Yahweh and people, it could only be of a cultic nature.

66. In the covenant forms, the acts of God have to do with His war, fundamentally, salvation from Egypt.

67. See the discussion above.

68. For a discussion of the meaning of the covenant theologically, see Walther Eichrodt, *Theologie des Alten Testaments*, I (1948), pp. 6ff.

69. Henry S. Gehman, "The Covenant--the Old Testament Foundation of the Church," *Theology Today*, Vol. 7 (1950-51), p. 28. Cf. R. E. Clements, *Prophecy and Covenant*, pp. 13f.; Delbert R. Hillers, *Treaty-Curses and the Old Testament Prophets*.

70. Joshua 24. Both Mendenhall, *op.cit.*, pp. 41ff., and Baltzer, *op.cit.*, pp. 29ff., discuss this chapter.

71. It is significant that long before Mendenhall, Martin Buber saw this as "the king's

covenant." Cf. Buber, *Königtum Gottes* (1936), pp. 111ff.

72. See Johannes Hempel, "Herrschaftsform und Ichbewusstsein," *The Sacral Kingship* (1959), pp. 302-315.

73. Treaty between Mursilis and Duppi-Tessub of Amurru. Cf. ANET, pp. 203ff. (italics added).

74. Italics added. I assume Exodus 20,1-17 to be the Sinai Covenant. It is called the Horeb Covenant in Deut. 6. See Mendenhall, *op.cit.* For those who do not accept this as a covenant form, the point of Yahweh's egoism is equally valid for Joshua 24 and Exodus 19,3-6.

75. 2 Kings 19,20-28 (italics added).

76. The Oriental Institute Prism Inscription (H2), Col. III, 1-10, D. D. Luckenbill, *The Annals of Sennacherib*, pp. 31f.

77. Isaiah 14,3-20. For the same type of taunt, see Ezekiel 28; Daniel 4,28ff.

78. Cf. E. O. James, "The Sacred Kingship and the Priesthood," *The Sacral Kingship*, p. 64.

79. Cf. Thorkild Jacobsen, "Mesopotamia" in *The Intellectual Adventure of Ancient Man*, H. and H. Frankfort, et.al., p. 192; John Gray, "Canaanite Kingship in Theory and Practice," VT, II (1952), pp. 193-220.

80. The meaning of kingship for the Mesopotamian is set forth in the Enuma Elish in which the memory of the origins of his own political organization governed his speculations about the origin of the organization of the unvierse. In this creation myth the origin of order developed from the conflict between two principles, inactivity and activity. Inactivity was first overcome by authority, the mere word of Ea (Tablet 1,60ff.). But to quell the second disturbance authority was no longer adequate (Tablet 2,50ff.). To authority had to be added force or physical compulsion (Tabler 4,35ff.). "The transition mirrors, on the one hand, a historical development from primitive social organization, in which only custom and authority unbacked by force are available to ensure concerted action by the community, to the organization of a real state, in which the rule commands both authority and force to ensure necessary concerted action"--Jacobsen, *op.cit.* p. 173. It was to meet this second threat that Marduk (earlier Enlil) was made king and was invested with all the powers of the gods (Tablet 4,1ff.). "What the assembly of the gods here confers upon Marduk is kingship: the combination of authority with powers of compulsion; a leading voice in the counsels of peace; leadership of the army in times of war; police powers to penalize evildoers"--*Ibid.*, p. 178. King of the gods, Marduk strode forth as war and storm god to overcome Tiamat (Tablet 4,30ff.). See NET, pp. 60ff.

81. KRT Epic, ANET, pp. 142ff.

82. George E. Mendenhall, "The Hebrew Conquest of Palestine," *The Biblical Archaeologist*, XXV (1962), p. 76. See also p. 75.

83. Perhaps the most serious work on warfare in the Old Testament is that of Gerhard von Rad, *Der heilige Krieg im alten Israel.* However, I feel that he fails to treat adequately the obvious context of covenant of many narratives on warfare, and the tensions which this causes.

84. Cf. Martin Noth, Die Gesetze im Pentateuch, *Gesammelte Studien zum Alten Testament*, pp. 9-141.

CHAPTER 13

MONOTHEISM, POWER, AND JUSTICE: A STUDY IN ISAIAH 40-55

Deutero-Isaiah elucidates the biblical teaching of monotheism, clearly stating its logical and climactic conclusion: Yahweh, God of Israel, is God alone; apart from him there is no other. This teaching involved more than a mere theoretical belief that Yahweh is one in contrast to the polytheism of the Near East. Hans Wildberger has defined Deutero-Isaiah's monotheism:

> To the concept of monotheism belongs the clear consciousness of the unity of the cosmos and history and the dependence of both upon the power of the one Lord, with all the consequences which such a world view brings with it for faith in one God.[1]

While this definition moves in the right direction by acknowledging the interrelationship of the oneness of God with the oneness of the cosmos and history, this paper will set forth one of the "consequences [or better, inherent components] which such a world view brings," viz., that the unity of the cosmos and history under the oneness of Yahweh includes a distinctive moral quality. This paper will seek to establish this thesis by showing that Deutero-Isaiah's only consistent and complete expression of this monotheistic claim is to be found not in the Cyrus poems, though these are essential to his argument, but only in the servant poems which testify to the moral quality of the unity toward which Yahweh is leading the nations, and thus also to the moral quality of the unity of God. The distinctive essence of this moral quality lies in the vocation, both in its task and method, to which the servant is called. The unity of the cosmos and history under the one Lord cannot be separated from this moral quality by which Yahweh's monotheistic claim is worked out in both the cosmos and history.

The method of this study, which seeks to substantiate this thesis, will be to examine, first, the trial speeches where the claim of Yahwistic monotheism against the divinity of the gods is stated most emphatically, especially 45:18-25, which, except for the servant poems, ends with Deutero-Isaiah's strongest universal note.[2] Second, I shall examine the Cyrus poems, some of which over-

From *The Catholic Biblical Quarterly*, 46, 1984.

lap with the trial speeches and are essential to their argument, even though Deutero-Isaiah recognized that they caused difficulty for his monotheism. Last, I shall explore the servant songs which, as I maintain, bring Deutero-Isaiah's argument for the monotheism of Yahweh to a satisfactory and consistent conclusion.[3]

Monotheism: Yahweh's Trial Speeches Against the Gods

Three trial speeches deal with the nations in regard to their gods: 41:21-29; 43:8-13; 45:18-25.[4] In all three speeches Yahweh is the speaker. In the first he addresses the gods (41:23); in the second, Israel in the assembly of the nations (43:8-10); and in the third, the survivors of the nations (45:20). The issue before the court in all three cases is monotheism (41:24; 43:10; 45:21). An either-or option is presented: either the divinity of Yahweh or of polytheism. The argument makes clear, however, that the issue is not the mere existence of one over against the many, but the effectiveness of only the one to present an understanding of history in terms of promise/threat and fulfillment[5] and to control the future in continuity with the promise of the historical past (41:22-23,25-27; 43:9,10; 45:21).[6] Obviously this argument has to do with the effectiveness of divinity in the political arena, not merely to project and control this or that event, but to control the present in continuity with the past in such a way as to insure continuity of communal life. The argument hinges on the issue of power.

But Deutero-Isaiah's argument for monotheism was not that Yahweh had a monopoly on violent political power and that the gods had none. Who among the exiles could buy that argument? Deutero-Isaiah's argument for Yahweh's monotheism claimed a unique kind of power and communal existence as well as the conviction that this kind of power alone is effective for survival. Deutero-Isaiah makes his argument by moving the proof for divinity from the arena of the battlefield to the arena of prophetic proclamation and its fulfillment. C. Westermann recognizes this fundamental break with Near Eastern thought but draws a conclusion from it which involves him in a contradiction that makes it impossible to understand the political thought of Deutero-Isaiah. He says,

> Since Israel had ceased to be an independent state, her God could not now prove his superiority to the gods of Babylon by means of victory over her foes. So Deutero-Isaiah shifts the arena of decision from the battlefield to the law court. This was a complete innovation on the prophet's part and it represents the first move in human history toward the dissolution of the link between 'religion' and politics. It does not, however, in any way imply a severance of the link between God's action and history; it only means that the hitherto accepted proof of a god's divinity, his power to win military victory for his own people, was replaced by another, the dependable and unremitting continuity between what a god says and what he does.[7]

The contradictory statements are (1) that the shift of the arena "from the battlefield to the law court" leads to the dissolution of the link between religion and politics, but (2) this does not "imply a severance...between God's action and history." While the second part is tenable in that there is a dependable and unremitting continuity between what "Yahweh says and does," the first statement cannot stand. The shift from "the battlefield to the law court" does not mean a renunciation of the control of the community and its future, which is what politics is about. Instead of divorcing politics from religion, Deutero-Isaiah is saying that the politics which tries to control by coercion is ineffective in terms of the continuity of community and that the "gods" of such communities are therefore not really divine. The only effective politics for the continuity of community is that based not on military might but rather upon the continuity of the creative word and deed of Yahweh, who therefore is alone God.

Israel might have understood Deutero-Isaiah's argument were it not "deaf and blind" (43:8), i.e., if it had faith to believe the prophetic word. From the time of Amos the great prophets had thundered with unanimous voice that the end had come for Israel and Judah. That word had come to pass.[8] Israel and Judah had been utterly defeated. The exiles could not hold to the monotheism of Yahweh on the basis of ancient Near Eastern power politics, but only on the basis of their own word-event theology. Their crushing defeat was evidence of the integrity of Yahweh's word through the prophets. Despite that defeat, Yahweh had been adequate for the continuity of their community, which even in exile experienced again that "I am he" (43:10-11).

Deutero-Isaiah did not reveal to the exiles something new, but only articulated their historical experience for them. His argument for the continuity of word-event was a part of Israel's experience all the way back to the exodus and had preoccupied Israel's writers from J to the deuteronomic historian. The law of Deuteronomy had insisted that even kingship must be based on Yahweh's torah rather than upon military power and state economics (Deut. 17:14-20). Because of this tradition the exiles should have had no problem understanding Deutero-Isaiah's argument for the monotheism of Yahweh though they might have had a problem of faith in the word of the new exodus, that their communal meetings of lament were now over.

The Babylonians, on the other hand, could not have understood Deutero-Isaiah's argument, just as most moderns cannot understand it. After the victory of Hammurabi's army over the city states of Mesopotamia, the political document, *Enuma Elish*, set forth the supremacy of Marduk, god of Babylon, in the Mesopotamian pantheon of world government.[9] Marduk, elected by the gods, had proved his supremacy on the battlefield. Also, the introduction to Hammurabi's law code explains how the great gods had elected Marduk and Hammurabi (after his military victory, of course) to bring justice to the Mesopotamian peoples.[10] Israel was thrust into this milieu of power politics more than a millennium later by the military victories of Nebuchadnezzar. It would have been impossible to argue for the ascendancy of the exiles' God on the basis of power politics. So far as Babylonian political values were concerned, Yahweh was hardly worth fitting into the lower echelons of the pantheon.

How might Deutero-Isaiah convince the Near Eastern mind, saturated with the mythology of violent power, of the monotheism of Yahweh based upon the argument of continuity of community by word-event? In the last trial speech the situation to which Deutero-Isaiah addresses himself has changed. Here he addresses the *pĕlîṭê haggôyim*, "the survivors of the nations" (45:20). The word *pālîṭ* when used of persons in the OT refers only to fugitives who have escaped after a defeat in battle (e.g., 2 Kgs. 9:15; Amos 9:1; Ezek. 24:26,27).[11] After Cyrus' victory, the nations, particularly the Babylonians, were in a similar state of that of the Jewish exiles. Historical experience had now demonstrated to them the inadequacy of their gods to provide political continuity, just as Deutero-Isaiah had prophesied.[12] This provided a basis for their understanding of Deutero-Isaiah's argument which he set forth to them:

> Who told this long ago?
>> Who declared it of old?
> Was it not I, Yahweh?
>> and there is no other god besides me,
> a righteous God and a Savior;
>> there is none besides me (45:21).[13]

This new situation provided an opportunity for a new turn in the prophet's preaching; addressing his oracle to the nations, he appealed to them to look to Yahweh for their continuity:[14]

> Turn to me and be saved,
>> all the ends of the earth!
> For I am God, and there is no other.
>> By myself I have sworn,
>> from my mouth has gone forth in righteousness
>> a word that shall not return;
> to me every knee shall bow,
>> every tongue shall swear (45:22,23).

Here military power is not involved, and the fulfillment of this appeal cannot be found in the Cyrus poems. The oath of Yahweh will go forth as a new word after Cyrus has worked his havoc upon the nations, a word which would also be effective (v.23).[15]

This new political order will consist of both Jewish and Gentile nations:

> To him shall come and be ashamed
>> all who were incensed against him.
> In the Lord all the offspring of Israel
>> shall triumph and glory (45:24).

Here again Westermann sees the radical character of this passage, but fails to understand Deutero-Isaiah's political concept of the kingdom of Yahweh, a concept essential to the understanding of the servant poems:

> As the verses before us make clear, he [Deutero-Isaiah] believed that in his day a final break has been made between the people of God and any form of its existence as a political entity. All men are invited to partake in the divine salvation, and membership of the people of God is based on the free confession of those who have discovered that he alone is God.[16]

In contradiction to Westermann's concept of a political entity but in congruence with Westermann's idea that "membership of the people of God is based on the free confession of those who have discovered that he alone is God," Deutero-Isaiah here develops the monotheism of Yahweh to its logical conclusion: God is one as expressed by the fact that all humankind will be one in their trust in his creative word-deed for continuity of community and in their voluntary commitment to his will, a radically new political kingdom which will arise upon the chaos created by Cyrus.

Though Cyrus was Yahweh's anointed, his military might was not to be the basis for the politics of the new world community. Just as Deutero-Isaiah had removed the case for Yahweh's monotheism from the arena of the battlefield, so here he has rejected military power for the persuasion of Yahweh's word as the foundation for the government of the new world-wide community. His concept of winning the allegiance of the total person corresponds to that of Jeremiah's where the law is written upon the heart, except that Deutero-Isaiah extends the concept beyond Israel to the nations.[17]

This oracle of Deutero-Isaiah is closer to the thought of the servant poems (especially poems one and two) than any other of his statements apart from those poems. It is surprising then that this oracle has seldom been compared with the poems. This comparison I propose to make, but I shall first examine the Cyrus poems, for they too are part of Yahweh's politics and represent the kind of power politics that the Babylonians could understand.

Monotheism and Power: The Cyrus Poems

The Cyrus poems as listed by K. Elliger are 41:1-4; 41:21-29; 42:5-9;[18] 44:24-28; 45:1-7; 45:9-13; 46:9-11; 48:12-15.[19] These poems are closely related to the trial speeches discussed above, with some of them actually overlapping those speeches;[20] others use much of the same terminology and presuppose the same ideas.[21] The Cyrus event was an essential part of the argument of the trial speeches, for this was the future event predicted by Yahweh's prophet; it thus formed a continuity with his word-event argument of the past. The Cyrus poems are closely related, therefore, to Deutero-Isaiah's claim for the monotheism of Yahweh.[22]

In examining these poems, I ask two closely related questions: (1) What relationship has Cyrus to Yahweh? and (2) What is the task of Cyrus? For an answer I shall examine Isaiah 45:1-7,[23] one of the two poems where Cyrus is named, and draw on some of the others for additional information.[24]

What is Cyrus' relationship to Yahweh? As a monotheist, Deutero-Isaiah must relate Cyrus to Yahweh. He does this deliberately by calling him Yahweh's anointed (45:1), his shepherd (44:28). In this context, both of these terms refer to kingship.[25] They describe Cyrus as Yahweh's agent who exercises violent political power to achieve his purpose.[26] Deutero-Isaiah bases this claim upon the realism of faith and not upon a blind dogmatism which flies in the face of facts. His argument that Cyrus is Yahweh's agent exercising violent power politics is not in discontinuity with his previous word-fulfillment argument based upon Israel's historical experience. It is rather the climactic point of that argument. The Cyrus poems point to the present demonstration of the word-event continuity of Israel's political history. According to Deutero-Isaiah, kingship, which in the thought of the ancient Near East was the office of violent power politics through which the gods gave continuity to the community, was made subservient to Yahweh who gave continuity to his community not by power politics but by his creative power of word-event, of promise/threat-fulfillment!

To understand more precisely the character of this paradox, it is necessary to examine further the relationship of Cyrus to Yahweh as stated in 45:4,5:

> I surname you, though you do not know me.
> . . . .
> I gird you, though you do not know me....

The clause "though you do not know me" is repeated for emphasis.[27] To know Yahweh in the thought of Deutero-Isaiah meant to have a present trust in the tradition of Yahweh's creative word-event, a tradition that went back to the beginning of Israel and that was now demonstrated in his choice of Cyrus. It meant also to believe that Yahweh is God, as demonstrated by this tradition, and that the gods of Cyrus, who are ineffective in achieving continuity of community, are not God. Put in such terms, it is obvious that neither Cyrus nor the Persians knew Yahweh. Nor could they know him without a radical rejection of their past and a restructuring of communal priorities in line with Israel's faith. Deutero-Isaiah's point is that Yahweh is perfectly capable of choosing a man (Cyrus) whose faith and office are based upon the false and ineffective gods of power politics for the continuance of Yahweh's own community, which is founded and based upon his creative word-event.

To pursue the paradox further we must ask the second question: If Cyrus was chosen as Yahweh's power instrument, what was his task? It is defined in this oracle mainly as a negative task performed upon the nations (45:1-3), a task not too different from that of the Assyrians as visualized by Isaiah of Jerusalem (10:5) or of Nebuchadnezzar as stated by Jeremiah (25:9; 27:6).[28] This task is fittingly designated by the title, "a bird of prey from the east" (46:11). However, this negative task against the nations was not also against

Israel which could exercise no violent political power; the task was rather in Israel's behalf (45:4).[29] Cyrus' task for Israel is most positively expressed in 45:13:

> He shall build my city
>   and set my exiles free....

There is no indication whatsoever in Deutero-Isaiah's thought that Yahweh would use Cyrus as his servant to extend his just rule over the nations.[30] As we shall see, this task was given to Yahweh's servant, to Israel and to Israel alone. For this task, Deutero-Isaiah stripped Israel of kingship and made the people themselves heir to the Davidic covenant (55:3), reflecting perhaps an influence of the pre-kingship traditions of Israel.[31] The promise of that covenant was transformed, for they were to call to the nations and the nations were to run to Israel because of Yahweh their God (55:4,5).[32]

Is Deutero-Isaiah satisfied to let his monotheism rest with the denial of the gods of violent power politics and to make that power politics itself Yahweh's instrument for the new exodus of his people? How can he be satisfied when Israel's continuity is dependent upon his creative word-event? Such a solution is too dualistic for Deutero-Isaiah, even though he has brought that dualism under Yahweh. At the end of the Cyrus oracle he articulates this dualism under Yahweh, denying thereby the dualism of the Persians (or more likely that of the Babylonians); at the same time he stretches biblical-monotheism beyond previous limits.[33]

> I form light and create darkness;
>   I make weal and create woe;
>   I am Yahweh, who do all these things (45:7).

Such "dualistic monotheism" would be known to all people, "from the rising of the sun and from the west" (v. 6). In oracles other than the Cyrus poems, Deutero-Isaiah recognized the dissatisfaction with this solution of "dualistic monotheism" (45:11-13):[34]

> Thus says the Lord,
>   the Holy One of Israel, and his Maker.
> Will you question me about my children,
>   or command me concerning the work of my hands?
> I made the earth
>   and created man upon it;
> it was my hand that stretched out the heavens,
>   and I commanded all their host.
> I have aroused him in righteousness,
>   and I will make straight all his ways;
> he shall build my city
>   and set my exiles free,

> not for price or reward,
>   says the Lord of hosts (45:11-13).

By this address to Israel Deutero-Isaiah himself, and perhaps his disciple (vv. 9,10), acknowledged the incongruity of this thought with Yahweh monotheism. The Creator God, however, can save as he chooses, though his methods may be paradoxical to the unity of his character.

But Deutero-Isaiah sees beyond this disputed solution of dualistic monotheism to an ultimately consistent monotheism, answering Yahweh's invitation and oath addressed to the nations, the survivors of the chaos left in the wake of Cyrus' victories (45:22-25).[35] It is precisely the effecting of this oath, climaxing the trial speeches, which occupies Deutero-Isaiah in his presentation of the servant poems.

Monotheism, Power, and Justice: The Servant Poems

Historically the servant poems have been designated as Isaiah 42:1-6; 49:1-5; 50:4-9; 52:13-53:12.[36] These poems can be removed from the book without leaving a break, but this is true also of individual oracles in other prophetic books. The present tendency of scholarship is to understand these poems in relation to the rest of the book (chaps. 40-55). One might argue that the number of the servant poems should be enlarged to include all those poems in the book which deal with Yahweh's servant.[37] My task, however, relates to these four traditional poems since they alone of the servant poems have to do with Yahweh's rule of the nations. It is my purpose to show how these servant poems are an essential part of Deutero-Isaiah's concept of monotheism, an monotheism which rejected the gods of power politics for the unity of Yahweh who alone can provide continuity of community by the politics of creative word-event. Though he may use those who know only the false gods of violent power as agents for his word-event, Yahweh's consistent expression of the unity of the cosmos and history will one day be expressed only by fulfillment of his invitation and oath that to him "every knee shall bow, every tongue shall swear."

In the history of the interpretation of these poems the servant has been seen as Israel, as an individual within Israel, or as some combination of the two.[38] What all of these possibilities have in common, however, is that through Israel or one within Israel designated by Yahweh, the word-event tradition to which Israel witnesses (43:10) will become the heritage of the nations.

The four servant poems may have a formal unity as a biography of a public servant, the first dealing with his installation into public life, the last discussing his end and evaluating his service.[39] Besides this possible formal unity, the unity of their themes and even of their language has been noted.[40] We shall now list some of the important themes of the poems and compare them with those of the final trial speech, Isaiah 45:18-25:

(1) The servant is Yahweh's agent to the nations (42:1,4; 49:1-6; 52:15), whom the servant addresses in the second poem (49:1).

(2) His commissioned task is to bring Yahweh's justice to the nations (42:1-4).[41]

(3) Equipped with Yahweh's spirit, the servant is to effect his ministry non-violently by means of Yahweh's word (42:2-3; 49:2; 50:4,5).[42]

(4) The servant faces growing opposition, persecution, and death, which he accepts patiently in pursuit of his task (42:4; 49:4; 50:6-9; 52:13-53:12).

(5) The servant achieves his purpose of bringing justice to the nations only by Yahweh's intervention, who reversed the judgment of the nations and elevates him to a place of rule (49:4; 52:13-15; 53:11-12).

(6) The kings and nations confess their rebellion and acknowledge that the suffering of the servant is on their behalf, that by his stripes they are healed (53:1-10).

Comparing these themes with the trial speech of 45:18-25, we note the following parallels:

(1) The oracle is addressed also to the nations (45:20,22).

(2) The oath declares that every person in the nations would acknowledge Yahweh's rule (45:23; cf. point 6 above).

(3) The only effective means to accomplish this rule was Yahweh's word which went forth from his mouth. (The trial speech lacks points 4-5).

(4) Opposition and suffering are not mentioned. However, the oath of Yahweh suggests that the prophet was well aware of the odds which would need to be overcome if the vision were to be achieved.

(5,6) The method of achievement is not stated by the oracle. However, the oath suggests that Yahweh would need to intervene if the vision is to be achieved, and the invitation suggests that the nations must respond by their own volition.

A most important element lacking in the trial speech is that there is no servant, an ingredient essential to all the servant poems. However, the oracle addressed to the nations was articulated by the prophet (45:22), considered by some to be the servant of the servant poems. Perhaps more important, in the second trial speech Israel is designated as Yahweh's servant, the witness through whom his case would be won against the gods of the nations (43:8-13).

This comparison would suggest that the roots of the servant poems are already present in the trial speeches, especially the last trial speech, and that the poems were a further development of the logic of the monotheism which is expressed there. What is involved in Yahweh's intervention in 52:13-53:12 is the elevation of the servant which led the nations to acknowledge a new kind of political leadership and authority based upon a new kind of political power.[43] Thus not merely peripherally but centrally the servant poems answer to the monotheism of the trial speeches.

I now compare the themes of the servant poems with those of the Cyrus poems:[44]

(1) Both present one who is designated by Yahweh to a public office. Cyrus is designated as Yahweh's anointed; Israel or a representative of Israel is designated as Yahweh's servant. With this the similarity ends and contrasts begin.

(2) Cyrus does not know Yahweh and is his instrumnent of violence, his "bird of prey." Even his positive acts, the freeing of Israel and building of Jerusalem, are possible because of his acts of violence. In contrast, the servant has intimate knowledge of Yahweh, is equipped by spirit and word to achieve his task, and comes to his end by violence perpetrated upon him.

(3) After his victory over the nations Cyrus, as Yahweh's king, should have established Yahweh's justice. The Cyrus poems are cut short from their logical conclusion. Instead, the servant poems take up this logical conclusion lacking in the Cyrus poems. The servant is equipped with Yahweh's word, a characteristic of the prophet rather than the king, and he, rather than Cyrus, is elevated as Yahweh's ruler.

This point, so important for an understanding of the servant poems, merits elaboration. The kingly characteristics of the servant may explain the addition of 42:5-8 to the servant poem. Some scholars regard this as a Cyrus poem; others regard it as originally a Cyrus poem now adapted as a supplement to the servant poem, 42:1-4.[45] The cause of confusion may well be due to the kingly task of the servant. There is no reason why a later writer or Deutero-Isaiah himself could not have adapted a Cyrus poem to the servant since the servant himself fulfills that positive function of kingship from which Cyrus was cut short.

This function of the servant is stated emphatically in 42:1-4:
v. 1. he shall bring forth justice (*mišpāṭ*) to the nations
v. 3. he will faithfully bring forth justice
v. 4. he will not fail...till he has established justice in the earth.

What is meant here by justice (*mišpāṭ*)? The word may denote judgment, sentence, or decision by a court. It may denote the justice or rectitude of a judge or of God. It may denote an ordinance or decision of a judge, a custom, or a plan.[46] In the context of 42:1-4 it has been given a variety of meanings by scholars.[47] Elliger is probably on the right track when he relates the word as used here to "politics, divine politics."[48] It is definitely related to the rule of Yahweh in 51:4,5, a paraphrase of the first servant poem. This justice can be understood only in terms of the tradition of biblical *tôrâ* in which Deutero-Isaiah speaks, a tradition which places law within the structures of covenant and worship rather than within the structures of kingship and coercion.[49] The kingly task of the servant is not peripheral but is central to his person and is in direct competition to the reign of kingly rulers such as Cyrus. It is little wonder that the servant met with opposition, persecution, and death.

The final denouement of the servant poems in 52:13-53:12 is the elevation of the servant kingly rule, a rule achieved not through violence and oppression, but through suffering and death. However strong the emphasis on expiation and vicarious suffering might be, the main point of the last servant poem is the kingly rule of the servant.

(4) The final contrast of the servant poems with the Cyrus poems is that Deutero-Isaiah recognizes a certain incongruity in Cyrus fulfilling Yahweh's monotheistic rule over history and cosmos. Although Yahweh alone is God, Cyrus left Deutero-Isaiah with a dualism under Yahweh, and he felt it neces-

sary to justify to his people the call of Cyrus (45:7,9-13).

There is no embarrassing incongruity in the servant poems. They, rather than the Cyrus poems, bring the monotheistic claims of the trial speeches to a satisfactory conclusion. The servant's elevation is the fulfillment of Yahweh's oath in 45:23. The oath is fulfilled as kings and nations acknowledge Yahweh's act for them through the suffering of his servant.

Conclusion

This comparison of the trial speeches, the Cyrus poems, and the servant poems has shown that while the monotheistic claim of Yahweh embraces the unity of historical and cosmic purpose in all three groups of oracles, only in the servant poems does Yahweh's oath to the nations find fulfillment: He shall bring forth justice to the nations; the coastlands wait for his *tôrâ*. Even as Yahweh's anointed, Cyrus, acting in accord with violent power politics, could not fulfill the oath to bring history and the nations into the unity of the worship of the one Lord. Only the servant through his suffering fulfills this oath. Hence the unity of the cosmos and history under Yahweh's one rule is rooted in a moral claim and confession: the politics of violent power falls short of fulfilling Yahweh's oath and purpose; only a new politics, disclosed in the work and the way of the servant, establishes and fulfills Yahweh's oath. For in the servant's mission the moral quality of Yahweh's rule of *tôrâ*-justice guarantees the continuity of community and evokes the acclaim of the nations that Yahweh alone is God, creator and redeemer.

NOTES

1. H. Wildberger, "Der Monotheismus Deuterojesajas," *Beiträge zur alttestamentlichen Theologie: Festschrift für W. Zimmerli zum 70. Geburtstag* (ed. H. Donner et al.; Göttingen: Vandenhoeck & Ruprecht, 1977) 509 (my translation).

2. Commentators such as R. N. Whybray (Isaiah 40-66 [NCB; London: Oliphants, 1975] 31-32, 112) see the universalistic message of Deutero-Isaiah to be only that the nations, Israel's oppressors and idol-worshippers, would in the future be Israel's oppressors, a feat achieved not by Israel's conquest, but by the nations' astonishment at God's acts for Israel. Other commentators, however, see universalism as the participation of the nations in the land and cult of Yahweh through Israel; see J. L. McKenzie, *Second Isaiah* (AB 20; Garden City, NY: Doubleday, 1968) lvii, lxv-lxvi. This paper accepts the latter view.

3. For a statement of the relationship of these literary types to the unity of the Book of Isaiah as set forth in the history of scholarship, see C. Westermann, "Sprache und Struktur der Prophetie Deuterojesajas, Erster Teil: Der Stand der Diskussion," *Forschung am Alten Testament: Gesammelte Studien* (TBü 24; Munich: Kaiser, 1964) 92-117. My discussion supports the essential unity of Deutero-Isaiah.

4. This is H. D. Preuss's listing, who is careful to distinguish between the trial speech and the disputation. See *Deuterojesaja: Eine Einführung in seine Botschaft* (Neukirchen-Vluyn: Neukirchener-V., 1976) 22. C. Westermann (*Isaiah 40-66* [London: SCM, 1969] 63 n.b) lists five trial speeches: 41:1-5; 41:21-29; 43:8-15; 44:6-8; 44:20-25. For a listing of other polemics of Deutero-Isaiah against the gods, see H. D. Preuss, *Deuterojesaja*, 61.

5. See B. W. Anderson, "Exodus Typology in Second Isaiah," *Israel's Prophetic Heritage* (ed. B. W. Anderson and W. Harrelson; New York: Harper, 1962) 177-95.

6. See C. *Westermann*, Isaiah 40-66, 84-85.

7. Ibid., 15.

8. The effectiveness and quality of Yahweh's word are stated in Deutero-Isaiah's prologue and epilogue, thereby denoting its importance for him; cf. Isa. 40:8; 55:10-11.

9. See NET, (1969) 60-72. The same is true of the political document, "Theology of Memphis" (*Ibid.*, 4-6) which rationalized the victory of the god of Memphis over the god of the older Egyptian center, Heliopolis.

10. *Ibid.*, 164.

11. See BDB, 812.

12. The Babylonian clergy were capable of explaining the Cyrus event in terms of their own mythology; see "The Cyrus Stele" (ANET, 315-16).

13. It is not my intention to deal here with the question of whether or how the prophet actually addressed the nations, but to note that this address was made in a historical situation in which the nations might have been able to understand his argument. See C. Westermann, *Isaiah 40-66*, 174-76.

14. This is Deutero-Isaiah's only such invitation apart from the Servant poems. See also Isa. 45:14; 49:23; 55:9.

15. Paul cites this passage twice, Rom. 4:11; Phil 2:10-11.

16. C. Westermann, *Isaiah 40-66*, 176.

17. Deutero-Isaiah seems to be acquainted with Jeremiah's thought; see Isa. 55:6; Jer. 29:12-14.

18. We will look at this classification of 42:5-9 later.

19. K. Elliger, *Deuterojesaja* (BKAT II/1; Neukirchen-Vluyn: Neukirchener-V., 1978) 117.

20. 41:21-29 is one of the trial speeches cited above, while 41:1-4 is cited as a trial speech by C. Westermann, *Isaiah 40-66*, 63.

21. See C. Westermann, *ibid.*, 155.

22. See 41:4,26; 44:24-26; 45:5; 45:12-13; 46:9; 48:12-13.

23. Westermann (*Isaiah 40-60*, 154) regards 44:24-45:7 as a unit. If this is true, then the two namings of Cyrus are found in this single unit.

24. This poem is a "royal oracle," a type represented broadly in Near Eastern literature as well as in the OT (Psalm 2). See C. Westermann, *Isaiah 40-66*, 153-54.

25. For Israel's king as Yahweh's anointed, see Ps. 2:2; for the use of the figure of the shepherd for kingship, see Ezekiel 34.

26. See 44:24-28; 45:1.

27. K. Elliger (*Deuterojesaja* 497) regards this oracle as an editorial unification of two original oracles, both of which emphasized this point. Its repetition here, according to Elliger, suggests its importance as an answer.

28. *Ibid.*, 492.

29. This demonstrates from both sides Jesus' classic aphorism, "All who take the sword shall perish by the sword" (Matt. 26:52). Israel, which unlike the nations would not take the sword, being defenseless, would be saved by the Cyrus event (see 41:1-20).

30. Those commentators who hold that Deutero-Isaiah originally hoped for Cyrus' conversion and was later disillusioned base their thought on 41:25, "and he shall call on my name." If the MT is accepted, this single colon is a slender thread on which to build a theory of Deutero-Isaiah's later disillusionment. There is nothing in Deutero-Isaiah's thought to indicate that Yahweh would use Cyrus and the Persians as his servant in behalf of the nations. 1QIs[a] reads "and he called him by his name." See C. Westermann, *Isaiah 40-66*, 84. For further discussion of the textual problem, see K. Elliger, *Deuterojesaja*, 173.

31. Judg. 8:23; 9:7-15. I agree with K. Elliger (*Deuterojesaja*, 152-56), R. N. Whybray (*Isaiah 40-66*, 65), and others that nowhere does Deutero-Isaiah see Israel as subjugating the nations by violence. Isa. 41:15-16 should be interpreted in the light of 40:4 as smoothing out the difficulties of the return but not as taking over the Cyrus function. Israel's historical task as agent of Yahweh is not the conquest of the nations but the destruction of the historic symbols of idol worship, the pride of the nations.

32. This thought of Deutero-Isaiah which transforms the promise of the Davidic covenant (55:3-5) is recognized by C. Westermann as a radical readaptation of the Davidic covenant (*Isaiah 40-66*, 285-86), but once again he sees it as "taken out of the political sphere," a concept which results in a misunderstanding of Deutero-Isaiah's reordering of politics.

33. C. Westermann in his discussion (*Isaiah 40-66*, 161-62) wonders why v. 7 does not disturb commentators more than it does.

34. In its present form Isa. 45:9-10 should be included. The text presents difficulties and C. Westermann (*Isaiah 40-66*, 165-66) holds with K. Elliger (*Deuterojesaja*) that a genuine utterance of Deutero-Isaiah has been reshaped by a later editor. However that may be, 45:11-13 speaks to essentially the same objection as does 45:9-10.

35. See above for my discussion of this passage.

36. As is well known this designation was made by B. Duhm in 1892. For a brief history of the interpretation, see C. R. North, *The Second Isaiah* (Oxford: Clarendon, 1964) 20-22.

37. See D. N. Freedman, "The Slave of Yahweh," *Western Watch* 10 (March 1959) 1-19.

38. For a discussion of these interpretations, see J. L. McKenzie, *Second Isaiah*, xliii-lv.

39. This is an important contribution of K. Baltzer, "Zur formgeschichtlichen Bestimmung der Texte vom Gottes-Knecht im Deutero-Jesaja-Buch," *Probleme biblischer Theologie: Festschrift für Gerhard von Rad zum 70. Geburtstag* (Munich: Kaiser, 1971) 27-43.

40. See C. Westermann, *Isaiah 40-66*, 92, 256, 258 and H. D. Preuss, *Deuterojesaja*, 94-96.

41. I discuss the meaning of this justice below.

42. Isa. 42:2-3 may refer to the concept that the servant's message was to be one of salvation instead of the usual oracle of prophetic doom; see K. Elliger, *Deuterojesaja*, 208-11.

43. The antecedent of the first person plural is debated. However, I think that C. Westermann (*Isaiah 40-66*, 260) is right when he points up the close relationship of the report (53:1-11, esp. v. 1) to 52:13-15.

44. Recent writers have been preoccupied with who the servant is but have seldom emphasized his contrast to Cyrus. For this contrast, see J. L. McKenzie, *Second Isaiah*, xlviii; M. Haller, "Die Kyros-Lieder Deuterojesajas, "*Eucharisterion: Studien zur Religion und Literatur des Alten und Neuen Testaments; Hermann Gunkel zum 60. Geburtstage, dem 23. Mai 1922 dargebracht...* (FRLANT 36; Göttingen: Vandenhoeck & Ruprecht, 1923), 1. 261-77; J. Hempel, "Vom irrenden Glauben,"ZST 7 (1929) 631-60. Mowinckel states the contrast in some detail, regarding the servant poems as the work of Deutero-Isaiah's disciples:

> Deutero-Isaiah had intended that Cyrus should lead back the exiles, and gather together the dispersed. In these Songs, it is the Servant who is to do this [n. Isa. 42:7; 45:13; with 49:5ff.]. For Deutero-Isaiah it is Cyrus whom Yahweh has 'called by name,' and who will 'fulfil Yahweh's will.' In the Songs, it is the Servant who has been called by Yahweh and entrusted with this mission [n. Isa. 45:3f.; 44:28, contrasted with 49:1; 53:10]. Deutero-Isaiah had thought that Cyrus would 'bring forth right order' by his sword [n. Isa. 41:2f; 42:6; 54:13)...
> In the Songs it is the Servant who will 'bring forth right religion' (judgment, right order) 'by his quiet and patient preaching' (42:1ff)... In short, what Deutero-Isaiah regarded and expected as a work of 'Yahweh's Anointed, Cyrus,' or as a direct result of the revelation of Yahweh's mighty power, to be seen in the fall of the Chaldean empire and the victories of Cyrus, all this the author of the Servant Songs expected to come from the Servant's prophetic preaching, his patient, vicarious, atoning suffering, and death, and the resurrection which Yahweh would grant to His 'righteous" Servant, in vindicating him before the eyes of all the world. Sometimes word for word, the poems echo thoughts and expressions from Deutero-Isaiah's preaching about Cyrus, and apply them to the Servant.... The Servant has been set up as a contrast to Cyrus, and, in general, as a contrast to the way in which the mode of restoration is presented in Deutero-Isaiah" (*He that Cometh* [New York: Abingdon, 1954] 244-46).

45. See H. D. Preuss, *Deuterojesaja*, 95.

46. See BDB, 1048-49. The word occurs eleven times in Isaiah 40-55, three times in the first Servant Song and once in each of the others (49:4; 50:8; 53:8). Since it also occurs once in a paraphrase of the first Song (51:4), it thus occurs only four times outside of the Servant Songs and related material.

47. See K. Elliger, *Deuterojesaja*, 206-10.

48. *Ibid.*, 206-7.

49. See my article, "Law in the Old Testament," *Occasional Papers* 3 (Elkhart, IN:

Institute of Mennonite Studies, 1982) 9-41, in this volume chapter number six.

III. WAR AND ECONOMICS

CHAPTER 14

PERSPECTIVES ON WAR AND PEACE IN THE HEBREW SCRIPTURES

My assignment is to give perspectives on war and peace in the Hebrew Scriptures which may be of important concern to contemporary communities of faith. Contemporary concern should prompt those who believe in the authority of Scripture to do careful, honest historical exegesis. At the same time, I would complain with Hans Walter Wolff that the exegetical work already done ought to have produced more unity among Christians on the question of disarmament than presently exists. Everybody wants peace; from this point of view, most everyone is a pacifist. But the real question is, how is this peace to be achieved?[1]

With this complaint before us, let us look at Scriptural perspectives on war and peace, first in the primary history (Genesis--Kings), and then in several of the prophetic books. A look at the Writings would also be profitable, but that takes me beyond the scope of my present investigation and time limits.

I. THE PRIMARY HISTORY

A. Yahweh's War, Yahweh's Kingship

Although there is a great deal of warfare and violence in the Hebrew Scriptures, a scholarly consensus exists that the war narratives are characterized by the exclusive prerogative of Yahweh's fighting and a denial of the efficacy of human fighting.[2] While all narratives are affected by this concept, many narratives present the case not as trust in Yahweh *and* human fighting, but trust in Yahweh which *excludes* human fighting.

Although there is scholarly unanimity on this important characteristic of Yahweh's war as presented in the war narratives, there is little agreement as to its explanation. Generally, three explanations are given. The first is that the piety of later centuries changed the tradition from synergism (that is, faith in God's miraculous action which resulted in humans fighting all the harder), to the present concept of the texts, a faith in divine miracle resulting in the ineffi-

---

Paper read at Society of Biblical Literature, Atlanta, Georgia, 1986.

cacy and even the unfaithfulness of human war activity.[3] A second explanation: this phenomenon was due to the influence of Near Eastern mythology upon the war narratives, mythology in which the gods won the battle over chaos (Enuma Elish, Memphite theology, Baal Epic), and that this as well as other important characteristics of biblical warfare is held in common with Near Eastern battle accounts.[4] The third explanation asserts that the Near Eastern war literature is only superficially comparable to the biblical war narratives on this issue. Israel's self-understanding was rooted in miraculous interventions in its early history, especially the miraculous experience of deliverance from Egypt, which formed the fundamental paradigm for Israel's subsequent interpretation of history, the history of a minority power among great coalitions of city states.

As you may know, in my book, *Yahweh is a Warrior*, I argue for the third position. I indicate that generally Israel's war literature, from the twelfth century poems through the tenth, ninth, eighth century narratives to the seventh-sixth century deuteronomic and deuteronomistic sources, points back to this first experience of deliverance as the event upon which later expectation and understanding was founded.[5] Congruent with this faith was Israel's social and political *minority* experience, stated so well by the Deuteronomist (that Israel was the least of the nations, Deut. 7:6-8) but apparent already in the patriarchal stories (Gen. 12:10-20, J). Furthermore, Israel did not live in a vacuum but within the general milieu of Near Eastern society, a society which had war concepts of miraculous deliverances, present in Assyrian, Hittite and other annals, though not radicalized as in Israel.

Important to this thesis is the early date of Exodus 15, which a growing number of scholars date approximately contemporaneous with the event.[6] Though important as a primary witness and as evidence to Israel's early understanding of Yahweh's fighting for Israel, the early dating is not necessarily essential to the thesis. My use of Martin Noth's argument for the historicity of the Sea event makes this evident. (His view is that though the various sources of the story of the sea miracle disagree in their representation of the details of the event, all agree on the essential element "in speaking of an act of God in which it was God alone who acted....")[7] My citing of Martin Noth further suggests that a conservative view of Israel's early history is not essential to the thesis; although Noth's view converges with the conservative view at the point of the Sea miracle, Noth does hold a rather minimal view of Israel's early history, that the unity of the exodus and Sinai tradition is due to an event of oral tradition in the time of the judges rather than to historical continuity in the wilderness period. For an historical assessment of his position the date of Exodus 15 is decisive, but the point I am making here is that a conservative view of Israel's early history, though compatible with, is not essential to my thesis.

Instead of lying between a "conservative" and "minimal" view of Israel's early history, the issue lies then between a "mythologized" view and an "historical" view (von Rad vs. M. Noth). Arguing for the "omnicompetence of analogy," von Rad held that Israel's beginnings were much the same as those of other nations, that in the case of the Sea event Israel fought hard, just as other peoples had done, and that the present text is due to later theological reflection that reconstructed history.[8] He maintained that the Sea episode was reconstructed by J as a result especially of the Solomonic "enlightenment" which reflected the influence of international wisdom literature on Israelite tradition. He maintained that the principle of Yahweh's prerogative to fight for Israel did not enter into Israel's historical situation until Isaiah, who, mistaking the 10th century mythologized history for the real event of Israel's early experience, counseled Ahaz and Hezekiah to deal with an historical situation according to the post-tenth century mythologization.[9] Martin Noth, on the other hand, held to an "historical" view of early Israel, that is, "at the very centre of the history of 'Israel' we encounter phenomena for which there is no parallel at all elsewhere, not because the material for comparison has not yet come to light but because, so far as we know, such things have simply never happened elsewhere."[10]

These divergent views of Israel's early history are profoundly significant not only for the past, but for the continuing political strategy of the faith community. Assuming that he is correct in his assessment of Isaiah's message, had von Rad been present in Isaiah's meeting with Ahaz, would he not have felt morally bound to correct Isaiah's presuppositions? Would he not have felt pressed to support the politics of Ahaz? Was not the independence of the prophet and Judah from the power politics of Ahaz dependent upon the reality of another kind of experience of power?[11]

Assuming the correctness of the intervention thesis, it is not surprising that Ahaz, Hezekiah and other kings rejected it (Isa. 7; 31:1-5). The surprising point is that this early intervention of Yahweh, rooted in the authentic memory and tradition of the community, remained throughout Israel's history the "canon" by which Israel's political policies were to be determined and evaluated.

This early emphasis upon Yahweh's miracle is accompanied with the substitution of warrior by prophetic word in Israel's wars. This is succinctly stated already in the 8th century by Hosea:

> By a prophet Yahweh brought Israel up from Egypt, and by a
> prophet he was preserved (Hos. 12:13).[12]

This tradition is corroborated by the prophetic figure of Moses in the earliest narrative traditions of the exodus, and makes very good sense if indeed a human warrior was not involved in the historical event. The unusual place of the prophet in Israel's war may thus be due to Israel's early history rather than to von Rad's claim of a later "spiritualization."[13] This substitution by ancient Israel of prophetic word and activity for the activity of warrior has major implications for handling conflict today.

B. Yahweh's Kingship

A second major point in my argument is that this principle of warfare

(Yahweh's prerogative) is inseparable from a specific theory of Israel's government. It is generally recognized that the Song of the Sea follows the pattern of the Baal epic. After Baal defeats Yam, a palace is built for him and he becomes king. So in Exodus 15, "Yahweh is a warrior" (v. 3) forms an inclusio with "Yahweh will reign forever and ever" (v. 18). Yahweh the warrior becomes Yahweh the king. Unlike the presuppositions of the Baal epic, however, (cf. the KRT Legend), Yahweh the king has no parallel human king. This testimony of the early poetry to the unparalleled kingship of Yahweh is supported by other traditions: Gideon's rejection of the Shechem offer (Judg. 8:22-23), Jotham's parable in which the trees reject the office (Judg. 9:7-15), the three speeches of Samuel at Rama, Mizpah, and Gilgal (1 Sam. 8; 10; 12). All three of Samuel's speeches connect the demand for human kingship with the rejection of the rule of Yahweh who had delivered Israel from Egypt (8:7-8; 10:18-19; 12:8-12). The sociologists have shown this early government of Israel to be quite plausible by their analyses of pre-industrial societies.[14]

What Yahwism rejected was "kingship like all the nations," that is, divinity mediated on the human scene chiefly by one who represented the "Enlil function," the violent power function.[15] Instead, Yahweh reserved the Enlil function to the divine self and was in immediate covenant relation to Israel, a covenant mediated by a prophetic type of person. The law codes of the Pentateuch (the law of Yahweh) were never reoriented to Israel's kingship. Characteristic of this law was the motive clause, Egyptian deliverance being the most used clause, an attempt to "write law upon the heart" (Cf. Ex. 22:21; Deut. 15:15).

This covenant structure of ancient Israel, and the fact that law and justice were found within such a structure rather than that of kingship, has profound meaning for social ethics; it is the foundation for both Synagogue and Ekklesia as independent legal entities with quite different structures from those of the state.

These two emphases, deliverance and justice, are brought together by the editor of the book of Exodus in chapter 18.[16] In the first part of this chapter (vss. 1-12), the word "to deliver," *nāṣal*, is used five times, looking backward to the deliverance from Egypt. Acknowledgement of this deliverance is the basis for foreign relations, shalom between Jethro and Israel (vv. 7-12). In the second part of the chapter (vv. 13-27), looking forward to Sinai, the word *šāpaṭ*, "to judge," is used six times, and is the basis for domestic relations, shalom between the households of Israel (v. 23).

II. THE PROPHETS

A. Introduction

Hugo Winckler (1903) began the German debate on the prophets and politics by proposing that all the great prophets were in the employ of the enemy: Isaiah in the employ of Assyria; Jeremiah, of Babylon; Amos, promoter of the policies of Uzziah (as the Bethel priest had charged). This dramatic thesis focused the attention of the German debate for this century, a debate which not only reveals much about the prophets but also reflects the political vicissitudes of Germany. In general, two positions are taken in this debate, that the prophet's political view was determined mainly by religion, or that it was determined mainly by political realism.[17]

E. Troeltsch (1917), widening the debate from the political to the social arena, set the pace for most of the conversations with the thesis that the prophets were "utopian," that is, that their politics was determined mainly by their religious view. K. Elliger, on the other hand, argued against the utopian view, claiming that the prophet was a "pneumatic realist," one who by religious experiences had gained a "long view" with unparalleled sobriety and objectivity for making political decisions; indeed, "the prophets were genuine politicians and even greater than their counterparts in the most varied times."[18]

H. Donner, Walter Dietrich and Freidrick Huber are among the first German scholars to take a careful exegetical approach to this question, working especially with Isaiah.[19] These all agree that the most basic influence upon the prophet was the religious. Dietrich and Huber conclude that the prophet Isaiah was essentially a pacifist (of his own variety), that Isaiah's exhortation to trust in Yahweh excluded any preparation for war by Judah's effectively arming itself or by making treaties with other nations.[20] Having worked carefully through the Hosean and Isaianic texts myself, I concur with this conclusion.

B. Isaiah and Hosea

Isaiah's message assumed that Judah was at the center of the nations: that the Assyrian threat against Judah was Yahweh's punishment for oppression of Judah's lower classes (Isa. 1-5); that Ahaz in 734/33 B.C.E. was not to enter into coalition with Assyria against the two Northern confederates (Isa. 7-8); that Hezekiah in 713-11 B.C.E. was not to join the Philistine-Egyptian coalition against Assyria (Sargon, Isa. 30:1-5); that Hezekiah in 705-3 B.C.E. was not to enter into treaty with Egypt against Assyria (Sennacherib, Isa. 31:1-3); and in that the end the arrogance of Assyria's claim to lead history would be punished by Yahweh's intervention (Isa. 10). Yahweh's first concern was justice for the weak, and only by reliance in isolated military weakness upon Yahweh's righteous strength could Judah expect Yahweh's political salvation.

As a successful policy of political self-interest must be guided realistically in the historical situation by power oriented wise men, so successful political reliance upon Yahweh required a wisdom informed not only by Yahweh's past acts of justice but also by a knowledge of the present political situation. Isaiah's foreign policy based on trust in Yahweh was the realistic foreign policy rather than the misguided "realistic" power politics of Ahaz or Hezekiah (who were unsuccessful). Based in the first instance on religion (trust in Yahweh, excluding effective military armaments and coalitions), it was a trust related successfully by the prophet to the political situation of the times. The only alternative realistic foreign policy based on political realism would have been that of the later Manasseh, complete subjection to Assyrian domination.

Isaiah 2:1-4 propounds that this break of Jerusalem from the power politics of Egypt and Assyria was not intended to isolate the city in a political ghetto, but was occasioned because Jerusalem was to lead the nations in a new international politics of voluntary obedience to Yahwistic torah, a politics which would render obsolete the sword and military college.[21]

Since Hosea's foreign policy (no arms race and no alliances with political power blocks) was remarkably similar to that of Isaiah, though based on a quite different northern theology, it must be assumed that both had a common earlier tradition, which necessarily must have been a pre-kingship tradition. Three common sources of this pre-kingship tradition may be pointed to:

1. A common source in Near Eastern mythology of warfare (Weippert).[22] This is inadequate because in Assyrian texts human and divine action are not mutually exclusive, but supplement each other.[23]

2. A common source in the anti-monarchic tradition of Shilo (1 Sam. 8-12). This northern tradition was directly available to Hosea and indirectly available to Isaiah through the ark tradition and the Zion tradition based upon it (cf. Pss. 46, 48, and 76). [24]

3. A common source in the traditions of holy war which ascribe victory solely to Yahweh's miraculous intervention.[25]

As I have noted in *Yahweh Is a Warrior*, options 2 and 3 are not mutually exclusive but are connected by the tradition and thus form the common root of the Hosea-Isaiah traditions. Von Rad sees Isaiah's tradition as rooted in the post-Solomonic novelistic presentation of Yahweh war,[26] which then cannot explain Hosea's similar position to that of Isaiah. Huber, agreeing with von Rad, contends that holy war as a source is inadequate "for it is universally accepted that this presentation does not correspond to the historical events."[27] It is curious that this denial is made on the basis of a "universally" held dogma. But as I have shown above, this dogma is not universally held. Those who accept the early date of Exodus 15 will find the roots of Hosea-Isaiah's position contemporary to the exodus event.[28] Those who do not accept this early date may accept the judgment of Martin Noth as to the essential historicity of the exodus accounts, with the first extant statement of the Hosea-Isaiah principle then made by J[29] (Ex. 14:13-14). The "anti-Enlil" power traditions of both Hosea and Isaiah point toward the essential authenticity of texts which witness to this phenomenon prior to kingship.

I have spent considerable time discussing Isaiah and Hosea to establish that both had a foreign policy based on their religion: trust in Yahweh, which excluded an arms race and integration into Near Eastern power politics. Isaiah 2:1-4 presented this policy not as a politics designed to isolate Jerusalem from the nations, but as the way to a new future for the nations.

It is from the perspective of this religious principle that we are to understand the foreign policies of Jeremiah, Ezekiel, Deutero-Isaiah, the book of Daniel, and finally of Jesus. Having said that, this does not mean that their policies were the same as those of Hosea-Isaiah, for this principle of trust must be worked out realistically in each political situation, just as the "wise men" who give themselves to the principle of self interest and balance of power must work out their principle in each new situation. In this essay we can give only brief perspectives of the policies of the prophets and literature listed above.

C. Jeremiah

In his oracles Jeremiah unlike Isaiah never advocated a foreign policy of complete independence from the foreign empires. We have no evidence that he cooperated with Josiah's reform, though he prophesied to Samaria, advocating a return to the rule of Yahweh on Zion (3:6-18). From the beginning of his ministry he scored Judah for its rebellion and prophesied that Yahweh would bring judgment from the North (4:5-31:6), a threat later identified with Babylon (25:8-9). In the temple sermon, Jeremiah emphasized that the people could remain in the land if they executed justice with one another, especially with the economically and politically weak and if they were loyal to Yahweh only (7:1-15). Like Hosea and Isaiah, Jeremiah opposed integration into a Western political power block, in this policy opposing the foreign envoys in Jerusalem, King Zedekiah, the prophet Hananiah, and the prophets and exiles in Babylon (Jer. 27-29; see also 2:14-19). When the revolt came, Jeremiah advocated surrender to Babylon (38:1-6).

For Jeremiah the future lay not with the power oriented nations, for Babylon itself would sink like a stone in the Euphrates. The future lay with Yahweh's new act of covenant with the people, a community in which law would be written upon the heart (31:31-34). Foreign nations would bless themselves with the Abrahamic blessing if Judah would be faithful to Yahweh's way of justice (4:1-2). The neighboring nations would be gathered back to their lands along with Israel as they learn the way of God's people and as they learn to swear by Yahweh's name (12:14).

Like Moses (as defined by Hosea) the prophet was to be the warrior of Yahweh's word, appointed over nations and kingdoms, "to pluck up and breakdown...to build and to plant (1:10)." He became "a fortified city, iron pillar and bronze walls" against kings, princes, priests and people (1:18).

D. Ezekiel

Ezekiel stated the prophetic protest against military relations with foreign nations succinctly and forcefully in an historical review of Samaria and Jerusalem's harlotrous relations with the great empires: Egypt, Assyria, Babylon, Egypt (chap. 23). He likened the harlotry of this military diplomacy to the harlotry of idol worship (see also chap. 16).[30] Despite, or perhaps because of this "utopian" concern, Ezekiel was ever a realist, as his politics in chapter 17 and 19 reveal.[31] Zedekiah, Jerusalem and the exiles were not to revolt against Babylon.

As with Jeremiah, the future lay not with Babylon but with Israelite exiles to whom Yahweh would give a new heart and spirit, causing them to walk in the divine statutes (Ezek. 36). Dealing with Israel *individually*, Yahweh would make of them an obedient *community*. The nations, represented by Gog, would be destroyed in Israel's land by Yahweh's intervening act (38-39). Ezekiel had no positive word for the nations other than that by Yahweh's dealings with Israel and with them, they would know that Yahweh, unrepresented by Judah's armies, is God. Israel's political future would be a temple community, centering in Jerusalem (40-48).

E. Deutero-Isaiah

Deutero-Isaiah's emphasis on monotheism is closely related to the question of violent Enlil power.[32] The gods of Babylon and of Persia, who had proved themselves by power of conquest, are no-gods (45:20-21). Yahweh of the defeated Hebrews, who had prophesied their defeat as well as the defeat of the Babylonians, is God alone, a claim based on the efficacy of Yahweh's word in history, rather than armies (45:20-25). But the anomaly of Yahweh's monotheism was a political dualism, for there were two divine representatives in history, Cyrus and Israel (or a representative of Israel). Cyrus was Yahweh's shepherd (anointed, 44:28-45:1), Yahweh's bird of prey from the East (46:11) who would rebuild Jerusalem and its temple and would return Israel to its land (45:13).

Cyrus, however, does not become Yahweh's "king of justice," the historical logic of any Near East conqueror. This is the task of Israel, Yahweh's servant, who on the chaos of Babylon's defeat, is sent to the nations to proclaim Yahweh's justice (Isa. 42:1-4). This justice is to be established, not by force of Cyrus' arms, but by Yahweh's word, by the suffering and death (?) of the servant. By a special revelation the kings and nations become aware of who the servant is, and accept his elevation to rule (52:13-53:12) Like Isaiah 2:1-4, Yahweh's torah goes international, and displaces Cyrus's violent power as the basis for the peace of the international community:

> Turn to me and be saved
> all the ends of the earth.
> By myself I have sworn,
> from my mouth has gone forth in righteousness
> a word that shall not return:
> "To me every knee shall bow,
> every tongue shall swear" (Isa. 45:22-23).

The illogical political dualism of Yahweh monism will one day come to an end.

F. Daniel

The book of Daniel may be understood as a series of political tracts which set forth an alternative to the Maccabees for resisting Greek culture.[33] The book forms a unit. Chapter 7 envisions Yahweh's judgment of the four empire beasts and the elevation of the son of man to place of rule. This dominion of Yahweh, however, which is to be achieved at the end of time (Dan. 7-12), is to be acknowledged by the great empires in the present by means of the martyr witness of the faithful and by Yahweh's intervention (Dan. 1-6).

Conclusion

My assignment was to give perspectives for peace from the Hebrew Scriptures. I have given only one perspective. From the book of Exodus through those of the Prophets, there may be found a shared principle based upon a corporate religious experience: trust in God which excludes both reliance upon armaments and integration into the power community. This trust is that obedience to the word of Yahweh rather than self-interest backed by violent power will pacify the nations, and will provide the base for a new system of justice.

It is beyond the scope of this paper to point up how this principle informed the vision of Jesus and the early Church (and that of Yohannan ben Zakkai), a principle they incorporated into the life of their contemporary communities. I leave it to you to decide what a commitment to this religious principle may mean for the faithful in terms of a realistic social and political policy for the human crisis today, a realism which may include the sacrifice of the servant, but a sacrifice made in the conviction that God will intervene even beyond death, that the God who rules not by military might but by word and spirit is lord of the political arena.

NOTES

1. Hans Walter Wolff, "Swords into Ploughshares, Misuse of a Word of Prophecy?" Trans. by Gary Stansell, *Currents in Theology and Mission*, 12 (1983), 133-147.

2. See my discussion on the scholarly positions in *Yahweh is a Warrior* (Scottdale, PA: Kitchener, Ont.: Herald Press, 1980), 24-31.

3. An example of this position is Patrick D. Miller, Jr., *The Divine Warrior in Early Israel* (Cambridge, Mass.: Harvard University Press, 1973), 209 n. 1. Miller has since changed his point of view. See his review of "Yahweh Is a Warrior," *Biblical Archaeologist*, 44 (1981), 188-189.

4. See Fritz Stolz, *Jahwes und Israels Krieg* (Zürich: Theologischer Verlag,1972), 153-154, who argues that the idea of divine power as contrasted with human powerlessness originated in such myths as the *Enuma Elish* and ancient Near Eastern hymnic literature where the god alone wins the victory. Manfred Weippert points up that this and other features emphasized by von Rad's work on holy war in Israel are found as well in Assyrian literature, that this feature has a mythological origin--Manfred Weippert, "'Heiliger Krieg' in Israel und Assyrien: Kritische Anmerkungen zu Gerhard von Rads Konzept des 'Heiligen Krieges im alten Israel,'" ZAW, 84; (1972), 460-493 .

5. Millard C. Lind, *Yahweh...*, especially pp. 74, 77-87.

6. For a general statement and literature, see David Noel Freedman, "Prolegomenon" in George Buchanan Gray, *The Forms of Hebrew Poetry* ([New York]: Ktav Publishing House, 1972), vii-lvi. Albright, Freedman and Cross were pioneers in this work. For recent scholarship, see David A. Robertson, *Linguistic Evidence in Dating Early Hebrew Poetry* (Missoula, Mont: Society of Biblical Literature, 1972).

7. Martin Noth, *Exodus* (Phila: The Westminster Press, 1962), 119.

8. Gerhard von Rad, *Old Testament Theology*, vol. I, trans. by D. M. G. Stalker (Edinburgh, London: Oliver and Boyd, 1962), 107, esp. n. 3.

9. Gerhard von Rad, *Der heilige Krieg im alten Israel* (Göttingen: Vandenhoeck & Ruprecht, 1952), 33-62.

10. Martin Noth, *The History of Israel* (2nd ed., rev. Eng. trans., New York: Harper & Brothers, 1960), 2,3.

11. H. L. Ginsburg prefers Ahaz rather than Isaiah as the politician to be followed by modern Israel: Don't leave everything to God except where there is nothing you can do for yourself. Fight a holding action against the north, pray, send a gift to Assyria. H. L. Ginsburg, *The Supernatural in the Prophets with Special Reference to Isaiah* (The Goldensen Lecture, 1978, Hebrew Union College, 1979).

12. RSV, except that *Yahweh* is used instead of *the Lord*.

13. von Rad, *Der heilige Krieg...*, 67-78.

14. See Norman A. Gottwald, *The Tribes of Yahweh, a Sociology of the Religion of Liberated Israel, 1250-1050 BCE* (SCM Press, LTD, 1979) 237-386. Georg Fohrer and others correctly rejected Martin Noth's concept of amphictyony, but not having any structure to replace it argued that there was no pre-kingship federation--Georg Fohrer, *History of Israelite Religion* (Nashville, New York: Abingdon Press, 1972), 89ff. An understanding of mišpaḥa, bêt ʾab, and cross-cutting associations such as the Levites who taught Yahwistic law and had occasional all-Israelite worship experiences by celebrating Yahweh's covenant with Israel, gives other possibilities. For a

sociological contribution to the understanding of the prophet, see David Charles Hester, "Authority Claims and Social Legitimation in the Book of Jeremiah" (Dissertation, Duke University, 1982).

15. See the introduction to the Code of Hammurabi in Pritchard, *Ancient Near Eastern Texts*, p. 164.

16. There is general agreement that Exodus 18 forms a basic unity, with only occasional signs of duplication. Most commentators ascribe the chapter to E, though some detect J influence. See Brevard S. Childs, *The Book of Exodus* (Philadelphia: The Westminster Press, 1974), 321.

17. Some of the names are: Hugo Winckler (1903), F. Küchler (1906), W. Staerk (1908), F. Wilke (1913), E. Troeltsch (1917), F. Weinrich (1932), K. Elliger (1935), H. J. Kraus (1952), E. Wurthwein (1954), H. Donner (1964), F. Huber (1976), W. Dietrich (1976). For summary statements and bibliographies of this debate, see Karl Elliger, "Prophet und Politik," ZAW, 53 (1935), 3-22; Walter Dietrich, *Jesaja und die Politik*,247-255.

18. Elliger, "Prophet...," 22.

19. Herbert Donner, *Israel unter den Völkern;die Stellung der klassischen Propheten des 8. Jahrhunderts v. chr. zur Aussenpolitik der Könige von Israel und Juda* (Leiden: E. J. Brill,1964); Dietrich, *Jesaja und die Politik*; Friedrick Huber, *Jahwe, Juda und die anderen Völker beim Propheten Jesaja* (Berlin, New York: Walter de Gruyter, 1976).

20. Dietrich, *Jesaja und die Politik*, 263-268, 289; Huber, *Jahwe, Juda...*, 138-139.

21. Wildberger.

22. See note 4.

23. See Huber, *Jahwe, Juda...*, 220.

24. Ben C. Ollenburger, *Zion, the City of the Great King, A Theological Symbol of the Jerusalem Cult*, (Journal for the study of the Old Testament, Supplement Series 41, 1987), 129-144..

25. Von Rad regards the holy war traditions as the source of Isaiah's concept, but not of Hosea's, since the holy war traditions were revised to their present state after the time of Solomon. If these traditions, essentially as they now stand, are pre-kingship, then they are a source of the Hosea-Isaiah tradition. See Lind, *Yahweh Is a Warrior*, 34. Also, David Noel Freedman, "Strophe and Meter in Exodus 15," *A Light unto My Path: Old Testament Studies in Honor of Jacob M. Myers*, ed. by Howard N. Bream, et. al. (Philadelphia: Temple University Press, 1974), 193.

26. See note 7, 8.

27. Huber, *Jahwe, Juda...*, 223; this translation was arrived at in consultation with Elizabeth Horsch Bender.

28. See Freedman, "Strophe and Meter...," 193.

29. See note 9 and Martin Noth as cited by Lind, *Yahweh is a Warrior*, 55-56.

30. For an exegesis of Ezekiel 23, and Ezekiel's fundamental principle of trust in Yahweh which excluded foreign military treaties, see Bernhard Lang, *Kein Aufstand in Jerusalem, Die Politik des Propheten Ezechiel* (Stuttgart: Verlag Katholisches Bibelwerk, 1978), 184-185.

31. See Lang, *Kein Aufstand...*, 28-131.

32. I draw here from my article, "Monotheism, Power, and Justice: A Study in Isaiah 40-55," *The Catholic Biblical Quarterly* 46 (1984) 432-446.

33. John J. Collins, *The Apocalyptic Vision of the Book of Daniel* (Missoula, Montana: Scholars Press for Harvard Semitic Museum, 1977) 191-215.

CHAPTER 15

PARADIGM OF HOLY WAR IN THE OLD TESTAMENT

In the Old Testament holy war and faith in the miracle of Yahweh are joined together; in some passages they are essentially one and the same.[1] Although this relationship is more apparent in some battle accounts than in others, it underlies all of Israel's understanding of holy war. In a time of military crisis, Israel was to have faith that Yahweh would act in a decisive way on her behalf. Other ancient Near Eastern peoples also believed that their gods would act for them in warfare.[2] However, they did not develop a concept that the army was therefore not to fight. Rather, because the gods fought, the army was to fight all the harder. In Israel, on the other hand, the miracle of Yahweh was so decisive that sword and spear were not efficacious for winning the battle.[3] In the Exodus from Egypt, the foundational event of Israel's history, faith demanded, not that the Israelites were to fight all the harder, but that they were to "stand still and see the victory of Yahweh."[4] It is my purpose to examine this unique concept in relation to Israel's early literature, and to discuss its possible origin. To delineate the issue further, it is necessary to give a short resume of the history of research on this subject.

Review of Works on Holy War

This unique concept of Israel's holy war was recognized in the first extensive treatment of this subject, that of Friederich Schwally in 1901.[5] For Schwally, the origin of Israel's concept was not due to an event of Israel's prehistory. He held that while Israel, like all other primitive peoples, believed in the magic value of the battle-cry, this did not mean that weapons were unnecessary, but that the warriors were duty bound to fight all the harder. Schwally believed the origin of Israel's unique concept (that the warrior was not to fight) was due to a theological event, a late Jewish reinterpretation of the ancient battles by writers whose purpose was to edify the community by emphasizing divine help, and who had therefore lost the realism of the earlier period. This explained for Schwally how these writings expressed the pietistic thought that the warrior bore the sword but did not need to use it, that shout-

---

From *Biblical Research*, 1971.

ing and trumpet blowing are better than shield and spear.[6]

Johannes Pedersen also acknowledged this peculiar aspect of Old Testament battle narratives, and like Schwally accounted for its origin not in an event but in a theological reinterpretation. Pedersen held that sword, spear, and lance were of great importance in early Israel, but the proper psychic force was of infinitely greater importance; both Israel and the enemy were under this same law.[7] Pedersen goes on to state, however, that by a slight change the narrator created a new picture of war from the old elements. Pedersen held that this corresponds to a change in the whole conception of divine action, a change of great importance for Israel's understanding of God and man. This new conception of Yahweh's activity in war is found "in the whole history of Israel's campaigns from the Exodus from Egypt to the conquest of Canaan (Ex. 14:24; 17:8ff; 23:27; Deut. 2:15; Josh. 10:10f; 24:12, etc.)."[8]

Gerhard von Rad's work on holy war dominates the present literature on the subject.[9] Von Rad points out that in some passages of the Old Testament holy war and absolute miracle are essentially equated.[10] Although he criticizes Schwally and Pedersen for regarding ancient Israel as too primitive a society,[11] he agrees with them that this recurrent emphasis of the Old Testament (that Israel was not to fight, that her fighting was inefficacious) was due to a theological reinterpretation of Israel's ancient wars. He sees the war camp as one of the major roots of Israel's faith, and holds that the down-grading of Israel's war-like participation was merely theological in origin, arising out of the Solomonic and post-Solomonic "enlightment" which was largely initiated by the impact of an international wisdom literature upon Israel.[12] To illustrate that only after Solomon's time the concepts of holy war and absolute miracle belonged inseparably together, he discusses four battle narratives as types of a much greater number: Joshua at Jericho (Josh. 6),[13] Gideon and the Midianites (Jud. 7), the miracle at the sea (Ex. 14), and David's conflict with Goliath (1 Sam. 17).[14] In all of these he regards the emphasis on the miraculous as a post-Solomonic reinterpretation of the ancient reality, except for the last where he sees even the miracle to be demythologized.[15]

According to von Rad's thought, the first attempt to apply the theory of holy war as absolute miracle to an actual political situation was made in the 8th century by the prophet Isaiah. Von Rad held that this great prophet counseled both Ahaz and Hezekiah, in times of political difficulty, to quit their frenzied activity and to rely on the ancient way of holy war, to trust in the miracle of Yahweh. Von Rad states that this prophet naively assumed the post-Solomonic reinterpretation of holy war to be indeed the way of ancient holy war itself.[16]

In the thought of von Rad, the prophets generally spiritualized the worn-out institution of holy war, seeing prophecy itself as the legal successor of the ancient institution and themselves as the executives of this tradition.[17] For him holy war was a major reason for the prophets' conflict with the kings, who secularized the institution and misused it for self-aggrandizement.[18]

Von Rad says that holy war began as an institution in the time of the judges, was spiritualized as a literary fiction in the time of the kings, and was again institutionalized in the time of Josiah (Deuteronomy) as an answer to the calamitous destruction of Judah's armed forces.[19] This attempt at reinstitutionalization came to its end, according to von Rad, with the death of Josiah, and after the catastrophes of 608, 598, and 587 a great new spiritualization took place with the deuteronomic reworking of history and the book of Chronicles.[20]

The theory that this unique unity of holy war and faith in miracle was due to late theological reflection has gone unchallenged. Patrick Miller corrects von Rad's depreciation of the historical value of the early biblical sources and therefore regards the main period of holy war to be in the time of the conquest rather than that of the judges.[21] In the biblical tradition, however, holy war begins neither with the period of the judges nor with the conquest, but with the Exodus and the wilderness.[22] If one accepts the Exodus and wilderness traditions as early, the argument that Israel's tradition of the inefficacy of human fighting was merely a late theological reflection would seem to be overthrown.[23]

Was Israel's Theologizing Based on an Early Event?

In view of the present tendency to treat the historical value of Israel's early traditions with greater respect, the question of the origin of Israel's unique equation of holy war and faith in miracle should be reexamined. Was this equation the result of late theologizing or was it early, perhaps even based upon an historical event?

Israel's ancient poetry witnesses to a nature miracle as Yahweh's act of war for his people. The Song of the Sea (Ex. 15:1-18), as indicated by its metric style, strophic structure, and archaic terminology, may in its original form have originated as early as the twelfth century, approximately contemporary with the Oracles of Baalam and the Song of Deborah.[24] This ancient poem presents Yahweh as a warrior God (vs. 3, *Yahweh ʾîsh milḥāmāh*) not in that he is merely leader of Israel's armies but in that he alone overthrows and destroys the army of Pharaoh in the Sea.[25] The relationship of any narrative to the event to which it points is debatable,[26] but in Israel's ancient poetic literature the tradition stands that Yahweh is known as warrior God when he alone annihilated Pharaoh's army.

It is also evident in the poem that this miracle is the paradigm for the march to and the conquest of Palestine, an event expressed in the language of holy war (vss. 13-16).[27] At the end of the march Israel is planted in Palestine from where Yahweh will reign eternally, much of which is expressed in terminology reminiscent of the Baal epic.[28] Thus the poem unites the march to Canaan, the conquest, and the eternal kingship of Yahweh with the dominant motif of the miracle at the Sea (over half the poem), as though this event sets the character both of the conquest and of Yahweh's kingship.[29] Yahweh as warrior God and King of Israel[30] is the object of the praise of the hymn throughout.

The Song of Deborah is a second ancient hymn dating to about the same period.[31] In contrast to the Song of the Sea its emphasis is on the cooperative action of the people, the subject of the poem (vs. 2):

> That the locks hung loose in Israel
> That the people volunteered, bless the Lord.[32]

This cooperative human effort occupies most of the space of the poem, indeed all of it except verses 3-5, 19-21, 28-31. In the absence of human kingship, Israel and many different persons and groups are named, a unique phenomenon in ancient Near Eastern war literature: Israel, the people, Shamgar, travelers, peasantry, Deborah, commanders of Israel, people of the Lord, Barak, remnant of the noble, Ephraim, Benjamin, Machir, Zebulon, Issachar, Reuben, Gilead, Dan, Asher, Naphtali, Meroz, Jael.

The poem is a complex one, and it is possible to overlook just how this cooperative action was viewed. Though this action was the subject of the poem, it was not the decisive factor in the winning of the battle. In the battle itself the human element is not even described. After the introduction the author pictures a theophany, Yahweh hastening from the south to the help of his people. This portrayal of the storm from the south is related to the definitive action of the battle which includes nothing of Israel's fighting. The stars fought, and the torrent Kishon swept the enemy away (19-21). Thus, already in this early poem the poet "downgrades" Israel's fighting to the extent that he does not even describe it. Certainly this does not mean that Israel did no fighting[33] but verse 21 is probably more than a mere poetic statement. It reflects an event of nature which, as at the sea, was decisive to the course of battle. "Victory was won when a torrential rainstorm bogged the Canaanite chariots down, enabling the Israelite footmen to slaughter their occupants."[34] Some advantage such as this was necessary if the Israelite infantry was to win over the Canaanite chariotry. The decisive action in the battle was seen as that of Yahweh who as covenant king of Israel again came to the aid of his people.

This leaves us with the question of the nature of the human participation. The only detailed description of human fighting is that of Jael who engages in the mop-up exercises after the main battle was won (24-27). This would seem to be the meaning of coming "to the help of Yahweh" (*lǝ'ezrat Yahweh*). The phrase does not mean that Yahweh fights the battle by human means, but that the human community engages in the mop-up exercises after the decisive defeat which was accomplished independently of human fighting. The cooperation was no doubt important to draw the enemy into the trap and to take political advantage of the event, but in the thought of our poet the trap itself was created and sprung by a force beyond and apart from the control of the human community.

This phrase (*lǝ'ezrat Yahweh*), made so much of by von Rad for his understanding of Israel's ancient warfare,[35] occurs only here in the Old Testament, while the opposite statement of Yahweh as the help of man occurs sixteen times.[36] In our poem it is not even used of the militia of the tribes, but of "Meroz," an entity which unfortunately is unknown to us. Meroz who is cursed, however, is parallel in the structure of the poem with Jael who is blessed.[37]

This parallelism would suggest that Meroz, like Jael, was friendly to Israel, but, unlike Jael, was afraid to participate in the battle because of reprisals if Israel were defeated.[38] If this analysis is correct, the phrase to come "to the help of Yahweh" is never used of the Israelite tribes but only of non-Israelites who lived among and were friendly to the tribes and who in times of crisis came to the help of Israel and Yahweh. The curse and blessing at the end of this poem are thus based upon the Abrahamic rather than the Mosaic covenant,[39] again witnessing to the complicated structure of the poem.

This leads us to a discussion of the curse in this poem and of its alleged relationship to the curse of the Mosaic covenant. The argument is made that even though the covenant forms of the Old Testament do not include the demand that the tribes come to the military aid of Yahweh, this is nevertheless to be assumed on the basis of the analogy with the Hittite international treaty where the demand that the vassal come to the help of the suzerain is an important part of the specifications.[40] While the analogy of the international treaty has made an important contribution to Old Testament studies, we must resist the temptation to fasten patterns upon the Old Testament from without, but rather to take seriously fundamental differences which are evident from within.[41]

The reason for the discussion of the point here is that the Song of Deborah is given as major supporting evidence that the biblical covenant assumed that which the Hittite treaty made explicit.[42] Two facts of the poem dispute this claim. The first is the emphasis on volunteerism, stated twice in the poem (vss. 2, 9: *b hitnaddēv ʿam; hammitnaddĕvim bāʿām*), and the second is the fact that the nonparticipating tribes, though derided, are not cursed.[43] While there is no absolute difference between a reproach and a curse, it is evident that there is a marked difference between the tone of vss. 15b-17 and vs. 23.[44] If it is impossible to distinguish absolutely between reproach and curse, so also it is impossible to distinguish absolutely between praise and blessing. Nevertheless, if a qualitative distinction exists between verses 15b-17 and 23, so a similar distinction exists between verses 14-15a, 18 and verses 24-27. If the tribes are not cursed, neither are they blessed. Only the unknown Meroz is cursed and the non-Israelite Jael is explicitly blessed.

Comparing the two songs, we note that the Song of the Sea sets forth Yahweh as the sole actor who by a nature miracle destroys the enemy while Israel fights not at all. This experience becomes the paradigm of Yahweh's future acts for his people (from the perspective of the poet): the march to Palestine and the conquest, the eternal reign of Yahweh. In contrast, the Song of Deborah has as its main theme the cooperative act of the people of Israel. However, this cooperative action is quite different from that set forth in other ancient Near Eastern literature in that the central actor is Yahweh rather than a human leader, whose decisive action is a nature miracle; the cooperative fighting of the people is not even mentioned in the battle description. While in the Song of the Sea the poet regards the experience at the sea as the paradigm for the future, in the Song of Deborah the poet would seem to be looking backward to the sea as the paradigm for the present event.[45]

This contrast of the two poems--warfare as Yahweh's action alone and warfare as cooperative action--marks the main difference also between the Sinai and Shechem covenants. The Sinai or Horeb covenant is given both in the Sinai pericope (Exodus 20:1-17) and in Deuteronomy (5:6-21).[46] It has been pointed out that the form of this material has certain fundamental parallels to the international treaties of the second millennium B.C.: the historical introduction (Ex. 20:1-2; Deut. 5:6), the specifications (Ex. 20:3-17; Deut. 5:7-21), and the blessing and curse formula attached to individual commandments (Ex. 20:5,6,7,12; Deut. 5:9,10,11,16).[47] While there are those who question whether there is a parallelism of the treaty form here,[48] the least that should be said is that the unity of history and law in the ancient Near East at an early period should call into question the denial by some form critics that the historical reference (Ex. 20:2; Deut. 5:6) was a part of the original form.[49] While no one would argue that the Ten Words were originally in their present form(s), there is no objective reason to challenge the ancient unity of history and law since such a unity was characteristic of Hittite treaties of the very time of Moses, treaties known in such diverse areas as Syria and Egypt.[50]

In the Ten Words, holy war is taken into the historical introduction as Yahweh's act of grace to which the specifications are to be a response. The act here set forth is the act which Israel everywhere confessed as foundational to their peoplehood, Yahweh's saving them from Egypt.[51]

On the other hand, the specifications have nothing to do with holy war. The non-martial character of the Ten Commandments has long been observed. This ancient document thus corresponds to the unique tradition of holy war in the Old Testament that Yahweh is the warrior God who fights for his people, that faith does not demand cooperative military action, but trust in Yahweh's action and obedience to specifications of a non-marital character.[52]

The covenant at Shechem (Joshua 24), generally regarded as derived from a very old tradition though touched up here and there by a Deuteronomic editor,[53] is more widely accepted as parallel in structure to the international treaties.[54] Unlike the covenant at Sinai, it sets forth the cooperative activity of holy war. Like the Sinai covenant, however, warfare--even cooperative warfare--is not placed among the specifications but in the historical introduction as the act demanded not of man but of God. Israel's fighting is freely acknowledged (24:8,9,11), although it is placed after the Exodus tradition (24:4-7)[55] in which no human fighting is acknowledged at all. As if ruled by the Exodus paradigm, the efficacy of the cooperative activity is denied. Yahweh gave the Amorites beyond the Jordan into Israel's hand; he destroyed them before Israel (24:8). Yahweh delivered Israel from Moab by causing Balaam to bless Israel rather than to curse (24:10); he also delivered Jericho into Israel's hand (24:11). The summary statement follows: "And I sent before you the hornet (?) and it drove them out from before you, the two kings of the Amorites: not with your sword and not with your bow" (24:12-13). It cannot be regarded as insignificant that even this cooperative warfare is dealt with in the covenant not in the specifications but in the historical introduction,[56] and that cooperative warfare, while acknowledged, is declared inefficacious as

though the theologian is ruled by the Exodus paradigm. It would seem that
while this is an adjustment of the Sinai covenant, yet it is not altogether a
denial of that covenant which rested upon the sole activity of the warrior
God.[57]

The narrative sources both of the Exodus and Conquest confirm the general picture which we have seen both from the ancient poetry and the covenant
forms. The account of Israel at the sea is generally regarded as composed of
the three traditional sources, though E is fragmentary. Two accounts seem to
be embedded in J, while P represents yet another.

That J considered the miracle at the Sea as Yahweh's war is suggested by
the pillar of cloud (ānān) which came between Israel and the Egyptian army
(Ex. 14:19b-20). The provenance of the ānān is to be found "in the Canaanite
mythology surrounding the storm deity, his messengers and weapons of divine
warfare...."[58] An interesting parallel to the statement of J is found in the
Annals of Mursilis where the Hittite king tells the story of his pursuit of the
Sunupassaer. The proud weather-god stood beside the king and it rained all
night so that the enemy could not see the king's troops. In the early morning
another storm suddenly came up and went before his troops, again making
them invisible to the enemy; the storm suddenly lifted to make possible an
attack.[59]

Of the various accounts, Martin Noth makes this judgment: "The different variants of the story of the miracle at the sea wrought by Yahweh which
are in part certain, in part only demonstrable with probability, clearly disagree
in their representation of the details of the event. But the essential elements of
the contents are the same in all forms of the story; and this similarity shows
itself all the more clearly against the background of the differences in the individual narratives. All agree in speaking of an act of God in which it was God
alone who acted...."[60] The oldest source, J, is most emphatic on this point:
"According to J, Moses meets the fear of the people with the cry of 'Fear not'
which used to introduce the powerful attack of Yahweh to protect his people.
Yahweh himself will lead the war, and Israel need only stand there and witness
the victory of Yahweh over the enemy (vss. 13f.). This then is what Moses
dares to say. Just as in J Moses is only the messenger sent to the Israelites in
Egypt to announce to them the acts of Yahweh (3:16f. J), so also now Yahweh
himself will do everything."[61]

For J then, so far as Israel's foundational event is concerned, faith does
not mean that the warrior is to have courage to fight in cooperation with Yahweh but to have courage not to fight, to stand still and wait for Yahweh's
miracle.[62] This is all the more astonishing if J took a "proud delight in kingdom and kings,"[63] and wrote in the wake of the time of David, when Israel was
involved in events which committed her to far-reaching commitments in foreign policy, and was influenced by all this theologically.[64] It would seem
incongruous for such a writer in such a time to originate a "pietistic" tradition.[65] It would seem more logical that he was writing under the influence of a
tradition, a tradition which continued to influence even his strong nationalistic
enthusiasm.

An examination and judgment of the sources are as far as the historian can go. The ancient poetry, the covenant forms, and the narratives all agree that Israel experienced at the sea a nature miracle in which Israel was saved from the Egyptian army by no act of her own. The ancient Song of the Sea goes beyond the Exodus narratives in that it sees the sea event as the paradigm for the march across the wilderness and the conquest.

Like the Song of Deborah, the narratives of the conquest set forth Israel's cooperative fighting with the miraculous activity of Yahweh. The mention of the sea in the material may be the work of the Deuteronomist.[66] However, the material itself suggests that which the Deuteronomist has made explicit. The crossing of the Jordan on dry land (chaps. 3,4),[67] the passover at Gilgal (5:10-12),[68] the visit of Joshua by the commander of the army of Yahweh (5:13-15), and the fall of Jericho,[69] are certainly a reminder to Israel of their escape from Egypt.

The decisive actor in these chapters is Yahweh. He occupies the position which the king occupies in the war annals of Egypt and Mesopotamia, the Legend of Keret, and the Moabite Stone. The account of the crossing of the Jordan, understood as a miracle, and the narrative of Joshua's meeting with "the commander of the army of Yahweh" (5:13-15) contribute to Yahweh's dominance. The battle narrative brings this leadership to a climax when it says that the ark, throne of the invisible Yahweh, was paraded about the city,[70] and at the trumpeting of the priests and shout of the people the wall of Jericho "fell down flat." It is only after the miracle that the militia engages in the "mop-up" activity.[71]

Both the ancient narratives of the sea and of the conquest agree with the theology of holy war of the ancient poetry. The narratives of the Exodus like the Song of the Sea set forth the sea event as an absolute miracle upon which Israel was to wait. The narratives of the conquest,[72] like the Songs of the Sea and of Deborah, set forth the conquest with the experience at the sea as the archetype. Like the song of Deborah, the conquest narratives of the battle of Jericho portray the Israelite militia as cooperating with Yahweh after he has delivered the decisive blow. It is not insignificant that the story of Jericho heads the battle narratives in this ancient material on the conquest.

The battle narratives of the Old Testament were affected by this theology in every period. Here is a list of the more dramatic episodes:

1. Deliverance from Egypt, Ex. 14.
2. Joshua's battle for Jericho, Josh. 6.
3. Deborah's victory over the Canaanite Coalition, Judg. 5.
4. Gideon against the Midianites, Judg. 6:7.
5. Samuel's battle with the Philistines, 1 Sam. 7:5ff.
6. David's battle with Goliath, 1 Sam. 17.
7. The king of Syria and Elisha, 2 Kings 6:15ff.
8. Benhadad and Elisha, 2 Kings 7.
9. Isaiah's counsel to Ahaz, Isa. 7:1-9.
10. Isaiah and Sennacherib, 2 Kings 19. Cf. Isa. 30:15; 31:1-4.

11. Jehoshaphat against the people of the East. 2 Chron. 20:1-30.

This tradition enters into the eschatological oracles of such prophets as Micah, Ezekiel, and Zechariah,[73] and finally into the New Testament.[74] It is no surprise that there is much in Israel's history and theology which contradicts this tradition.[75] It is remarkable that the tradition survived a long and bloody history at all.

Conclusion

It has long been recognized that in the Old Testament the law of mythological correspondence between the earthly and heavenly has been broken.[76] The radical consequences of this are evident when it is realized that the break in the area of metaphysics was also a break in the practical area of ethics and political science. Ancient Israel witnessed that this break occurred in nothing less than the institution of warfare itself when at the sea Israel stood still and beheld the victory of Yahweh. This radicalism was institutionalized in early Israel in a covenant form which recited this event as Yahweh's act of war upon which Israel's existence was founded and which excluded human kingship, accepting only the kingship of Yahweh.[77] As heavenly king and divine warrior he had need not of an earthly counterpart but of a messenger who would communicate his will, a messenger of whom Moses became the type.[78]

This faith in the immediacy of Yahweh's political leadership was more than a mere belief. It was an experience to which Israel witnessed, an experience from which Israel fell away especially in her first and second adaptive periods,[79] an experience to which Israel was called back again and again by the great prophets. This response of faith and unfaith to the political leadership of Yahweh is both the glory and the tragedy of Israel's history.

NOTES

1. This is particularly true of the Exodus narratives. See Ex. 14:13-14. Gerhard von Rad says in his discussion of the Gideon Narrative: "Also hier erst bei diesen nach-solomonischen Novellisten stossen wir auf jene Auffassung für die heiliger Krieg und das absolute Yahwewunder unabtrennbar zusammengehören, ja eigentlich ein und dasselbe sind"--von Rad, *Der Heilige Krieg im alten Israel* (1952) p. 45. His particular reinterpretation is discussed below.

2. For an example of miracles outside of Israel, see below, note 26. Despite these miracles, no Near Eastern army outside of Israel was exhorted to "stand still and see the victory" of its gods. The self-interest of a leader, or even of a people, could hardly afford the development of such a tradition.

3. See Joshua 24:12 and the discussion below.

4. Ex. 14:13-14. My statement here assumes that the Sea event is the climax of the Exodus theme. See M. Noth, *Exodus* trans. by J. S. Bowden (1962) pp. 104f. J. W. Coats challenges this, holding that both J and P regard the Sea tradition not as the nucleus of the Exodus theme but as the beginning of the wilderness theme. See George W. Coats, "The Traditio-Historical Character of the Reed Sea Motif," VT, Vol. 17 (1967), p.258. B. S. Childs agrees with Coats in regard to JE, but holds that P places the Sea event with the Exodus tradition. See B. S. Childs, "A Traditio-Historical Study of the Reed Sea Tradition," VT XX (1970), p. 407. Thomas W. Mann holds that the view of Coats does not adequately deal with the complexities of the tradition and that "while the Jordan crossing (Joshua 3-4) and the Reed Sea event (Exodus 14) are dependent in their transmission on other traditions, they became of such individual importance that neither could be subsumed under one tradition." Thus each comprised "*both the beginning and the end* of a crucial segment of Israel's history." See Thomas W. Mann, "The Pillar of Cloud in the Reed Sea Narrative," JBL, Vol. XC (1971), pp. 27, 28 (italics mine).

5. Friederich Schwally, *Der Heilige Krieg im alten Israel* (1901), pp. 27f.

6. "Wenn auch die alte Zeit alle Erignisse des Krieges der Gottheit bezw, aller Art Schlachtensauber zuschreibt, so besitz sie doch Naivetät genung, die Mitwirkung der Waffen nicht unnötig zu finden. Im gegenteil, der Mensch füllt sich, im Bewusstsein göttlicher Hilfe, zu um so grosser Tapferkeit nicht nur befähigt, sondern auch verpflichtet. Dagegen hat die spätere jüdische Geschichtsschreibung, ganz von erbaulichen Tendenzen beherrscht, diese Naivetäte verloren und den glauben an die göttliche Hilfe überspannt. Sie ist auf den pietisteischen Gedanken geraten, dass der Krieger zwar das Schwert führen, aber nicht gebrauchen dürfe, dass Schreien und Trompetenblasen besser sei als Schild und Speer." *Ibid.*

7. Johs. Pedersen, *Israel, Its Life and Culture* (1940, reprint 1953), III-IV, p. 18.

8. *Ibid.*, p. 21.

9. Von Rad, *op. cit.*

10. Cf. note 1, above.

11. Von Rad, *op.cit.*, pp. 29ff.

12. *Ibid.*, pp. 33ff.

13. While von Rad criticizes Pedersen and Schwally for their primitive, magical understanding of Israel's ancient wars, yet he sees the ancient concept of the Jericho war as magically based. *Ibid.*, p. 43.

14. *Ibid.*, pp. 43-50.

15. *Ibid.*, p. 48.

16. *Ibid.*, p. 16.

17. *Ibid.*, p. 67.

18. *Ibid.*, pp. 50ff.

19. *Ibid.*, pp. 68ff.

20. I. J. Seeligmann adds an important contribution to the literature in his article, "Menschliches Heldentum und göttliche Hilfe, Die doppelte Kausalität im alttestamentlichen Geschichtsdenken," *Theologische Zeitschrift*, XIX (1963), pp. 385-411. He finds in the Bible the human hero who was responsible for victory, the help of God who aided the human heroes or who left room for human initiative, and finally also the idea of God as the *only* actor who permitted no human initiative or deed beside that done by himself. He feels unjustified to press these elements of thought into one schema of biblical thought regarding history. They stand beside one another in varied forms of unity. While uncertain, he feels that in their respective appearance in Israelite thought they might answer the order given here. *Ibid.*, p. 411.

21. Patrick Dwight Miller, Jr., "Holy and Cosmic War in Early Israel," unpublished dissertation, Harvard University, Cambridge, Massachusetts (1963), pp. 68ff.

22. Exodus 15:3. See the discussion in the text. Also Exodus 14:24J. The *'ānān* is an image connected with divine warfare, which has a mythological background in the Ugaritic texts. See Mann, *op.cit.*, pp. 23ff.

23. Miller follows von Rad in explaining any such tendencies in the early literature as later theologizing. *Op. cit.*, pp. 200, 265, 268.

24. Cf. Frank M.Cross Jr., and David Noel Freedman, "The Song of Miriam," JNES, Vol. XIV (1955), pp. 237-250. Among older writers, Ewald and Dillman saw the poem as having a genuine Mosaic kernel. But Bruno Baentsch held that it was hardly written before Deuteronomic times because of what he considered to be a reference to the Jerusalem temple. See *Exodus, Leviticus, Numeri* (HAT, 1903). Martin Noth also sees the poem as relatively late, but takes no account of the new evidence of the Ugaritic literature--*Das Zweite Buch Moses,* Exodus (ATD,1959), p. 98. B. S. Childs challenges Cross and Freedman's early dating. On the basis of tradition-historical criticism he dates the poem, with Mowinckel, in the ninth century. See Childs, *op.cit.*, p. 411, note 1. However, Childs holds that a common tradition lies behind J and the poem and that the Sea tradition was therefore ancient: "...the fact that in the prose account the sea was transmitted with the wilderness tradition while in the poetic account with the exodus would point to the antiquity of the sea tradition. The common tradition preceded the period in which the prose tradition was transmitted within a larger traditional complex". *Ibid.*, p. 412. In his article, "The Song of the Sea and Canaanite Myth" (*Journal for Theology and the Church*, Vol. V, 1968, pp. 1-25), Frank M. Cross goes far beyond his cooperative statement with Freedman, cited above, in his discussion of the date of the Song. He states that the poem is to be dated by (1) the typology of its language, (2) the typology of its prosody, (3) orthographic analysis, (4) the typology of the development of Israel's religion, (5) the history of tradition, and (6) historical allusions (p. 10). On the basis of these considerations, he sees the hymn not merely as "one of the oldest compositions preserved by biblical sources" but also as "a primary source for the central event in Israel's history, the Exodus-Conquest" (p. 11).

25. Cross and Freedman point out that this oldest tradition, independent of JE and P, presents the event as a sudden squall which overturned the barges or vessels of the Egyptian army on which they had apparently set out, *op.cit.*, p. 239. Childs, however, interprets the poem as describing similar phenomena as chapter 14--J. Childs, *op. cit.*, p. 411.

26. Lewis S. Hays challenges the historicity of the tradition, holding that Israel actually

fought as in the battle of Deborah-Barak (Judges 5); but there is no question as to what the tradition itself says. See "What Really Happened at the Sea of Reeds," JBL, LXXXIII (1964), pp. 397-403. Miracles are recorded in extra-biblical narratives of the ancient NE, and it would seem probable that at least some of them may have been grounded in fact. Mursilis II reported in the annals of the first ten years of his reign that his army camp saw an object (*kalmišanaš*) and that this object destroyed the land of the cities of Arzawwa and Apašaš. See Friedrich Hrozny, *Hethitische Keilschrifttexte aus Boghazköi* (Leipzig: J. C. Hinrick'sche Buchhandlung, 1919), Nr. VI, K Bo III, Col. II (16). In the same annals this king tells how the gods seized his enemies who had broken the oath of the covenant and that brother cast down brother, *Ibid.*, Nr. VII, K Bo. II, Nr. 5, 5a, Col. IV (11-15). In his annals of the 27th (?) year, Mursilis tells how the people of Kalašma broke their oath, how they were seized by the gods, that brother betrayed brother, friend betrayed friend, and the one killed the other. See Albrecht Götze, *Die Annalen des Mursilis* (Leipzig: J. C. Hinrichs'sche Buchhandlung, 1933), p. 193. Mursilis also tells of a miracle while pursuing the Sunupassäer. The proud weather-god stood beside the king and it rained all night so that the enemy could not see the king's troops. In the early morning another storm suddenly came up and went before his troops, again making them invisible to the enemy; the storm suddenly lifted so as to make possible an attack. *Ibid.*, p. 195.

27. George W. Coats says that the Song of the Sea constitutes a basic whole, and that the miracle at the sea (4-10) is in parallel relationship to the conquest (14-17). I would therefore regard the framework to be Exodus-Conquest (with Cross) as against Coats who proposes the framework as sea-river--George W. Coats, "The Song of the Sea,"CBQ, Vol. 31 (1969), pp. 1-17. In this parallelism, it is obvious that the miracle of the Sea rules the concept of the conquest so far as the fighting is concerned. Certain details may move the other way. For example, the drying up of the Sea may be the result of influence from the narrative of the crossing of the Jordan. See Coats, *Ibid.*, p. 17.

28. Ex. 15:17, 18; cf. Gordon, Text 51; V ABC:26ff. See Cross and Freedman, *op.cit.*, pp. 249-250. For an extensive treatment of Canaanite myth and the hymn of Exodus 15, see Cross, "The Song of the Sea and Canaanite Myth," *op. cit.* Cross is careful to state that the rites and religious ethos of pre-kingship Israel were shaped fundamentally by the celebration of historical events which were conceived as Yahweh's acts, creating a new community. On the other hand, he does not posit a radical break "between Israel's mythological and cultic past and the historical cultus of the league." It seems to me that the nature of this break is inadequately assessed without seeing its sociological counterpart, Israel's new experiment regarding political power. I treat this briefly in my conclusion. See note 77.

29. See note 27.

30. In the thought of the ancient NE, warrior and kingship are closely related. See ANET, p. 60ff. Also 1 Sam. 8:20.

31. For the early dating of this poem, see Otto Eissfeldt, *Einleitung in das Alte Testament*, (1956), pp. 118-119; W. F. Albright, "The Song of Deborah in the Light of Archaeology," BASOR 62 (1936), pp. 26-31. For a reconstruction of the history behind the poem see Engberg and Albright, "Historical Analysis of Archeological Evidence: Megiddo and the Song of Deborah," BASOR, 78 (1940), pp. 4-9; y. *'hroni, "mlhmt me-mrom umlhmt dvorh," historyh sv'it sl 'rs-ysr'l bime hmqr'*, editor, *y'qv livr*, pp. 91-109.

32. For the translation of the first colon, see Jacob Meyer, "The Book of Judges" (IB, Vol. II), p. 719. The RSV follows the Greek: "That the leaders took the lead in Israel." The noun as "long hair" or "locks" occurs in Ezekiel 44:20, Numbers 6:5, and Deuteronomy 32:42. The verb

occurs often in the sense of "to let go," "let loose," "let alone." The Syriac, Akkadian, and Arabic cognates support this. The practice was symbolic of the people's vow, of their dedication to Yahweh for his purpose. See Acts 18:18.

33. Judges 4:14-16. Wellhausen saw chapter 4 as a narrative based upon the poem in chapter 5. However, the writer may have had other sources. See G. F. Moore, *A Critical and Exegetical Commentary on Judges.*

34. John Bright, *A History of Israel* (1959), p. 158.

35. Von Rad sees this coming "to the help of Yahweh" as the ancient reality of holy war, a reality which was later changed by theological reflection—*op. cit.* pp. 12, 13.

36. Exclusively in the Psalms: 46:2; 27:9; 40:18; 35:2; 22:20; 38:23; 40:14; 70:2; 71:12; 60:13; 108:13; 44:27; 63:8; 94:17; 70:2; 108:13. Seldom if ever in the Assyrian or Hittite Annals is it said that the king helps the god. Repeatedly, however, the god comes to the help of the king: *i-na tukulti(ti) dAššur bēli-ia it-ti-šu-un am-da-ḫi-iṣ-ma.* D. D. Luckenbill, *The Annals of Sennacherib* (1924), p. 31 (The Oriental Institute Prism Inscription (H2), Col. III, 1, 2).

37. Patrick Miller sees the praise of the tribes as a blessing which is then paralled with the curse of Meroz. Meroz is presumed to have been an Israelite entity which, unlike the previous tribes, violated the covenant demand to come to the aid of the suzerain and thus was cursed, *Op. cit.*, pp.207ff. This, however, violates the explicit parallel of the curse of Meroz with the blessing of Jael, the non-Israelite.

38. Cf. Jacob Meyer, *op. cit.*, p. 727.

39. See Genesis 12:3.

40. James Pritchard, ANET (1955), p. 204. Cf. Patrick Miller, *op. cit.*, pp. 76ff.

41. For example, although the Hittite treaty is a form of feudalism, Israel's covenant rejected feudalism.

42. As an example, see Patrick Miller, *op. cit.*, pp. 77ff.

43. Cf. Roland de Vaux, *Ancient Israel, Its Life and Institutions,* (1961) pp. 215f. While he holds that the tribes as units were free to decide, he explains that Meroz, a town in Naphtali, was cursed because it did not follow the decision of its tribe. See my suggestion above.

44. Cf. Patrick Miller, *op. cit.*, pp. 204ff.

45. The Sea event is not specifically stated. However, the comparison of the description of the Kishon event to the Sea event, the former coming as a climax of Yahweh's march from Sinai in a storm cloud to wash away the enemy, would seem self-evident.

46. Called *berit* in Deuteronomy 5:2, 3.

47. See George E. Mendenhall, *Law and Covenant in Israel and the Ancient Near East* (1955); Walter Beyerlin, *Origins and History of the Oldest Sinaitic Traditions,* (1966).

48. Dennis J. McCarthy in *Treaty and Covenant* (1963), p. 161, fails to see the reference to Egypt as an historical introduction but as an identification of Yahweh, even if it may have been original. He does not see the Ten Words as a parallel of the international treaty form. Klaus Baltzer hesitates to work with the Sinai pericope because of its difficulties, but sees in Ex. 19:3-8 a short parallel form. This form also has as its introduction the Exodus experience—*Das Bundesformular* (1960), pp. 37f.

49. Cf. Eduard Nielsen, *The Ten Commandments in New Perspective* (1968), p. 140.

50. Cf. ANET, pp. 201-205. As to the age of the Ten commandments themselves, few scholars would challenge the possibility of their pre-settlement origin since Albrecht Alt's article, "Die Ürsprünge des Israelitischen Rechts." For a history of research, cf. J. J. Stamm with M. E. Andrew, *The Ten Commandments in Recent Research* (Naperville: Alec R. Allenson, Inc. 1967),

pp.22ff.

51. For a discussion of the use of this theme in the Old Testament, see Aarre Lauha, "Das Schilfmeermotiv im Alten Testament," *Supplement to Vetus Testament, Congress Volume*, Bonn, 1962 (Leiden: E. J. Brill, 1963), pp. 32-46. He holds that the Sea theme was a separate ingredient of the Exodus tradition.

52. See the discussion above.

53. The Chapter is conventionally regarded as E with strong D editing--John Bright, "The Book of Joshua," IB (1953), p. 544. Albrecht Alt acknowledged its relation to history in 1936--"Joshua" in KS (1953) vol. I, pp. 191f. See G. E. Wright, *Shechem* (1965), pp. 134f.

54. See Klaus Baltzer, *op. cit.* pp. 28ff; Dennis J. McCarthy, *op. cit.*, pp. 145ff.

55. Note how this recital lifts out the Sea tradition, vs. 6.

56. See above.

57. For a discussion of the periods of Judges and Kings as the first and second adaptive periods of the creative period of Moses, see George E. Mendenhall, "Biblical History in Transition" in *The Bible and the Ancient Near East*, ed. by G. Ernest Wright, pp. 38-49.

58. Mann, *op. cit.*, p. 23.

59. See note 26.

60. Martin Noth, *Exodus* in the Old Testament Library (1962), p. 119.

61. *Ibid.*, p. 113.

62. See the discussion above.

63. Otto Eissfelt, *The Old Testament, An Introduction* (1965), p. 200.

64. Martin Noth, *Op. cit.*, p. 15.

65. See discussion above.

66. 2:9-11; 4:21-5:1; 9:9. For the Deuteronomic material, cf. John Bright, "The Book of Joshua," IB, p. 543.

67. See note 27.

68. While the passover (5:10-12) is edited by a priestly hand, the narrative rests on an old tradition. See John Bright, *The Book of Joshua*.

69. M. Noth held that the narratives in Joshua 2-11 were originally separate etiological tales arising about the holy place at Gilgal, and tribal war narratives from Judah and Galilee, which were made the concerns of all Israel and were attached to the Ephraimite leader. Cf. Martin Noth, *Das Buch Joshua* (1953), pp. 11ff. While etiologies abound in the material, they were attached to older narratives, probably JE, which the Deuteronomist revised and inserted in his history. See John Bright, *op. cit.*, pp. 541f.

70. The LXX states that the Israelites "surround" rather than "go around" the city.

71. von Rad sees this narrative as rooted originally in magic, but reinterpreted after the Solominic enlightenment as an "absolute miracle"--*op. cit.*, p. 43. Although the work of Kathleen Kenyon leaves the story in question, we cannot be sure that an unusual event does not lie behind the narrative. See Kathleen M. Kenyon, *Digging up Jericho* (1957).

72. The older sources were writtten down no later than 900 B.C. See note 68.

73. Von Rad, *op. cit.*, pp. 63ff.

74. See Matthew 26:53 and Revelation 20:7-10.

75. Rudolph Smend sees the covenant and holy war traditions divided from the beginning, the one forming the foundation for the churchly and the other the stately character of Israel. While it seems evident to me that the institution of holy war was gathered up into covenant (see above), this was not a smooth event. The past traditions of the pre-Israelite tribes had great

power, and were constantly breaking out of the strictures of covenant. See Smend, *Yahweh War and Tribal Confederation* (1970).

76. See Von Rad, "Typological Interpretation of the Old Testament" in *Essays on Old Testament Hermeneutics* edited by C. Westermann (1963), Eng. translation edited by James Luther Mays (1964), pp. 18ff. Also James Barr, "The Meaning of 'Mythology' in Relation to the Old Testament," VT, IX (1959), pp. 1-10.

77. I have written of this in "The Concept of Politics in the Old Testament," *Annual of the Swedish Theological Institute*, Vol. VII. The relationship between warfare and kingship is recognized in the early poetry (Es. 15). See above, note 30.

78. See above. Cf. Deut. 18:18.

79. See above, note 57.

CHAPTER 16

EXASPERATED LOVE
an Exposition of Hosea 5:8-6:6

In 1983 two events on two continents struck me as bringing the prophet Hosea dramatically to center stage. The first event I experienced in London, the televised debate of the General Synod of the Church of England on the report, "The Church and the Bomb" (February 8-11). The result was disappointing for me, since the Church of England practically removed itself as a restraining voice in British and European international relations.

The second event was the publication of the pastoral letter on war and peace by the National Conference of Catholic Bishops, USA (*The Challenge of Peace: God's Promise and Our Response* [May 3, 1983]). This report was more rigorous, in part because the bishops addressed two audiences, the Catholic faithful "formed by the premises of the Gospel," and then the more pluralistic civil community.

Perhaps it was the critical nature of the times which led Hosea to direct his message only to Israel and Judah, the two communities which shared the traditions of Yahweh's grace and law. It is the communities of faith, after all, which Yahweh has called to lead the world in a new kind of religious-political experience. If our world collapses as a result of a misguided power politics, it ought not be because the community "formed by the premises of the Gospel" does not know God's new political leadership in Christ (cf. Mark 10:42-45).

Albrecht Alt made a breakthrough in the understanding of Hosea 5:8-6:6 when he saw it as a unit relating to the Syro-Ephraimite war. Though this relationship is challenged by some, the passage is nevertheless a literary unit giving (1) a prophetic indictment of a war of Judah against Ephraim (5:8-11), (2) a prophetic rebuke of each state's appeal to the Assyrian emperor for help against the other (5:12-15), (3) a liturgy of political repentance for the two wounded states (6:1-3), and (4) a soliloquy on the difficulties of their political salvation (6:4-6).

From *Interpretation, A Journal of Bible and Theology*, October, 1984, Vol. XXXVIII, No. 4, pp. 398-403.

1. Prophetic Indictment Against the Judah-Ephraim War (5:8-11)

The passage begins by portraying an army moving across the tribal territory of Benjamin, from south to north. Four phrases in this segment are archaisms from pre-kingship Israel: "After you Benjamin" (v. 8; cf. Judg. 5:14), "the day of accusation" (v. 9; cf. Judg. 19; 20), "the tribes of Israel" (v. 9) and "the princes of Judah" (v. 10). We will examine the second archaism as that reflected an alternative to the kingship structures of Hosea's own time.

"The day of accusation" is a "picture of a general assize in the assembly of tribes, where the performance of each tribe is under scrutiny" (Frances I. Andersen and David Noel Freedman, *Hosea, A New Translation with Introduction and Commentary*, AB [Garden City, NY: Doubleday & Co., Inc., 1980], p. 408). Just how this had functioned, we do not know (cf. Judg. 19; 20). Now, however, Hosea used it imaginatively to present his indictments against Ephraim and Judah.

The indictment against Ephraim beginning at verse 9 is not given until the end of verse 11. There the fault is what we would regard not as a political but as a cultic sin: "He has persistently gone after vanity." One commentator translates the Hebrew word underlying "vanity" by a four letter word not printed in most theological journals. It is probably Hosea's epithet for an idol and has to do with the first and second commandments.

The connection of this cultic sin with politics is a close one, for the great gods of the ancient Near East were associated both with fertility (economics) and power politics (the "Enlil" function). As one scholar has stated, the god Ashur was a projection into the heavens of the Assyrian state. The god Ashur was a projection into the heavens of the Assyrian state. The god Ephraim followed was not a projection of Ephraim's higher nature, but a projection of Ephraim's excrement and filth. According to Hosea, the god of power politics stinks.

While the indictment against Ephraim was cultic-political, the indictment against Judah was straightforwardly political: "The princes of Judah are like removers of the boundary [stones]." Hosea evidently adapted a law regulating the boundaries of private real estate to regulate international boundaries (cf. Deut. 27:17).

By the use of this figure, the all-Israelite assize, Hosea challenged the autonomy of the politics of Ephraim and Judah by proclaiming anew the sovereignty of ancient torah: the first/second commandment and the boundary law against stealing. The prophet saw himself not as an individualist but as guardian of torah which, adapted and applied to the present moment, was an expression of Yahweh's sovereign will.

2. Power Politics for the Wounds of War (5:12-14)?

Hosea 5:8-11 deals with the international difficulties of the Yahwistic states, Judah and Ephraim. Verses 12-14 deal with the foreign international scene to which the two siblings appeal for redress of the wounds each had inflicted upon the other.

The attention of Ephraim and Judah was upon their wounds, the devastating effect of their resort to power politics. To heal their wounds they did not repent of their act of warfare, accepting the decision of Yahweh's international assembly, but compounded their violence by appealing to an international politics quite foreign to Yahwism. Each against the other appealed for help from the king of Assyria. This is stated as a prophetic indictment rebelled against them.

The attention of the prophet, on the other hand, was upon the cause of their wounds: the sin of Ephraim who worshipped the projection of its own national ego into the world of the divine; the sin of Judah who rebelled against Yahweh's torah to remove the boundary marker. These wounds would not be healed by an appeal to a foreign international politics, a kind of politics which had caused their wounds in the first place, but only by forsaking that and returning to the mediating international politics of Yahweh's assize.

The prophet says a resounding NO to Ephraim-Judah's involvement in conventional Near Eastern politics, whether of Egypt or of Assyria. A recent study by Herbert Donner (*Israel unter den Völkern, die Stellung der Klassischen Propheten der 8. Jahr-hunderts v. Chr. zur Auussenpolitik der Könige von Israel und Juda*, Supp. to Vetus Tetamentum, XI [Leiden: E. J. Brill, 1964]) has shown that Hosea, Isaiah, and Micah agree on this point: The people of Yahweh were not to make covenants with foreign powers. This was not a policy of isolation. Yahweh's covenant was a new type of international politics based upon the mutual acceptance of Yahweh's authority, the torah, and prophetic mediation in the assize. This covenant, implicitly international from the beginning in that it was intertribal, continued in its international character as a covenant between the two states. Isaiah envisioned this new covenant-politics as the international politics of the future for the entire world of nations (Isa. 2:1-4). The great prophets championed this Yahwistic politics against kings and princes, kings and princes who too often sold out Ephraim and Judah by adopting the coventional politics of the Near East.

Verse 15b is the climax of this segment. Yahweh who calls Israel to a new kind of politics is alone God and therefore Sovereign Lord even of conventional politics. He thus guarantees the ineffectiveness of Assyria's politics for the survival of the two states. Conventional politics will not rescue Israel from Yahweh's destructive power (cf. Isa. 10:5).

3. A Liturgy for Political Repentance (6:1-3)

The eighth century prophets distinguished themselves from earlier prophets by their message that the END was upon Israel and Judah. Their message was not fatalistic however, for the END was a matter of the people's choice. The wounds of Ephraim and Judah could yet be healed, indeed not by Assyrian politics but by a return to the politics of Yahweh.

Albrecht Alt was the first to see the obvious, that Hosea or his editor connected this liturgy of confession to 5:12-14 by adding 5:15, presenting the confession as healing for the political wounds of Ephraim and Judah. The cult was not to multiply sacrifices but was to be a major institution for the promotion of Yahwistic politics (cf. 6:6). Those politics were to be the decision, not of a few leaders, but of the people. By an emphatic third person singular pronoun in verse 1, the people acknowledge that Yahweh rather than the king of Assyria is their political healer.

Alt says of Hosea's message, "It is the prophet's religious consideration of history which here opposes powerfully the nation's political consideration of history; not false and true politics, but politics and religion stand opposed to each other" ("Hosea 5:8-6:6, Ein Krieg und seine Folgen in Prophetischer Beleuchtung" [1919], *Kleine Schriften des Volkes Israels* III [München: Beck, 1983], 182, my translation). But is that the way Hosea saw it? In ancient Israel, religion and politics were one. Yahweh as political leader to whom the people committed themselves in obedience made his will known through the prophet. Thus torah and word of Yahweh through the prophet, rather than kingship as an institution representing violent power (the "Enlil" function), were at the center of Yahwistic politics.

For the Assyrians, religion and politics were also one. The king of Assyria, leader of the armed forces, was the servant of the god Ashur. Thus the institution of violent power was at the center of Assyrian politics *and* religion. As servant of Ashur it was the king's responsibility to manipulate that power to make evident Ashur's rule in the world.

When Ephraim's and Judah's leaders turned to Assyria's king for political healing, they turned to both a false religion and a false politics, a politics which, if left unhindered, would be the end of Yahwistic international politics. From the prophetic viewpoint, Ashur was a "no god," and the king of Assyria represented the arrogance of human leadership which was elevated to the place of divinity in order to control Assyria's future by the manipulation of power (Isa. 37:22-29; cf. 14:4-15). Thus, contra Alt, the people's choice was between a true and false religion *and* a true and false politics. The religions of Baal and Ashur as well as of Yahweh had their political dimension.

Verse 3 sets forth the nature of the political dimension of Yahweh. "To live in Yahweh's presence" was a contemporary idiom for living "by Yahweh's will" (cf. Andersen and Freedman, *Hosea*, p. 522). The "knowledge of Yahweh" was a knowledge of Yahweh's way, a way beginning with exodus and Sinai. It was the way to freedom, all of which was lost when Ephraim and Judah fought each other and integrated themselves into the conventional politics of the Assyrian empire.

The stakes were high for Ephraim and Judah. The confession ends by comparing Yahweh's leadership to fall and spring rain (6:3). The gentle rain of fertility was the alternative to the cosmic flood which conventional politics was about to let loose on Ephraim and Judah (cf. 5:10).

4. Prophetic Reflection: The Pathos of Yahweh (6:4-6)

In this oracle, Hosea regarded himself not as a unique entity, but as one in the succession of the prophets (6:5; cf. Deut. 18:18). Since Hosea regarded Moses as the prophet through whom Yahweh had brought Israel up from Egypt (12:14), it is likely that he saw this succession as beginning with Moses. His positive message on the prophets may be contrasted with his negative critique of kings (13:9-11).

Hosea saw this succession as a line of negative prophets (cf. Jer. 28:8,9). This negativism was not a product of negative psychology but was caused by Yahweh's frustrated purpose. Israel and Judah were inclined to assert their own sovereignty rather than to respond to Yahweh by steadfast love (6:4).

The prophet represented the divine pathos to Ephraim and Judah. This exasperated love of Yahweh is expressed even more fully in 11:8. Israel had been called out from the self-serving politics of Egypt to a politics of steadfast love, the "knowledge of God," the way of their deliverer. Celebrations in the cult only added to the guilt of the two states which refused to acknowledge Yahweh's sovereignty in the new international order.

Conclusion

There is a trajectory of Hosea's thought on international politics which spans the Testaments. We have seen how Isaiah expanded Hosea's thought in his vision of the nations who flowed up to Zion to submit to Yahweh's torah and decision, rejecting the sword as an instrument of international policy (Isa. 2:1-4). The trajectory is evident again in such great passages as Ephesians 1:21, where the resurrected Lord is placed "far above all rule and authority, power and dominion, and every title that can be given, not only in the present age but also in the one to come."

In view of this trajectory I would note insights from Hosea which may yet be pertinent to our present situation, especially to those persons on every continent who would be "formed by the premises of the gospel."

1. Now that the END is upon us, may we see it as God's positive act confronting us again with the alternative of the gospel and its meaning for international politics. The END for some is a time for fatalism, for despair. For Hosea and us it is a time for turning, a new choice.

2. It is time for all of Yahweh's people to listen to Hosea's, Isaiah's, and Micah's firm NO to conventional Near Eastern politics, a politics which has brought us to the precipice.

3. We need to focus attention not upon the terror of nuclear holocaust but upon the prophet's indictment: our idolatries, our rejection of the Sovereign Lord revealed in Jesus, one who has taught us to love our enemies.

4. We ought to use our worship services as an instrument of the church's political repentance, that the sovereignty we profess in worship may be that which we acknowledge in life, that we may indeed be those "formed by the premises of the gospel."

5. We need prophetic leaders who share in Yahweh's pathos, to confront humanity with the good news of God's leadership in Christ.

In our haste for a quick remedy, let the church not turn to conventional politics for healing. Let us rather give thanks that the futility of conventional politics again lies exposed. Let us affirm our international unity in Christ. From this new ground we may then address what the sovereignty of God means in a pluralistic world, a sovereignty which both leads those who accept the good news in Christ and gathers up all pluralisms in providential care and concern.

CHAPTER 17

POWER AND POWERLESSNESS IN THE OLD TESTAMENT
A Book Analysis

GEWALT UND GEWALTLOSIGKEIT IM ALTEN TESTAMENT. Norbert Lohfink, ed. Freiberg/Basel/Wien: Herder, 1983.

Introduction

This book is another evidence of the growing interest of the ecumenical church in the question of war and violence. It is made up of four essays read at a Catholic Conference, "Arbeitsgemeinschaft deutschsprachiger katholischer Alttestamentlicher," August 24-28, 1981 in Neustift bei Brixon.

The essays read at the conference were:

1. "'Gewalt' als Thema alttestamentlicher Forschung," Lohfink;
2. "Die Schichten des Pentateuch und der Krieg," Lohfink;
3. "Klagelieder in Israel und Babylonien-verschiedene Deutungen der Gewalt," Lothar Ruppert;
4. "Die Botschaft von Gottesknecht--ein Weg zur Überwindung der Gewalt," Ernst Haag.

The book ends with a short essay written shortly after the conference by a dogmatic theologian, Raymund Schwager, a conference guest.

The book includes a foreword and bibliography written and compiled by Lohfink. The book does not pretend to be a comprehensive treatment of the theme but a beginning discussion by Catholic Old Testament scholars of a question thrust upon them by the present international scene.

It is significant that the conference and book received its impetus and direction not only from outside the field of Old Testament scholarship, but also of theological scholarship. Although the four essays are written by competent Old Testament scholars according to generally accepted historical-critical methods, the theory of violence developed by René Girard from his study of world literature, psychological analysis, ethnology and social theory provided the writers with new and better questions to ask of the Old Testament text.

From *Essays on War and Peace: Bible and Early Church*, Willard Swartley, ed., *Occasional Papers* No. 9, 1986.

Without the provocation of Girard, the conference would never have happened. For the purpose of the conference his two important books were, *La violence et le sacre* (1972) and *Des choses chashées depuis la fondation du monde* (1978).

Girard's theory is important to Old Testament studies in stating that violence is not merely one drive among many, but is above all that which separates humans from animals. Human greed gives birth to conflict which then moves toward violence. This original cause of conflict was soon lost to humanity and violence became blind. At the same time it was infectious and threatened humanity with chaos. To contain this chaos, all ancient societies developed the scapegoat mechanism which concentrated the aggressions of all upon one individual whom they considered guilty and who by this was destroyed. Over the cadaver of this person, the community came to peace. This took on religious significance in that the offering provided freedom from guilt and at the same time became the embodiment of the ones saved. In these two aspects was experienced the two aspects of the holy, *Tremendum* and *Fascinosum*. The experience was regularized in a repeated ritual of universal atonement which usually climaxed with a ritual meal, celebrating the new harmony of the community. By this mechanism, violence was ever and again contained.

Although Girard's viewpoint was essentially atheistic, in 1973 he wrote an essay claiming that only the Christian gospel did not follow the structure of all other religions on the point of violence. Unlike them, it does not cover up or veil the scapegoat mechanism by which violence was contained socially, but exposed it.

Girard's thought was introduced to German theological circles by the Catholic dogmatician, Raymund Schwager. Schwager saw Girard as the thinker by whom European spiritual development in consequence of its own logic and from its own presuppositions, had arrived where the evangelists had already stood some 2000 years ago, a period when humanity was not yet ripe for it. The Christian in a pluralistic society, Schwager held, was not to withdraw from society as a sect-type, nor to give up the faith by melting into the society, but was to be maintained by "high faith consciousness" as a disciple of Jesus. Norbert Lohfink qualified Schwager's reception of Girard's thought somewhat (at a 1978 academic conference at Munich), saying that "we the disciples of Jesus sought to understand ourselves not in the 'heightened faith-consciousness' of individual Christians but in transformed, interdependent, powerless Christian congregations which stood as an alternative society to the universal society."

1. "Violence (Gewalt) as a Theme of Old Testament Research" (Lohfink)

Lohfink begins his history of research by pointing up that no other theme fills the OT like that of violence, giving statistics provided by Schwager. He points out that already in the second century Marcion saw this and responded by excluding the Old Testament from the canon. This solution is accepted today in a practical way by the recent exclusion of Psalms of violence from the Catholic lectionary. This solution, however, the church did not buy historically, holding, as did the New Testament, to the essential unity of both Testaments. Contrary to this self-evident fact of the predominant theme of violence, OT theologies do not deal with the theme, due, he thinks, to an unconscious mechanism at work which excludes everything dealing with violence.

After discussing secondary literature mainly known to us, Lohfink concludes that the question is discussed too narrowly. Is it anywhere discussed that violence is united with the legal order and the state, and that one cannot be discussed without the other? Can the problem of violence be discussed marginally, or must it come central to the discussion of the traditional themes of theology, especially since it is intricately involved in central Old Testament themes, such as the exodus, occupation, kingship, and eschatology?

It is interesting that Lohfink does not mention those Catholic orders which historically rejected the practice of violence. Also, his discussion of the Reformation includes the Lutheran and Reformed approaches, but omits entirely the Anabaptists. He includes some writings from Mennonite authors, but indicates that such writings were mostly unavailable to him. Norbert concludes the chapter by discussing the contribution to Old Testament scholarship from the outside, namely that of Girard and his disciples. He feels that no theory lightens up the meaning of OT texts like that of Girard.

2. "The Pentateuchal Sources and Warfare" (Lohfink)

Lohfink holds that there is an oriental commonality in regard to war which holds that divinity alone is the effective actor. J and E have a "natural" attitude toward war; warfare is not central but is accepted as a "fact of life." Although J consciously excluded war from the patriarchal narratives, this may have been because of their placement before the exodus and occupation traditions, so that they could not have been involved in the conquest.

Lohfink does not discuss why J omits war in the primeval history.

Deuteronomy, on the other hand, shifts the weight from the "natural" attitude of J and E to an aggressive one. Lohfink regards Deuteronomy 1-Joshua 22 (DtrL) as essentially one source with two major themes, conquest and law. Since these were the two chief interests of Josiah, he assumes this to have been written late in Josiah's reign as propaganda and legitimation for Josiah's actions. (1) DtrL's theory of holy war was that beside having faith, Israel was to fight--as Lohfink notes, quite the opposite of Isaiah 7:9 where faith for the prophet meant the rejection of normal politics. (2) DtrL included the special oath of ḥērem as a part of warfare and then generalized it to mean the destruction of the total population. (3) DtrL had a juristic-theological territorial concept: that God allotted to each nation its land, which each nation then had to possess, as receiver of a fief. This theory gave moral courage to Josiah against Assyria. It united justice and power in that justice is achieved by power and that behind all stands divinity. This then was a change from older Israelite anti-state ideas to the legitimation of state power, a change which collapsed, however, under the weight of the reality of Near Eastern politics.

In contrast to J to whom war was "natural" and certainly to DtrL to whom war was central to Yahwistic faith, P omits warfare from its recounting of Israel's history. "In the priestly historical narrative there is no war." In this respect P resembles the Chronicler who omits or even denies the conquest, not because of a pacifistic interest (nowhere in the OT is holy war so devotedly described as in the Chronicler), but because of a bias of a mythological tendency to link land and people from the time of creation. P lacks war narratives entirely in Genesis. In the Exodus Yahweh's judgment is substituted for war; the Israelite camp in the wilderness was not at all a military camp; the spy history had as its purpose to divide the land which had been given as God's gift; the instituting of Joshua was not a military action; the entrance to Canaan was accomplished without an army, God did it alone. God's judgment was tied to the divine uniqueness of the Creator.

This rejection of war by P was matched by a construct of a world which functions without the use of violence. P knows no state but assumes an egalitarian, tribal enclave or sub-society gathered around the Jerusalem temple. Holy war exists not between humans but between humans and animals; the inter-human peace is maintained by cultic ritual, the scape-goat mechanism of animal sacrifice (Girard). This absence of war is substituted by the presence of the *kābôd* of Yahweh which consumes all that is sinful.

This warless character of P is obscured by the final redactor of the Pentateuch who unites the cultic interest of P with the holy war interest of D as a way of acting for the future (cf. Num. 31; 32-34). Thus the final Pentateuchal redaction qualifies the temple society of P.

P, as noted above, is followed by the Chronicler who rejected the conquest, by the Maccabees, and especially by the Qumran Community which saw warfare only as an eschatological event and that they themselves were to live "pacifistically" in the parenthesis. The basis for all this was the Pentateuch, but the law rather than the narrative. This then became the basis for Jesus' Sermon on the Mount.

3. "Laments in Israel and Babylon: Different Meanings of Power" (Ruppert)

In this essay Ruppert compares laments mainly from the Psalms which deal with the enemy and violence (Ps. 109; 59; 10; 7; 26; 27; 57; 142; 53, etc.) with the most relevant Babylonian-Assyrian prayers of lament, especially the Assyrian Maqlu collection (Maqlu I, 73-86; II, 38-49).

Although he finds an undeniable relationship between the two religions, he rejects the earlier results of Mowinckel and more lately of Vorländer and Gerstenberger which by analogy with the Babylonian laments identify the enemy in the Psalms with practitioners of magic (hexers) and with demons. Comparison of religions is valid, but ultimately each religion must be interpreted within its own context. Ruppert concludes that the setting of the Mesopotamian laments was magic, while the Psalms had a wisdom setting.

In the Babylonian lament, sickness plays a major role, in contrast with the laments of the Psalms which are mainly directed at actions of the enemy. Since in both cultures the natural causes of sickness were unrecognized, numinous powers were regarded as responsible. In Mesopotamia, (sickness) demons, incited by hexers, could be warded off by sacrifices which would propitiate an angered divinity. In Israelite Psalms it was Yahweh's own self who caused sickness, whether for punishment or for unknown reasons, without the help of practitioners of magic (hexers). The experience of sickness was essentially demythologized in Israel, with the result that the image of God, who alone was to be worshipped, took on characteristics of the irrational (Job).

With this demythologizing also, the human petitioners in the Psalms recognized much more clearly than their Mesopotamian contemporaries that humans were responsible for violence, perversion of justice, and oppression in the inter-human and social arena. In the Psalm lament, the enemies were mainly public rather than private enemies, oppressors of the socially weak, of the poor who needed on their side to trust in Yahweh, the God of justice (especially in the later Psalms). Violence was the misuse of human freedom. This means that the grotesque and demonic was shifted almost exclusively to humans themselves, especially to humans as sinners. In contrast to Mesopotamia, violence was therefore considered not merely as hostility to humans, but especially as hostility directed against God. Because that is so, violence, while it can be understood by the faithful, can be overcome only by Yahweh's own self, by divine judgment which creates justice for the threatened and punishes the enemy, who opposes God's rule.

Statements which scandalize Christians from the point of view of the Sermon on the Mount should be seen in this light (perhaps they should be compared with the *woes* of Jesus directed against those who do not receive the gospel message?). In any case, they are not (at least for the most part), to be regarded as requests for personal vengeance, but as a cry of the oppressed and powerless, that God might act to redress injustice.

4. "The Message of the Servant of God: A Way to Overcome Violence" (Haag)

In this section Haag deals with the four traditional Servant Songs. He has a long section on their literary criticism which results in a form critical presentation of the four poems as one poem made up of seven speeches, each with ten stichoi. He regards this as the "basic stratum of the Ebed-Yahweh Poem" which should be regarded as a literary whole (unit), a "prophetic liturgy." His most radical excision to achieve this remarkable result, is the removal of the two Yahweh speeches from Isaiah 53 (52:13-15; 53:12), ascribing them to a revision which in turn was later added to with "additions and supplements."

Haag deals with the tradition criticisms of this "prophetic liturgy" by discussing the three speeches. He finds the poem dependent upon three traditions: the David tradition, the ancient tradition of the judges, and the deuteronomistic tradition of Jeremiah. The Davidic tradition was a deuteronomistic idealization of David developed in the exilic period. The Judges tradition had to do mainly with holy war elements of the poem, such as the "cry" of 42:2 (which the servant does not do) which he regards as the cry marshalling the militia, though the prophetic use of this cry marshalled the enemy of Israel. The Jeremiah tradition is credited as the background for the servant's non-violent reliance upon the word, which Haag traces especially to the deuteronomistic call of Jeremiah where this prophet of the word is placed over the nations. Also, Haag sees the statements of the opposition of the servant as influenced by Jeremiah's confessions.

Haag regards Deutero-Isaiah as author also of the Servant Poem. With a later redaction of Deutero-Isaiah, the Ebed-Yahweh poetry lost its original form. The biggest change was that the servant (originally an individual) was related not to Israel itself, but to the remnant saved by Yahweh, which then took on a collective meaning. The reason for the reinterpretation was the dis-illusionment suffered after the Exile when it was impossible to set up a Davidide, and therefore the message regarding the political structure was changed to one of an immediate theocracy.

The poem was a reflection begun in Israel's exile, caused by the fact that the Davidic mediator of Yahweh's rule no longer existed. This crisis, partly filled by the older prophetic authority, led to a continuing conversation regard-ing the reality and fulfillment of the theocracy and the destiny of the mediator.

Fundamental to this contribution is the unmasking of violence as an expression of sin and of the misuse of creation power, an unmasking accomplished by prophetic authority. This violence toward fellow humans is bound up with the lie (the opposite of knowledge of God grounded on repentance) which like violence is also an expression of sin. Because the sinner has lost sight of the norm for a morally good relation by rejection of God, in an attempt to maintain him or herself as a sinner, he or she falls under the delu-sion of violence. Instead of the hoped for heightening of power this attempt brings only the chaos of destruction and annihilation.

Salvation from violence is due to the divine initiative, the work of salva-tion creating communion with God, which sets aside the situation of sin, the cause of the lie and violence. The effect of this new saving communion with God is shown already in the behavior of the divine servant who, confronting the attack of violent sinners, does not imitate violence nor vie with evil. The ser-vant's decisive deed for overcoming violence is vicarious atonement for the sin-ner which is supported by God's self-communication (Selbstmitteilung). This opposition the servant recognized as directed as against God's own self, whom the servant represented. However, when God personally opposed the servant by making of the servant an offering of vicarious atonement, this mediator no longer stood before the violence of the sinner but before God who enabled him by communication with God's own self to complete his mission. At this point (Isa. 53), what astonishes the people is no longer the rejection of violence but the servant's obedience before God unto death. This unrestricted obedience before God makes possible that rejection of violence by the mediator, which constitutes his martyrdom.

Although Haag seems to hedge a bit about the right of defense so that the Servant Songs are not a rule of action valid for all cases, he does say that the

servant, while an individual of unique meaning, is at the same time a representative of universal obligation. The right to one's own self-assertion and defense
can only come under the scrutiny of the highest norm, the revelation of the
saving love of God.

Evaluation

One can only rejoice that the Catholics are so interested in peace that
they call together a conference of Old Testament scholars to discuss violence
and powerlessness. The participants in the conference accepted the unity of
the testaments as well as their authority for the church today. The matter of
authority makes the violence of the Old Testament a pressing matter.

While generally appreciative, I raise the following questions about the
work:

1. The three authors are unanimous about their acceptance of the theory
of Girard, though they all used the theory mainly to ask new questions of the
biblical material. Does the theory, however, narrow the scope of their interest
too narrowly to the issue of sacrifice? Can one relate this interest to the historic Catholic emphasis on the mass? Has this narrowing of interest caused
their lack of interest in history to the extent that they do not mention those
Catholic orders and other Christian groups who have historically rejected the
practice of violence?

2. Schwager complains about the amount of time given to textual
criticism by the writers and the piece-meal results this tends to give. While I
would not be critical of this per se, yet I feel that it is pushed beyond the limits
of probability at certain points. Can we be sure that DtrL was oriented only to
fit the political "needs" of the time of Josiah, that the ḥērem had no basis in
Israel's early history as a part of warfare, that P's rejection of warfare was
obscured by a pentateuchal redactor who united P's ideas with those of DtrL?
A differentiation of sources in the Pentateuch is difficult enough that one
should not discredit the process by pushing the method to the point where it
appears to be manipulation.

This is especially true of Haag where he radically alters the meaning of
Isaiah 53 toward emphasis on vicarious atonement, effectively qualifying its
political emphasis by removing the two Yahweh speeches.

But more important, the question beyond this is one of method. Does the
tension of Yahweh's judgment and human violence lie essentially between the
sources (DtrL and P, etc.), or is it found within each of the sources themselves? I would hold to the latter view?

3. Lohfink is correct in saying that the question of violence should be
seen more broadly in terms of structural violence, that violence is indissolubly
connected with the state, and that both should be looked at together. It seems
to me, however, that Girard's theory has distracted them from this broader
approach.

4. Is Deuteronomy that well adapted to the power needs of Josiah? Why
is the militia in the laws of warfare in no way connected to kingship? Why do

these laws protect the voluntary status of the individual militiaman rather than emphasize the power needs of kingship? Above all, why is the king restricted as to army and wealth, and his "power base" made his obedience to Yahweh's word? These restrictions in praxis are accompanied by the doctrine that Israel is powerless and must depend upon Yahweh for victory. The unity of this restrictive praxis with this doctrine makes the doctrine quite different from seemingly similar doctrines of other Near Eastern states.

5. The setting of the Psalms of violence within a wisdom rather than in a magical context (as in Babylon) is probably a correct understanding. The Christian is left, however, with the task of justifying these Psalms in light of the Sermon on the Mount.

6. Of the three essays, the final essay on the Servant Songs gave the greatest promise of unity with the New Testament. As noted above, the implication for the poet's attitude toward structural violence is blunted some-what by the removal of the Yahweh speeches. Even more unfortunate is the tempering of the authority of the servant as a universal pattern by legitimating self-defense, a tempering which the New Testament does not do.

As stated above, these criticisms do not mean that I am unappreciative of the book. It is an important addition to a growing peace literature on the Old Testament.

CHAPTER 18

PRINCE OF PEACE: TEMPLE OR PALACE?

"Astronomers in orbit over new planet." I saw this headline in the *Chicago Tribune*, December 11, 1984. It introduced a story of astronomers, jubilant over their discovery of the first planet to be detected outside our solar system. Twenty-one light years away from earth, it promises that there may be many planets outside our system, and that some of them may possibly support life.

As Columbus sailed what for him was a boundless ocean, we too have found a new frontier. It is an exciting time to live, a time of new perspectives, of new economic and spatial possibilities, a time of exploration and possible exploitation of the universe. Human progress continues in our first halting steps beyond earth. With these halting steps, however, the military is already talking of star wars. If this happens, progress may be not toward life but toward death.

This essay, celebrating the Christmas season, is about progress toward life. It is a homily on the last of Isaiah's four names of the future king: Wonderful Counselor, suggesting God's new strategy for international relations; Mighty God, suggesting how this new strategy is to be implemented; Everlasting Father, suggesting God's persistence and patience in its implementation; and finally, Prince of Peace, suggesting the goal of the strategy, a strategy that is God's answer to star wars.

A prince is usually connected with a palace. Isaiah 1-12 portrays two major institutions: the leading institution, the temple (chapters 2 and 6) and the secondary institution, the palace (chapters 9 and 11). Isaiah is a great artist. His artistry in this book (one of Jesus' favorites) may be traced if one follows the flow between temple and palace.

I propose that we examine these two institutions first in the ministry of Jesus, then of Isaiah. From this examination I will raise a few considerations both for the problem of star wars, and for the church as we celebrate this advent season.

Not at the palace

From *Gospel Herald*, December 8, 1987.

Jesus did not spend much time in palaces. I memorized Matthew 2 one summer as a boy, while spreading manure on my father's farm. It tells how wise men came searching for Jesus: "Now when Jesus was born in Bethlehem of Judea in the days of Herod the king, behold, there came wise men from the east to Jerusalem, saying, 'Where is he that is born King of the Jews? for we have seen his star in the east, and are come to worship him.'" The wisdom of the astrologers led them to the palace. But they did not find Jesus at the palace. Only the special wisdom of Judah's priests and scribes could redirect them to an ordinary house in Bethlehem where they found the baby Jesus.

The only time that we read about Jesus in palaces was at the end of his earthly life. In Herod's palace Jesus was mocked and treated with contempt (Luke 23:11). In Pilate's palace, Jesus was sentenced to die (Luke 23:24). Though Jesus was legitimately called "Prince of Peace" by the later church, none of the four names of Isaiah 9 were given him by New Testament writers. And Jesus certainly did not spend his time in palaces.

Jesus' relationship to the temple was quite different. Luke tells us that Jesus as a baby was presented to God in the temple (2:22-38). Then when twelve years old, Jesus went with his parents to the passover feast in Jerusalem. There in the temple he sat among teachers, listening and asking questions. When anxious parents rebuked him he replied, "How is it that you sought me? Did you not know that I must be in my Father's house" (Luke 2:41-49)?

The Gospel of John intimates that Jesus regularly attended the yearly festival seasons in the temple. He healed in the temple precincts, often taught the people there.

The synoptic Gospels tell how at the end of his ministry, he drove out those who bought and sold, overturned the seats of money changers and of those who sold pigeons. "It is written," he cried out, "my house shall be called a house of prayer for all nations" (Mark 11:11).

Quite differently from the Gospels, Isaiah (chapter 9 and 11) portrays idyllic scenes which emanate from the palace. The Quaker minister, Edward Hicks felt deeply about the prophecy in Isaiah 11, that lion would lie down with lamb. Obsessed with this *Peaceable Kingdom*, he painted more than 100 versions of this scene.

Chapter 9, from which our text is taken, tells of the child born to the palace: "For to us a child is born...And his name shall be called...Prince of Peace."

But the peaceable kingdom was not what Isaiah found in Judah's palace. Sent forth from the temple (Isaiah 6), Isaiah met the rebel kings Ahaz and Hezekiah who, each in his time, were preparing for war. As a protest against Judah's rebellious palace, Isaiah portrayed his *Peaceable Kingdom* of the future, when palace would again listen to the message from the temple.

Besides the two scenes of the palace, Isaiah also paints two scenes of the temple. In chapter 6 he sees in a vision God, sitting upon a throne. "Woe is me," he cries, "for my eyes have seen the king, the LORD of hosts."

What makes Isaiah's flow between temple and palace different from that between temple and palace in the surrounding ancient Near Eastern states? In

Babylon and Egypt, the temple supported and undergirded the palace. In Judah, however, just as portrayed in Isaiah, temple was often *against* palace. Judah's different relationship between temple and palace was founded when David brought the ark (a small wooden chest) into Jerusalem.

The Lost ark

The story of how the ark had been lost to its northern home, Shilo, where the boy Samuel had been prophet, might be titled *Ichabod*. Israel's militia had been defeated by the Philistines. The priesthood was all but wiped out. The ark was taken captive. Then the daughter-in-law of Eli, her own husband dead in battle, gave birth to a son whom she named Ichabod--no glory. The ark, the glory of Israel, was housed in the pagan temples of the Philistines.

But there was a mystery about the ark. The Philistines suffered a series of plagues, characteristic of the early iron age, and they were glad to get rid of it. They turned it loose on a cart drawn by oxen, and the oxen drew their burden into the hill-country of Judah. When David later took it to Jerusalem, the mystery of the ark was again experienced when Uzzah, touching the ark to steady it, collapsed in death.

It was a fateful moment in biblical religion when David brought this ark to Jerusalem. For the ark was a symbol of the rule of God, Yahweh enthroned upon the cherubim. It was the rule of God from the tabernacle, a rule which had known no palace. On the day when David brought the ark to Jerusalem, he subjected the foreign tradition of Judah's kingship to the mysterious, holy power of the reign of Yahweh. This is why Isaiah dared to go to Ahaz and Hezekiah and cry: "No foreign alliances! No trusting in armaments! You must trust in Yahweh alone. For Yahweh rules from the temple."

Divine paths

So much for chapter 6. Isaiah's second temple scene is found in chapter 2:1-4. It is the celebrated passage where swords are beaten into plowshares and spears into pruning hooks. But the real issue of the passage is that the nations go up not to the palace but to the temple. They choose there the law, Yahweh's teaching, as a basis for setting their differences instead of reliance upon human wisdom backed by threat of sword and spear. They want to learn the ways of the God of Jacob, to walk in divine paths.

Please note that this is a people's movement. Isaiah does not say that kings and political leaders shall go up. Perhaps some shall. Isaiah says that *many peoples* shall say, "Come, *let us* go up...." Humanity's hope, says Isaiah, lies not with political leaders but with a people's movement. Political leaders obsessed with manipulation of power, with learning the art of star wars, are not about to say, "Come, let us go up to the house of the Lord that we might learn God's ways." This may be why Jesus, Prince of Peace, chose the temple instead of palace, for he found there the common people, who heard him gladly. A new approach to world problems requires a new kind of leader.

When nations learn the way of Yahweh to settle their differences in inter-national relations, Isaiah says, sword and spear become obsolete. Armaments are beaten into instruments of economic productivity.

This also means that our war colleges are obsolete: "Neither shall they learn war any more." This means West Point, Annapolis, the Air Force Academy at Colorado Springs, and the Royal Military College of Kingston, Ontario. All these, with their Moscow equivalents, will go when the peoples of the world wake up and the movement of the Prince of Peace really gets under way: "We ain't a gonna study war no more."

Micah extends this picture not only to international but also to internal relationships (4:1-4). He says that every householder shall sit under their vines and fig trees, "and none shall make them afraid."

When the temple becomes the center of reconciliation, when the people's movement of the prince of peace gets going, it will render obsolete my town's county jail, the armored building of concrete and steel with which national planners have burdened thousands of small towns across America--all to house a few hundred people most of whom are poor, nonviolent, and sinned against. All of the armor, and all of our war colleges will be rendered irrelevant when the advent movement really gets under way.

Beyond this vision of the future which we have already noted, what does this temple versus palace imagery mean for us today? The key is found at the end of Isaiah's prophecy (2:5): "O house of Jacob, Come, let us walk in the light of the Lord."

Our Dordrecht Confession cites this Scripture as to why the temple com-munity is to beat its swords into plow shares *now*.

Healing balm

In 70 A.D. the temple was swept away by Roman armor. But both Jews and Christians had prepared for this eventuality by transferring temple imagery to synagogue and congregation. The church, says Ephesians, is joined together and growing into a holy temple in the Lord (2:21). From all our gathered assemblies throughout every land, the teaching of the Prince of Peace is to go forth throughout every land. As the ruined atomic reactors of Russia and America may some day spew their poisons over the surrounding areas of our countries, so the temples of the Prince are to shed God's healing balm over city and countryside.

With the Prince of Peace going before us, congregations are to lead the nations in a new internationalism. As Deuteronomy says, the people of God are called to be the head and not the tail. We are not to limp along behind the international politics of Ahaz and Hezekiah, of Reagan and Schultz, the palace politics of star wars. We are to follow instead the holy power of the ark, the holy power of the crucified and risen Lord, Prince of Peace, so that when the world's peoples awaken they will find an alternative way in which to walk.

CHAPTER 19

ECONOMICS AMONG THE PEOPLE OF GOD IN THE OLD TESTAMENT

Introduction

My purpose in this paper is to take a holistic approach to the question of economics in the Old Testament. While this would seem to be the logical approach, it has not often been the approach to biblical economics heretofore, either in profession of biblical studies nor in popular presentations such as this. The approach usually has been to examine a single aspect or institution such as the laws of tithing, the sabbath, or jubilee. We may then try to transfer the partial results to an alien economic system and may miss the radical goal to which all the institutions of Israel were dedicated.' By a holistic overview, we may then have more freedom to borrow and adapt institutions from our own history as well as more insight as to which biblical economic-social institutions might be used to express the historical continuity of the people of God to achieve the ancient, yet ever futuristic goal of biblical economics.

This is not a definitive paper on biblical economics. Such a paper cannot be written in snatches of time stolen from students the first month of a new school year. Furthermore, I am not sure that biblical studies are at a point where such a definitive study can be written. The best I can do is to give something of an overview as I see it, with the hope that it will stimulate more adequate studies in the future. My purpose in this paper is to project an overview of the economics of the people of God in the Old Testament in relation to their religious-social goal(s), assuming that those goals, and their basic institutions have some relevance for understanding Jesus and the early church's teaching about economics, and are therefore relevant to the people of God in the 1980's.

I. ISRAEL AS A RELIGIOUS-SOCIAL/ECONOMIC ENTITY

Ancient Israel has meaning for us not simply because of its theology but

---

From *Occasional Papers* of the Council of Mennonite Seminaries and Institute of Mennonite Studies, No. 1, 1981.

also because of its sociology and economics. To try to "cream off" the theology of the Bible does violence to the Bible, and misconstrues the theology itself. For in the Bible theology and sociology, theology and economics are integrally related. It is probably wrong even to say that theology created the sociology. Both biblical theology and biblical sociology were created by certain prophetic experiences of Israel within a particular theological and socio-economic environment. For an understanding of biblical theology, it is necessary to understand the effect of that experience also upon sociology and economics. Anything less than this is a kind of irrelevant pietism.

II. ISRAEL AS AN EGALITARIAN SEGMENTED SOCIETY

Israel was an egalitarian, segmented society rather than an hierarchically centralized society. This is another way of saying Israel's structure was tribal rather than that of a city state. The most obvious option for Israel in Canaan was that of the city-state. The society of the city state was highly stratified, with its higher and lower classes, a stratification reflected even in law. Its economic and political power was concentrated in the hands of a few, and was inclined as it developed to build an empire, to dominate the country-side and weaker city-states.

In the midst of the Canaanite city-state system, Israel deliberately chose the tribal system and resisted the hierarchical city-state structure for over 200 years. Even when the Israelites accepted something of this structure, they attempted to qualify it with the more egalitarian structures of covenant tribalism.

What does tribalism mean? Ever since the late 19th century, biblical sociologists have assumed that tribalism was characteristic of a nomadic society; they have compared ancient Israel to the camel nomads of the Arabian desert (Robertson, Pedersen, de Vaux). This is a major error. Tribal life is characteristic not of a nomadic society but of a settled agricultural and village society. The step below the tribal society was the band society, associated with food gathering and hunting. Israel's agriculture-village society was much too specialized for that. The next stage above it was the state, where further specialization meant the hierarchical concentration of economic and political power, with domination of the many by the few. It was this hierarchical domination which Israel's faith in the one Lord rejected.

The structure of Israel is set forth in the story of Achan, in the verse which tells how Achan was discovered: "In the morning therefore you shall be brought near by your *tribes*; and the tribe which Yahweh takes shall come near by *families*; and the family which Yahweh takes shall come near by *households*, and the household which Yahweh takes shall come near *man by man*" (RSV). The three structures named here are the tribe, the family, and the household, ending with the individual.

A. The Tribes of Israel

Let us now examine the largest unit of this structure, the tribe. Israel was not made up of one tribe but was inter-tribal. This inter-tribal organization was a "bottom-up" organization rather than an hierarchical one. According to Exodus (19; 20; 24) all Israel was gathered before Yahweh and each household entered into covenant with him. In Joshua 24, Joshua gathered the tribes of Israel to Shechem with their elders, heads, judges and officers, and the entire people covenanted with Yahweh. At least in later gatherings for reading of the law and covenant-making, women and children were also present (Deut. 31:9-13; Neh. 10:28-29). The main centralizing force among the tribes was thus religious rather than an economic or political organization. (There may have been a judge or judges who arose periodically from different tribes.) However, the covenant-making of all Israel before Yahweh was also a political act in which each household accepted the "TOP," Yahweh's Lordship which included responsibility for Yahweh's "bottom-up" system, especially for those fellow households and others who were financially ailing.

B. The Household

We will now discuss the smallest unit of the organizational structure stated in Joshua 7:14, the household.

The household was the extended family who lived together or in close proximity. It was usually made up of three or four generations (Ex. 20:5). In the case of Elimelech in the story of Ruth it numbered only six members (Ruth 1:1-4), but more generally would number between 50 and 100 persons.

This smallest institution in early Israel was given greatest significance from the socio-economic point of view, for it was the primary socio-economic unit in Israel.

In Israelite economics, all land belonged to Yahweh, and was under his centralized control (Lev. 25:23). This was not just a theological idea but was an economic reality to which the Israelites committed themselves in their covenant-making. This centralized authority had parcelled out the land to each of his households for their inalienable heritage (Josh. 13ff.). The relationship of this centralized authority to the prosperity of the household is portrayed in Micah 4:1-4. As stated in this passage, all nations will some day go up to Jerusalem to be instructed in Yahweh's *tôrāh* for the arbitration of their disputes, rather then relying upon the sword and diplomacy based upon the balance of power, just as the tribes had gone up for such a purpose in the time of the judges. Then Yahwism had been inter-tribal; now it had taken the next cultural step to become international. However, this passage on the internationalism of this *"pax* Yahweh" ends not with a centralized system but with the economic primacy of each and every household: "they shall sit every man under his vine and under his fig tree, and none shall make them afraid."

Note that it was not the land but that which was produced from the land which belonged to the household. Yahweh owned the land and had distributed its use to each householder among the nations. The individual householders experienced both freedom from fear and freedom from want because the international people's movement had committed themselves to the way of Yahweh, to his justice and teaching.

That this economic principle of Yahweh's ownership of the land was valid even under kingship is evident from the story of Naboth's vineyard (1 Kings 21). The point of the story is not that king Ahab was a cheat. He offered Naboth a better vineyard than his, or if Naboth preferred, its money value. But Naboth would not be tempted; he was true to his covenant oath: "The Lord forbid that I should give you the inheritance of my fathers." The king, bound by Yahwistic law and tradition, was helpless in the situation and could only sulk. Action was taken by Jezebel as a former Canaanite princess had been reared in a tradition where kings were kings.

The clash in the story was between two systems of economics. In the Israelite system, land belonged to Yahweh and had been parceled out to the individual householders as their inalienable right. In the Canaanite system, the ownership of land was concentrated in the hands of the king and his feudal lords and individual householders labored on that land as serfs. Whatever justice there was, was mediated by the crown who rewarded those who served him well with estates. The Israelite king, however, had sworn to uphold Yahwistic economics. After Ahab had violated his covenant oath, the guardian of Yahwistic law, the prophet, suddenly appeared like an apparition before Ahab: Ahab said, "Have you found me, O my enemy?" Elijah replied, "I have found you."

C. The Association of Households, the "Family" or Clan

The above socio-economic primacy of the individual household in Israel was not characteristic of tribalism of pre-industrial societies as known by sociologists and anthropologists, and may have been a deliberate qualification of tribalism by ancient Israel. In tribalism as it is practiced around the world, land is usually held not by the household but by the clan. The clan of these societies is a large structure cross-cutting every household (each husband and wife belonging to a different clan), every larger family grouping, and the tribe(s). It is a sodality structure, that is, its function is to bind the segments of the society together. In the usual tribal society, the household, instead of being the primary socio-economic unit, is little more than the clan's fertility mechanism. Even responsibilities for fathering and mothering are distributed somewhat, according to the clan structure.

In Israel, on the other hand, where the household was the primary socio-economic institution, the family (Josh. 7:14, RSV) or clan (JB, NIV) was simply an association of households who lived in proximity. This association might number into the hundreds or even thousands. Instead of being a cross-cutting sodality which owned and controlled the society's property, its primary economic function was to stimulate mutual help among the households or in the case of larger disasters, the mutual help of other clans or even tribes. The tithes and the first-fruits of the household were brought to the regional altar to be distributed to the orphan, widow, Levite, or alien who resided in the territory of the clan (see Deut. 14:28,29). The reapers of the various households were to leave some of the grain in the field so that the poor of the clan might glean for their own needs. The attention of the clan, and of the association of the clans which made up the tribe, was to focus upon the financially ailing household, lending it money without interest and selling it food without profit (Lev. 25:35ff.), so that the household could continue to live among them. This obligation of the clan was the teaching of Israel's inter-tribal authority, Yahweh the God of Israel who had saved them from the slavery of Egypt and who therefore would not permit them to make slaves or serfs of each other (Lev. 25:38-43).

The book of Deuteronomy is realistic in its assessment of Israel's socio-economic possibilities. In 15:11 the writer states, "For the poor will never cease out of the land." It was recognized that some households in Israel would periodically be in financial trouble, or that some widows, orphans or resident aliens would fall outside the economic structure. This was not to be the occasion however for becoming weary of mutual aid, but the opposite. The writer continues his statement, "...therefore I command you, you shall open wide your hand to your brother, to the needy and to the poor, in the land" (15:11).

While Deuteronomy was realistic in recognizing that there would always be poverty in the land, and that therefore the Israelite should always be generous, the objective of mutual help was to eliminate poverty. In the same chapter the Deuteronomist writes, "But there will be no poor among you..., if only you will obey the voice of Yahweh your God, being careful to do all this commandment which I command you this day" (15:4,5). The command referred to here is evidently the command of release, as that is the context of the statement: "Every creditor shall release what he has lent to his neighbor; he shall not exact it of his neighbor, his brother, because Yahweh's release has been proclaimed" (15:2). I shall discuss the year of release later; the point I am making here is that the objective of Israel's mutual help was not to create a body of perpetual poor, but to integrate each person into a household economy and to enable each household to stand on its own financial feet. By obeying such commandments as Yahweh's release, the Israelites would constantly be eliminating poverty so that there would not develop a class of perpetual poor among them.

The book of Ruth is the story of how the clan offered mutual aid to rescue a household from extinction and to place it upon a sound financial basis. This household's difficulties began with a famine which caused it to migrate from Bethlehem to Moab where, after the sons had intermarried with Moabite women, all male members of the household died. The household was revived only by the determined effort of the mother who returned to Bethlehem with her Moabite daughter-in-law to make use of the Israelite institutions of mutual aid. Naomi began the process by taking advantage of the law of gleaning, sending her daughter-in-law to glean in the barley fields of Bethlehem. When Ruth was successful in attracting the favor of a wealthy member of the clan to which the household of Elimelech had belonged, Naomi pressed her claim by demanding through Ruth that Boaz do the part of a *go'ēl* by taking to wife "Ruth the Moabitess, widow of the dead, in order to restore the name of the dead to his inheritance" Ruth 3:1-4:7). The transaction also involved the buying of Elimelech's parcel of ground, which Naomi was selling to the go'ēl, evidently to redeem it for Elimelech's household by paying the debt which was upon it (4:1-6). When after Ruth's marriage a child was born to Ruth, the neighboring women celebrated the event with Naomi because her household had been saved from extinction and financial disaster.

In this story it is evident that the duty of the go'ēl (redeemer) was the obligation of the able male member most closely related to the head of the troubled household. The obligation included both "the raising up of an heir" for the household, and the restoration of its parcel of land.

It is significant that this term go'ēl from Israel's mutual aid system was used of Yahweh as redeemer (go'ēl) of his people from Egypt (Ex. 6:6; 15:13) and finally entered into the New Testament concept of atonement (lútron, āntílutron, Matt. 20:28; Mark 10:45; 1 Tim. 2:6). As we have noted in the laws of Leviticus 25, Israel saw a close relationship between God's act of freeing them from slavery in Egypt and their act of mutual help for one another.

D. The Cross-Cutting Association(s)

In ancient Israel, centralized power was in the hands of Yahweh alone. This centralized power was then distributed to this "bottom-up" society as we have described. This means that in Israel's tribal society there was no tight hierarchical, organizational structure on household, clan, tribe and inter-tribal levels. Instead, the unity of the society was achieved by cross-cutting associations. The most important of these was the tribe of the Levites who were divested of land (though they could own a house in the city) and were responsible to teach Yahwism as well as to arrange for worship celebrations. They may have been responsible for meetings of all Israel held once every seven years (Deut. 31:9-13) or perhaps yearly. At these general meetings, besides feasting and worship celebrations, laws were adjusted to meet contemporary needs and covenant renewal reenacted.

These laws and teaching included provision for the weekly sabbath, the sabbatical year, and the year of jubilee, all of which were very important to Israel's economic and social life. The weekly sabbath was a time of household celebration, a day of freedom from work, freedom extended to all household members, the resident alien, including even the animals (Ex. 20:8-10). In Deuteronomy the rationale of this important social law was the memory of Israel's slavery in Egypt (5:15).

Every seventh year was a sabbatical year of rest for the land. In this year no crops were to be planted (Lev. 25:1-7). According to Deuteronomy, this was also the year of Yahweh's release, when every creditor was to release his debtors from obligation for their debts (15:1-13).

The year of Jubilee occurred every 49th year and included all the stipulations of the seventh year besides a unique feature, the redistribution of land to its original households (Lev. 25:8ff.). This law was discounted by Western scholars as an idealistic curiosity, who knew only their own economic system and could not imagine how such an institution might work. Today we know that redistribution was occasionally proclaimed by Near Eastern kings all the way back to the Middle Bronze Age in Mesopotamia (2,000-1500 B.C.). The seller simply sold the crops rather than the land, which could not be sold in perpetuity. In Israel, the law was a regular institution of every 49th year, a matter of obedience to Yahweh, rather than an institution proclaimed irregularly by kings. This law had to resist social and economic pressures as did also the law of the weekly sabbath (Jer. 17:19-27). Of the ancient character of the law, however, and of its practicality there no longer should be any doubt. It was an important institution in Israel's emphasis upon the economic freedom of the household and in her struggle against the feudalism of the Canaanite city-state.

III. ISRAEL'S ADJUSTMENTS AND STRUGGLE

Much of the story of Israel is the story of her adjustments to the city-state system and the struggle to maintain her religious, segmented, egalitarian structure over against that of the hierarchical, centralized, city-state. The leaders of ancient Israel knew that if they were to adopt Canaanite kingship, the Israelite households would lose their economic freedom, and would be reduced to the slavery which they had experienced in Egypt (1 Sam. 8:10-18). Their attempt was then to adopt a modified and even a transformed kingship, a transformation which reached its climax when Jesus of Nazareth was proclaimed by the early church as the fulfillment of Yahweh's covenant with David.

All of Israel's institutions, including kingship, were to resist the feudalistic structures of the Canaanite city-states. One of the ancient sources of the Pentateuch, though its editor-writer may have been a member of the king's court in the time of Solomon, reveals a strong anti-city-state bias (Gen. 4; 11). He also set forth an Israelite alternative to the empire building of David and Solomon (Gen. 12:1-3).

The Deuteronomist recognized kingship as an institution essentially foreign to Israel, and demanded its radical transformation from an institution based upon military power, international diplomacy and state commerce, to an institution whose political base was the fear of Yahweh and the doing of his law (Deut. 17:14-20). The Deuteronomist is so radical in his opposition to the centralization of military power and its tie with economics that he refused to associate the militia with kingship, but insisted instead on the revival of the ancient tribal mechanisms for its expression. His emphasis on the militia even then is primarily weighted to protect the freedom and interests of the individual householder (Deut. 20).

The key word in regard to Israelite kingship for the Deuteronomist is the word *brother*: "One from among your brethren you shall set as king over you; you may not put a foreigner over you, who is not your brother" (17:15). The king must be someone who knows the Israelite tradition. Furthermore, he must steep himself in this tradition by writing, reading and keeping "the words of this law and these statutes" all the days of his life, "that his heart may not be lifted up above his *brethren*" (17:20). A brother in Israel is an equal who is under covenant law. Kingship in Israel was not to result in a stratified, hierarchical society.

The Hebrew word translated *brother* is used twenty-five times in Deuteronomy, and is used especially in the legal section to insure economic equality. A *brother* is one who in the year of release frees his fellow Israelite from slavery (15:1ff.), rescues him from poverty (15:7,9,11), helps him maintain his property (22:1-4), lends him money without interest (23:19), deals honestly with him (19:18-19). If the king is under the rule of Yahweh and observes the fraternal law of brotherhood, the theocratic rule of Yahweh is maintained. Kingship is permitted only if such a centralized office helps to maintain Israel's "bottom-up" society. The ultimate fulfillment of such a transformation of kingship is the suffering servant of Isaiah 40-55 who was elevated to universal kingship, and the servant who came "not to be ministered unto but to minister and to give his life a ransom for many" (Mark 10:35; the Greek *lútron* translated *ransom* is the Hebrew equivalent of the word borrowed from Israel's mutual aid system, *go'ēl*).

With the adoption of kingship in Israel, the prophetic office proliferated under the guidance of Samuel. By activating Israel's ancient covenant tradition in the new situation, the prophets withstood the powerful economic and political pressures which were catapulting Israel toward a hierarchical society. In the 9th century, Elijah opposed Ahab and his political-economic alliance with Tyre as represented by his marriage with the Tyrenian princess, Jezebel. The scheme was to revive the ancient commercial land-bridge between the Mediterranean and the Red seas (the land equivalent of the Suez Canal) by political and economic treaties between Tyre, Israel and Judah. The price was that Yahweh would be remade to fit into the Canaanite pantheon along with Baal, with all that that meant in terms of religious and societal values.

The societal values of Baalism are symbolized in a bas-relief of Baal found in 1932 in Ugarit, an ancient Canaanite city on the Mediterranean coast in present day Syria just north of the Lebanese border. The left hand of the god Baal grasps a lance which at the top flowers into a plant. This represents Baal as god of fertility and plant life, the foundation of economics. The lance itself symbolizes that Baal unites this economic interest with the coercive political interest. This coercive, political character of Baal is further emphasized by his right hand which swings a club over his head. By use of his club and lance, Baal beats all recalcitrant forces into line which interfere with his economic interest. The representative of Baal is the king who as servant of the god thus united in his office the "military-industrial" and religious complex of ancient times.

Elijah opposed Ahab's Baalization of Yahweh by reviving Israel's ancient practice of the all-Israelite meeting where the people were again confronted with the decision of covenanting with Yahweh. If Baal is God, represented by the Tyrenian alliance of economic-religious interests and backed in Israel by the coercive power of Ahab-Jezebel, let Israel worship him. If Yahweh is God, represented only by his word through Elijah and dependent for support upon the voluntary loyalty of the Israelite households, then let Israel worship him. The issue for Israel was a choice between a divinity who represented an alliance of economic and religious hierarchal interests backed by political coercion, and a divinity who represented the moral-social-spiritual egalitarian values of Exodus-Sinai, whose economics consisted of faith in his word of promise, and whose politics consisted of voluntary commitment of Israel's households to his word through Elijah.

The 8th century prophets proclaimed their opposition to the growing hierarchical structures of Israel. Amos challenged the economic and political alliance of the north:

> You who loll on beds inlaid with ivory
> and sprawl over your couches,
> feasting on lambs from the flock
> and fatter calves,
> You who bawl to the sound of the harp (JB),
> and invent musical instruments like David,
> You who drink wine by the bowlful
> and lard yourselves with the richest of oils,
> but are not grieved at the ruin of Joseph--
> now, therefore,
> You shall lead the column of exiles;
> that will be the end of sprawling and revelry. (6:4-7 NEB)

To the idle women of these political leaders, Amos said,

> Listen to this,
> You cows of Bashan who live on the hill of Samaria,
> You who oppress the poor and crush the destitute,
> who say to your lords, 'Bring us drink':
> Yahweh God has sworn by his holiness that your time is
> coming.... (4:1-2).

Isaiah of Jerusalem spoke against the violation of Yahwistic tradition by the commercial interests of his day:

> Woe to you who add house to house
> and join field to field
> until everything belongs to you
> and you are the sole inhabitants of the land.
> Yahweh Sabaoth has sworn in my hearing,
> 'Many houses shall be brought to ruin,
> great and fine, but left without habitant;
> ten acres of vineyard will yield only one barrel,
> ten bushels of seed will yield only one bushel. (Isa. 5:8-10, JB, NEB)

Micah, patron saint of 19th century American labor unions, would sound like a rabble rouser were he to confront us on the streets of Goshen:

> Hear, you heads of Jacob
> > and rulers of the house of Israel!
> Is it not for you to know justice?
> > You who hate the good and love the evil
> Who tear the skin from off my people,
> > and their flesh from off their bones;
> who eat the flesh of my people,
> > and flay their skin from off them,
> and break their bones in pieces,
> > and chop them up like meat in a kettle,
> > like flesh in a caldron (3:1-3, RSV).

I end this sampling of the prophetic witness by quoting from the prophecy of Malachi of the 5th century B.C., the final book of the Old Testament:

> Behold, I send my messenger to prepare the way before me,
> and Yahweh whom you seek will suddenly come to his temple;
> the messenger of the covenant in whom you delight, behold,
> he is coming, says the Lord of hosts. But who can endure
> the day of his coming, and who can stand when he appears?
> For he is like refiner's fire and the fuller's soap....

> Then I will draw near to you for judgment;
> I will be a swift witness against the sorcerers, against
> the adulterers, against those who swear falsely, against
> those who oppress the hireling in his wages, the widow
> and the orphan, against those who thrust aside the
> sojourner, and do not fear me, says Yahweh of hosts (3:1-2,5).

Archaeological evidence indicates that this thundering of the prophets was not without its economic effect, as Israel moved from an agricultural society toward a commercial and handicraft economy. Judean towns of the late eighth century give evidence of a remarkable homogeneity of population and "yield few signs of extremes of wealth or poverty. Concentrations of craftsmen seem to have existed, with whole towns devoted almost exclusively to the pursuit of a single industry, such as the weaving or dyeing industry at Debir...; some evidences of a common prosperity may be observed. The disintegration of social patterns and the concentration of wealth in the hands of a few had clearly not yet gone to extremes in Judah, as it had in Israel" (John Bright, 1959, p. 260).

Conclusion

When one glimpses something of the totality of Israel's socio-economic system, one recognizes the inadequacy of seeing the system only in terms of one or two institutions and of then trying to graft these institutions into our capitalistic or socialistic models. Furthermore, without understanding what the prophets were aiming at, some of their prophecies may be misunderstood as only economic nihilism. The "bottom-up" economic system of ancient Israel which emphasizes the economic freedom and primacy of the individual household, and which nevertheless brings those households out of economic isolation and vulnerability by cross-cutting associations and commitment to one God (to whom they owe mutual help and love to the neighbor) is a system difficult to understand by those who know only the centralizing models of capitalism or socialism. Yet it is a simple system and quite adaptable to a variety of situations, perhaps more to rural areas and the inner city than to suburbia, though not impossible even there.

Christians who are interested in biblical economics should be devoted to the economic freedom and primacy of the individual household, whether that household is represented by the nuclear family, the extended family, or a fellowship of faith. The household may be a relatively small unit or as large as 100 or more. The larger household may need to be especially responsive to the development of financial responsibility in all of its members.

These households should be brought out of their economic isolation and vulnerability by conversion and commitment to the covenant God, who demands of each householder a repudiation of the hierarchical city-state or imperial economics, and commitment to a system of mutual aid which emphasizes the economic freedom of individual households who are gathered together in congregations. Openness of households on financial matters should be encouraged by the example of the New Testament church, especially the Jerusalem church.

Besides the teaching and mutual aid of the congregation, there should be cross-cutting associations responsible for teaching and mutual aid between congregations. Local, regional and centralized meetings should occur periodically in which the anti-hierarchical, bottom-up economics should be discussed. Attention should be given to the cross-cutting associations themselves that their structures do not become hierarchical, overly centralized or bureaucratized. We should be free to choose and adapt economic structures of our day which may move us toward the biblical vision. We should unite such structures, however, with certain key social-economic structures of the Bible so as to give to our congregations a sense of continuity with biblical faith.

It remains to be seen how much of Israel's socio-economic system is background for understanding the radical economic sayings of Jesus, and for understanding the economic practices of the early church.

The poor and disadvantaged of this world need religious and economic/social leadership if they are to be led out of their slavery existence. The socially and economic advantaged of this world may escape boredom and the meaninglessness of their existence by following the example of Moses: "By faith Moses, when he was grown up, refused to be called the son of Pharaoh's daughter, choosing rather to share ill-treatment with the people of God than to enjoy the fleeting pleasures of sin. He considered abuse suffered for the Christ greater wealth than the treasures of Egypt.... By faith he left Egypt, not being afraid of the anger of the king; he held to his purpose like a man who could see the Invisible. By faith he kept the Passover and sprinkled the blood, so that the Destroyer of the first born might not touch them. By faith the people crossed the Red Sea as if on dry land; but the Egyptians, when they attempted to do the same were drowned" (Heb. 11:24-29).

CHAPTER 20

THE MONEY TREE

Let me begin by congratulating James Mott on his paper. It is rare indeed that a social ethicist, even a Christian social ethicist, derives a social ethic from both a careful study of the Biblical text and a careful analysis of the present situation.

Certainly I would agree 1) that the Bible is historically and economically oriented; 2) that biblical law is to be understood positively as rooted in the character of God and as an expression of God's desired ways for human conduct; 3) that the NT is in fundamental continuity with the Old, though within continuity there are also significant discontinuities; 4) that the economic regulations of Israel apply to the church and have relevance for the nations; 5) that these regulations should be understood in terms of the writer's intention, within the context of God's redemptive acts, the great theological affirmations of the reign of God, sensitivity to the powerless, of creation, of explicit moral teachings such as love, justice, mercy and faith.

I affirm Mott's more specific radical statements, 1) that Israel's egalitarian land distribution means that the Bible is opposed to elitist ownership or control of productive property, whether of the private capitalistic or state capitalistic variety; 2) that commands such as loaning money at no interest meant both then and today the economic empowerment of the poor brother/sister; 3) that the law is paradigmatic and so was never meant to cover every case, but points the specific direction which the more general principles of love and justice should take.

I am not so sure of the cultural irrelevance of the family as the basic economic unit (p. 20). It may be quite relevant to note that Israel's basic economic unit was neither the individual nor a large centralized body, but a small group of persons bonded together by a common economic and familial destiny.

Mott touches the heart of our problem of relating the biblical vision to economics in his discussion of eschatology. With Jesus, the new form of social existence has broken out from Israel upon the world. We live in a situation where the dawn is breaking, but high noon has not yet arrived. Does this leave

---

Response to Stephen R. Mott: "How Should Christian Economists Use the Bible? A Study in Hermeneutics," Wheaton, Illinois, September 16, 1987.

us then with (1) an ethical dilemma faced by each individual Christian as citizen of both the kingdom of God and of the nation-state (certainly an unbiblial concept), or (2) do we disregard the NT as the fulfillment of the Old to build our ethic upon the Old in isolation from the New; or (3) do we see the tension within the church itself, between an elite who follow the NT injunctions on economics while the laity follows only from afar; or (4) does the biblical tension lie between the congregation and the world, a congregation which is in the world but not of it? Of these alternatives, I think Jesus would have us choose the fourth.

Mott comes close to the key question on pages 8 and 9: "Do the regulations of Israel apply to the church and do provisions in the unique theocracy of Israel have relevance among the nations, including ours, who lack the worship of God at their center?" Here our essay, like the Catholic bishop's letter on the American economy, recognizes two audiences: those who commit themselves as disciples of Jesus, and the larger pluralistic society which makes no such commitment. But the question is not whether the regulations apply (I suppose most people here would say they do), but (1) how Israel's regulations (as exposited by Dr. Mott) apply to the church and (2) how do these faithful relate them to our nation "which does not have the worship of God at the center."

"The worship of God at the center" is the key to the economic structure both of ancient Israel and the early church, as Sinai and Pentecost emphasize. As Mott has shown, ancient Israel regarded Yahweh as the owner of productive property, with each Israelite household enjoying inalienable access to its use. At Pentecost also, "no one said that any of the things which he possessed was his own" (Acts 4:32). Property was utilized for "the needy person among them;" the needs of socially marginal members soon resulted in a new corporate structure (Acts 6). What ancient Israel and the early church held in common was that their economic structures were created by and dependent upon their *spirituality*, their corporate and individual ability to respond to motive clause, the act of God among them, an act which eventuated in covenant community. A modern parallel to this structural phenomenon is dependent upon the spirituality of the legally autonomous congregation, legally autonomous not from God in Christ, but from the legal, social and economic powers of this world. From this "worship of God at the center' one should expect of the congregation all kinds of economic experimentation along the lines that Mott has so clearly pointed. By their experience of the Holy, it is the vocation of the Abraham people to lead the world in actualizing in communal life something of Yahweh's justice. In the midst of the horrendous impersonal powers of our twentieth century life, to have faith like Jesus and Paul is first of all to think and act small ("like a grain of mustard seed," Matt. 13:31), if we are to participate in the growth of the money tree that one day will fill the earth.

The answer to this first question, (do Israel's regulations apply to the church?) is already on the way toward an answer to the second: How do disciples relate Israel's economic regulations to our nation which, unlike Israel and the modern congregation, "does not have the worship of God at the center?" We do not need to be theoretical here about our serious situation. I have recently read Norman Cousin's book, *The Pathology of Power* (1987). Cousin writes not as a Christian but as a secularist, deeply committed to the system, believing that it can reform itself and function better. The economic theme comes through ever and again in discussing America's pathology:

> "Nothing manufactured in the world today is in as great abundance as destructive force" (p. 26).
> "There is danger in creating a military welfare state" (p. 30).
> "The prospect of domination of the nation's scholars by Federal employment, project allocations, and the power of money is ever present--and gravely to be regarded" (p. 74, quoting Eisenhower).
> "Salesmen representing the Pentagon travel the world, pressing the merits of American weapons in competition with salesmen from other governments.... What is most disturbing is that questions of moral principle, which at one time were held to be central in American policy, have hardly been raised" (p. 95).

The money tree of American militarism has become morally autonomous. Is there no Daniel who might get through to the promoters of this mad nightmare that there are divine Watchers who may decree that the tree be cut down (Dan. 4:23)? Is there no one who might give acceptable counsel, "break off your sins by practicing justice, and your iniquities by showing mercy to the oppressed, that there may perhaps be a lengthening of your tranquility" (Dan. 4:27)?

There is today a tendency among Bible students to reinterpret the "conversion" of Nebuchadnezzar, not that he was converted to Yahwistic monotheism but that as an enlightened pagan he recognized the God of feeble Israel to be higher in the pantheon than his own power god, Marduk. The realism of biblical faith does not expect the nations of this world to place the worship of the God of Israel at the center. Only the second coming will do that. But the congregation by participating in the new community of Yahweh's agape love and justice, by setting up alternative economic structures, by faithful participation in secular business, economic and political structures which are not impervious to the biblical vision of love and justice, may expect some of these nations to acknowledge the values of the God and Father of Jesus Christ as above the values of their own power gods, may expect some of these nations to break off their sins by practicing justice and showing mercy to the oppressed. And as for those nations which flaunt the moral autonomy of their money tree, the congregation must warn that there are Holy Watchers who at any moment may give the word to cut the tree down!

IV. WORSHIP, MISSION AND COMMUNITY

CHAPTER 21

WORSHIP: RETELLING THE STORY AND COVENANTING

Many narratives of worship experiences in the Bible include story as an important ingredient. One of these narratives is Joshua's covenant-making between God and people at Shechem. At this covenant-making, recital of the story is prominent: the ancestoral events, the exodus, wilderness wandering and finally entrance into the land. Worship settings for such story telling are common throughout the Bible: Deuteronomy 26, the feast of the first-fruits: "A wandering Aramean was my father"; Deuteronomy 6, a family worship setting where the parent recites the story to the child: "We were Pharaoh's slaves in Egypt; and the Lord brought us out of Egypt with a mighty hand..."; Psalm 105, a Psalm used in temple worship:

> He is mindful of his covenant forever,
> of the word he commanded,
> for a thousand generations,
> the covenant which he made with Abraham,
> his sworn promise to Isaac
> which he confirmed to Jacob as a statute,
> to Israel as an everlasting covenant
> saying, "To you I will give the land of Canaan
> as your portion for an inheritance."
> When you were few in number,
> of little account, and sojourners in it,
> wandering from nation to nation,
> from one kingdom to another people,
> he allowed no one to oppress them;
> he rebuked kings on their account,
> saying, "Touch not my anointed ones,
> do my prophets no harm!"

In Acts 13, Paul speaks to the synagogue: "The God of this people Israel chose our fathers and made the people great during their stay in the land of Egypt,

Presentation made at a Worship Festival, Goshen College, May 18, 1986.

and with uplifted arm he led them out of it" (vs. 14). Then there is the story of Jesus repeatedly told in the New Testament, stated in synoptic form in Peter's sermon at Caesarea: "The word which was proclaimed throughout all Judea, beginning from Galilee after the baptism which John preached: how God anointed Jesus of Nazareth with the Holy Spirit and with power; how he went about doing good and healing all that were oppressed by the devil, for God was with him. And we are witnesses of all that he did both in the country of the Jews and in Jerusalem. They put him to death by hanging him on a tree; but God raised him on the third day..." (Acts 10:37).

The Bible is made up of law, wisdom, prophecy. But story dominates and provides context for all of these. This is especially true in worship settings like Joshua 24, settings which punctuate their way through the Bible from Genesis to Revelation.

Let us look then at some of the features of this story telling, exemplified in the covenant making of Joshua 24, and characteristic of the use of the story in worship throughout the Bible. I will discuss three points:

First, the story's personal, corporate character.

Second, the story's demand for individual decision.

Third, the story's unity with law and ethics, a call to righteousness and justice.

These stories in their worship settings throughout the Bible tell of God's love to Israel. They are stories of a personal relationship: of God and people. Students of Near Eastern history tell us that in the 4th millennium B.C. humanity's need was for food. Therefore human worship centered on gods representing the impersonal power of economics: fertility of flock, field and family and the powers of nature such as storms which made fertility possible. The need of the third millennium B.C. was for ordered political relations, the development of the city and of empire. Therefore human worship, centered on the gods representing the impersonal power of politics: Father Anu the sky god who caused people to submit in awe before him; the gods Enlil and Baal who threatened the rebellious with lightening and thunder, and whose power was represented by their servant, the king and his army. By the 2nd millennium B.C., the time of Abraham, these great gods had grown distant and inaccessible so that human need was for a personal god, one who cared about the individual and who would represent individual needs to the great gods. Such a God appeared to Abraham and Sarah. But this personal One of Israel was different from all others in that this God is personal not merely in relation to the individual but above all in relation to the nation. The story is a personal one of God and people, a corporate body, a story which eventuates in land.

This is not so obvious but is true also of the New Testament. The stories of Jesus in the gospels are stories not merely of a private person, but of Jesus who is Lord of all. Jesus is leader of the corporate body the church, and the stories of his ministry are there to show the personal way his Lordship takes in leading the world to God. His personal, corporate leadership he announced in a synagogue worship service in Luke 4:18:

"The Spirit of the Lord is upon me, because he has anointed me to preach good news to the poor. He has sent me to proclaim release to the captives and recovery of sight to the blind, to set at liberty those who are oppressed."

That is the personal corporate program of the head of the church, the one whom we meet in public worship. With the advent of the God of Israel in the call of Abraham and Sarah, humanity is called to forsake the gods representing the impersonal powers of economics and violent politics, and to serve instead the personal God of the story: "Then I took your father Abraham from beyond the River..." (Josh. 24:3); "Then I brought you to the land of the Amorites..." (24:8). If we worship this God of the story we cannot also worship mammon (Matt. 6:24) or Caesar.

This introduces us to a second characteristic of the story, the demand for individual decision. The story is of a corporate people, Israel, but its demand is for individual decision: "Now therefore, serve the Lord...and if you be unwilling to serve the Lord, choose this day whom you will serve, whether the gods your fathers served in the region beyond the River, or the gods of the Amorites in whose land you dwell; but as for me and my house, we will serve the Lord" (Josh. 24:14-15). The story gives us a choice, for the story in this passage begins with the fathers who served other gods. It was only because God called Abraham out from those pagan fathers that Israel had a choice to serve Yahweh.

As Brethren and Mennonites, we rightly gain inspiration and nourishment from our Anabaptist roots. But lest we become proud of that heritage, let us remember also our pagan ancestors who lived a few generations behind those Anabaptist fathers and mothers. Our roots are also in them and our story gives us a choice. We can serve the gods of our pagan ancestors. Or the impersonal powers of our contemporary environment (24:15). Or we can serve the Lord of Menno and of Mack. Like Joshua's congregation of old, we should regularly confront ourselves with this choice as we tell the story in our worship service.

And now let us discuss point three, the unity of this story with law and ethics, with God's demand for righteousness and justice. Joshua said to the people, "You cannot serve the Lord; for he is a holy God; he is a jealous God..." (24:19). Israel replied, "No, but we will serve the Lord..." (vs. 21). "So Joshua made a covenant with the people that day, and made statutes and ordinances for them at Shechem" (vs. 25). The recital of the story of God's mercy ends with *now therefore*, the response to God's grace by obedience to law, to torah. In the New Testament, Paul's recounting of God's grace in the book of Romans ends with, "I appeal to you therefore..." (Rom. 12:1).

In the Protestant tradition we have denigrated law. Our mood is too often measured by the song, "Free from the law O happy condition!" But the mood of those who know law as response to story is stated by the Psalmist, "O how I love thy law; it is my meditation all the day!" (119:97).

This link of law with story is found even in the Ten Commandments.

These commandments begin with identifying who God is: "I am the Lord your God who brought you out of the land of Egypt, out of the house of bondage." The proper response to this, God's act of freedom is: "Thou shalt have no other gods in my worship." The God of freedom is alone our authority for life; the worship of all other gods leads to bondage.

Unfortunately, the traditional Christian enumeration of the Ten Commandments has omitted the story: we usually begin with "Thou shalt...." Little wonder that our mood is anti-law. We have lost the connection of law with story, and therefore know law only as ethnic law, as state law, law with its burden, its threat of police and burgeoning prisons. We do need freedom from law as burden, from law as the law of sin and death. That freedom is offered us in a new kind of law, a law given us in the context of story, the story of God's love which forms both model and motive for law. If our worship is to have continuity with biblical worship, it must include teaching of the way of Yahweh, the way of Jesus, the way of righteousness and justice.

We have considered three characteristics of biblical story: 1) the story's personal corporate character, 2) its demand for individual decision, 3) its unity with law and ethics. Let us close by a consideration of the congregation's worship calendar, how the story should form our congregational life by periodic celebrations throughout the year.

Many people do not know that the Bible gives us a worship calendar (see Ex. 23:14-17; Lev. 23; Deut. 16). Years ago, one of my students in Hebrew Exegesis exegeted this calendar. Afterward a fellow student gently asked, "I don't mean to offend you, but what is the relevance of this exegesis?" His answer was also gentle, "I think our congregations ought to adopt this calendar."

The calendar starts in September with the beginning of our school and church year, the festival of Tabernacles or Booths. This festive season includes the New Year (Lev. 23:24), and the day of atonement (23:27). This Feast of Booths celebrates the new beginning in the wilderness, a new beginning recapitulated by ancient Israel, Jesus, and John the Baptist (Matt. 3; cf. John 7). The second festive season is the Feast of Dedication associated with Christmas. This festival is not found in the Old Testament; but Jesus celebrated it as stated in the Gospel of John (10:22-39), when Jesus declared his unity with the Father.

The third celebration is the Festival of Passover, celebrating the exodus and Jesus' death and resurrection (see John 6:1-19). The fourth yearly celebration is the Festival of Weeks, fifty days after Easter, associated in late Old Testament times with Sinai, and by the New Testament church with the advent of the Spirit (see Acts 2).

By observing these Festivals the congregation can enter intellectually and existentially into the reality of biblical story. Since we are about to celebrate communion and footwashing, let us take Passover as an example. Note first the unity of the Testaments. The synoptics tell us that on passover night Jesus instituted communion (Matt. 26:17-29; Mark 14:12-25; Lk. 22:14-23). Passover celebrated freedom from state slavery. In this context, the New Covenant celebrates freedom in Christ from the impersonal powers (see Col. 2:14-15).

As part of the passover service Jesus broke bread and said, "*This* (the broken-ness) is my body which is for you." "This cup is the new covenant in my blood" (1 Cor. 11:23-25). Jesus universalized this freedom; in his body and blood all peoples are free from enslavement to the powers.

Today we celebrate with communion the washing of feet. The story in the Gospel of John stands at the approximate place where the synoptics report communion (John 13:1-17). Using a little different calendar, John emphasizes a lesson that the church has needed in every age; certainly we need it today: impersonal power struggles are not to be a part of our congregational life, nor of life in our denominations. The church, a corporate entity, is not to be like the corporate nation-state. Jesus said, "You know that those who are supposed to rule over the nations lord it over them, and their great men exercise author-ity over them. But it shall not be so among you; but whoever would be great among you must be your servant, and whoever would be first among you must be slave of all. For the Son of man also came not to be served but to serve, and to give his life a ransom for many (Mk. 10:42-44).

John saw the relationship between the covenant of the new corporate community and this teaching of Jesus on the exercise of power. Therefore he displaced the communion story in his Gospel with the story of the washing of feet. We join both acts together this morning, celebrating them as two mutual and reciprocal acts. Sisters and brothers: the brokenness and shed blood of Christ's body inaugurates a new covenant, a new corporate community, whose characteristic is a renunciation of impersonal power struggle for the personal act of the servant. What began with Moses and Israel is fulfilled and effected anew in Jesus. And what was effected anew in Jesus is effected today in us as we partake of Christ's brokenness, as we enter into Christ's death, and as we are resurrected to a new corporate life, a life celebrated by the washing of one another's feet. It is effected anew in us as we enter again into the story, celebrated today in the event of passover-communion, the first in our yearly cycle of the biblical calendar.

CHAPTER 22

THE RULE OF GOD: AGENDA FOR THE CITY

It is my purpose in this paper to set forth the nature of the rule of God and what that may mean for the strategy of a congregation in the city. In pursuing this purpose, I will first examine the nature of the biblical critique of the city; second, the model of the new political structure which is set over against that of the city; and third, leadership for the new political world order. My fourth point is a short discussion of Jesus and the *ecclesia* as the fulfillment of this order, a fulfillment which, though partially hidden, I assume even now to be in process. In my conclusion I list a few things which this may mean for the strategy of the congregation in the city. Since I am not involved in an inner city ministry (the closest I have come to this is seven years as a pastor in the Allegheny area), the immediate strategy for such a ministry must develop out of a discussion of those who are so involved.

RULE OF GOD AND THE CITY

A. Is the Biblical critique "Christ against Culture?"

A biblical critique of the city has been presented by Jacques Ellul's book, *The Meaning of the City*.[1] Ellul is unsparing in presenting the biblical case against the city. He begins with the narrative of the murderer Cain who builds the first city, discusses the Bible's negativism to Babylon as a type of the city (Daniel, Revelation), and treats Israel's unfavorable result in trying also to build the city. On the other hand, Ellul points out that God accepts the city, that it is within this very city that God struggles with humanity, and that the issue of that struggle is the triumph of the city of God, a triumph due finally not to the work of the saints but to the final intervention of God in human history: the city of God is let down from heaven.

While Ellul has rendered a valuable service by his courage in presenting the Bible's negativism toward the city,[2] he does not probe the Bible's specific objection to the city; nor does he show Yahweh's challenge to that objection through Israel. He rightly rejects the simplistic solution of Renan who held

---

From *The Covenant Quarterly*, 1982.

that "the Yahwistic author has a kind of hate for civilization which he considers to be a downfall from the patriarchal life. Every step in what we would call progress is for him a crime, followed by immediate punishment. The punishment of civilization is found in the labors and divisions of humanity. The search for worldly, secular, monumental and artistic culture at Babel is the crime *par excellence*."[3] According to Renan, Israel later became accustomed to civilization and accepted it along with the city.

Most "Christ against culture" understandings of the biblical critique take more sophisticated forms. Such explanations of the biblical critique of the city and civilization should now give way to more specific and adequate explanations arising out of recent historical studies of the ancient Near Eastern city. It is within the context of such studies that Israel's critique should be placed.

B. The Biblical Critique and Near Eastern Rural-Urban Tensions

Israel's negative critique of the city is unique in ancient Near Eastern literature.[4] Was this uniqueness due to the fact that elsewhere there was no conflict between the city and outlying rural areas or was it because only Israel articulated that conflict?

Studies in ancient Mari reveal that this conflict was present between the city and villages of the Middle Euphrates River in the 18th century B.C., and was probably a type of conflict which was widely spread.[5] The fact that the Mari tribal people were North-West Semites, closely related to the Abraham people, is also significant. This study challenges the theory that the conflict was due to nomadic pressure on the settled areas, a deeply-rooted theory propounded by biblical scholars for over a century but which now should be discarded. The pressure flowed in the opposite direction, from the urban centers to the tribal territories, as the urban authorities infringed upon tribal territorial claims, migration patterns, and independence of the tribes. These tribes were not nomadic but village people who specialized in animal husbandry, raising of grain, etc. The tribe DUMU.MES, Iaminites (Benjaminites), were in continual conflict with the rulers of Mari, yet were permitted to occupy villages along the central Euphrates and to engage in seasonal migration. Mari officials had to be careful about drawing up a census list of the people, designed for the purpose of military service, the corveé, and taxes.[6]

This conflict is not to be confused with our modern day rural-urban tensions. The Amarna letters reveal that the urban lower class were often challenged to merge their efforts with "all the lands" to overthrow oppressive city-state rulers.[7] The small elite upper class of the city dominated both the lower class and the outlying peasantry.[8] The usual conflict was not between the rural and urban population, but the rural-urban population against the oppressive rulers. *It was a conflict between rulers and the ruled.*[9]

C. The Biblical Critique

The Hebrew term translated "city" in the Old Testament ('îr, 1090 times) is usually used of a greater or lesser walled settlement, but may refer also to a simple fortified enclosure or citadel used by a rural people in an emergency.[10] The "city" built by the murderer Cain was probably a simple fort, built because he did not trust the protection of Yahweh's mark (Genesis 4:15-17, J). J observed that the city-fort and the development of specialized trades and arts resulted in an increase of violence (4:17-24). Even in such a world, however, a new beginning could be made. After the birth of Seth, people began "to call upon the name of Yahweh" (4:25,26).

J's criticism of the city-state in Genesis 11 is a profound statement to be understood in terms of his concept of Yahweh's new post-flood order. In this order, Yahweh had made his peace with the human race as expressed by his gracious providential promise (8:21,22). This providential promise might be considered the base line of a triangle, the apex of which is found in Yahweh's special grace, the call of the Abraham people in whom all mankind might bless themselves.

J saw the call of Abram (Gen. 12) as Yahweh's answer to humanity's vain attempt to insure unity in chapter 11 establishing a city-state. The "tower" (migdal) of the city was probably not the temple tower or zigurrat as assumed by older commentators, but denoted monumental architecture, the symbol of the city's power.[11] The city here was the Mesopotamian Babel, a prototype of all cities which became centers of the centralized authority of empire. J's message to the religious and political elite of Jerusalem was that the unity of mankind cannot be achieved by a power oriented city-state with its tendency toward empire, but by a new kind of Yahwistic leadership to which the Abraham people had been called. For J, the human power politics of the city-state was in direct and unsuccessful competition with Yaheh's new political order in which all of the earth's families would find unity and blessing (cf. Colossians, Ephesians).

J's negative attitude toward the city continues with the story of Sodom and Gomorrah (Genesis 18; 19). Within the context of that story, however, J presents the relationship of the Abraham people to the Canaanite city (Genesis 18:16-33). It is likely that J is here challenging the ancient practice of ḥērem, the utter destruction of the Canaanite city.[12] The Abraham people are not to be Yahweh's instrument of wrath, to "utterly destroy" the Canaanite cities as depicted in the conquest narratives. On the contrary, Yahweh had elected Abraham and his children "to keep the way of Yahweh by doing righteousness and justice" (18:19) so that "all the nations of the earth might bless themselves in him" (18:18). "To keep the way of Yahweh by doing righteousness and justice" meant that the Abraham people must challenge the very justice of Yahweh's wrath as it is directed against the Canaanite city: "Shall not the judge of all the earth do justice?" (18:25).

Israel's vocation was not to act as Yahweh's agent of wrath, but to challenge that wrath, to stand up against the justice of the Almighty himself.[13] Thus while J was negative toward the city, he was positive in his concept of Israel's vocation to the city. That vocation was to do justice by opposing Yahweh's wrath, to thus fulfill the promise that all nations would find blessing in the Abraham people.

The biblical critique of the city climaxes in the critique of Nineveh (Nahum) and of Babylon (Habakkuk), the latter used as the symbol of Rome in the New Testament (Apocalypse of John). Surely this critique is not adequately understood as "Christ against culture." The Bible is not against humankind and culture; the Bible gives to humanity the mandate to rule over the animals and earth. But humanity has fallen, so that the male uses his powers over nature to subjugate women (J, Genesis 3) and his fellowman (Genesis 4). The critique of the Bible is not that God and Israel are against culture, the solution being the return to a primeval or rural society. It is rather the critique of the ruler by the ruled. The solution is more than a critique; is an experience, the overthrow of humanity's unjust rule by the rule of the warrior God. Israel witnesses to the beginning of this overthrow and to the establishment of Yahweh's rule at the exodus and Sinai. The *ecclesia* witnessed to its fulfillment and establishment among the nations by the story of the ministry, resurrection, and ascension of Jesus of Nazareth. Both Sinai and the Jesus event provide for *qāhāl* (synagogue) and *ecclesia* (church) the high ground to experience and interpret the victory of Yahweh's rule over the injustice of humanity.

THE BIBLICAL MODEL FOR THE NEW POLITICAL STRUCTURE

A. Israel as a Theopolitical[14] Entity

The two central pillars of the Old Testament are the exodus and Sinai events. These two events deal with the fundamental needs of any state: freedom from foreign powers and internal order. The different character of these two primary events from the usual origins and structure of a state set Israel apart from the ancient states of the Near East (cf. Nm. 23:9; Deut. 4:32-34). Their relevancy for the church in the city is that they clearly establish the independent political character of the people of God.

B. The Exodus (Exodus 1-15)

1. Political Legitimacy (Exodus 3,4)

The problem of Moses was the problem of a leader of any state, that of political legitimacy. Confronted with the question of legitimacy after killing the Hebrew, Moses fled (Exodus 2:14). This question is the concern of the call: "Who am I that I should go to Pharaoh, and bring the sons of Israel out of Egypt?" (3:11). Moses' political task was legitimated by the fact that Yahweh had sent him, that he would be with him (3:10,12). All prophetic calls in the Bible should be understood as answering this question of political legitimation (cf. Amos 7:10-15). This made possible Moses' confrontation of the elders of Israel and Pharaoh, the prophet's confrontation of people and king. Political legitimation is also a modern problem for the church in the city, but a problem upon which the Bible is explicit. The political authority of the *ecclesia* in the city is independent of the politics of the city. It is an authority grounded upon the commission and presence of the political leader, Yahweh.

2. Nonviolent Resistance

The narrative of the exodus is by far the earliest and best narrative of a nonviolent resistance movement in ancient history. The story begins with the account of five women who oppose the decree of a totalitarian state. The issue of the narrative is stated simply: "But the midwives feared God, and did not do as the king of Egypt commanded..." (1:17).

Chapter 5 sets forth the pattern of resistance with such clarity of detail that a thoughtful reader might wonder whether it formed something of a pattern for a conflict situation. First, Moses and Aaron as Yahweh's messengers state his demand (5:1). Second, Pharaoh denies knowledge of Yahweh and refuses the request (5:2). Third, the request is repeated with more detail and with the consequences for Israel if they do not obey Yahweh; the demand entails freedom to worship Yahweh (5:3). Fourth, Pharaoh accused the leaders of a slow-down of the people's work. He responded by demanding an increase in the people's work and a maintenance of the work quota (5:6-9). Fifth, the Hebrew foremen, caught in the middle, were flogged by the Egyptian taskmasters when the people failed to achieve their quota (5:10-14). Sixth, the Hebrew foremen appealed to Pharaoh for redress, but Pharaoh repeated his charge of a work slow-down and his increase of the work demand with no decrease of the quota (5:15-18). Seventh, the foremen recognized their impossible situation so they turned on their leaders, Moses and Aaron. Finally, Moses complained to Yahweh and received the promise of divine intervention (5:22-6:1).[15]

The entire story of the Exodus sets forth Yahweh's answer to the problem of injustice. Israel's celebration of Yahweh's intervention (Exodus 15) was an acknowledgement that he had liberated them from Pharaoh's slave policy and genocide, from the power of a city culture which used its technology to dominate a foreign population as well as its own citizens. It was this deliverance which formed the charter of Israel's independence, the foundation for its self-understanding as a nation.

C. Sinai (Exodus 19-Numbers 10)

1. The Law and the Prophets

After being liberated from the enemy, Yahweh's freedom movement was provided with internal order. Like the progressive, contemporary Near Eastern states, early Israel had law collections. Unlike those states, however, its law was immediately linked to Yahweh, Israel's only king. This meant that law was mediated by the prophetic personality in the Bible, rather than by king. As spokesman for Yahweh, the prophet was guardian of the law. The New Testament reflects this close connection between prophet and law by the repetitious phrase, "the law and the prophets" (Matthew 7:12; 22:40; Acts 24:18, etc.).[16] Law in the Bible is thus linked with Yahweh's messenger, one who communicates his word, rather than with the coercive office of kingship to which most Near Eastern law collections are closely linked.[17] Although later Israel accepted kingship, law in the Old Testament is never reoriented to the kingship office. This is remarkable when it is considered that the king was Israel's highest judge, and that his duty was to do justice (cf. Jeremiah 22:13-17).

2. The Law and Covenant Structure: God and People

To do justice was the duty which the prophet laid upon every Israelite, since law in the Bible is within the covenant structure of God and people (see Micah 6:1-8). Justice in the Bible was therefore intensely personal, the proper response of every individual to the saving deeds of Yahweh. This intensely personal nature of law is reflected in the prophecy of Jeremiah who foretold Yahweh's new act for his people, the writing of the law upon every heart (Jeremiah 31:31-34). It is reflected also in the close link of the Deuteronomist between love for God and the keeping of his commandments: "...and you shall love Yahweh your God with all your heart.... And these words which I command you this day shall be upon your heart..." (Deuteronomy 6:4,5).

3. Foundation for law

The foundation for biblical law is Yahweh's saving acts, especially the exodus from Egypt. The prophet Micah in a *ñb* (lawsuit) oracle against Israel, proclaimed Yahweh's righteous, saving acts, acts to which Israel was to respond by keeping his revealed law (Micah 6:1-8). The Ten Commandments begin with the foundational word: "I am Yahweh your God who brought you out of the land of Egypt, out of the house of bondage" (Exodus 20:2). In the Jewish enumeration this is the first and most important word, a word which unfortunately is omitted in all Christian enumerations.

This characteristic of biblical law is contrasted with Mesopotamian law which was an expression of *kittim*, defined as "the sum of cosmic laws and truths."[18] This corresponds to the doctrine of natural law of the Greek Stoics, a notion which entered Christian thought in the early church fathers and which was systematized by Thomas Aquinas.[19] Such doctrine reinforces the conservative character of law. The good news of the act of God, on the other hand, sustains a justice which puts "down the mighty from their thrones, and exalts those of low degree" (Luke 1:52). Biblical law which is within the structures of God and people, and is proclaimed by the prophetic community, is a revolutionary expression of Yahweh's new order.

A consequence of the gospel as the foundation of law is that justice does not arise out of the market place; nor does it arise out of the law of supply and demand. Governments have had to interfere in order to mitigate some of the injustices which develop from the concept of the free market place. From the point of view of the church in the city, the economic practices of society must be subjected to the gospel which gives a norm for justice in the relativities of the market place.

The fact that the gospel forms the foundation for human justice means that the church in the city must be unalterably opposed to the idea that the state is the final arbiter and dispenser of justice. The transformation of law from Moses to Jesus is predicated on the proposition that state law is unjust and must therefore be replaced by a new order. We must take Paul seriously when he wrote to the church in the city of Corinth, "How dare one of your members take up a complaint against another in the law courts of the unjust..." (1 Cor. 6:1, JB). The "unjust" here refers to the courts of the pagan society which refuse to accept the gospel as the foundation for justice. The church in the city dare not leave matters of justice to the unjust courts, courts which do not accept the gospel as norm and foundation for justice.

4. The Character of Israel's Society: Covenant Egalitarianism

Biblical law tried to maintain a covenant egalitarian structure over against the hierarchical, feudal structure of the Canaanite city-state. Contrary to Near Eastern law, Israel's law did not recognize different social classes. Israelite society was a "bottom-up" society, a society in which the individual household (numbering from 50-100) was the most important economic and social unit.[20] Israelite laws of land tenure protected the individual household's inalienable right to the use of a plot of land, in ancient times the most important of capital goods. The law of Jubilee, Sabbatical year, and lending of money without interest (Leviticus 25) were mutual aid laws to help maintain a basic economic equality.

The Hebrew word *ăḥ* translated "brother" is used twenty-five times in Deuteronomy, especially in the legal section of the purpose of insuring economic equality. A *brother* is one who in the year of release frees his fellow Israelite from slavery (15:1ff), rescues him from poverty (15:7,9,11), helps him maintain his property (22:1-4), lends him money without interest (23:19), deals honestly with him (19:18,19). When Israelite society changed from an agriculture to a handicraft society, the law of brotherhood was applied to the new economic situation. Entire cities were given over to a handicraft such as the purple die industry or to a clothing industry. The archaeological remains of the Judean towns of the late eighth century reveal a remarkable homogeneity of population and "yield few signs of extremes of wealth or poverty."[21]

Israelite law was especially concerned for the orphan, widow, Levite, or alien who were not integrated into the economic system and therefore had a right to special help. The law of the tithe (Deuteronomy 14:28.29), the law of gleaning, and the command to open wide the hand to the poor (Deuteronomy 15:11) were regarded as the rights of the poor to life in the land. Where possible, the objective of such help was to integrate the poor within the economic system rather than to perpetuate their poverty (Deuteronomy 15:4).

The sharp words of the prophets against the merchants and ruling classes who pushed Israelite society toward the hierarchical feudal city-state, should be interpreted against this background of Israel's egalitarian law (Amos 6:4-7; 4:1,2; Isaiah 5:8-10; Micah 3:1-3; Malachi 3:1-2,5 etc.). The teaching of Jesus and the early church on riches should not be interpreted as economic nihilism, but should be understood against the background of Israelite egalitarian law. For example Jesus' command to the rich young ruler to sell and give his wealth to the poor was probably intended as a responsible distribution based on the law of economic brotherhood (Mark 10:17-22).

LEADERSHIP AND THE NEW POLITICAL ORDER

A. Commitment of Every Person to Yahweh's Rule

We have already indicated the socio-economic primacy of the household, a four generation association of about 50-100 members. The clan or "family," an association of households, was the next larger unit, while the tribe was an association of the clans (cf. Joshua 7:14). Yahwism was inter-tribal. But this did not mean that there was a strong organizational pyramid from the household to the inter-tribal level. On the contrary, unity was promoted by cross-cutting associations, especially the Levites whose chief function was to teach Yahwism and perhaps to lead in occasional covenant ceremonies which included all Israel. It was probably to protect against a centralization of power that the Levites were not a landed tribe. Scattered throughout the tribes, their inheritance was Yahweh; that is, he would care for them through the gifts of his people. Centralization depended upon the commitment of each Israelite to Yahweh, a commitment made periodically at the all-Israelite Covenant renewal ceremony (Deuteronomy 31:9-13). This commitment included the loyalty of each household to Yahweh which meant loyalty also to the brother, the mutual aid system of Yahwistic law. At least in later times, this assembly included men, women, children, and aliens, assembled to hear the law as read by the Levites (Deuteronomy 31:11,12). Jeremiah looked forward to the time when even the Levite as teacher would no longer be needed (31:34).

It appears that from time to time judges also would be raised up to meet "all-Israelite" needs. The influence of the judge often extended beyond the borders of his own tribe.

B. The Adoption of Kingship

When Israel demanded a king "like the nations" it was warned against the hierarchical structures of the Canaanite city-states (1 Samuel 8:10-18). Israel was granted kingship, not like that of the nations, but the king was to be chosen by Yahweh through the prophet. The law of kingship in Deuteronomy sets forth how kingship was to be different from that of the nations. The king's political base was not to be an up-to-date army, diplomacy, or state wealth, but obedience to the torah which he was to copy and to read all the days of his life. The key word in the law is *brother* (17:15,20). As we noted earlier, a brother as used in Deuteronomy is one who practices jubilee, releases fellow Israelites from slavery, rescues them from poverty. Thus Israel's centralized office of kingship according to this law was to promote Yahweh's justice, his "bottom-up" society. While kingship usually violated this law, its radical reorientation represented a tradition upon which the prophet could stand as guardian of Yahwistic justice. Elijah's confrontation with Ahab in Naboth's vineyard is evidence that the adoption of kingship was not to mean the desertion of Yahweh's "bottom-up" system for structures of the Canaanite city-state (1 Kings 21).

C. Leadership for Yahweh's World-Wide Political Order

It is generally accepted that Deutero-Isaiah (DI) brings to a climax the biblical teaching on monotheism. This monotheism, however, is not merely that Yahweh of Israel is alone God, but that he alone rules in the universe and the nations.[22] This rule included the question of human leadership: how is Yahweh's rule of the nations to be achieved?

In three trial speeches of Yahweh against the gods, DI sets forth the either-or option of the divinity of Yahweh against polytheism (41:21-29; 43:8-13; 48:1;18-25). The issue is not the mere existence of the one over against the many, however, but the effectiveness of only Israel's God to present an understanding of history in terms of promise/threat and fulfillment and to control the future in continuity with the historical past (41:22,23,25-27; 43:9,10; 45:21). While the gods of the nations claimed superiority by giving victory to their martial representatives on the battlefield,[23] Yahweh argued that he alone is God on the basis of the fulfillment of his word given through his prophetic representative, his word of defeat first of all, but continuity of community through defeat and beyond. Obviously, this argument has to do with power, the effectiveness of the gods in the political arena, not merely to project or control this event or that, but to control the present in continuity with the past in such a way as to insure continuity of communal life. The argument has to do with power.

The Jews, though not without their problems with Deutero-Isaiah, had no difficulty understanding this argument. They had known about Yahweh's promise-fulfillment from their oldest writings. Above all, they had experienced fulfillment of two centuries of prophetic threats by their exile in Babylon (Isaiah and Micah; Zephaniah, Jeremiah, and Ezekiel).

But how could the Babylonians understand the prophet's arguments, steeped as they were in the concept that divinity is expressed by the supremacy of violent political power? The prophet's answer is given in the third trial speech. This speech is given not to Babylon in victory but to Babylon in defeat.[24] Now the Babylonians were in the same defeated situation as the Jewish exiles, just as Deutero-Isaiah had previously prophesied to them. This new situation would provide an opportunity for a new turn in the prophet's preaching, his oracle to the nations appealing to them to look to Yahweh for their continuity:

Turn to me and be saved,
all the ends of the earth!
For I am God, and there is no other.
By myself I have sworn,
from my mouth has gone forth in righteousness
a word that shall not return:
'To me every knee shall bow,
every tongue shall swear' (45:22f).

How would Yahweh achieve this voluntaristic rule over the nations? As in Genesis 11 and 12, there are two competitors;[25] but this time both are related to Yahweh. The first is Cyrus who in the Cyrus poems is called Yahweh's anointed (Messiah), his shepherd king (45:1; 44:28). This means that Cyrus was Yahweh's agent to exercise violent political power to achieve Yahweh's purpose. But after his victory, Cyrus never proceeds to become Yahweh's representative ruler over the nations, which was what every kingly representative of the NE gods was expected to do. Cyrus was chosen by Yahweh mainly for a negative purpose, to defeat the nations so that he could return Israel to her land (45:4,13). His negative task is best described by the title, "a bird of prey from the east" (46:11).

The fact that Cyrus as a "bird of prey" could do a positive deed for Yahweh by returning his people to their land should not be overlooked, however. The national state is here judged on the basis of how it treated Yahweh's people.

The second competitor was Yahweh's servant Israel (or representative of Israel) whose task was to bring *justice* to the nations (43:1-4). This is what Cyrus thought he was doing by his conquests. From the perspective of Yahwism, however, the justice of Cyrus was the epitome of injustice. The instrument of Yahweh's servant was not to be violent political power but the word of Yahweh (42:2,3; 49:2; 50:4,5). The servant himself would meet with opposition, persecution and death in the pursuit of his task (42:4; 49:4; 50:6-9; 52:13-53:12). Justice to the nations would be achieved only by Yahweh's intervention, by reversing the negative judgment of the nations and by elevating the servant to a place of rule (49:4; 52:13-15; 52:11,12). Because of Yahweh's intervention the kings and nations will confess their rebellion and acknowledge that the suffering of the servant was for them, that by his stripes they are healed (53:1-10). Yahweh's oath of victory in his trial speech is fulfilled not through Cyrus (though as a bird of prey he had his positive function), but only by Yahweh's intervention on behalf of his servant Israel. Yahweh's monotheism, his rule over the nations, can come to its victorious conclusion only by means of the leadership of his *ecclesia*, or by one representing his *ecclesia*. This fundamental insight has profound meaning for the church in the city.

A. A Social Ethic

An examination of its content suggests that we should take seriously the

New Testament claim that it fulfills the Old. The nativity hymns herald the advent of Jesus as a social and political revolution, fulfilling the promise to the fathers (Luke 1:46-55, 68-79; 2:29-32). Jesus' strictures against wealth and riches should not be regarded as economic nihilism, but more probably are to be interpreted against the background of covenant egalitarianism. It may be that he advocated the enforcement of such institutions as Jubilee (Luke 4:18.19).[26] Thus his proclamation of the kingdom of God, while emphasizing Yahweh's intervention, had an immediate as well as a future reference.

The kingdom or rule of God is defined in the Lord's prayer: that the will of God might be done on earth as it is done in heaven. As one would expect when this teaching is contemplated against the background of exodus and Sinai, this concept had both its realized and futurist dimensions. The ecclesia is to play a major part in its realized dimension, for it is to live in the present in light of the resurrection, the future which has burst in upon the present (cf. Colossians 3).

As a result of Pentecost, the Jerusalem church practiced a continuing redistribution of wealth (Acts 2:42-47; 4:32-35). Paul went about the churches of Greece and Asia Minor to collect an offering for the poor in Jerusalem. Paul saw this offering as more significant than a one time event. He explains to the church in the city of Corinth: "There is no question of relieving others at the cost of hardship to yourselves; it is a question of equality. At the moment your surplus meets their need, but one day your need may be met from their surplus. The aim is equality; as the Scripture has it, 'The man who got much had no more than enough, and the man who got little did not go short'" (2 Corinthians 8:13-15, NEB).

B. The Leadership of Jesus

At the beginning of his ministry Jesus considered and rejected the role of state leadership (Matthew 4:8-10; Luke 4:5-8). Instead, he took a way which opposed the social order and the state, a way resulting in capital punishment. The church in the Roman empire dared to preach the good news of Christ crucified, that the one whom Rome and Jerusalem had rejected God vindicated by resurrection (Acts 2:22-24). This Jesus whom they had crucified was made both Lord and Messiah (Acts 2:36). This general picture of ministry, rejection, and Yahweh's intervention compares positively with the portrait of the servant of Yahweh of Deutero-Isaiah.

The writer to the church at Colossae says that by his act on the cross, Christ disarmed "the powers and authorities," which includes all those powers which oppose the kingdom of God, including the power of the *pôlis* (Colossians 2:15; cf. Romans 8:38).

C. Leadership in the Church

This leadership of Jesus, as contrasted with leadership of nation-states, is the pattern for leadership in the *ecclesia:*

"Jesus...said, 'you know that among the nations their so-called leaders lord it over them, and their great men make their authority felt. This is not to happen among you. No; anyone who wants to become great among you must be your servant, and anyone who wants to be first among you must be slave to all. For the Son of man himself did not come to be served but to serve, and to give his life as a ransom for many'" (Mark 10:42-45; cf. Matthew 20:25; Luke 22:25).[27] Against the background of covenant egalitarianism one can understand what such leadership means. It is significant that the Greek word for *ransom* (*lútron*) translates the Hebrew word *gā'al* and this may be derived originally from the Hebrew mutual aid system.[28]

Ephesians 4 includes one of the greatest New Testament passages on unity and leadership in the church. The writer begins his letter by saying that the church was elected before creation to be God's forgiven people in Christ, to whom he made known the mystery of his will to "bring all things in heaven and on earth together under one head, even Christ." This statement obviously deals with the theme of monotheism, the unity of Yahweh's rule, and may be compared to the argument of Deutero-Isaiah.

The writer then prays that God will give them wisdom that they may know the hope of this calling and the power by which it is to be achieved, namely, the power which raised Christ from the dead and has given to him his place of authority, "far above all rule and authority, power, and dominion, and every title that can be given...." The writer continues, "and God has placed all things under his feet and appointed him to be head over everything for the church, which is his body...."

The writer continues in chapter 2, saying that the church itself is elevated with Christ to the place of his rule, a rule which is to be expressed by doing good works (2:9). Christ has reconciled the Gentile-Jewish division in the church by abolishing the law, creating in himself a unity which is "built on the foundation of the apostles and prophets, with Christ Jesus himself as the chief cornerstone" (2:20).

The writer then discusses the place of Paul's leadership, who is presently a prisoner for the sake of the nations. The church is not to be discouraged because of his sufferings. He prays rather that they may have power with all the saints to comprehend the dimension of the love of Christ and to know this love.

In chapter 4 the writer urges that the ecclesia live a life worthy of their calling, to be humble, gentle, patient, and to keep the unity of the Spirit. This unity is not to be expressed in a hierarchy of leadership, however. The authority of ministry is given by the ruling Christ to "God's people" (*laós*).[29] Within this body he has given some to be apostles, prophets, evangelists, pastors, and teachers to prepare God's people for ministry, the goal of which is maturity, "the fullness of Christ" (4:13).

The organization structure here is egalitarian, against the hierarchical structure of the city-state or of empire, just as we have seen that early Israel was against such a hierarchical structure.[30] It is based upon a power given to the body, a power different from that known by the nations.

CONCLUSION

As indicated in the introduction my purpose here is not to spell out a detailed strategy for a congregation in the city. That must be done by those involved in the task as they interact with both the city and the Scripture. I do present the few following suggestions on the basis of our above discussion.

1. The congregation should understand the biblical critique of the city, the rule and exploitation of men and women by their fellowmen. They should understand that this exploitation has certain cosmic dimensions, and is expressed in the present politics, economics and social stratification of the city as well as in the relationship of the city to the "hinterland."

2. While the congregation should understand the nature of the city which it is *in*, it should understand also that is not *of* the city, that its own political legitimacy is derived elsewhere and is of a prophetic nature.

3. The congregation should experience freedom from the oppressive powers of the city by "going through the sea," by baptism into the death and resurrection of Jesus, a victory achieved by God's response to Christ's non-violent resistance to evil.

4. The congregation should nurture its covenant experience in Christ by a mutual ministry in the exercise of spiritual gifts and in a vigorous program of mutual aid which works toward equality.

5. The congregation should experience the radical character of a justice based upon the gospel and within covenant structures and how this justice brings into tension and qualifies the law of the market place and the laws of the city. Members need to recapture something of the spirit of Tertullian who held that it was possible and necessary to examine and evaluate each law individually to see what may be inherently tyrannical.[31] The examination should be both an individual and congregational process.

6. The congregation should discern the special gifts of each person within it and nurture these gifts for the development of the entire body toward the maturity of Christ, that it might fulfill its mission of a new type of leadership within the city. Special ministries should arise from the congregation and sister congregations to cultivate the ministry of each member in the exercise of their Christian vocation. This ministry will include the resources of their Christian vocation. This ministry will include the resources of the psychological and social sciences; the ministry of the word is important for qualifying and orienting all of these.

7. The ministry of the congregation includes also outreach. The justice of Yahweh practiced in the congregation is to be proclaimed and practiced also in the city. This includes both evangelism and good works. When members of the congregation penetrate the social, economic, and political structures of the city, those structures are also penetrated by covenant structure. It is the challenge of every Christian to see that Covenant and gospel draw into tension the laws and mores of the social and political structures where they are involved.

8. The congregation should be home base for each member's ministry of outreach. What secular vocations should be taken, what should be done about

problems of witness in one's vocation, where one should withdraw, where advance, what corporate witness for peace and justice should be made, these and many others are questions for discussion by small groups and/or the congregational meeting.

9. The congregation, while recognizing its individual character and responsibility before Christ, should be eager to express its unity by cooperation with other congregations who are like-minded in dedication to the way of Yahweh as revealed by the historical Jesus. Congregations which are not like-minded in following this way of peace and justice should be brought into dialogue wherever possible, as an expression of Christian unity. For appropriate social concerns, a congregation might cooperate with men and women of good will wherever they may be found. Such cooperation will demand all the more that each member is able to communicate his or her faith and that the cooperation is for limited objectives.

10. The congregation in the city should regard itself as the *ecclesia* of God, a minority community representing his way of justice open to all classes of the city, whose task is to preach good news to the poor, healing to the sick and blind, release to the prisoner, enfranchisement and possession to the disenfranchised and dispossessed.

NOTES

1. Jacques Ellul, *The Meaning of the City* (William R. Eerdmans Publishing Company, Grand Rapids, Michigan, 1970).

2. Compare the optimism of Harvey Cox toward the city, *The Secular City* (New York, Macmillan, 1966).

3. Renan, *Historie d'Israel* II, p. 341, quoted by Ellul, *op. cit.,* p. 71.

4. Argument between Dumuzi and the farmer and other conflicts between trades and values are debated in Mesopotamian literature, but there is no rural-urban debate. See John Martin Halligan, "*A Critique of the City in the Yahweh Corpus*" (dissertation, U. of Notre Dame, 1975), pp. 47-54.

5. See John Tracy Luke, "Pastoralism and Politics in the Mari Period, a Re-examination of the Character and Political Significance of the Major West Semitic Tribal Groups on the Middle Euphrates, ca. 1828-1758 B.C." (Dissertation, University of Michigan, 1965).

6. *Ibid.*, p. 252.

7. See the translation of a letter by Ronald Fred Youngblood, "The Amarna Correspondence of Rib-Haddi, Prince of Byblos" (dissertation, Dropsie College for Hebrew and Cognate Learning, Philadelphia, 1961), pp. 127f.

8. See Frank S. Frick, *The City in Ancient Israel* (Scholars Press for the Society of Biblical Literature, 1977), p. 97.

9. *Ibid.*, pp. 102-112.

10. *Ibid.*, p. 25-31.

11. *Ibid.*, p. 208

12. Martin Noth held that this narrative is the independent contribution of J, but one cannot be sure. See *The History of Pentateuchal Traditions* (N.J.: Prentice-Hall, 1972), p. 238.

13. See Isaiah 63:5 where Yahweh searches for someone to stay his wrath, but cannot find anyone.

14. Martin Buber is the first to use this term, to my knowledge. See *Kingship of God*, trans. by R. Scheimann, 3rd ed. (London: George Allan and Unwin, Ltd., 1967), pp. 56,57; 126,139,40.

15. The question of the nature of the conquest is beyond the scope of this paper.

16. See Walther Zimmerli, *The Law and the Prophets* (Oxford: Basil Blackwell, 1965). See also the suggestive work of Hans-Joachin Kraus, *Die prophetische Verkundigung des Rechts in Israel* (Evangelischer Verlag AG. Zollikon, 1957).

17. See for example the prologue to Hammurabi's law collection where Hammurabi is chosen by the gods "to cause justice to prevail in the land." In the epilogue he is called "king of justice." See ANET, pp. 164, 178.

18. E.A. Speiser, "Authority and Law in Mesopotamia," J. A. Wilson, et. al., *Authority and Law in the Ancient Orient* (Baltimore: American Oriental Society, 1937), p. 12.

19. For this insight I am indebted to a conversation with J. R. Burkholder, Goshen, Indiana. See Brenden Brown, *The Natural Law Reader* (Ocena Publications, N.Y., 1960), pp. V,IX.

20. See Norman K. Gottwald, *The Tribes of Yahweh* (Maryknoll, N.Y.: Orbis Books, 1979), pp. 237-341.

21. John Bright, *A History of Israel* (Philadelphia: The Westminster Press, 1959), p. 260. See also Frick, *op. cit.*, pp. 113,114.

22. For a definition of monotheism which includes the unity of the cosmos and history, see Hans Wildenberger, "Der Monotheismus Deuterojesaijas," *Beitrage zur alttestamentlichen Theologie*, Festschrift for Walther Zimmerli zum 70 Geburtstag, hrsg. Herbert Donner, et. al. (Gottingen: Vandenhoeck und Ruprecht, 1977), p. 509.

23. As an example, see the prologue of Hammurabi's law, *ANET*, p. 164. Also, Enuma Elis, *ANET* (1969), 60-72.

24. The word translated "remnant" is used in the Bible of those who are left after a defeat. See BDB, 812.

25. See above, IC.

26. See John Howard Yoder, *The Politics of Jesus* (Grand Rapids, Mich.: William B. Eerdmans Pub. Co., 1972), pp. 64-77. But John's main argument, the possibility of a Messianic ethic, does not rest on the slender argument of Jesus' attitude toward jubilee; it is broadly based. See pp. 11ff.

27. This translation is from the Jerusalem Bible except for the word *nations*, which I use instead of JB's *pagans*.

28. Cf. H. Berkhof, *Christ and the Powers*, trans. by John Howard Yoder (Scottdale, PA., Herald Press, 1962).

29. See David Daube, *Studies in Biblical Law* (Cambridge: at the University Press, 1947), pp. 40-53.

30. See Ross Bender, "Ministry in the Believer's Church," Memorandum to Marlin Miller, March 8, 1977, p. 1.

31. See above II C4.

CHAPTER 23

YAHWEH AND FEMININE LIBERATION, A FEW OBSERVATIONS FROM THE HEBREW TEXT

INTRODUCTION

The militant wing of the feminist movement of the 1970's revolted against the "male god" of biblical faith to return to a goddess and nature religion which feminists believed was the original cult of a matriarchal society prior to Yahwism.[1] Writers like Ruether, and especially Trible and Byrd, support the feminine liberation movement not as a revolt against biblical faith but by a reinterpretation of the Bible. We should support such writers who are reexamining the Bible on this question. We must be honest, however, by asking whether theirs is a true exegesis or whether it is reading a modern movement back into the text.

I will center my thoughts around the first two commandments:

> Thou shalt have no other gods before me.
> Thou shalt not make unto thee any graven image.
> (Ex 20:3,4; Dt 5:7,8).

These two commandments are correctly regarded as one, protecting the unity and character of Yahweh. In some enumerations they are counted as the first commandment.

1. The structure an inclusio: the two motive clauses.

The structure of Exodus 20:2-6; Deuteronomy 5:6-10 is an inclusio; that is, the two commandments are contained within two motive clauses (Ex 20:2,5-6), both beginning with exactly the same words, "I (am) Yahweh your God." The first clause refers to Yahweh's past action; the second refers to Yahweh's present and future rule. It is significant for interpreting these two commandments prohibiting the worship of any God other than Yahweh that they are enclosed by two motive clauses, the first denoting this God as one who has

---

A presentation at the Institute of Mennonite Studies Consultation, June 1986.

freed Israel from slavery, the second denoting Yahweh as one whose holy love, rather than wrath, rules to infinity. Since the first clause is the more relevant to our present interest, I will deal only with it.

The first motive clause identifies Yahweh as Israel's God who freed Israel from state oppression. This is the most fundamental identification of Yahweh in the Old Testament. It gave to Israel a different view toward slavery than the views of other Near Eastern nations, as demonstrated in Leviticus 25 where it penetrates the Holiness Law Code as a motive clause: "For they are my slaves, whom I brought forth out of the land of Egypt; they shall not be sold as slaves" (25:42).

This motive clause was extended to other kinds of oppressions, especially to the economic oppression of the resident alien, of the child and of women (Ex 22:21-23). Its aggressive character is documented by Deuteronomy 15:12-18, a later revision of the older law of slavery in Exodus 21:2-6. The older law liberated only the male slave sold for a debt; the new law liberated "a Hebrew man, or a Hebrew woman" sold for a debt. The old law made no economic provision for the released slave; the new law provided for a liberal gift, recognizing the oppressive character of poverty. The old law had no motive clause; the new law supplies the historic motive clause: "You shall remember that you were a slave in the land of Egypt, and Yahweh your God redeemed you; therefore I command you today." In summary, "servitude has been reduced to ownership of a person's labor, not of the persons."[2] Our interest here is to note that the "Hebrew woman" and the motive clause are inserted into the revised law. It is likely that there is a relationship between these two insertions.

2. The Mosaic Covenant and Women

In the larger segment of the present structure in the book of Exodus, the Ten Commandments and the covenant code are introduced by the negotiation of covenant (19:4-6) and are concluded by the ratification of covenant (24:3-8). This covenant was a democratic one in that Moses spoke to "all the people" (24:3), the "twelve tribes of Israel" (24:4), who were then party to the covenant-making ceremony (24:8). The text does not expressly say that this ceremony included women. However, Deuteronomy states that the seven year ceremony at the feast of booths when the law was to be read (probably a recapitulation of covenant) was to include "the people, men, women, and the little ones, and the sojourner..." (Deut 31:12). The recapitulation of covenant in the time of Ezra included wives, sons, daughters, "all who have knowledge and understanding" (Neh 10:28-29). It is therefore likely that women were included at the original covenant ceremony. If not, then covenant logic caused them to be included in later ceremonies. This inclusion meant that women along with men were persons of the covenant, with privileges and responsibilities pertaining thereto. These privileges and responsibilities may have fluctuated in the vicissitudes of history, but the basic fact remained that women along with men participated before God in the legal covenant-making ceremony which was foundational to the Israelite societal order.

3. The Two Commandments

Let us now examine these two commandments themselves:

> Thou shalt have no other gods before me.
> Thou shalt not make unto thee any graven image.

The first command prohibits the worship of any god other than that One who delivers from state bondage. The second rejects the making and worship of images. Although there were tendencies toward monotheism in the Near East, so far as we know monotheism elsewhere was never expressed in a law code. These laws are unique to extant Near Eastern law.

The law of monotheism did away with the male or female consort, of the god eliminating from worship the sexual act, a ceremonial act which was quite central to Near Eastern worship (cf. Judah-Tamar, Gen. 38), and which expressed the economic concerns of Near Eastern religion, a concern which developed at least by the 4th millenium B.C.[3] Near Eastern divinities were to a large extent the personification of impersonal powers, in this case of economics.

For our interests, the first commandment means that divinity is transcendent to the sexual relationship. Since ultimate reality includes no female divinity, this means that it includes no male divinity either, in the commonly accepted meaning of that word. In contrast to the mythologies of the gods of Canaanite and other Near Eastern literature, the Bible includes no Yahwistic sex orgies, obviously because there was neither a male nor female consort. Neither does Yahweh masturbate, as do the gods of Egyptian cosmogonic literature.[4] Nowhere in the Bible, to my knowledge, is there a description of or reference to Yahweh's sex organs. Divinity in the Bible is transcendent to the relationship of sexual intercourse, and thus divinity is understood as neither male nor female in the commonly accepted meaning of those terms.

This conception of divinity represents a break with the pre-Platonic mythological law of correspondences: what is on the earth has its correspondence in the heavens (or really vice versa).[5] Because this mythological analogy is broken in the Bible's conception of divinity, it is difficult to understand the biblical concept.

God as father in the Bible is not to be understood in the mythological sense of the Egyptian god, Amon, who engendered the Pharaoh by copulation with the Queen Mother.[6] Modern popular concepts of approaching God through the analogy of the human father, are based upon a misconception of the biblical concept of God as Father, and are essentially a return to paganism.

Most of the classical prophets charged that Israel and Judah had broken the first and second commandments, loyalty to Yahweh only. This was the special emphasis of Hosea who used the heart of Baal mythology, the male and female relationship, to communicate to his largely Baalistic audience that they had broken covenant with Yahweh. While this language may reinforce biblical literature a personal concept of the covenant relation between God and people, it should be regarded as secondary figurative language which points to the primary event of covenant.

A similar example in the New Testament is the imagery of Christ and the Church. When males use this language of Christ and the church they should remember that they are identified with the female side of the equation, the church, rather than with Christ. If their action is identified with that of Christ as in Ephesians, it is identification with Christ's self-emptying act of love which elevated the church to equality with his own life--a meaningful identification in a society where males have a superior status.

The secondary character of Hosea's figurative language is demonstrated in Hosea 9:1 where the pronouns for Israel are in masculine gender. This is entirely appropriate when the relationship of God and people is removed from the figure of Hosea and his wife, for *Israel* is a masculine noun, a name of the patriarch Jacob.

> *Do not rejoice* (Imperf. 2 *masc.* sg. jussive) O Israel.
> *Do not exult* (Imperative, 2 *masc.* sing.) like other peoples.
> *For you have committed adultery* (Imperf., 2nd *masc.* sing.!!)
>   like other peoples by deserting God.
> *You have loved* (perfect. 2nd *masc.* sing.!!) the wages of a prostitute at every threshing floor.

If one were to regard the relationship here as a primary figure, then Yahweh has married a male. That conclusion seems rather absurd when it is obvious that Hosea throughout uses these figures (as well as others, such that of the rebellious son, Hos. 11) to point to Israel's unfaithful covenant relationship with Yahweh.

This leaves us with the question of why the Bible uses the second and third masculine singular pronoun of Yahweh. That question is answered by the linguists who point out that the so-called masculine pronoun is actually unmarked according to gender, while the feminine pronoun is marked.[7] Given the choice between only these two, it is fitting that the Israelites used the unmarked pronoun of Yahweh who is transcendent to either gender.[8]

4. Humans Created in the Image of God

It is appropriate to discuss Genesis 1:26,27 with the first two commandments because of the words *image* and *likeness*. The first word is a synonym of the Hebrew word used in the commandment (Ex. 20:4) while the second is the same Hebrew word. This is daring mythic language used by the P strata which is the most demythologizing strata of the Pentateuch. Although humans are not to make God in the image of any likeness in the universe, P says that God made humans in the divine likeness.

Relating to our subject, there are two mutually exclusive interpretations of this passage. One is represented by Barth, that the image represents the male-female characteristic incorporated within God's own person: "in his image, male and female created he them."[9] The second interpretation is that *image/likeness* here is kingship language along with *dominion over, subdue* (cf. Ps 6:5,6).[10] The Pharaoh is often spoken of as the image of the god Re, all the way from the late first millennium back to the early second millennium B.C. Probably in a democratization of this language, Egyptian wisdom literature speaks of humanity as made in the image of the divine, as early as the third millennium B.C. More than this, when Near Eastern kings conquered new territory, they often set up their images when they departed, as representatives of their own rule.

Looking at our text again in the light of these Near Eastern possibilities, image/likeness might mean the human as representative of God ruling over the earth. The uniqueness of P's statement, then, is that both male and female share in this rule, a concept not found elsewhere in Near Eastern literature. This is a rather remarkable concept for a priestly class which included only males.

In summary, the Bible developed in the ancient Near Eastern and Mediterranean worlds, in a society within which the male dominated the overarching public institutions. This male domination of public institutions was characteristic of all ancient societies, so far as we know. This characteristic was penetrated however, by the heart of the biblical faith: by motive clause (*history*) which recognized that women with men experienced deliverance from state slavery; by *covenant*, in which women and men shared privilege and responsibility before God (though these fluctuated in the vicissitudes of history); by *law*, which excluded from the experience of God the male-female consort relationship and its emphasis upon magic and impersonality in the divine-human relationship of worship, replacing this with the I-Thou relationship ("I am...Thou shalt"). This penetration of history, covenant, and law was the seed of promise for God's act in Christ, an act which is yet to come to full fruition in the freedom and responsibility of male and female in the presence of God.

NOTES

1. Rosemary Radford Ruether, "The Female Nature of God: A Problem in Contemporary Religious Life," Johannes-Baptist Metz and Edward Schillebeeckx, editors, *God as Father* (New York: The Seabury Press, 1981), 64.

2. Dale Patrick, *Old Testament Law* (Atlanta: John Knox Press, 1985), 113.

3. Thorkild Jacobsen, *The Treasures of Darkness, a History of Mesopotamian Religion* (New Haven and London: Yale University Press, 1976).

4. See Pritchard, *ANET*, p. 6.

5. James Barr, "The Meaning of 'Mythology' in Relation to the Old Testament," *Vetus Testamentum*, IX (1959) 1-10.

6. Henri Frankfort, *Kingship and the Gods, a Study of Ancient Near Eastern Religion as the Integration of Society and Nature* (Chicago: The University of Chicago Press, 1948), 45.

7. All English pronouns are unmarked outside of context except for the third person singular pronoun. An example of the use of the unmarked third person singular "masculine" pronoun is, "The person who is honest in *his* relationships does not need to fear exposure." I had noticed this character of the pronoun in reading the Hebrew Bible, but was introduced to the linguistic terminology by my colleague, Perry Yoder. See John Lyons, *Introduction to Theoretical Linguistics* (Cambridge University Press, 1968), 79.

8. Perhaps it would be better to use the grammatical terms *unmarked* and *marked* of Hebrew pronouns instead of *masculine* and *feminine*.

9. For a history of interpretation of "image" and "likeness" of Genesis 1:26-27, see Claus Westermann, *Genesis 1-11, A Commentary* (Minneapolis: Augsburg Publishing House, 1984), 147-155.

10. See Hans Wildberger, "Das Abbild Gottes, Gen. 1:30, II," *Theologische Zeitschrift* 6 (1965) 481-501.

CHAPTER 24

A POLITICAL ALTERNATIVE: AN EXAMINATION OF EZEKIEL'S RECOGNITION STATEMENTS

No revolt in Jerusalem! With this understanding of Ezekiel's intention to head off Zedekiah's revolt against Babylon, Bernhard Lang (1978, pp. 152-180) challenges Zimmerli's pastoral and theological interpretation of the pre-exilic oracles. It is the thesis of this essay that Lang's practical reorientation of Ezekiel studies reflects part of Ezekiel's larger intention focused in the recognition statements: "you shall know that I am Yahweh" means not a mere exchange of one nationalism for another, but the acknowledgment by Israel and the nations of an alternative politics to the realpolitik[1] of the Near East (NE).

Each recognition statement has been examined within the context of its oracle or narrative unit (the "recognition oracle" or "unit") to determine the nature of the goal which it sets forth for Yahweh's acts (cf. Zimmerli 1954, pp. 9-16; Takiya 1964, p. XIV). My focus is not upon the fact of Yahweh's action but upon 1) the prophetic political structure of the announced action, 2) its character as expressed in judgment oracles by threat/indictment and in salvation oracles by promise, 3) finally, I examine the recognition oracles against Zedekiah and the nations, especially against Gog.[2] Though I have examined all the recognition statements, I limit this presentation to illustrate these three considerations.

I. PROPHETIC POLITICAL STRUCTURE AND THE RECOGNITION STATEMENT: "they will know that there has been a prophet among them."

Though this recognition statement occurs only twice in Ezekiel (2:5; 33:33) it is essential for understanding the recognition of Yahweh (cf. Zimmerli 1954, p. 67). Occurring first in the call narrative[3] the statement acknowledges that Yahweh's universal rule (1:26-28) is mediated not by Jerusalem's coercive politics (cf. Lind 1980, p. 63) but by Ezekiel's prophetic word.

This universal ruler addresses Ezekiel as "son of man" (2:1), a term here associated with human weakness (1:28c-2:2). Political authority is vested not in Ezekiel's person or office, but in the word/spirit of the one by whom he has been sent (2:3,4), authority clarified by the messenger formula, "thus says Yahweh...." Israel is in a state of rebellion against this authority (*mārad* and *pāśaʿ*, 2:3,4)[4], a rebellion which would issue in Ezekiel's torment (vss 6-7). But whether Israel would hear or reject Ezekiel, they would recognize that their enthroned leader had given them political direction by this prophet (vs 5).

The second recognition statement involving the prophet (oracle, 33:30-33)[5] indicates that when his dissembling hearers experience the judgment Ezekiel had prophesied, "then they will know that a prophet has been among them." Fulfillment of prophetic word rather than victory in battle was the primary criterion by which Israel would recognize that Yahweh is indeed God (cf. Westermann 1969, pp. 15, 84, 85).

The concept of fulfillment of threat/promise as basis for recognition is found in other statements: "and they shall know that I, Yahweh, have spoken in my jealousy, when I spend my fury upon them" (5:13* cf. 37:14; 17:21*, 24*; 24:24).[6] As a reflective reading will show, this is a presupposition underlying all recognition statements.

In summary, Yahweh's immediate rule by prophetic messenger to the people and their leaders is the theopolitical order (cf. Buber 1952, p. 139) set forth in Ezekiel's oracles, forming an essential part of the word-fulfillment schema by which Yahweh's recognition will be achieved.

II. THE CHARACTER OF YAHWEH'S ANNOUNCED POLITICAL ACTION

Since Yahweh's action has recognition as its goal, the nature of this action/goal will now be examined in two types of oracles: threat/indictment and promise of political salvation.

A. The Announced Action: Threat of Yahweh's Judgment

Yahweh's basic action announced against Israel is defeat in war. Within the recognition oracles and narrative units the word *ḥereb* 'sword' occurs twenty-seven times as judgment against Israel and Jerusalem.[7] This and other war-like expressions indicate the political realism of Ezekiel's message, that the expanding Babylonian empire would engulf the Judean state.

Though Ezekiel's message of defeat is politically realistic, the human cause of defeat, indicated by the indictments,[8] is spiritual and moral. The fundamental indictment of the recognition oracle/unit is rebellion against Yahweh's political leadership (2:5-7, *bêt mĕrî* 'house of rebellion'; 5:6; 20:21a *mārâ* 'rebel'; 20:38, *mārad* 'rebel', *pāšaʿ* 'transgress').[9] The rebellion is against Yahweh's ordinances/statutes (5:6; 20:18-21a).[10] Such negative behavior is further delineated as worship of idols (6:5-6*, 13; cf. 20:18*, 24*; 23:49*),[11] Israel's ways (7:27; 14:22,23; 20:43,44)[12] and abominations (5:9*; 7:3,4,9; 12:16*),[13] profaning sabbaths (20:20),[14] defiling the sanctuary (5:11*),[15] bloody crimes, violence (7:23; 12:19),[16] multiplying the slain (11:6),[17] shedding blood (33:25),[18] resorting to the sword (33:26),[19] dishonest gain, blood in their midst (22:13*),[20] eating flesh with blood (33:25),[21] defiling neighbor's wives (33:26),[22] iniquity, dealing treacherously (39:23*),[23] uncleanness and transgressions (39:24*).[24]

Ezekiel indicts Israel's political leaders--prophets, elders, Davidic dynasty.

He indicts male prophets who are not sent by Yahweh, who divine lies and cry peace when there is no peace (13:1-16).[25] For these reasons, their whitewashed wall would collapse; the prophets will then recognize that the God who rules history by moral and spiritual directives (13:11*,14) is indeed Yahweh. Ezekiel indicts female prophets whose magic performance disheartens the righteous and encourages the wicked so that there is no repentance (13:17-23).[26] When delivered from these prophets, the people would recognize that Ezekiel's God is indeed the liberating Yahweh (13:21).

Ezekiel indicts the exiled elders who, though alienated from Yahweh by mental idolatry, had come to Ezekiel for an oracle (14:1-11).[27] He indicts the Davidic dynasty who with the people were a rebellious house (bêt-hammerî, 12:2)[28]: having eyes and ears (prophets) they neither "saw nor heard." He warns Zedekiah who had broken covenant with Nebuchadnezzar and with Yahweh (17:11-21)[29] that when his rebellious policy will fail, they (Israel/nations?) will know that the God Ezekiel represents determines their political future (12:15; cf. 17:21).[30]

Except for those against Zedekiah, these indictments are less realistic from a conventional political viewpoint than are the threats of defeat. Was Israel's political difficulty due to their theological and domestic sins, or was it due to Babylon's westward expansion, for which there was no possible cure other than capitulation or alliance with Egypt? This "spiritualization" tendency of his indictments is compounded by Ezekiel's oracles of political salvation.

B. The Announced Action: Political Salvation

The editorial summary states the case: "Then they shall know that I am Yahweh their God because I sent them into exile among the nations, and then gathered them into their own land" (39:28*).[31] Exile and return make up the cycle by which Yahweh will be recognized as political leader.

Ezekiel prophesies that Yahweh will reconstitute Israel by resurrection and will place them in their own land (37:6,13,14).[32] He makes no hint that Israel would do this by military prowess, nor even that Yahweh would do it because of their repentance. Yahweh must act to vindicate the holy name, a name profaned by Israel when the nations interpret the exile as due to Yahweh's political impotence (36:16-23;[33] cf. 20:40-44).[34]

Though Yahweh would reinstate Israel not because of Israel's repentance but to vindicate the divine name, Israel may not continue its rebellion. The recognition goal will be achieved only when Yahweh is king over Israel: gathering Israel from the nations, Yahweh will purge out the rebels in the wilderness (20:33-38;[35] cf. Nu 14:20-24); Yahweh will renew Israel that they might walk in the divine statutes (36:22-32).[36] Yahweh also will renew the devastated land (36:33-36), will increase Israel "like a flock" (36:37-38); then Israel and surrounding nations will recognize Yahweh as political leader.

In his critique of Israel's kingship and promise of a new "servant David," Ezekiel proclaims that Israel will recognize Yahweh when they are delivered from political servitude, both domestic and foreign (34:20-21);[37] "And they shall know that I am Yahweh, when I break the bars of their yoke, and deliver them from the hand of those who enslave them. They shall no longer be a prey to the nations...; they shall dwell securely and none shall make them afraid" (34:27*, 28). There is no hint that Israel's domestic pacification is to be achieved by the coercive power of the Davidic prince; rather, it is to be achieved by Yahweh's act of humanization, by replacing Israel's "heart of stone" with a "heart of flesh" (36:26).

In summary, Ezekiel's threat of military defeat proved more realistic in the course of history than did the politics of the Jerusalem court. However, ascribing the cause of this debacle solely to Israel's theological and domestic relationship, declaring that it might be avoided by repentance, would seem less than realistic. Further, Ezekiel's concept that Israel will be reestablished by Yahweh's power of resurrection and humanization breaks the mold of conventional politics.

As indicated above, an exception to the "spiritualization" tendency of Ezekiel's indictments is found in the two recognition oracles against Zedekiah's political policy, "no revolt in Jerusalem." Is this exception based upon NE real-politik or, like the more spiritual/moral indictments, is it based upon religion (theopolitics)? Again, if in Ezekiel's oracles the Davidic prince plays no role in pacifying the domestic situation, how is the international community pacified? The two oracles against Zedekiah and the recognition oracles against the nations (especially against Gog) will now be examined.

THEOPOLITICS AND REALPOLITIK

A. Two Oracles Against Zedekiah's International Policy

1. 12:1-16[38]
Consisting of a prophetic act (vss 1-7) and its interpretation (vss 8-16) and directed "to the house of Israel,"[39] this oracle was made near the beginning of Zedekiah's revolt against Nebuchadnezzar (cf. Zimmerli, 1, 1983, p. 269).

a. Yahwistic Political Structure
Prophetic political structure in this oracle compares to that of the previous discussion. Ezekiel's authority is Yahweh's word, indicated by the revelation (vss 1,8) and messenger (vs 10)* formulae. As a *môpet* 'sign', Ezekiel embodies this word in action (vs. 11). As messenger and sign, Ezekiel is addressed as "son of man" (vss. 2,3,9; cf. 2:1,2), an indication of dependence, an indication augmented by the first personal singular pronoun, used by the prophet only when professing obedience (vs 7) as Yahweh's sign (vs 11), but used by Yahweh to dominate the action immediately before the recognition statement (vss. 13,14).

b. Yahwistic Politics and Realpolitik
Ezekiel's oracle is directed at "the prince" and "all the house of Israel," a "rebellious house" (vss. 2,3,9*) against the prophetic political structure: "who have eyes to see but see not [eg., the prophetic sign, vs. 11], who have ears to

hear, but hear not" [eg. the prophetic word, vs. 1]. Ezekiel's determined confrontation to make them see is indicated by *lĕ-ênêhem* 'in their sight,' a phrase repeated six times (vss. 3,3*,4*,4*,5,6*,7). Their inability to see and hear was not their improper discernment of the current political winds, but their deliberate rejection of the prophet's directives for the nation (see Greenberg, 1983, p. 220). From the standpoint of conventional politics, Ezekiel's public demonstration (vss. 3-11), designed to change Israel's international policy, was rebellion against "the prince" (cf. Amos 7:10-13); but from the standpoint of Ezekiel (and Amos), Jerusalem's prince was the rebel.

To "know Yahweh" meant that Jerusalem must recognize Yahweh as political leader, a leadership not by human power but by prophetic word, and must acknowledge that reliance upon Egyptian armament is an autonomous policy that leads to disintegration (vss. 13,14). The recognition statements (12:15,16*) form an inclusio for the exiles' confession of their *tô-ēbôt* 'abominations' (vs. 16*). This word 'abominations' belongs "to the vocabulary of the Deuteronomic polemic against idolatry" (e.g., Deut 7:25f.; 13:15; 17:4, Greenberg, p. 113), and is used by Ezekiel of Judah's life-style (cf. 5:9-11*). The exiles will confess that because Judah had shaped its domestic life after the demands of the power gods of the NE, Yahweh has given them over to those powers.

2. 17:1-24

This chapter, both a *ḥîdâ* 'riddle' which hides the message and *māšāl* 'allegory' which illuminates it (vs. 2; see Greenberg, p. 309), has a political viewpoint similar to that of chapter 12: Yahweh is ruler (vss. 19-21; 22-24*), Ezekiel is prophetic messenger (vss. 1,3,11,19,22a*), who as such is vulnerable (vs. 2a); the recognition of Yahweh's rule is entirely dependent upon the fulfilled word (vss. 21,24)*. The chapter is different, however, in the clarity of its description and critique of Israel's integration into NE politics (17:1-21),[40] and in its statement of the future success of Yahwistic politics (17:22-24)*.[41]

a. Ezekiel's Description and Critique of Jerusalem's Integration Into NE Power Politics (17:1-21)

In this allegory Ezekiel describes Jerusalem's international situation: a small vine between eagle-headed cherubim (Nebuchadnezzar and Pharaoh), Jerusalem, planted and watered by Nebuchadnezzar, prefers Pharaoh (vss. 3-8). Ezekiel articulates well the difference between a sovereign and client state (vss. 2-6), the means by which the client relationship is established (vss. 13,14), the consequences of violating the relationship (vs. 15), and the futility of military reliance upon Egypt (v. 17*).[42] Even from Zedekiah's own position of power politics, Ezekiel perceives the situation much more realistically than did the Jerusalem court.

Ezekiel juxtaposes to this NE political perception, however, his perception from the Yahwistic point of view: "Indeed (*lākēn*),[43] thus says Yahweh God: as I live, surely my oath which he despised, and my covenant which he broke, I will requite upon his head" (vs. 19). Yahweh will bring Zedekiah to

Babylon and judge him for the *ma'al* 'treason'[44] committed against the divine suzerain. When this threat is fulfilled, Israel will recognize "that I, Yahweh have spoken" (vs. 21).[45]

The traditional interpretation of this juxtaposition identifies the Zedekiah-Nebuchadnezzar covenant with Yahweh's covenant (Zimmerli 1, 1979, pp. 365, 366; cf. Tsevat 1959, pp. 199-204). Lang (pp. 54-60, 182-184) accepts this view, but argues that this broken treaty with Babylon was a superficial criticism made only here by Ezekiel; that underlying most of Ezekiel's work is the critique that military reliance upon Egypt is idolatrous. Greenberg (pp. 320-323) however, rejects the traditional interpretation, arguing that Ezekiel here views the situation from two planes, the human (vss. 11-18) and the divine (vss. 19-21), and that the broken divine covenant is Ezekiel's fundamental reason for the future collapse of Zedekiah's foreign policy.

A reexamination of the Massoretic text reveals that the pronouns distinguish between the two covenants: in *'ālātô, běrîtô* 'his oath,' 'his covenant' (vs. 16*), the Babylonian king is the pronoun's antecedent;[46] in *'ālātî, běrîtî* 'my oath,' 'my covenant' (v. 19), Yahweh is the pronoun's antecedent (cf. 16:59). Though juxtaposed, the two covenants are not necessarily the same since *lākēn* (vs. 19) may emphasize the new oracle.[47]

While both covenants are not identical, they do share the same indictment: "but he rebelled against him by sending ambassadors to Egypt, that they might give him horses and a large army" (v. 15). Although here directed to rebellion against Babylon, it is also the traditional indictment of Israel's diplomatic rebellion against Yahweh (Hos 5:8-6:6; Isa 30:1-5; 31:1-3; Jer 2:14-19), a rebellion which Ezekiel traces throughout Israel's history (23:1-21). After stating the two kingdoms' common unfaithfulness in their Egyptian beginnings, Ezekiel details the diplomatic history of the North: "she doted on her lovers, the Assyrians, warriors clothed in purple,... all of them desirable young men, horsemen riding on horses" (23:5,6). Ezekiel continues this diplomatic history by detailing the unfaithfulness of the South: relations with the Assyrians (23:12), Chaldeans and Babylonians (23:14,15), and in full circle, with Egypt (vs. 19; cf. vs. 3). Ezekiel relates this military unfaithfulness to cultic harlotry (23:7; cf. 16:26-29 where diplomatic harlotry is inserted in a survey of cultic harlotry). That this relationship is not adequately explained by the observation that ancient NE diplomatic relations could not be made without recognition of each others gods (Fohrer, p. 134), is evident from this text itself which states it quite differently: having been seduced to harlotry by attraction to military power, Israel then "defiled herself with all the idols of every one on whom she doted" (23:7*). The objective of Yahweh's judgment is "so that you shall not lift up your eyes" to the Egyptians (vs. 27), an expression used of idolatry in 18:12. The national gods of the NE empires were power oriented gods; alliance with these military powers is synonymous with trust in these gods, a trust which is incompatible with Yahwistic politics (cf. Lang 1978, pp. 183-186).

What then does this interpretation mean for the recognition statement (17:21)? Ezekiel's *hîdâ* 'riddle' analyzes the results of Jerusalem's action from

two perspectives, the first from that of conventional politics, Zedekiah's violation of the Babylonian covenant; the second, which is emphasized, from the
perspective of violated covenant with Yahweh. Yahweh is lord in the NE
political arena: because Zedekiah had committed treason (*ma'alô*) against
Yahweh by sending ambassadors to Egypt, Yahweh will requite upon Zedekiah
the military violence in which he has trusted (17:19,20*; cf. 23:22-27). Israel
will then know that Yahweh has spoken in the allegory of this "son of man" (vs.
2).

b. Future Success of Yahwistic Politics: The Proverb (17:22-24)

Ezekiel's recognition statement is concerned ultimately with the establishment of a Yahwistic governmental structure (17:22-24)*.[48] An enlargement
of the statement as in 37:14, the second statement (vs. 24) is split in two to
form an inclusio for the proverb, a proverb building on the allegory as
indictated by the reversals, language drawn from the vine imagery (Greenberg
1983, p. 317): "I, Yahweh, bring low [*hišpaltî*, cf. *šiplat*, vs. 6, *šĕpālâ*, vs. 14] the
high tree, and make high the low tree [*ʾēs šāpāl*, cf. vss. 6,14], dry up [*hôbašî*, cf.
yābēš ʾîbos, vs. 9], the green tree, and make the dry tree flourish [*ʾēs yābēš*, cf.
vs. 10]. If one follows this interpretive lead (see Lang 1978, pp. 83-88 for other
arguments), the proverb is concerned throughout with the Davidic dynasty, that
Yahweh first frustrates its autonomous political pretensions then replants it
according to the sovereignty of Yahweh's word (cf. Deut 32:39).

This recognition of Yahweh involves the nations: "All the trees of the
field shall know..." (see Greenberg 1983, pp. 316-317). Nowhere in the book of
Ezekiel is there a concept of the prince ruling over the nations (see Lang 1978,
72-80); instead, there is a concept of the universal recognition of another kind
of political existence, the rule of Yahweh's word as demonstrated by a prince
who in the midst of the nations functions under Yahweh's covenant.[49]

If in Ezekiel the revived Davidic dynasty plays no role in the pacification
either of Israel or the nations, how then are the nations to be pacified?

B. The Oracles Against the Nations, Gog

1. The Recognition Oracles Against the Nations

The foreign recognition oracles are against Ammon (25:1-7),[50] Moab
(25:8-11), Edom (25:12-14)[51] and Mount Seir (35:1-9, 10-15),[52] Philistia (25:15-
17), Tyre (26:1-6),[53] Sidon (28:20-23*) and Egypt (29:1-6a; 29:6b-9, 13-16;[54]
30:1-8; 13-19*, 20-26[55]; 32:1-16).[56]

Like the domestic oracles, these are realistic in their threat of defeat in
war.[57] Again like the domestic oracles, the indictments give spiritual/moral
reasons for the nations' defeat: Ammonites and Moabites gloat over the deso-
late land (25:3,8); Edom and Philistia avenge themselves upon defeated Judah
(25:12,15; cf. 35:5); Tyre exults over vistas of commercial opportunity occasioned by Jerusalem's fall (26:2); Egypt has been an unrealiable reed-staff to
Israel (29:6,7). Do these oracles arise from Ezekiel's patriotic fervor, or is a
spiritual/moral principle involved? The funeral lament against Egypt (32:17-

32) by its universal polemic against militarism points in the latter direction: Egypt, Assyria, Elam, Meshech and Tubal, princes of the north and Sidonians are sent down to the *bôr* 'Pit', slain by the sword, because they "spread terror in the land of the living" (*'ăšer-nātĕnû hittîtām bĕ'ereṣ ḥayyîm*, or variant, 32:23,24,25*,26,30*,32*). Also, in the recognition oracles against Egypt, generalized reasons are given for the threats of defeat: arrogance (29:3), *gĕ'ôn 'uzzāh* 'proud might' (30:6,18*); fouling the nations' rivers with its feet (32:2; cf. vss. 13*,14*). As we shall see, the Gog oracles also point toward a moral/spiritual rather than a patriotic motivation. Ezekiel proclaimed that the nations will recognize Yahweh as universal political leader who opposes imperialistic militarism, especially as directed against Yahweh's representative, defeated, powerless Judah.

The oracle against Edom (25:12-14), the only oracle in the book where Israel is to be the instrument of Yahweh's vengeance, compares to the recognition narrative, 1 Kings 20:26-30. In this battle description, though Syria's military superiority is emphasized, Yahweh intervenes only after Israel had annihilated most of the Syrian army (20:29,30). The recognition statement is found also in the plague narratives (see Zimmerli 1954, pp. 19-26)[58] and is the goal of Yahweh's intervention in which Israel will be led from Egypt without a human battle. This intervention became paradigmatic for Yahweh's war (Lind, 1980, p. 34), an intervention comparing to that in the Gog narrative, discussed below. The uniqueness of Ezekiel's statement of Yahweh's vengeance "by the hand" of Israel may be matched by the fact that this is not a genuine recognition statement: "and they shall experience my vengeance, says Yahweh God" (25:14).[59]

A second unusual oracle in this segment against the nations is the political salvation oracle concerning Egypt (29:13-16). Israel's historic imperialist enemy will be restored, but stripped of its imperialism, its politics no more a temptation to Israel. With this unburdening they (Israel/Egypt?) will recognize Yahweh.

2. The Recognition Statement and the Gog Oracles (Ezek 38-39)

The fifth recognition statement of the oracles against Gog (39:21-22) is the goal of the entire Gog event, whose "story line" (38:1-13; 39:1-5, 9-20)[60] is supplemented by four recognition units enlarging on individual aspects of the main event (38:14-16*, 17-23*; 39:6*, 7-8*). I will deal primarily with the goal of the "story line," the fifth statement, and secondarily with the "supplements."

a. Israel's Yahwistic International Politics

Ezekiel 38:1-13 presents two types of politics, that of Israel and of Gog. The time is "after many days" (v. 8), after the restoration and humanization described in chapters 33-37. Contrary to the previous situation, the land, once a "continual waste" is now "revived from the power of the sword;" the people "dwell securely..." (*lābeṭaḥ*, vs. 8).

Ezekiel presents the land as militarily defenseless (vs. 11): a land "of unwalled villages" (*pĕrāzôt*), a people "dwelling without walls" (*bĕ'ên ḥômâ*) and "having no bars or gates" (*bĕrîḥ ûdĕlātayim 'ên lāhem*). Since this contradicts

36:35 (*bĕṣûrôt yāšābû*), Fohrer (pp. 215,216) regards all this as a gloss, the unwalled villages describing a period when Israel had not yet had time nor wealth to rebuild the walls. Zimmerli (1985, 2, p. 310; cf. Zech 2:5-9) regards the entire reference (38:10-13) as the addition of a post-exilic writer (c. 520 B.C.E.) who opted with Zechariah against walls, satisfied with Yahweh's protection only. But if a disciple could have been satisfied with trust in Yahweh instead of walls, may not Ezekiel also have been? As for Fohrer's argument, Ezekiel 38-39 may originally have been independent of chapter 36, and more congruent with his criticism against power alliances (23:2-20).

In the land long enough to collect cattle and goods sufficient to awaken the greed of far off Gog and the merchants (vss. 11-13), Israel had not bothered to build fortifications. They are portrayed as the *quiet* people who dwell *securely (haššoqĕṭîm yošĕbê lābĕtah)*, two words with the same root as those of Isaiah 30:15: "In *quietness (bĕhašqēṭ)* and *confidence (ûbĕbithâ)* shall be your (military) strength (*gĕbûrâ)*," part of a pericope counseling trust in God to the exclusion of armaments and alliances (see Huber, 1976, pp. 140-160, 226). Ezekiel's portrayal is one of Israel's deliberate political policy, motivated by trust in Yahweh.

b. The Recognition Statement and the Imperialistic Politics of Gog

To identify Gog, it is best to begin with his function, that of a militarist, typical of the imperialists with which Israel had dealt since 8th century Assyria and before (Ezek 23:1-21).[61] Gog's advancing army is described in images typically used of military campaigns in NE annals: "You will advance, coming on like a storm, you will be like a cloud covering the land..." (38:9, cf. Luckenbill, 1924, p. 44). Like NE imperialists, Gog will be motivated by economic interests: "to seize spoil and carry off plunder"... (38:12). This economic prospect will incite international merchants who profit from such campaigns by barter and trade (38:13).

Who then is Gog? A comparison of the Gog indictments with those made against the nations can readily be made, indictments which condemn both arrogance and violence of nations who violate helpless Judah (25:3,8,12,15; 26:2), and imperialists who spread international terror (32:2,17-32). With mythological imagery, Ezekiel denounces the political autonomy and self-aggrandizement of the great commercial and military empires (28:1-10,11-19; 29:2,3; 31:10-11). However, instead of using Israel's historic enemy, Egypt, upon which to vent his final invective against imperialism, Ezekiel restores Egypt (shorn of its imperialism) and chooses Gog and the half-mythic peoples of *yarkĕtê ṣāpôn*, the "far-off north" (38:6).[62] Ezekiel's proto-apocalypticism is not a flight from history but a polemic against history's perennial problem, imperialistic politics and oppression. The polemic is made in such a way that Israel's historical enemies might participate with Israel in acknowledgment of the politics of quietness and confidence (39:21)![63]

Though Ezekiel portrays dualistic politics, both are controlled by Yahweh. Yahweh is the aggressive protagonist who sets Gog in motion against the quiet political stance of Israel (38:4). Nevertheless, Gog himself devises "an evil scheme" (38:10) and throughout the pericope is never the instrument but the antagonist of Yahweh. The "supplement" also emphasizes Gog's autonomous politics (38:14-16a*), then presents Yahweh initiating its demise (38:16b*).

c. The Demise of Gog's Politics (39:1-5,9-20).

The oracle of 39:1-5 begins by repeating 38:2-4: in control of Gog's driving forces, Yahweh will turn Gog from his military successes and send him toward his end (vs. 2*). Yahweh controls violent autonomous politics, even though Yahweh is represented by a militarily defenseless people, by a mere spokesman, the prophet.

Yahweh's battle with Gog is stated low-key: Yahweh will strike the war implements from Gog's hands (v.3). Gog's imperial politics will meet its end on "the mountains of Israel" (vs. 4; cf. Isa 14:24-27), the land whose foreign relations are based upon quietness and trust in Yahweh. The "supplements" (38:17-23*; 39:6*, see Fohrer 1955, pp. 215,217) enlarge upon this battle with apocalyptic imagery, a portrayal of an eschatological holy war (see von Rad 1959, pp. 99, 100). As in the Exodus story, basic text and "supplement" agree that the defeat is due solely to Yahweh's act; the "quiet people" do not raise a hand.

Though they do not participate in battle, "the quiet people" are involved with its aftermath (39:9-20),[64] the apogee of Ezekiel's polemic against Gog's imperialism. As in the early conquest narratives (Josh 11:9, Lind, 1980, p. 64), the weapons are burned (cf. Isa 9:5), though here the burning is for a productive purpose (39:10; cf. Isa 2:4). The denigration of war implements as useless waste corresponds with the early tradition of Jothan's fable: the fruit trees refuse to reign over the forest because they are engaged in socially useful occupations (Judg 9:7-15).

The sacrificial feast presents a reversal: ordinarily, human beings participate in animal sacrifices; here, animals participate in human sacrifices. The victuals are described as "flesh of the mighty" (*gibbôrîm*, professional soldiers) and "the blood of...princes" (*nĕsî᾽ê*, 39:18a), called "rams" (*᾽êlîm*), "lambs" (*kārîm*), "goats" (*᾽attûdîm*) and "bulls" (*pārîm* 39:18b)*. This corresponds with Ezekiel's polemic against the "shepherds of Israel," "rams" and "he-goats" (*᾽êlîm*, *᾽attûdîm*, 34:17-19, cf. 20-21). Ezekiel's critique against Gog's international politics is essentially the same as that against Israel's rebellious domestic politics.

The pericope begins (38:1-9) with a description of the violent political apparatus of the nations, represented by Gog, on the march against "the quiet people who dwell securely." The march ends with this political apparatus as fuel for burning by "the quiet people" and as carrion for vultures and wild beasts (39:9-20). It may not be inappropriate to contrast these less than human images with the *kābôd* 'glory' of Yahweh "set among the nations" (39:21), a glory which in the first vision is a "likeness as it were of a *mar᾽ēh ᾽ādām*, 'human form' (1:26); or to compare them to the prophet who in the Gog pericope is addressed as *ben-᾽ādām* 'son of man' (38:2,14*; 39:1,17).

d. The Recognition of Yahweh (39:21-22; 39:23-24*)

The term "glory" here refers to Yahweh's judgment on Gog's armies. By Yahweh's judgment the nations will perceive (*wĕ rā᾽û*) that autonomous, violent politics end in the death of the international community; and Israel will recognize (wĕ yādĕʿû) that Yahweh is savior God. The recognition statement involves not merely the victory of one nationalism over another, but the acknowledgment of an alternative way in the midst of the imperialisms of the NE: trust in Yahweh which rejects the politics of the sword as less than human.

Ezekiel 39:23,24,* usually regarded as a "supplement" related to Ezekiel's total message (Zimmerli, 2 1983, p. 17), may refer specifically to the Gog pericope, relating Yahwistic domestic policy to Yahwistic foreign policy. Israel went into exile not because of Yahweh's political impotence (cf. 36:16-21), but because like Gog, Judah had governed itself by greed and violent power politics.

CONCLUSION

If Ezekiel's recognition statements are interpreted within the context of their oracle and narrative units, then the recognition of Yahweh involves acknowledgment of a prophetic political structure which provides an alternative to the realpolitik of the ancient NE. This theopolitic was realistic in that it predicted military defeat for Israel and the death of the international community. Ezekiel broke the boundaries of conventional politics, however, by proclaiming that Judah might be saved by obedience to Yahwistic prescriptions and prophetic word, and that beyond exile Judah will be restored by resurrection and humanization. Ezekiel's ultimate optimism was his portrayal of the final collapse of imperialistic politics as represented by Gog's semi-mythic hords on the march against Yahweh's quiet and confident people. The genius of this portrayal was that it made possible that Israel and its historic enemies, both small states and empires, would acknowledge the efficacy of the politics of nonviolence and trust.

NOTES

1. See Morganthau (1985, pp. 31-51) for a definition of *realpolitik* as a politics whose concern is power to control, based on threat of military or police power. For ancient mythologies of *realpolitik*, see "The Theology of Memphis," "The Creation Epic," "The Code of Hammurabi" in Pritchard (1955, pp. 4-6, 60-72, 163-165). (Cf. Lind 1980, pp. 50-53).

2. For statistics of the recognition statement in Ezekiel and Tanach, see Zimmerli (1954 pp. 6-7, 17-38).

3. On the inner unity of vision, call and commission, see Fohrer (1955 p. 6). I regard the recognition unit as 1:26-2:7.

4. For a discussion of the political significance of *mārēd* and *pāšać*, see Greenberg (1983, p. 63).

5. Fohrer (1955, 190) agrees with the definition of this unit. Where he disagrees substantially, I indicate this with a footnote.

6. Although my study is based on the present Massoretic text, I note with a star * any portion of the text which Fohrer regards as a non-Ezekiel supplement, if it is essential to my point. Any unstarred text indicates that my point is founded on his basic text. His choice of basic texts do not essentially alter my argument. Translations are from the *Revised Standard Version* (1952). Variations from this are my translations.

7. Recognition oracles (or units) followed by the verse with *hereb* as judgment are: *5:1-17*, vss. 1, 2, 2*, 12, 12*, 17*. (Fohrer 1955, p. 35, regards the recognition statement, vs. 13, as supplementary); *6:1-10*, vss. 3, 8* (Fohrer 1955, p. 37, regards the recognition statements, vss. 7, 8-10 as supplements); *6:11-14*, vss. 11, 12 (Fohrer: p. 39, regards the second recognition statement, vs. 14, as supplement); *7:10-27*, vss. 15, 15*; *11:5-12* vss. 8*, 8*, 10 (Fohrer, p. 59: the second recognition statement, vs. 12, is supplement); *12:1-16*, vss. 14, 16* (Fohrer 1955, p. 65: the second recognition statement, vs. 16, is supplement); *14:12-23*, vss. 17, 17, 21; *17:1-21*, vs. 21; *21:6-12* [Eng. 21:1-7], vss. 8[3], 9*[4], 10[5] (Fohrer 1955, pp. 118, 120, divides: 21:1-10; 21:11-12); *24:15-24*, vs. 21; *33:23-29*, vs. 27; *39:23-24*; vs. 23*. (Fohrer 1955, p. 217: 39:23-29 is supplement. His "supplements" do not invalidate my point).

8. "Indictment" is here used in a general rather than technical literary sense.

9. See note 4 for political connotations of these words. For the recognition units of the first two references, see notes 3 and 7; *20:18-21a, 33-38* are the immediate recognition contexts of the last two references.

10. Notes 7, 9.

11. Notes 7,9; *20:18-21b; 20:21b-26; 23:45-49**, recognition units.

12. Note 7; *20:40-44*, recognition unit.

13. Note 7; *7:1-4, 5-9*, recognition oracles.

14. Note 9.

15. Note 7.

16. Note 7; *12:17-20*, recognition oracle.

17. Note 7.

18. Note 7.

19. Note 7.

20. *22:13-16*, recognition unit.

21. Note 7.

22. Note 7.
23. Note 7.
24. Note 7.
25. Recognition oracle, *13:1-16*. Fohrer 1955, pp. 68, 71-72 divides this into three segments; threats against salvation prophets (vss. 1-2, 5, 7-8), false prophets (vss. 3-4, 6, 9) and again, salvation prophets (10-16).
26. Recognition oracle, *13:17-23*. Fohrer 1955, pp. 73, 74 divides: 13:17-18a, 22-23; 13:18b-21.
27. *14:1-11*, recognition oracle.
28. Note 7.
29. Note 7.
30. Note 7.
31. For a discussion of 39:23-29, see Zimmerli 1983, p. 319.
32. *37:1-14*, recognition unit.
33. *36:16-38*, recognition unit.
34. Note 12.
35. Note 9.
36. Note 33.
37. *34:17-31*, recognition unit. Fohrer 1955, p. 195 regards the first recognition statement (vs. 27) as supplement.
38. Note 7.
39. See Lang 1978, pp. 160-163 for Ezekiel's speaking to both exiles and Jerusalem against the Babylonian revolt.
40. Note 7.
41. Fohrer 1955, 97, regards this as a comparatively young oracle with numerous late parallels; Zimmerli 1979, p. 368 argues for an exilic date; Greenberg 1983, pp. 323, 324 and Lang 1978, pp. 65, 88 argue for an Ezekiel provenience of this segment which both in content and form fits chapter 17.
42. *Par oh* 'Pharaoh' may be secondary Greenberg 1983, p. 315. The "mighty army" of Zedekiah and confederates, however, was dependent upon Egypt for armaments.
43. *Laken* 'indeed' may here be an emphatic introduction to a new oracle rather than a particle of consequence, Lang 1978, pp. 52, 53.
44. Fohrer 1955, p. 95 regards vs. 20 as supplement.
45. Fohrer 1955, p. 95 omits *dibbarti* 'have spoken.'
46. The Greek and Syriac texts use the first person singular pronoun; the identification of the two covenants was an early one.
47. Note 43.
48. Note 41.
49. Lang 1978, pp. 63-65 discusses the diverse interpretations of this segment. For an extended argument against a military interpretation, see Lang 1978,(pp. 65-88.
50. Fohrer 1955, pp. 144, 146: two oracles, vss. 1-5; 6-7.
51. See note 59.
52. Fohrer 1955, p. 197: 1-4; 5-9; 10-12a; 12b-15.
53. Fohrer 1955, p. 149: the recognition statement is a supplement (v. 6).
54. Fohrer 1955, p. 168: 29:9b-16.
55. Fohrer 1955, pp. 173-174: 30:22-26; recognition statement (v. 26) a supplement.

56. Fohrer, 1955, p. 178: 32:1-8; 9-16 (supplement).

57. *Ḥereb* 'sword' occurs 17 times in these recognition oracles: 25:13[*]; 26:6[*]; 28:23[*]; 29:8; 30:4,5[*],6,17[*],21,22,24,25; 32:10[*],11[*],12[*]; 35:5,8[*].

58. Exod 6:7(P); 7:5(P), 17(JE); 8:10(JE), 22(JE); 9:14 (Supp. JE), 29(JE); 10:2(JE); 11:7(Supp. JE); 14:4(P), 18(P). See Noth 1962, pp. 56-57, 62-66, 84, 103. P is rooted in the older sources.

59. Fohrer 1955, p. 147 translates, "dass sie (Israel) mit Edom verfahren nach meinem Zorn und Grimm" (cf. 25:17).

60. Fohrer's 1955, p. 212 basic text: 38:1-13 (with minor omissions); 39:1-5, 9-10, 17-22 (with minor omissions); he treats this as a unit. He includes only the fifth recognition statement (39:21-22) in this text.

61. See above on 17:1-21.

62. See Gordon 1955, p. 141 (Text 51, IV, 19).

63. If this is true, it qualifies the present negativism toward Tanach's universalism. For a discussion, see Holmgren 1973, Clements 1975.

64. Fohrer 1955, p. 217: vss. 11-16, a supplement.

BIBLIOGRAPHY

Buber, M. 1952. *Moses*. Heidelberg.
Clements, R. 1974. "The Purpose of the book of Jonah." *Congress Volume, Edinburgh*, pp. 16--28. Leiden.
Fohrer, G. 1955. *Ezechiel*. Tübingen.
Gordon, Cyrus H. 1955. *Ugaritic Manual*. Roma.
Greenberg, M. 1983. *Ezekiel 1-20*. New York.
Holmgren, F. 1973. *With Wings as Eagles, Isaiah 40/55*. Chappaqua.
Huber, F. 1976. *Jahwe, Juda und die Anderen Volker beim Prophet Isaiah*. Berlin, New York.
Lang, B. 1978. *Kein Aufstand in Jerusalem*. Stuttgart.
Lind, M. 1980. *Yahweh Is a Warrior*. Scottdale.
Luckenbill, D. 1924. *The Annals of Sennacherib*. Chicago.
Morganthau, H., Thompson, K. 1985. *Politics Among Nations*. New York.
Noth, M. 1962. *Exodus*. Philadelphia.
Pritchard, J. 1955. *Ancient Near Eastern Texts Relating to the Old Testament*. Princeton.
Takiya, Y. 1964. "Relation Between Knowledge of God, Covenant and History in the Thought of Isaiah." Dissertation, Drew University.
Tsevat, M. 1959. "The Neo-Assyrian and New Babylonian Vassal Oaths and the prophet Ezekiel." *Journal of Biblical Literature* 78:199-204.
von Rad, G. 1959. "The Origin of the concept of the Day of Yahweh." *Journal of Semitic Studies* 4:97-108.
Westermann, C. 1969. *Isaiah 40-66*. London.
Zimmerli, W.1954. *Erkenntnis Gottes nach dem Buch Ezechiel*. Zurich.
Zimmerli, W. 1979, *Ezekiel 1*, trans. by Ronald E. Clements. Philadelphia.
-----. 1983. *Ezeliek 2*. Philadelphia.